MACMILLAN HISTORY OF LITERATURE
General Editor: A. NORMAN JEFFARES

MACMILLAN HISTORY OF LITERATURE
General Editor: A. Norman Jeffares

Published

OLD ENGLISH LITERATURE
Michael Alexander

ENGLISH GOTHIC LITERATURE
Derek Brewer

SIXTEENTH-CENTURY ENGLISH LITERATURE
Murray Roston

SEVENTEENTH-CENTURY ENGLISH LITERATURE
Bruce King

EIGHTEENTH-CENTURY ENGLISH LITERATURE
Maximillian Novak

NINETEENTH-CENTURY ENGLISH LITERATURE
Margaret Stonyk

TWENTIETH-CENTURY ENGLISH LITERATURE
Harry Blamires

ANGLO-IRISH LITERATURE
A. Norman Jeffares

THE LITERATURE OF SCOTLAND
Rory Watson

THE LITERATURE OF THE UNITED STATES
Marshall Walker

COMMONWEALTH LITERATURE
Alistair Niven

A HISTORY OF LITERATURE IN THE IRISH LANGUAGE
Declan Kiberd

A HISTORY OF AUSTRALIAN LITERATURE
Kenneth Goodwin

A HISTORY OF LITERARY CRITICISM
A. Ashe

A HISTORY OF CANADIAN LITERATURE
W. New

MACMILLAN HISTORY OF LITERATURE

A HISTORY OF AUSTRALIAN LITERATURE

Ken Goodwin

MACMILLAN
EDUCATION

First published 1986
Reprinted 1988

Published by
MACMILLAN EDUCATION LTD
Houndmills, Basingstoke, Hampshire RG21 2XS
and London
Companies and representatives
throughout the world

Printed in Hong Kong

British Library Cataloguing in Publication Data
Goodwin, K. L.
A history of Australian literature.
1. Australian literature — History and criticism
I. Title
820.9′994   PR9604.3
ISBN 0—333—36405—8 (hc)
ISBN 0—333—36406—6 (pbk)

Contents

List of plates

1. Map of Australia (© Division of National Mapping, Department of Resources and Energy, Canberra)
2. *Landing at Botany Bay* (1786), engraving by John Boyne (© Mitchell Library, Sydney, as by permission of the Library Council of New South Wales)
3. *The Kangaroo*, drawing by Arthur Bowes (Smyth) in his *A Journal of a Voyage from Portsmouth to New South Wales . . . 1787–1789* (© Mitchell Library, Sydney, as by permission of the Library Council of New South Wales)
4. *Death of Constable Scanlon* (1946), enamel on composition board by Sidney Nolan (© Australian National Gallery, Canberra, as by permission of Sidney Nolan)
5. *Attacking the Mail*, lithograph, from *The Australian Sketchbook* (1865) of Samuel Thomas Gill (© Mitchell Library, Sydney, by permission of the Library Council of New South Wales)
6. A shopkeeper in the gold-mining town of Gulgong, 145 miles north-west of Sydney (1872) (© Holtermann Collection, Mitchell Library, Sydney, by permission of the Library Council of New South Wales)
7. *A Curiosity in Her Own Country*, cartoon by Phil May in *The Bulletin*, 3 March 1888 (reproduced by courtesy of the Fryer Library, University of Queensland)
8. *Bourke Street*, Melbourne (1885–6), oil painting by Tom Roberts (© National Library of Australia, Canberra)
9. *Shearing the Rams* (1890), oil painting by Tom Roberts (© Felton Bequest, reproduced by permission of the National Gallery of Victoria, Melbourne)
10. Cover-design of *The Lone Hand* (1914) by May Gibbs, using the gumnut babies later developed as characters for her children's stories (by courtesy of the Hayes Collection, Fryer Library, University of Queensland)

Every effort has been made to trace all the copyright-holders,
but if any have been inadvertently overlooked the publishers
will be pleased to make the necessary arrangement at the first
opportunity.

Editor's preface

THE study of literature requires knowledge of contexts as well as of texts. What kind of person wrote the poem, the play, the novel, the essay? What forces acted upon them as they wrote? What was the historical, the political, the philosophical, the economic, the cultural background? Was the writer accepting or rejecting the literary conventions of the time, or developing them, or creating entirely new kinds of literary expression? Are there interactions between literature and the art, music or architecture of its period? Was the writer affected by contemporaries or isolated?

Such questions stress the need for students to go beyond the reading of set texts, to extend their knowledge by developing a sense of chronology, of action and reaction, and of the varying relationships between writers and society.

Histories of literature can encourage students to make comparisons, can aid in understanding the purposes of individual authors and in assessing the totality of their achievements. Their development can be better understood and appreciated with some knowledge of the background of their time. And histories of literature, apart from their valuable function as reference books, can demonstrate the great wealth of writing in English that there is to be enjoyed. They can guide the reader who wishes to explore it more fully and to gain in the process deeper insights into the rich diversity not only of literature but of human life itself.

A. NORMAN JEFFARES

Acknowledgements

I am grateful to the University of Queensland, which provided me with time and facilities to write this book. Colleagues in the Department of English and staff in the University of Queensland Library were unfailingly helpful. Dr Stephen Torre is owed a particular debt of gratitude for his very substantial work on the Chronological Table.

1

The nature of
Australian literature

LAND and language have been the two major rival
determinants of written literature in Australia. Two hundred
years ago, in 1788, white settlers, bringing with them an
alphabetically written language, the concept of a distinction
between literature and utilitarian or ephemeral writing, and
the technology for producing multiple copies of what needed to
be widely disseminated, came to establish a penal colony for
Britain. A colony, penal or otherwise, immediately establishes
a tension between the introduced culture, with its language,
law, education and scale of values, and the indigenous qualities
of the land that is settled and its existing inhabitants. A sense of
exile may, through the perspective of distance, sharpen
appreciation and assessment of the homeland, but it can also be
an inhibiting factor in coming to terms with the new
circumstances. The initial puzzlement, incomprehension and
near-despair of some of the first white colonists in Australia was
offset by the enterprise, curiosity, and wonderment of others.
Many convicts and free settlers, together with some officers and
soldiers, soon realised that this was no temporary exile but a
new home, with qualities different from those of the British
Isles.

The contrast between gloom and hope runs roughly parallel
to the contrast between colonialism and nationalism in the first
century or so of settlement. Language, with its often
unrecognized cultural biases, tended to pull the settlers back
towards British values. The land, with its many phenomena
unnamable in the English language, tended to pull them
towards a sense of national uniqueness.

British values were, of course, often disguised as universal values, though from at least the last two decades of the nineteenth century a genuine internationalism was advocated by J. F. Archibald and others as an antidote to purely British literary and cultural values. Opposition to British values was often also a disguised form of support for Irish culture and political aspirations. From early in the period of transportation a high proportion of convicts were of Irish origin and they, with Irish settlers and officers, formed the nucleus of a vociferous and influential element in Australian culture. While the present-day population of Australia has fewer than 20 per cent of Irish origin, the contribution of the Irish to Australian literature has been very substantially greater.

Australia still contains substantial numbers of advocates for cultural colonialism (the 'cultural cringe'), who emphasize commonality with and derivativeness from Britain. They exist alongside vociferous nationalists – advocates, for instance, of republicanism and a new national flag – and those who reject both colonialism and nationalism in favour either of internationalism (that is, emancipation from the pull of both language and land) or of personal withdrawal and self-identification (that is, emancipation from all social pressures, expectations and categories).

These divisions in Australian culture, literature, and criticism bear no close correlation with the purely literary division between the solid descriptiveness of social realism on the one hand and a more ironic, poetic, romantic or comic mode on the other. Social realists tend to be left-wing nationalists, but many left-wing nationalists (such as Xavier Herbert) are far from being social realists, and some would-be social realists, such as Katharine Susannah Prichard, are really romance writers. In any case, the modes of fiction in Australian writing, as in other literatures, became very mixed from the 1960s onwards, and all one can say now is that pure social realism is a discredited mode.

The same period is also one in which two groups of writers, Aborigines and non-English-speaking migrants, have come to prominence. Both groups have cause to express a sense of alienation from land and from language. Both have lost their homelands and both are required to use an alien tongue.

For at least a hundred years, there has also been another kind of alienation from the land expressed by settlers of British and

Irish origin. The early sense of the land's hostility was replaced by a sense of its possibilities for the creation of agricultural, pastoral and mineral wealth, but the success of large ventures of this type enabled substantial numbers of people to become urbanized. As a result, from the latter part of the nineteenth century onwards literature reflects a continuing opposition between the interests of country-dwellers and those of city-dwellers. The expression 'Sydney or the bush' is a product of urban preference for the easier life of a city and contempt for the discomforts and lack of pastimes in the bush. Even today, writers often align themselves in their preference for subjects and values with one side or the other of this choice.

For a variety of reasons and from a variety of cultural backgrounds, writers in Australia have emphasized such themes as the search for identity by a wanderer or explorer, the establishment of a habitation and family line, the quest to recover the past, the sense of being an outcast, and the threat of impending violence. The wanderer or explorer, in the work of such writers as Furphy, Brennan, Herbert, McAuley, White or Stow, is likely to be more engaged on a metaphysical quest than a topographical one, though it is often the strangeness and featurelessness of what he encounters that leads to dissociation from previous accepted standards and even to madness. The exploratory quest to discover what lay at the heart of the continent – a quest not completed until the early twentieth century – provided a natural metaphor for the exploration of the country of the mind.

The urge to settle the country, to tame the frontier, to acquire such tracts of land as the Old Country could not provide and to found a dynasty was both an historical fact and a literary commonplace – as it was in the prairie literature of Canada. One difference between the more popular and romantic treatments of this myth and the treatment by such writers as Henry Handel Richardson, Brian Penton and Patrick White is that the former tend towards triumphant success, the latter towards ironic incapacity by nature or human genetics.

The quest for the past, associated through the operation of memory with the attempt to align chronological and experiential measurements of time or to escape entirely from the dominance of chronological measurement, has been a major feature of Australian literature, especially from the 1930s onwards. Historical novels from at least *His Natural Life* pursue this theme, but so too do poets such as FitzGerald, Wright, Shapcott and Malouf. The search is rarely, however, for a lost Eden, for historically the beginnings of white settlement in Australia were brutal and dismal.

The outcast figure may be a runaway convict, a bushranger, an Aboriginal or a new migrant. *His Natural Life* is the quintessential escaped-convict novel, *Robbery under Arms* probably the best of the bushranger novels. *Capricornia, Poor Fellow my Country, The Chant of Jimmie Blacksmith,* and *A Kindness Cup* are competent treatments of Aborigines by white writers, and the novels of Colin Johnson the best historical works by an Aboriginal writer. The new migrant is represented by treatments both of the 'new chum' in literature of the 1890s and of the non-English-speaking newcomer in the work of many recent ethnic writers.

A sense of oppression, loneliness, alienation, and fear is often symbolized by or is preliminary to violence or the threat of violence. Australian literature, in novels, stories, plays and poems, is a literature of violence in its treatment of judicial punishment, male–female relationships, gang warfare and declared war. Literature about convicts is inevitably full of brutality; what is more surprising is a similar brutality in the work of writers as diverse as Patrick White, Thea Astley, David Ireland, Roger McDonald, Colin Johnson and Archie Weller. Its presence is often associated with a sense of the absence or fragility of culture, a sense that culture is never here and now but always elsewhere or at another time.

Whatever its theme, Australian literature in its characterization and its own literary character is in large measure a literature of persistence, endurance and repetition almost beyond endurance. These are qualities of man's experience against the continent, of course, and they are the qualities often evident in its fictional representation. But they are also qualities of construction and style. Australian authors wear down and wear out their readers by the repetition of horrors, instances of similar incidents, lists of details, or stylistic mannerisms. Bush ballads, with their insistent, inevitable refrains, practise seduction by exhaustion. Marcus Clarke piles sensation on sensation, horror on horror, sorrow on sorrow to produce an effect of weariness of spirit and a sense of the insupportability of life. Joseph Furphy makes his story-telling so heavy-laden with its recondite references that a similar sense of surrender by the reader to the impression willed by the writer occurs. There is a similar unrelenting quality in Henry Handel Richardson and Xavier Herbert. In the modern short story many writers amass detail to nullify resistance by the reader or to reduce the reader to a state of nervous tension, waiting for the repeated pattern to be lifted. Patrick White characterizes his creations with detail after detail, long after the general impression has been gained. Hal Porter amasses stroke after feline stroke. John Bryson creates through repetition a sense of nervous tension, of fearful expectation. Peter Carey sometimes seems merciless in his tolerance of repetition. Frank Moorhouse uses repetition for his characteristic mixture of black humour and nervous strain.

Perhaps this stylistic quality operates as an analogue of the land itself. Whatever the reason though, Australian literature has within it frequently an air of infinitude, timelessness, changelessness, endless space, the still moment out of time, and the endless progress through space. It is, once again, a characteristic found also in the Canadian prairie novel. It is, in fact, a common characteristic of imperial-pioneering literature in various countries. Boundlessness and timelessness can represent either absence of cultural landmarks or a return to the void of Nature or the loss of self-identity or a mystical union with the divine. All of these possibilities are laid out in Australian writing – all can, for instance, be found in the novels of Patrick White and Randolph Stow, as they can in various degrees in the late Romanticism of Harpur, Kendall, Gordon, Clarke, Lawson and Furphy. Such writers often begin from the premise that Australia is a materialistic society, bordering on philistinism, and hence liable to alienate and despise its writers. Novels about writers or other artists who are ill at ease with their environment have been a staple of Australian writing since the 1930s.

Writing in Australia obviously began as a literature metaphorically in chains, the shackles of British expectations of what a colony and its writing should be. New South Wales was a colony founded before the Romantic revival had made an impact in Britain, and it is not surprising that in modes of writing, as in styles of architecture, the new colony clung to

eighteenth-century Georgian models long after they had fallen
out of fashion in Britain. In time, the Romantic ethos spread
from Britain to Australia. Because of its emphasis on the
communion of the poet with the surroundings, on spontaneity
and on the individual alone in the landscape it was perhaps a
more appropriate model for describing a newly discovered kind
of nature. At any rate Romanticism and post-Romanticism
served as the prevailing modes for poetry and prose until the
second half of the twentieth century. *Le néant*, the void, the
essential hollowness of existence is a characteristic concern of
post-Romantic nineteenth-century Europe. In Australia the
bush in its melancholy aspects and the oppressed or fugitive
nature of convictism are the commonest symbols of personal
solitude and despair. Whatever symbols are used, however, the
void is a central concern of such writers as Harpur, Lawson,
Brennan, Richardson, Wright, Hope and White as it is of
mid-twentieth-century painters such as Russell Drysdale,
Sidney Nolan and Arthur Boyd.

Twentieth-century modernism was a late arrival, in visual
art and in literature. Despite some flutterings of
experimentalism by Slessor and a small number of others in the
1930s and the efforts of the *Angry Penguins* group in the 1940s,
most Australian poets wrote in a Romantic style into the 1960s.
Then, in a sudden bound that bypassed such modern masters
as T. S. Eliot, the mode changed to the American tradition of
William Carlos Williams, Black Mountain and the New York
poets. At about the same time fiction writers discovered the
ludic and ironic modes, and playwrights caught up with
Brecht.

Some chauvinistic critics would find such statements
contentious. There is some hostility in Australia to the
whiggish notion that Australian literature has experienced
'development', partly on ideological grounds about the nature
of literary history, partly on xenophobic, especially
anglophobic, grounds that development may imply imitation
at a temporal distance of some external model. Antipathy to
such tendentious statements as 'Australian literature is a
branch of English literature, and however great it may become
and whatever characteristics it may develop, it will remain a
branch' is understandable. It is understandable too that much
structuralist theory, with its emphasis on synchronic pattern, is

not easily able to accommodate long periods of history. This account of Australian literary history does not, however, seek to avoid notions of periodicity. Nor does it accept the crasser forms of either the theory that literature is determined by its social origins or the theory that literature is entirely self-referential. It is a study that seeks to be eclectic in its notion of what constitutes a literary work and in its acceptance of the value of both plain and tropological modes. Australian literature in its rich variety is not amenable to critical reductionism.

This brief history is unique in its concentration on the literature of the last fifty years. While there are historical and social reasons for detailed study of nineteenth-century Australian literature, the aesthetic value and general interest of many of the standard texts is not high. This account concentrates therefore on more recent works that need no special pleading to justify their place in world literature. They emerge from and often express a different Australia from that of the nineteenth century, one where the spread of settlement inland has long ago been completed, where there is a substantial drift back to the cities of the coast, and where the distribution of population, far from being spread throughout a boundless landscape, is one of the most urbanized in the world. The account of the multifarious kinds of writing existing in Australia is descriptive rather than judicial. While many themes and theories are suggested, an attempt has been made to provide counter-evidence, so that every reader can have the materials for finding individual patterns in the literary history of Australia.

2
The first hundred years of colonization

Colonial beginnings

HUMAN language has existed in Australia for some 40,000 years. In that time the Aboriginal peoples of Australia – perhaps from the beginning of their occupancy of the land, perhaps much more recently – developed a very rich oral literature. It contains long song cycles (many of them dealing with hidden sacred meanings), shorter communal songs for dancing and entertainment, songs of love and of mourning, songs on contemporary events, spoken poems, and prose tales. Those who perform them believe that the inspiration for the sacred song cycles came from the mythical time of the Dreaming and that in his dreams and in performance the poet is in contact with the ancestral spirits. In contemporary poems, too, the songman or songwoman is thought to have attained material and inspiration through communion with his or her personal spirit in dreams. It is not surprising, then, that much of the material concerns the mythical time of the making of the earth, sun, and moon, the making of human beings and their arrival in their own land, and the making of trees, birds and animals. Much also concerns the right relationships that human beings must have with the land, its creatures, relatives and others in the clan, and the spirits: some of it is concerned with sacred sites, some of it with secret symbols whose meaning is known only to the initiated; some of it with the rituals expressing the meaning of puberty, marriage, old age and death.

Almost nothing of this rich imaginative life was appreciated by the first European voyagers to visit Australia. Portuguese navigators may have landed during the sixteenth century on their way to or from Timor, Sumatra and Java, but we have no documentary evidence. The first authenticated European sightings of and landings on Australia were made by Dutch explorers early in the seventeenth century. They made landings in the west and north of Australia, often in places that seemed virtually uninhabitable to them. The Aborigines seemed hopelessly primitive and savage. Their literature, their art and even their technology remained hidden to the prejudiced eyes of the Europeans. Even the efficiency of Aboriginal hatchets, boomerangs, spears and spearthrowers, fishing-nets and grinding-stones were not appreciated. The people seemed entirely alien and even dangerous. In 1623, Jan Carstensz, having landed on a Cape York beach, became alarmed by the behaviour of Aborigines and fired on them, killing some. Later in the century William Dampier, encountering Aborigines on the north-west coast, described them as 'the miserablest people in the world', and seemed surprised that 'we could not understand one word that they said'.

More favourable reports of the inhabitants came from Lieutenant James Cook and Joseph Banks, the naturalist, when they encountered Aborigines on the east coast of Australia in 1770. Both commented on the philosophical happiness of the Aborigines, in so far as they had few wants and no luxuries. Cook recorded in his journal that clothing given by the Englishmen to the Aborigines was left 'carelessly upon the sea beach and in the woods, as a thing they had no manner of use for; in short, they seemed to set no value upon anything we gave them, nor would they ever part with anything of their own for any one article we could offer them'.

Partly because of Banks's favourable reports – presented some years after his visit – the British Government determined to establish a colony at the site of Cook's first landing, Botany Bay, in the territory known to the British as New South Wales. It was to be a penal colony, intended to clear the overcrowded and insanitary prison hulks, which could no longer siphon off prisoners to Britain's lost American colonies. The reasons for choosing a land so far from Britain and so difficult to service and administer almost certainly included thoughts of establishing a post for trade with China and a base for collecting strategic materials for the Royal Navy – wood for masts and flax for ropes and sails.

The convict settlement established early in 1788 under the governorship of Captain Arthur Phillip consisted of just over 1000 people, nearly three-quarters of them convicts, the remainder officers, marines, seamen, wives and children. It was established a little to the north of Botany Bay, at Sydney Cove, on the shores of a fine harbour for ships. The British Government hoped that the colony would become self-supporting within three years. Phillip tried to disabuse them. He found the soil poor, the rains unreliable, the seasons unpredictable, the tools brought out for agriculture unsuitable and of poor quality, and the pests almost intolerable. No plough arrived in the colony for fifteen years; the convicts – described as 'dreadful banditti' by one English official – mostly lacked even a modicum of farming skills. More than once, while waiting for supply ships, the colony almost starved.

Of the books taken to the colony we know little. The chaplain took with him a supply of Bibles, prayer books, and tracts against lying, swearing and fornication. Some officers kept journals or diaries, but they make no mention of their reading. Someone had a copy of George Farquhar's *The Recruiting Officer* (1706), because it was performed by convicts before an audience of officers and their wives to celebrate the birthday of George III, in mid 1789. The first theatre was built by convicts in 1796; its first production (also staged by convicts) was *The Revenge* by Edward Young, a tragedy first performed at Drury Lane in 1721: 'their efforts to please were not unattended with applause' says a contemporary account.

The sentiments, moral, political and religious, expressed in the diaries and in the first printed accounts of the colony reflect those of late-eighteenth-century British society. Where style departs from that of official or informal report, it too takes on the conventional eighteenth-century apparatus. James Tuckey's *An Account of a Voyage to Establish a Colony at Port Philip* (London, 1805) includes descriptions of the author listening to 'the last hymn of the feathered choiristers [*sic*] to the setting sun' in a place where 'Contemplation, with her musing sister Melancholy, might find an undisturbed retreat'.

Such flourishes are, however, not common in the earliest official and semi-official reports, annals and surveys. Their

sober, unadorned prose, devoid of imaginative creativity but
not of intelligence, may be seen as the beginnings of a worthy
tradition of discursive writing in Australia. Watkin Tench
(?1758–1833) was a captain-lieutenant of marines in the First
Fleet; he remained in the colony until the end of 1791. His *A
Narrative of the Expedition to Botany Bay* (London, 1789) helped to
supply the appetite of Europeans for accurate information
about the Antipodes; it had three London editions within a
year, was published in Dublin and New York, and, like other
early accounts, was translated into several European
languages. Tench's *A Complete Account of the Settlement at Port
Jackson* (London, 1793) is a perceptive, lively and orderly report
beginning with the dispatch of the first ships from the new
colony in July 1788. He records skirmishes with Aborigines, the
capture of one of them, Arabanoo ('of a countenance which,
under happier circumstances, I thought would display
manliness and sensibility'), the attempts to 'civilise' him
('strong liquors he would never taste, turning from them with
disgust and abhorrence'), and his death in 1789 from smallpox.
The excursions to explore beyond the colony, the movement of
the main agricultural effort to Rose Hill, where the soil was
better, punishments of convicts (who 'continue to behave
pretty well; three only have been hanged' in his account of one
five-month period), brick-making and building operations, his
leading of a party of marines into a bog of mud with near-fatal
results, the anxious wait for long-delayed supply ships from
England, and the eventual recall of the marine battalion to
England are all narrated in a tone that is neither opinionated
nor undiscriminating. His prognostications were optimistic,
but not unduly so. He obviously disapproved of the absence of
free settlers, but applauded emancipation, found the soil only
moderate in quality but good for vines, especially grapes,
thought the climate 'changeable beyond any other I ever heard
of' and enervatingly hot in summer, and was fascinated by the
customs of Aborigines.

One of the items in the First Fleet was a wooden
printing-press, intended for the production of Government
Orders. It was first operated by a semi-skilled young man,
George Hughes, but on the arrival of the skilled convict printer
George Howe in 1800 the office of government printer passed to
him. Howe was more ambitious than Hughes. In 1802 he

produced the first book printed in the colony, *New South Wales General Standing Orders*. On 5 March 1803 he began publication of the colony's first newspaper, the *Sydney Gazette*, despite having only one old press, a mere twenty pounds of type, a constant shortage of paper and ink, and subscribers resistant to paying.

It was almost exactly a year before the first consciously literary item appeared in the *Gazette*. It was a poem, 'The Vision of Melancholy, A Fragment' by 'C. S.' After that beginning, verse appeared from time to time, some pretentious, some comic or satirical, all anonymous or pseudonymous, at least for the first few years. The first identifiable contributor was Michael Massey Robinson (1744–1826), transported for a conviction of blackmail arising from one of his poetical quips, and subsequently convicted of forgery while a civil servant in the colony. From 1810 he formed the habit of publishing in the *Gazette* rather forced and rhetorical odes on public anniversaries, especially the birthdays of the king and queen. News of the deaths of Queen Charlotte in 1818 and George III in 1820 arrived too late to halt the publication of Robinson's dutiful celebration of their next birthdays. Howe was also responsible for the publication of the first book of verse, *First Fruits of Australian Poetry* (1819), consisting of two poems by the Supreme Court judge Barron Field (1786–1846). The poems were 'Botany-Bay Flowers' and 'The Kangaroo', with the second of which Wordsworth and Coleridge were reported by Field's friend Charles Lamb as being 'hugely taken'.

Field was also in some measure the discoverer and editor of the *Memoirs of the First Thirty-two Years of the Life of James Hardy Vaux*, which he arranged to be published in London, by John Murray (1819). Vaux (1782–after 1841), a convict transported three times to Australia for theft and forgery, compiled both the *Memoirs* and a dictionary of convict slang for the aid of magistrates, *Vocabulary of the Flash Language*, the two being published together. Vaux's *Memoirs* unconsciously reveal him as an egocentric, vain and venal person, an imaginative rogue, but one with a good ear for reporting dialogue and personal mannerisms. As the first extended account of the colony from a convict's point of view the *Memoir* has substantial historical interest. The *Vocabulary*, similarly, as probably the first dictionary compiled in the colony (apart from brief glossaries of Aboriginal words) is also historically important.

Vaux was an unwilling inhabitant of Australia who returned at least twice to England. Some officials and emancipated convicts by this time were, however, able to regard Australia as their homeland. William Charles Wentworth (1790–1872) was born on Norfolk Island, which had been settled, along with Sydney Cove, in 1788. He was the son of a somewhat disreputable Irish surgeon and a convict woman. His father sent him to England for his education. In 1823 at Cambridge, where, as a barrister, he was 'keeping a few terms', he entered a poem, *Australia*, for the Chancellor's Medal, and was placed second. In it he describes the white discoverers of Australia, Aboriginal life and customs, the town of Sydney and its environs, and the prospects for the establishment of a new nation, which, should Britain decline in power might, as

> thy last-born infant, then arise,
> To glad thy heart, and greet thy parent eyes;
> And Australasia float, with flag unfurl'd,
> A new Britannia in another world.

Wentworth's poem, with dedication to Lachlan Macquarie, a former governor of New South Wales, was published in England. Charles Tompson (1806–83) has the distinction of being the first Australian-born writer to have a volume of verse published in his homeland. The themes of *Wild Notes, from the Lyre of a Native Minstrel*, published in Sydney by Robert Howe (George Howe's son) in 1826, are largely those derived from his experiences, even if the imagery is often conventionally Augustan. He writes of captivity and 'the bliss of freedom'; of fetters, whips and chains; of his sense of loss at seeing the forests cut down and Aboriginal camp sites destroyed; and of the brutality of the convict system. Like Field and Wentworth, and like the early white artists in Australia, Tompson lacked the skill and confidence to emancipate himself from European categories in attempting to describe the landscape, the animals and the birds. Such categories were obviously inappropriate, but there seemed no alternative. Field in 'The Kangaroo' invoked the 'sphynx', mermaid, centaur, minotaur, Pegasus and the hippogriff in a vain attempt to account for the 'anomalous' animal. Wentworth described an Aboriginal corroboree as a

'Pyrrhic dance'. By the time of Tompson, however, Australian readers had begun to feel that a new language needed to be wrought. The reviewer of *Wild Notes* in the *Sydney Gazette* (1 Nov 1826) said

> we will merely suggest to Mr Tompson the propriety of letting his similes and metaphors be purely Australian. He will soon find his account in doing so, as they will infallibly possess all the freshness of originality. In this respect he has a decided advantage over all European poets, because here nature has an entirely different aspect.

Four years later the first novel written or published in Australia appeared. It was *Quintus Servinton, a Tale Founded upon Incidents of Real Occurrence* by Henry Savery (1791–1842). Savery, a sugar-refiner in Bristol, was convicted of forgery and transported to Hobart Town in Van Diemen's Land (modern Tasmania), the convict settlement established in 1803 to support the sealing trade and to forestall the French. There he was imprisoned for debt, and it was while in prison that he wrote a set of thirty sketches and essays that were published in the *Colonial Times* of Hobart in 1829 under the title *The Hermit in Van Diemen's Land*. Book publication followed later in the same year.

Quintus Servinton was written after Savery's release and published in Hobart in three volumes (1830–1). It is a disguised and fictionalized autobiography, a work, like Vaux's, of self-justification. In the first two volumes the righteousness and probity of the hero's life as a schoolboy and businessman in England are insisted upon. In the third volume, victim of a temporary lapse, he is transported to a vaguely described penal colony in New South Wales. Resentful of being included in the single opprobrious term 'convict', he nevertheless learns to curb his recklessness and desire for independence, to accept the harsh convict discipline, and to nudge the system of authority in his favour. In the end, he is on the point of being granted a pardon.

The question of relationships between the governing class and the governed is also central to several of the plays of David Burn (?1799–1875), a Van Diemen's Land farmer who had migrated from Scotland in 1826. One of his earliest plays, *The Bushrangers*, was performed twice in Edinburgh in 1829. The subject is derived from the exploits of Matthew Brady, the leader of a bushranging gang of escaped convicts in Van Diemen's Land between 1824 and 1826. Brady is romanticized as an upholder of liberty and civil rights against the arbitrary tyranny of the Governor (clearly based on Governor Arthur). The purpose is less to glamorize bushranging than to expose the Governor's oppression of free settlers such as Burn. The Aboriginals in the play are presented as stupid, amoral and unworthy of consideration.

Henry Melville (1799–1873) was the author of another play of the same title. It has the distinction of being the first local play performed in Australia. It was produced in Hobart and Launceston in 1834. Burn, who wrote eight plays in all, received few Australian productions, perhaps because he considered that the anti-establishment political content of some of the plays would not meet favour with official censorship. He did, however, publish five of them in a two-volume edition, *Plays and Fugitive Pieces* (Hobart, 1842), together with poems and prose. This was the first collection of plays published in Australia.

Charles Harpur and some early novelists

Yet another play called *The Bushrangers* (1853) was written by Charles Harpur (1813–68), but he is more justly famous for writing the first sonnet sequence published in Australia. *Thoughts: A Series of Sonnets* (Sydney, 1845) is a work of much greater competence and inspiration than any so far discussed. Like Tompson, Harpur was a child of convict parents, still a substantial social disability. His father, an Irishman, was a schoolmaster at Windsor, one of the prosperous Hawkesbury River settlements established by Governor Macquarie to the west of Sydney. Charles Harpur began contributing poetry and sketches to Sydney newspapers while earning a precarious living as a clerk and journalist. Early in the 1840s he was in and near Singleton, some 100 miles north of Sydney in the Hunter River valley. Many of his poems were published in the *Maitland Mercury*, established in a nearby town. In this district he met Mary Ann Doyle, the 'Rosa' of his sonnets and his future wife.

Thoughts contained just sixteen sonnets. *The Bushrangers, a Play in Five Acts, and Other Poems* (Sydney, 1853) was Harpur's only substantial publication during his lifetime. It was not until 1984 that a full, competently edited collection of his manuscript and printed poems was published. The play, originally written in blank verse in the early 1830s as 'The Tragedy of Donohoe', has the distinction of being the first play written and published by a native-born writer. Its hero is the bushranger of several ballads, such as 'Bold Jack Donahoe'.

Harpur was a better observer of nature and a better poet than earlier versifiers, but the influence of the eighteenth-century cultivation of the sublime and the picturesque, and the prophetic orotundities of Milton, Wordsworth and Emerson ('Thou giant minded mystic', as he called him) were still an oppressive legacy. His landscape poems, such as 'The Bush Fire' and 'A Storm in the Mountains', emphasize the relationships between elemental nature and the human mind and between the human and the supernatural elements. In 'A Storm in the Mountains', after describing the wind, thunder, lightning and torrential rain, he reflects on the sublime imagination generated by the storm:

> Strange darings seize me, witnessing this strife
> Of Nature; while, as heedless of my life,
> I stand exposed. And does some destined charm
> Hold me secure from elemental harm,
> That in the mighty riot I may find
> How through all being works the light of Mind?
> Yea, though the strikingly eternal see
> My novel Soul's divulging energy!
> Spirit transmuting into forms of thought
> What but for its cognition were *as nought*!

Harpur can be an intrusive poet, directing and instructing the reader with 'hark' and 'lo' and 'see how', he can be over-anxious, strained, and didactic, but he can also achieve the contented Marvellianism of 'A Midsummer Noon in the Australian Forest', where he is in sympathy with 'Tired Summer', which

> Turning with the noontide hour,
> Heaves a slumbrous breath, ere she
> Once more slumbers peacefully.

Harpur's Emersonian transcendentalism and vague unitarianism as expressed in such poems as 'The World and the Soul' are less impressive. But the sense of loneliness and displacement expressed by Harpur (and by Kendall and Gordon), though it may be symptomatic of a mid-nineteenth-century European malaise, is different in expression from Heine's concept of *les enfants perdus* or Arnold's notion of standing helplessly between two ages. Harpur's Egremont in 'The Creek of the Four Graves' feels

> As if his blood were charged with insect life
> And writhed along in clots . . . .

The ominous silence is broken by Aboriginal 'Beings':

> from the long grass
> And nearer brakes, a semi-belt of stript
> And painted Savages divulge at once
> Their bounding forms!

They club the four white sleepers to death, despite slight resistance of

> one
> Who had with Misery nearly all his days
> Lived lonely, and who therefore, in his soul,
> Did hunger after hope, and thirst for what
> Hope still had promised him, – some taste at least
> Of human good however long deferred . . . .

This hopeless hope, this stubborn clinging to some promise in life, this refusal to believe that the world is given over to violence and misery except in so far as man makes it so, is characteristic of Harpur.

His political poems have a similar tough resistance to man's unjust political activities. 'To Myself June 1855' describes the Crimean War as part of 'the Old World's dirt' that must be insulated from 'The virgin nature of the New'. 'Wellington' derides its subject as 'Great minion of the Crown', 'a man without a heart',

> an Irishman,
> Who for a hireling's meed and ministry,
> Could tear away from his inhuman heart
> The pleading image of his Native Land!

Harpur's radicalism, his support of the franchise, political independence from Britain, republicanism, and land reform, hindered his gaining any permanent or well-paid office. So did his frequent bouts of drunkenness and querulousness. But the same querulousness made him a vigorous satirist, and he was a skilful user of post-Popian couplets. His chief literary antagonist was James Martin, whom he caricatured in 'Marvellous Martin':

> see him creep
> Into our Parliament, and dare to prate
> About the god-like principles of State;
> With this sole claim address him to the work,
> That he has read that prince of sophists, Burke!

Harpur's sources of inspiration were chiefly literary, though his landscape and characters were Australian. Though proud of his Irish descent he does not seem to have drawn much from the strong ballad and song tradition brought to Australia by Irish convicts and settlers. Convicts and sailors had work songs, of course, and there were English and Scottish ballads sung in the colony by those of that tradition, but it is the Irish originals in words and music that had the strongest influence on the anonymous ballads that flourished as recensions and adaptations of various Old World models, at least from the 1820s. They concern guiltless convicts, harsh overseers, brave bushrangers, and brutal police and magistrates. The jovial English-based 'Botany Bay', with its refrain of 'Singing too-ral, li-ooral, li-addity', contrasts strikingly with the Irish sombreness of 'A Convict's Lament on the Death of Captain Logan' with its imprecation of

> Our overseers and superintendents –
> These tyrants' orders we must obey,
> Or else at the triangles our flesh is mangled –
> Such are our wages at Moreton Bay!

The convict and bush ballads are for the most part anonymous, exist often in substantially different versions, were presumably often composed or modified collectively, are popular in style and democratic in outlook, and can be both self-righteous and sentimental. They formed a large part of the musical entertainment of working men and convicts deprived of or unable to read books and newspapers. They are a background to the literary bush ballads composed by Gordon, Paterson, and Lawson from the 1870s onwards.

A similar working-class point of view is expressed by Alexander Harris (1805–74), who spent the years between 1825 and 1841 in New South Wales. His *Settlers and Convicts; or, Recollections of Sixteen Years' Labour in the Australian Backwoods* was published in London in 1847 as by 'an Emigrant Mechanic'. It is the only substantial description of what life in the colony was like for a free working-man in the 1830s. It tells in a lightly fictionalized way of Harris's experiences as a rural labourer and farmer. Harris won some respect as an authority on emigration to New South Wales, a subject on which he wrote for working-class and religious journals. His guidebook novel, *The Emigrant Family; or, The Story of an Australian Settler*, published in three volumes in 1849, was referred to by Charlotte Brontë in several letters, but chiefly as a handbook for migrants. Like *Settlers and Convicts* it is conscientious in its accuracy about places, customs and language in the colony, judicious in its judgements, sensitive to the needs of Aborigines, and outraged by the practice of flogging. Where *The Emigrant Family* fails is in its adoption of a clumsy romantic plot that sits uncomfortably on the realistic material.

The division between realistic experience and literary romance is even more striking in James Tucker's *Ralph Rashleigh* (written between 1844 and 1850), which falls stylistically into two distinct parts, the first containing Ralph's early career as a thief in London, his convict experiences, his escape and forcible adoption by a gang of bushrangers, the second containing his escape from the Coal River settlement, his subduing overwhelming numbers of Aborigines and his life with an Aboriginal tribe in north Queensland. James Tucker (1808–?88) was a Bristol man transported for threatening violence to a cousin. After eight years in the colony he was given a ticket-of-leave, but was subsequently reconvicted and transferred to the penal colony at Port Macquarie, 200 miles north-east of Sydney. While there he wrote – or at least copied out, for there are still some doubts about the true authorship – a novel, published directly from the manuscript in 1952 as *Ralph Rashleigh; or, The Life of an Exile*; a play, published in 1955 as

Jemmy Green in Australia; and a historical drama, 'The Grahames' Vengeance'.

Like Vaux and Savery, Tucker writes from the inside of the system; like them he is concerned to vindicate his own life; but *Ralph Rashleigh* is told in the third person and there is at times an impersonal detachment in the narrative. The convict scenes, with their brutality and degrading struggle to survive, the setting of convict gang in rivalry with convict gang, overseer against overseer, convict against convict, emancipist master against free-settler master, offer a graphic account of the system. Rashleigh in his escape falls into the hands of bushrangers, a ferocious gang of former convicts, who are quite the equal of overseers in brutality and injustice.

The Aboriginal scenes in the second half of the novel lack this level of authenticity. They seem in fact, to be partly derived from Fenimore Cooper's depiction of American Indians or even from eighteenth-century British accounts of exotic tribes. The Aborigines are 'sable warriors', 'sable sons of nature', 'fleet as kangaroos'; a tribal elder ends his advice with 'I have spoken. Do I say well, my brothers?' The hero comes to behave in a manner derived from late-eighteenth-century notions of sensibility, displaying previously unaccustomed sentiment and generosity.

Romanticism of the popular kind is alien to the fiction works of Catherine Helen Spence (1825–1910). An accomplished speaker and writer on matters such as migration, reforms in the treatment of orphans, schooling, evolution, electoral reform (including proportional representation) and Unitarianism, she wrote eight novels. They are sober works that achieved little renown in her own lifetime; indeed, only five of them were published in volume form.

Catherine Spence migrated with her family from Scotland to South Australia when she was fourteen. She became a governess and later a writer and lecturer, devoting her life to her many causes. She rejected two proposals of marriage, but brought up three separate families of orphans by herself. Her novels are influenced in tone and substance by Jane Austen (whose works she read through every year), Scott, George Eliot (whom she met), Harriet Martineau and the Brownings. Most of her novels are set in both England and Australia and deal with the problems of the female immigrant. She has thus the distinction of being the first woman novelist to write about Australia and the first to deal with women's problems.

Her first novel, *Clara Morison: A Tale of South Australia During the Gold Fever* (2 vols, London, 1854), is, despite its title, set in a domestic circle in Adelaide. There are no scenes of goldfields life, though the author moralizes about the demographic, social, financial and moral problems posed for the colony by the flight from Adelaide to the Victorian goldfields. It is in fact a discussion novel; public issues gradually push aside the early interest in setting and the tepid love story. The best chapters are the earliest ones, dealing with Clara's voyage to the colony and her search for suitable work. *Clara Morison* was highly praised by Frederick Sinnett (1830–66) in his two-part article 'The Fiction Fields of Australia', which appeared in the *Journal of Australasia* (Melbourne) in 1856. Sinnett considered it 'Decidedly the best Australian novel that we have met with', 'free from the defect of being a book of travels in disguise'. Catherine Spence also wrote two utopian novels, the first of which, *Handfasted – A Romance*, remained in manuscript until 1984. About 1880 it was submitted to the *Sydney Mail* in a competition, but was rejected as 'calculated to loosen the marriage tie . . . too socialistic and therefore dangerous'. The second, *A Week in the Future*, was serialized in the *Centennial Magazine* in 1889. Both were influenced by Malthus, Darwin and Herbert Spencer. *Handfasted* daringly anticipated by over a decade advocacy of the notion of trial marriage, a subject still dangerous for Gissing and Hardy in the 1890s.

Gathered In, considered by Catherine Spence to be her best novel, was serialized in the *Adelaide Observer* in 1881–2, but not published in volume form until 1977. It attacks some of the assumptions of romantic fiction. Kenneth Oswald sets forth to make his fortune and develop his character in an alien land (in much the same way as Kingsley's Geoffry Hamlyn). Catherine Spence has great tolerance for misunderstandings and coincidences as plot devices. In this novel she steers the hero through them to a happy ending. But romantic convention is jettisoned in so far as Oswald's legitimacy is not established. The heroine accepts him knowing that his birth was illegitimate.

Kingsley, Kendall and Gordon

Catherine Spence depicts a series of hard-working, respectable, middle-class migrants. Her women are determined to make the most of the opportunities offered by Australia and she obviously shares their strong national pride. Her dogged realism is in stark contrast to the highly coloured romanticism of Henry Kingsley's *The Recollections of Geoffry Hamlyn* (3 vols, Cambridge and London, 1859). Far from being confined to domestic circles, *Geoffry Hamlyn* ranged widely over generations and over a large tract of the pastoral land of Victoria. It is concerned with outback-station life, male equestrianism, dynastic longings and epic grandeur. Henry Kingsley (1830–76) spent only four years in the colony (1853–7), always intended to return to his homeland, and in *Geoffry Hamlyn* created aristocratic characters whose object was to undertake heroic exploits in the leadership of a barely civilized community.

Their extensive landholdings, relaxed if adventurous life, snobbish attitude to those not privileged to be born in England, and heroic exploits in fire, storm, earthquake, hunt and fight are the stuff of pastoral romance given an open-air Australian vastness but with many concessions to the understanding and prejudices of the British reader. To some extent this is due to Kingsley's publisher, Macmillan, who disliked 'scenes of darkness', and to Charles Kingsley, who considered some scenes indelicate.

Contrary to the satiric intentions of Kingsley and his narrator, Hamlyn, the currency lad, John, who makes a brief appearance to give Jim Burton a letter, comes out of the episode more credibly and creditably than the landowner. John was 'one of those long-legged, slab-sided, lean, sunburnt, cabbage-tree-hatted lads', who fails to touch his hat to his employer because 'an Australian never touches his hat if he is a free man, because the prisoners are forced to'. Kingsley had something of an ear for Australian expressions, even if he tended to be condescending. The currency lad's conversation has a plausible nonchalance and unpretentiousness that contrasts with Burton's formal periods.

Kingsley wrote some twenty-four novels and volumes of belles-lettres, but he never succeeded so well artistically or commercially as with his first novel, which was highly praised by Marcus Clarke and 'Rolf Boldrewood'. Decades later, however, Joseph Furphy, who seems to have derived enjoyment out of what he disliked in the book, allowed his character Tom Collins to ridicule it as an entirely false portrayal of bush life, a romantic delusion. Collins refers to the 'slender-witted, virgin-souled, overgrown schoolboys who fill Henry Kingsley's exceedingly trashy and misleading novel with their insufferable twaddle'.

Kingsley developed some of the dynastic material of *Geoffry Hamlyn* in *The Hillyars and the Burtons* (*Macmillan's Magazine*, 1863–5; 3 vols, London, 1865). It is a novel greatly flawed by the clumsy handling of the various strands of the plot, but idealistic about the values of the English landed gentry. The Hillyar family, though wealthy, are morally cankered; they remain aristocratic colonial visitors. The Burtons are tradespeople and they decide to stay and make their life in the colony.

Geoffry Hamlyn is a novel of the squatting-age in Australia – that is, the 1830s and 1840s, a time of the opening-up of vast tracts for sheep-farming. *The Hillyars and the Burtons* deals with Australia after the goldrushes began in 1851. It describes the Victorian goldfields which form so large a part of Adelaide discussion in *Clara Morison*. Both Spence and Kingsley were writing from their own experience, Kingsley having been an unsuccessful gold-miner for much of his stay in Australia.

Nationalist critics of Australia literature tend to dispraise Kingsley for his condescension to Australian society and his adherence to the English romance formula. The Australian-born poet Henry Kendall (1839–82) fell under similar strictures in the 1890s for deriving his versification and imagery from British (and American) models. Kendall himself felt that literature was neglected in the colonies and he frequently alluded to the paucity of patronage and the slightness of encouragement he received. He was chronically in debt, partly because of the extravagance of his widowed mother and his three sisters and the irresponsibility of his twin brother. He left a poorly paid clerkship in the Surveyor General's office in Sydney for fear of impending bankruptcy and dismissal, failed to make a living as a journalist, lapsed into alcoholism, opium addiction and intermittent bouts of insanity, and was left by his wife. With the help of friends he managed to rehabilitate himself and was reunited with his wife and children. In the last six years of his life he achieved some success as a public poet and satirist.

The most persistent basis of Kendall's reputation has been his bushland verse. He knew and loved the temperate rain-forest country on the central north coast of New South Wales, where he spent many periods of recovery from his physical and mental problems. It is the landscape of 'Bell-birds' and 'September in Australia'. Yet, although Kendall at times regarded himself as a descriptive poet, he wrote very few poems in which his eye is fixed on the landscape. He is a frustrated mystic, using nature as suggestive of, symbolic of, or simply as a mnemonic for, contemplation of states of mind and the nature of eternity.

Influenced by Emerson and Poe, he writes a great deal about a desirable but unattainable goal, worlds just beyond his grasp or understanding, as in 'After Many Years:

> My spirit fancies it can hear
>   The song I cannot sing . . . .

or in 'Orara', where he describes the mystic 'rose-red' brook which he desires but will never reach and the unattainability of which is part of its value, for

> The slightest glimpse of yonder place,
>   Untrodden and alone,
> Might wholly kill that nameless grace
>   The charm of the Unknown.

The elusive spirit of nature is sometimes expressed in a fascination for oblivion and death by water, as in 'Outre Mer', which also hints at sexual loss or failure.

Kendall's heavy-handed sense of verse music, his heavy accents, insistent alliteration, strong internal and end rhyming, and fondness for anapaestic rhythms are reminiscent of Swinburne. But, though Kendall admired Swinburne, he himself began to write in this style before Swinburne had published, and the most obvious source of his style is Poe. The style was parodied from early in his career, most notably by a

writer in *Sydney Punch* in May 1865 who set his sights on
Kendall's poem 'Safi':

> Was he light in the head that he wandered,
>   That he sang in this ludicrous way,
> Of the 'distances dim' and the 'spaces'
>   As of friends that we meet every day.
>
> . . .
>
> His rhymes are the rhymes of a jingler,
>   Like the wavelet's monotonous wash;
> His words are the words of a dreamer,
>   In love with the beauty of Bosh!

Kendall retaliated with 'The Bronze Trumpet', published
anonymously in the following year. In it he eschewed the
parodied style in favour of late-eighteenth-century couplets,
distributing much vigorous blame and a little praise among his
poetic contemporaries, defending 'Safi', acknowledging his
immaturity, but characterizing his verse as akin to what

> a traveller sees in windy nights
> Swift water-moons blown into golden lights,
> . . .
> The swift delights of thoughts that are no more!

Ten-syllable couplets are also the medium he uses for the best
of his longer narrative poems, 'King Saul at Gilboa', relating
the death of Saul. (Indeed all the longish narrative poems tell of
a heroic or pathetic death.) This time the couplets are
sometimes like Dryden's, end-stopped with a varying caesura,
sometimes like the looser narrative couplets of the late
eighteenth century. The variability gives Kendall great scope
for describing the movement of battle, the despair of the
defeated and disheartened king, the majestic horror of his *coup
de grace* at the hands of 'a black Amalekite', and the sorrow of his
dejected people.

Kendall's prize-winning poem 'The Sydney International
Exhibition' (1879) takes up Harpur's theme of lament for what
has been lost through the white settlement of Australia in a
sustained *ubi sunt* passage:

Where are the woods that, ninety summers back,
Stood hoar with ages by the water-track?
Where are the valleys of the flashing wing,
The dim green margins, and the glimmering spring?
Where now the warrior of the forest race,
His glaring war-paint, and his fearless face?
The banks of April, and the groves of bird,
The glades of silence, and the pools unstirred,
The gleaming savage, and the whistling spear?
Passed with the passing of a wild old year!

Compared with the neglect of Harpur and Kendall, Adam Lindsay Gordon (1833–70) achieved prodigious renown. He was the only Australian to be included in the Oxford Standard Authors series and the only Australian to be given a place in Poets' Corner in Westminster Abbey (1934). His fame locally was equally high for a couple of decades after his death. Thereafter he came to seem more an English balladist in a colony than an Australian national poet.

Gordon came to Australia in his early twenties, worked as a mounted trooper in South Australia, then as a horse-breaker and rider in steeplechases, later becoming a land-speculator and, briefly, a member of the South Australian parliament. He failed as a grazier in Western Australia and subsequently as the keeper of livery stables in Victoria. His first two volumes, *Ashtaroth: A Dramatic Lyric* and *Sea Spray and Smoke Drift*, were both published in Melbourne in 1867, but failed to sell. His third, *Bush Ballads and Galloping Rhymes*, was published, also in Melbourne, in 1870. Henry Kendall wrote a laudatory review which he showed to Gordon in proof. The next day, however, Gordon shot himself. His reckless riding had caused him several bad accidents, he was dejected by the failure of his claim to a Scottish estate, the loss of his only child had increased his melancholy tendencies, and he was habitually worried by debt.

Marcus Clarke wrote a Preface for the second edition of *Sea Spray and Smoke Drift* (Melbourne, 1876) in which, although making Gordon more in his own image than the poems justify, he offered some shrewd comments. 'The influence of Browning and Swinburne', the satisfaction in 'duty' and 'labour', the depiction of 'the lonely horseman' are all qualities to be found in the verse. But the most famous passage in the Preface is Clarke's paean to melancholy:

What is the dominant note of Australian scenery? That which is the dominant note of Edgar Allan Poe's poetry – Weird Melancholy. A poem like 'L'Allegro' could never be written by an Australian. It is too airy, too sweet, too freshly happy. The Australian mountain forests are funereal, secret, stern. Their solitude is desolation. They seem to stifle, in their black gorges, a story of sullen despair. No tender sentiment is nourished in their shade. In other lands the dying year is mourned, the falling leaves drop lightly on his bier. In the Australian forests no leaves fall. The savage winds shout among the rock clefts. From the melancholy gum strips of white bark hang and rustle. The very animal life of these frowning hills is either grotesque or ghostly. Great grey kangaroos hop noiselessly over the coarse grass. Flights of white cockatoos stream out, shrieking like evil souls. The sun suddenly sinks, and the mopokes burst out into horrible peals of semi-human laughter. The natives aver that, when night comes, from out the bottomless depth of some lagoon the Bunyip rises, and, in form like monstrous sea-calf, drags his loathsome length from out the ooze. From a corner of the silent forest rises a dismal chant, and around a fire dance natives painted like skeletons. All is fear-inspiring and gloomy.

This is recognizably Clarke, recognizably Australia in some of its moods. It is not recognizably Gordon. His is a more open countryside, less the prey of primeval gloom. It is not closely observed. In 'A Dedication' for instance, he offers the extraordinary error, hardly perpetrated since Cook's voyage of 1770, that he was literally writing

In lands where bright blossoms are scentless
And songless bright birds . . . .

He is really more at home with the Arthurian environs of 'The Rhyme of Joyous Garde', where 'The brown thrush sang through the briar and bower'.

The prevailing note of Gordon's poetry is a rather shallow pessimism and pathos. At his best he is able to justify these moods as plausibly arising from circumstance; at other times they seem rootless. 'The Sick Stockrider', a dramatic monologue by a dying man reviewing his life and times, may have its moments of sentimentality, but it is not maudlin. The theme is not original; it had been around for at least twenty years in bush songs such as 'The Dying Stockman', but Gordon expands his vision into an elegy for a whole way of life that was giving way before the urbanization of Australia. The stockrider reviews without self-pity the exploits in which he has been involved: droving, exploring, chasing dingoes (a detail also found in 'The Dying Stockman'), wheeling 'the wild scrub cattle at the yard' (a detail that Paterson made a feature of 'The Man from Snowy River'), chasing bushrangers (a dying breed by the late 1860s), playing cards, drinking, working hard, and dying with few regrets. 'The Dying Stockman' has a sentimental end: the adjuration to 'Sometimes think of the stockman below'; Gordon is more consistent:

> At least it makes no difference to the dead man underground
> What the living men remember or forget.

Gordon seems, almost unconsciously, to have sensed what the sea-coast and the surf mean to Australia. In poems such as 'The Song of the Surf' and 'The Swimmer' he uses the surf as symbol of mystery, cosmic power and annihilation, themes close to his heart, and he is not unaware of the work of nineteenth-century British balladists of the sea, but he depicts his images with a graphic eye for the turbulence and unpredictability of the surf that is true to Australian experience.

Marcus Clarke

Like Gordon, Marcus Clarke (1846–81) has the distinction of encapsulating a past phase of Australian social history, a phase that had, however, lasted longer and been more traumatic than the pastoral expansion celebrated by Gordon. British settlement was in the form of penal colonies, an increasingly irksome system to the free settlers and emancipationists. Before Clarke, two other novelists had depicted the convict system. One was James Tucker, whose work had not been published. The other was Caroline Leakey (1827–81), whose novel, *The Broad Arrow* (1859), Clarke knew well.

Clarke arrived in Australia in 1863 at the age of seventeen, having gone to school with Gerard Manley Hopkins at Cholmeley Grammar School, Highgate. For a time he worked in a bank in Melbourne, then tried life on the land, and finally settled into journalism for a variety of newspapers and magazines. His first novel, *Long Odds*, was written as a serial for the *Colonial Monthly* (1868–9), in which briefly he held a financial interest. His second novel, *His Natural Life*, appeared in the *Australian Journal* (1870–2), which, again briefly, he edited.

In January 1870 the *Argus* newspaper group sent Clarke to Tasmania to undertake research for a series of articles on the convict days. Fourteen of them appeared in the *Australasian* in 1870–1, and, with the addition of a fifteenth, as a book entitled *Old Tales of a Young Country* later in 1871. The convict records, diaries, letters, and official reports that Clarke consulted in Tasmania and in the Victorian Public Library formed the basis for his great convict novel.

His Natural Life survives, despite its improbable, episodic plot and its gruesome melodrama, partly because of the unremitting sense of horror occasionally trembling on the brink of hope and humanity, and partly because of the author's profound sense of compassion. It is perhaps not the book that might have been expected from a witty, urbane, high-spirited journalist with a penchant for organizing extravagant spoofs. But Clarke was absorbed by the spectacle of suffering, outraged by injustice, and obsessed by the workings of authority and officialdom.

When *His Natural Life* was prepared for book publication (Melbourne, 1874), substantial structural and thematic changes took place. The original Book I of the serial form, amounting to 40,000 words, was replaced by a 3000-word Prologue. This disposed of the garrulous and implausible melodramatic explanation of how Richard Devine, under the pseudonym of Rufus Dawes, came to be unjustly transported. At the end of the serial another 100,000 words were jettisoned. In them Dawes survives the Norfolk Island hurricane and assumes a new life as shepherd, store-keeper and man of property. The events cover the period after the ending of transportation, including the Eureka Stockade rising on the Ballarat goldfields in 1854. In the end, like the plot of a Henry Kingsley novel, Dawes returns to England to assume his rightful propertied inheritance. In the book-form revision he drowns in the hurricane with his companion Sylvia:

> Borne before the returning whirlwind, an immense wave, which glimmered in the darkness, spouted up and towered above the wreck. The wretches who yet clung to the deck looked shuddering up from the bellying greenness, and knew that the end was come.

In the morning light, tangled in the mainmast rigging were 'two corpses – a man and a woman. The arms of the man were clasped round the body of the woman, and her head lay on his breast.'

A three-volume English edition, including a detailed stylistic revision, was published in London in 1875 by Richard Bentley. One of Bentley's readers suggested that the death of the hero in the Melbourne book-text was too painful and that an additional chapter should be supplied in which Dawes survives, for 'it is *too* bad to let him be drowned just as the tide is beginning to turn in his favour'. On learning of Bentley's wishes Clarke replied, 'It would be monstrous to make the hero – a convict – *marry* his love, so I have given the woman a daughter and contrived that the hero shall rescue the daughter from death and see in her the mother whom he once loved.' In the end, however, the Bentley edition did not use the alternative ending.

The novel proved to be very popular. Almost 45,000 copies were sold in the twenty-three years from 1875. In 1884 and 1885 Bentley produced further editions under the longer title *For the Term of his Natural Life*. There were further stylistic changes and corrections of inconsistencies in the 1885 edition. Clarke's widow insisted that Bentley's Australian edition of 1885 should be sold at two shillings and six pence, compared with the standard price of six shillings for the one-volume English edition.

In the following year, a proposal in the Victorian Parliament to provide a pension for the indigent Mrs Clarke and her children – an early attempt to replicate the Royal Literary Fund – was opposed by Thomas Bent with the words that the novel was 'unfit to be read in a decent house' and was 'all sharks, bulldogs and lacerated flesh'. The bill was narrowly defeated.

In its 200,000-word book form, *His Natural Life* tells the story of Richard Devine, disinherited by his nominal father when he is found to be a bastard, wrongly accused and convicted of murdering his true father, and transported to Van Diemen's Land under the assumed name of Rufus Dawes. From then on his life as a convict is full of the malignancy of his fellow convicts, brutal and undeserved punishments, several escapes from custody, missed opportunities genuinely to escape, and thwarted love for Sylvia Vickers, the daughter of a military officer.

Dawes saves Sylvia, her witless mother, and his persecutor, Captain Frere, from almost certain death on the deserted west coast of Tasmania. When they return to society Frere takes the credit and subsequently marries Sylvia. Dawes tries to protect a young convict, Kirkland, from being raped by the older men, but is forced judicially to flog him, to see him die from the flogging, and to be flogged himself for insubordination. His friend the drunken clergyman North makes himself incapable of intervening to ensure justice through another bout of alcoholism. Sylvia's interest in two convict boys and her words, which they remember as 'Lord, have pity on them two fatherless children!', give them the courage to escape from their miserable existence by suicide.

On Norfolk Island, where Dawes, Frere and North are reunited in their accustomed roles, Sylvia becomes dissatisfied with the 'barren' and 'solitary' life that is her fate. Aware of her husband's unreasonable antipathy and cruelty to Dawes, she finds him being slowly tortured to death on a suspended frame. She has him released from punishment, and leaves her husband to return to her father. North, infatuated with her, plans to leave too. But in his self-laceration and confusion he allows Dawes to impersonate him and escape. The escape is, however, only into a fatal storm and shipwreck.

His Natural Life has the same kind of absorbing miasmic gloom as Victor Hugo's *Les Misérables* (1862). The account of the romantic hero fated by the relentless cruelty and indifference of a world in which 'there is no God', occasionally buoyed up by his own compassion or, more rarely, by the prospect of love, is given rhythmic structure by the paralleling of lives and plots. The assumption of false identity – overtly by Dawes and by his half-brother, who subsequently impersonates him to his mother for the sake of the inheritance, spiritually by those who are brutalized or forced into sanctimoniousness by the system – is a recurring aspect. So is the failure of good and noble intentions, whether by Dawes, Sylvia or North. There is a strong sense of convict settlements as emblems of the cosmic fate to which all humanity is doomed.

Clarke wrote two more novels after this, *'Twixt Shadow and*

Shine (Melbourne, 1875) and *Chidiock Tichbourne; or the Catholic Conspiracy* (*Australian Journal*, 1874–5; London, 1893). They and the many short stories he wrote – mostly collected in *Holiday Peak and Other Tales* (Melbourne, 1873), *Four Stories High* (Melbourne, 1877), and *The Mystery of Major Molineux and Human Repetends* (Melbourne, 1881) – are competent and lively, but lack the brooding intensity of *His Natural Life*. The outback stories are urbane, civilized, sometimes condescending to the locals, sometimes admiring of their laconic good sense. Glenorchy, in the Wimmera district, where Clarke worked as a jackeroo between the ages of nineteen and twenty-one, is thinly disguised in some stories as Bullocktown. Its society is dull, monotonous, drunken and unintellectual, and Clarke's attitudes to his material are similar to Bret Harte's.

Clarke was a brilliant city journalist, with a satirist's interest in the pretentiousness of the nobs or nabobs of Toorak and a reporter's eye for the low life of the music hall, opium dens and immigrant homes. He also wrote four dramatic pieces of a light-hearted satirical and burlesque character. One of them, *The Happy Land* (1880), was partially censored by the government on the ground that it was defamatory. When the actors came to the passages complained of they stopped the action and shouted out 'Prohibited', to the mirth of the audience.

Other novelists

Robbery under Arms by 'Rolf Boldrewood' (Thomas Alexander Browne, 1826–1915) was once as popular as *His Natural Life*, but now seems merely an old-fashioned English romance with an Australian setting and vernacular language. Boldrewood came with his parents to Australia when he was five, supporting his mother and six unmarried sisters after his father's breakdown in 1846 by running a cattle station and later a sheep station in Victoria. He was subsequently a police magistrate and goldfields commissioner in New South Wales.

His first publication, a story in the *Cornhill Magazine* (London), did not occur till he was forty. From 1870 on, however, he supported his family by writing, producing seventeen novels in all.

Robbery under Arms, his second novel, was published in the weekly *Sydney Mail* in 1882–3 and in book form in London in 1888. Narrated by Dick Marston, it covers in sensational fashion cattle-duffing, bushranging, horse theft, convictism and Aborigines. Walter Scott provides not only Boldrewood's adopted pen name (from *Marmion*) but also much of the romantic inspiration for this and other novels.

Marston, a garrulous and moralizing 'Sydney-side native', is in chains in the condemned cell, awaiting execution for bushranging (an art that by the time Boldrewood wrote had left the country road and found more immediate pickings in the commercial and political world of the cities). He relates the story of his life up to his last-minute reprieve, followed by twelve years in gaol, release and marriage to his faithful childhood sweetheart, Gracey Storefield. The book closes with his sententious statement that 'in any part of Australia, once a chap shows that he's given up cross doings and means to go straight for the future, the people of the country will always lend him a helping hand, particularly if he's married to such a wife as Gracey'. The centre of attention of many of the bushranging episodes is the dashing Captain Starlight, first encountered by Marston after he has been shot in the shoulder by the aptly named Sergeant Goring. The scene of the encounter stays long in Marston's mind; 'Starlight, with the blood dripping on to his horse's shoulder, and the half-caste [Warrigal], with his hawk's eye and glittering teeth' supporting him in the saddle.

In the scene of Starlight's final stand they are all together again. Starlight kills Goring, now a sub-inspector, but is himself mortally wounded. With his dying breath he exchanges honorific pleasantries with his old London clubmate, Sir Ferdinand Morringer, Inspector of Police, and breathes the name of Aileen Marston, his sweetheart. The faithful Warrigal rides up furiously to pour out a lament over his dead mate.

The vigorous narrative is to some extent impeded by the garrulity of the narrator, though his demotic language has its own interest. Nothing is to be taken too seriously in this romantic entertainment, just as the local and Sydney papers do not take too seriously the exploits of Starlight and the efforts of the police to track him down. There is an air of the school practical joke about it all. The result is a good deal better than anything in 'Ouida', but inferior to the best of Robert Louis Stevenson.

Ada Cambridge (1844–1926) began publishing before Boldrewood, which may account for her contemporary reputation. Coming to Australia in 1870 as the wife of an Anglican clergyman, she went on to write twenty-four novels, a volume of short stories, three volumes of poetry and two of autobiography. She writes about recent arrivals in the colony, their establishment in respectable society, marriages, and the sense of family and cultural exile. She is a conscientious story-teller, but one unable to break from the confines of the standard romance plot.

Rosa Praed (1851–1935), born in Queensland, was equally committed to the romance (a commitment fostered by her English publishers) and even more prolific. She produced almost fifty novels and collections of stories, about twenty of them dealing to some extent with Australia. All were published after she and her husband went to live in England in 1876 and they mostly adopt a colonial attitude to Australian society.

In *Policy and Passion* (1881), as in most of her novels, the rivalry of two suitors is a prominent theme. The heroine Honoria is the daughter of a colonial premier but is bored with Australia and restless for European culture. She tells her aristocratic English suitor, 'I am always fancying that we Australians are like children playing at being grown up. It is in Europe that people live . . . .' But the Englishman turns out to be a bounder, and Honoria eventually marries the Australian suitor she had previously rejected. Despite a certain exterior roughness, he proves to possess 'chivalry' and 'instinctive good breeding'. Years later she is able to say 'I have never regretted having married an Australian; and wish for no better fate than to cast in my lot with [Australia].' It is hardly as subtle as the national comparisons of Henry James or Henry Handel Richardson (who criticizes both English and colonial society in *The Way Home*).

A third woman novelist of this period, 'Tasma' (Jessie Catherine Couvreur, 1848–97), migrated with her parents to Tasmania when a child. Her marriage to a profligate, neglectful, adulterous husband was dissolved in 1883, when she went to live permanently in Europe. Four of her six novels are identifiable with the life of this man. It is, however, her first novel, *Uncle Piper of Piper's Hill* (London, 1889), that succeeded best in her own day and by which she is still remembered. It is the story of a family presided over by a rich, intolerant old Australian, Uncle Piper, who is 'coarse and contradictory'. A novel of romance and marriage in respectable society, it is enlivened by brisk, smart dialogue and by the ironic commentary of the narrator.

3
The *Bulletin* school

Founding of the *Bulletin*

IT will be evident that the Australian novelists in the second half of the nineteenth century had the options of publishing serially in any one of a number of newspapers and periodicals supported by the various colonies, book publication in London or book publication in Melbourne or Sydney. In 1880 the most famous of all Australian periodicals, the Sydney *Bulletin*, was founded. At first it seemed much like its predecessors and contemporaries, opening with a serial entitled 'Adrienne, a Love Story of the Lancashire Cotton Distress'. But it was politically and economically chauvinistic and satirically opposed to colonial pretentiousness. It favoured the federation of the Australian colonies, republicanism, Home Rule for Ireland, a White Australia policy, and protectionism. It was bohemian, radical, socialist, anglophobe, pro-Irish, and opposed to both capital punishment and 'flogging'. Its chief effects on literature were to popularize bush life as a subject, to encourage amateurs to write, and effectively to move the literary capital of Australia from Melbourne to Sydney. Its demonology included John Bull, the Chow (Chinese labourers who were prepared to work for low wages), the new Chum, and the Fatman capitalist. Its angelology (though it was a secularist, anti-Church magazine) centred on the bushman – tall, athletic, hard working, sceptical of bosses and imposed creeds.

The *Bulletin*, chiefly under the direction of J. F. Archibald in its first two decades, used a bright comic style. Most of its contributions were thoroughly sub-edited and boiled down to this characteristic and attractive house style. The *Bulletin* was founded at a time when the Australian population was predominantly urban (to a much greater extent than in England or America), but much of its fiction was set in the bush, and this, together with its sketches and paragraphs and its tone, caused it to be known as 'the bushman's bible'. It was read and contributed to by drovers, shearers, miners, fencing-contractors, bullock-team drivers ('bullockies') and small farmers.

Archibald and his fellow proprietors were not, however, chauvinistic in their literary tastes. Archibald was, in fact, so much a francophile that he changed his Christian names to Jules François, and he regarded the *Bulletin* as an international cultural review.

In 1894 Archibald appointed A. G. Stephens to the staff. He had come to notice through his contributions to the literary section of the Queensland *Boomerang* from 1891 onwards. Archibald was attracted by his praise of French and American literature, and allowed him to develop the inside-front-cover literary column of the *Bulletin* into the 'Red Page' in 1896. The title, devised from the pink cover which the magazine had adopted, lasted through the editorship of Stephens (1896–1906) until the editorship of Douglas Stewart (1939–61), being unceremoniously jettisoned shortly after the financially ailing magazine was taken over and redesigned into a journal of political and social comment by Sir Frank Packer's Consolidated Press.

Stephens's creed is summed up in his Red Page comments of 25 June 1898:

> To filter Australian ideas through English modes alone would be the depth of folly. We have the right and the duty – if we are developing a literature – to found it on the widest basis, the world-widest basis. We are heirs not only to English literature, but to every other literature as well.

Half of Stephens's contributions to the *Bulletin* were on non-Australian literature. His favoured models were French, German, Italian and American. Like Archibald, he considered English literature decadent. One of the critical writers to whom he gave space was the poet and academic Christopher Brennan, who contributed articles on French, German, Italian and classical poets – Mallarmé, Verlaine and Rimbaud; Heine; Ariosto; Homer, Sappho and Horace, for example.

It is, however, Australian poetry and fiction, particularly of the nationalistic kind, with which the *Bulletin* came to be identified. The exclusion of non-Australian influences began in the first decade of the new century. A sense of national identity was called for in the wake of the federation of the six colonies in 1901. The bush was the best source of such a characteristic Australian individuality so it was bush art that should be cultivated. As this view found expression in the *Bulletin*, the retrospective view of the 1890s – the decade when the conditions for federation were established – became that of a golden age of literary achievement. The major droughts, floods, bank crashes, low commodity prices, economic depression and strikes in the pastoral and maritime industries were forgotten, and the cultural qualities were extended into a notion of economic and cultural prosperity.

Some idea of the way the *Bulletin* viewed Australian literature can be gained from the anthologies it produced in book form. The first of them, *A Golden Shanty* (1890), contained 172 pages of literary content. Thirty-one were given over to the lyrics of Victor Daley, a follower of Harpur and Kendall. Two works, the long story 'His Father's Mate', and the city poem 'Faces in the Street', amounting to fourteen pages in all, were contributed by Henry Lawson. Two poems (amounting to ten pages) were by 'Banjo' (i.e. Andrew Barton Paterson) – 'Old Pardon, the Son of Reprieve' and 'Clancy of the Overflow'. Henry Kendall's poem 'In Memoriam: Marcus Clarke' was also included.

In 1901 the *Bulletin* published two more anthologies, *The Bulletin Story Book* and *The Bulletin Reciter*. In an introductory note to the *Story Book*, A. G. Stephens berates 'The grotesque English prejudice against things Australian', using as his main exemplar 'Englishman Marcus Clarke'. Clarke 'knew nothing of this country beyond Victoria and Tasmania', but he 'multiplied a Wimmera station by the literary imagination and called the product Australia', falsely calling the gum tree 'melancholy' and the forests 'funereal'. The collection includes 'The Drover's Wife' by Lawson, 'The Tramp' by Barbara Baynton, 'On Our Selection' by Arthur H. Davis (better known later by the pseudonym 'Steele Rudd'), and Paterson's 'White-When-He's-Wanted'. In all, it includes the work of sixty-two prose-writers, evidence of the way in which the

Bulletin attracted a large number of amateur writers. *The Bulletin Reciter* is an even more popular work, with a large number of ballads and of humorous and pathetic recitation pieces. In this instance, though, several contributors are represented by three or four pieces.

Henry Lawson and Barbara Baynton

The best-known of all the *Bulletin* contributors was Henry Lawson (1867–1922). He was the son of Louisa Lawson, a writer of short stories (some on similar subjects to those of her son) and proprietor and editor of a radical women's magazine, *Dawn* (1888–1905). Henry Lawson grew up in poverty on a small selection (a block of Crown land being bought by instalments) and worked as a coach-painter before becoming a writer and outback swagman, and then for much of the last twenty years of his life an alcoholic beggar.

The best of his work was done in the first fifteen years of his writing career. His prose was published in the story collections *Short Stories in Prose and Verse* (published by his mother, 1894), *While the Billy Boils* (1896), *On the Track* (1900), *Over the Sliprails* (1900), *The Country I Come From* (a retrospective selection published in Edinburgh, 1901), *Joe Wilson and his Mates* (another Edinburgh collection, 1901), and *Children of the Bush* (London, 1902). His verse appeared in *In the Days when the World was Wide, and Other Verses* (1896), *Verses Popular and Humorous* (1900) and *When I Was King, and Other Verses* (1905).

The Edinburgh (and subsequently London) publications came about through Lawson's two-year stay in England, 1900–2, a period in which he secured publication in several important British journals (including *Blackwood's*, *Cassell's*, and *Chambers'*) but worked himself out psychologically and artistically.

Although in 1917 Lawson told an interviewer, 'I never look upon poetry as my forte. I'm better at prose', his reputation in the early years rested on his poetry. He secured publication as a poet in the *Bulletin* when he was twenty with 'A Song of the Republic', an exclamatory exhortation to 'Sons of the South' to avoid 'the wrongs of the North and Past'. 'Faces in the Street' is an insistent lament for the unemployed, who are 'Mammon's

Slaves'. He has an apocalyptic vision of the unemployed being transformed into 'a swollen river that has broken bank and wall', advancing 'with the red flags over all . . . bright with revolution's heat'. But the vision quickly fades, and he contents himself with the belief that only 'Red Revolution' will end 'the terrors of the street'.

A similar social conscience is at work in 'One-Hundred-and-Three', a ballad of prison life, though it is overlaid by a Dickensian maudlin ending. Lawson's diatribe is directed against both the gaol conditions and the administration of justice. There is also a sense of personal justification in stanzas such as:

> The champagne lady comes home from the course
>   in charge of the criminal swell –
> They carry her in from the motor-car
>   to the lift in the Grand Hotel;
> But armed with the savage Habituals Act
>   they are waiting for you and me –
> But drunkards in judgment on drunkards sit
>   (Keep step, One-Hundred-and-Three!).

> The clever scoundrels are all outside,
>   and the moneyless mugs in gaol –
> Men do twelve months for a mad wife's lies
>   or Life for a strumpet's tale.
> If people knew what the warders know,
>   and felt as the prisoners feel –
> If the people knew, they would storm their gaols
>   as they stormed the old Bastille.

Some of the rural poems have the same kind of bitterness – 'Out Back', the ballad of a worn-out swagman's death, is an example – but others are full of the heroism of endurance or even the romance of love and mateship. 'The Teams', a poem in praise of bullocks and bullockies, presents bullock-drivers as having more to say to their charges than to human beings, for their minds are set on a fight against heat and flood:

> And thus – 'tis a thankless life at the best! –
> Is Distance fought in the mighty West,
> And the lonely battle won.

Endurance against seemingly impossible odds is also

characteristic of the reckless long-distance coach-drivers in 'The Lights of Cobb and Co'.

Both these poems have glimpses of women and the comfort of home which are more developed in 'The Sliprails and the Spur' and 'Andy's Gone with Cattle'. Such poems have a sense of heartache and the improbability of reunion, and they provide clear evidence of the falseness of the popular belief that Lawson (and other bush balladists) never write of love.

Lawson's stories express loneliness and isolation, but also, if somewhat warily, gregariousness and mateship. A sense of profound unease and dismay at the nature of existence is evident in many of the stories of *While the Billy Boils*. Contemporary critics found the volume (which sold only moderately well) gloomy, dreary and fragmentary. They were puzzled by the appearance of the same character in more than one story, with inconsistent biographies attached. Other characters were intermittently referred to, but never actually appeared. And the order of stories was unchronological, apparently random. In one story, 'Drifted Back', Mary Wild is the grocer's wife, inquired after rather mysteriously by a passing swagman. Five stories later, in 'An Echo from the Old Bark School', Mary Wild is a child who has died during the school holidays. Such evidence leads plausibly to the conclusion that for Lawson literal truth and consistency are unimportant features of the world. There is a sense of nihilism in the ending of stories such as 'The Union Buries its Dead', where the drowned young union labourer's identity dissolves. 'Most of us didn't know the name till we saw it on the coffin', says the narrator, but in any case it wasn't his real name, 'only "the name he went by" '. Later they hear what his real name was, 'but if we ever chance to read it in the "Missing Friends Column" we shall not be able to give any information to heart-broken mother or sister or wife, nor to anyone who could let him hear something to his advantage – for we have already forgotten the name'.

This is not the only story of this period in which characters are reduced to silence, to a turning-away from issues that are too deep for words. Another is 'The Bush Undertaker', in which the old shepherd provides a makeshift burial for his mate, Brummy. He feels that 'Theer oughter be somethin' said. . . . Theer oughter be some sort o' sarmin', but the only ceremonial words he can recall are 'I am the rassaraction', and then, in a final burst of solemnity, 'Hashes ter hashes, dus ter dus, Brummy – an' – an' in hopes of a great an' gerlorious rassaraction!'

The sense of inevitability and powerlessness is strong in these stories, as it is in 'The Drover's Wife'. But there is also the sense of physical and mental endurance. The drover's wife, whose husband has been away for six months, is used to coping with childbirth, sickness, death, fire, drought, marauders and snakes. She is a type of the worn-out, flat-chested, resourceful countrywoman that Lawson may have derived from his mother's prose sketches. She stays awake all night, guarding her children against a poisonous snake sighted at dusk. Like many of Lawson's stories it manages wry laughs at points where horror and the temptation to pity become almost too crushing. Near daylight she recalls her sense of hurt at finding an Aboriginal had built her a hollow woodheap. Tears spring to her eyes. 'She takes up a handkerchief to wipe the tears away, but pokes her eyes with her bare fingers instead. The handkerchief is full of holes, and she finds that she has put her thumb through one and her forefinger through another.' This makes her laugh – to the surprise of the dog.

From Lawson's time in London come the Joe Wilson stories, 'Joe Wilson's Courtship', 'Brighten's Sister-in-Law', 'Water them Geraniums', and 'A Double Buggy at Lahey's Creek'. They are much longer and much more dependent on dialogue than the early slight sketches. In 'Water them Geraniums' Mrs Spicer is 'gaunt and flat-chested', a woman who has lived through a phase of suspicion and curiosity and grown out of it through sheer tiredness. She is so much the same type as the drover's wife that she even tells the story of the handkerchief with holes that made her laugh when she wanted to cry. She manages to stave off madness, but not depression, and eventually dies. Counterpointed against this story is that of the younger and smarter Joe and Mary Wilson. Despite Mary's fears – and her argument with Joe on the matter is painfully vivid – they manage to prosper, and Mary seems to overcome her justified resentment at being brought to make a life in such a hopeless, isolated spot.

The Joe Wilson stories are memorable accounts of the decay of romantic love and the drifting-apart of husband and wife.

Where Lawson was incomparably better than most of his contemporaries was in his development away from the main lines of the Australian short story, which remained rhetorical in style and formal in construction (including the fashionable English story-within-a-story form popularized by the *English Review* and Conrad). He came to write with a lightly sketched but unmistakable authorial voice and a self-awareness of the playfulness inherent in story-telling. He distances himself from his contemporaries by accusing them of optimistic romanticism, 'craving for the ideal', and depicting imaginary 'shining rivers and grassy plains'. With his loosely linked stories – notably those told by 'Mitchell' and the Joe Wilson stories – he also established a mode somewhere between the coherence of the novel and the individuality of the short story. It is a mode generally called 'discontinuous narrative', and it is found not only in Lawson but also in Joseph Furphy, Christina Stead, Judah Waten, Gavin Casey, Hal Porter, Frank Hardy, Shirley Hazzard, Frank Moorhouse and Robert Drewe.

A writer with some affinities to Lawson in her gloomily realistic view of life in the bush and her sense of vulnerability and horror was Barbara Baynton (1857–1929). A carpenter's daughter from Scone, NSW, she married as her third husband an English baron and travelled regularly between the Melbourne suburb of Toorak and London in her search for antiques and fine china. Where she differs from Lawson is in her unrelieved focus on the women of the bush. Lawson writes sympathetically about them, but can surprise by a sudden off-hand comment. Baynton is concerned with their endurance amidst hardships and their resourcefulness. In what is probably her best story, 'Squeaker's Mate' (from *Bush Studies*, London, 1902), she concentrates on the tragic loss of bush capability by 'Squeaker's mate', commonly agreed to be 'the best long-haired mate that ever stepped in petticoats'. Her back is broken by a falling branch, and she is permanently deprived of movement, independence and usefulness. But her will and the power of her upper body remain and she uses them to terrible effect in wreaking vengeance, with the help of her faithful dog, on Squeaker's selfish new mate and on the weak-willed snivelling Squeaker himself. The ending is bitter and violent. Squeaker's mate draws the new woman to her like a tigress holding her prey; Squeaker returns and beats off the relentless tightening arms with a pole; then the dog savages Squeaker. Here is rage externally suppressed and then breaking out in a more positive and frightening way than anything in Lawson. It is, moreover, vengeance approved of by the author, not the fierce predatoriness of a peripheral marauder.

A similarly intense and outraged tone is found in the convict stories of 'Price Warung' (William Astley, 1855–1911). He contributed some ninety stories of convict life to the *Bulletin* from 1890 to 1892. They deal with convicts who are persecuted, sentenced to transportation for naïve political radicalism or minor theft, or simply as scapegoats. They are guarded by brutal warders under a harsh code of penal torture that degrades both prisoners and warders into animals. The scenes are more grotesque and highly coloured than in Marcus Clarke, the authorial guidance and moralizing more obtrusive. The suggestion is constantly made that the repressive forces of convict days have merged imperceptibly into the contemporary neo-colonialism exercised by English imperialism and capitalism. One is never in doubt of Warung's socialism, anglophobia and radical republicanism: his stories are cautionary parables for his beliefs.

'Banjo' Paterson

The view of bush life offered by Andrew Barton Paterson or 'The Banjo' (1864–1941) is very remote from the desolation and despair of Lawson and Baynton. He had grown up in the grazing country of the southern slopes of New South Wales, but in comfortable circumstances amid rich pasturelands. He was a trained solicitor, a profession he practised intermittently. His ballads and short stories were considered by Lawson to be over-optimistic and unrealistic.

Paterson's poetry is collected in *The Man from Snowy River, and Other Verses* (1895), *Rio Grande's Last Race, and Other Verses* (1902), *Saltbush Bill, JP, and Other Verses* (1917), *The Collected Verse of A. B. Paterson* (1921) and *The Animals Noah Forgot* (children's verse, illustrated by Norman Lindsay, 1933). His stories are most collected in *Three Elephant Power, and Other Stories* (1917).

Some time in 1892 Lawson suggested to Paterson that they should engage in a verse contest in the *Bulletin*. By this time Paterson had become well known as a bush balladist in the style of Adam Lindsay Gordon, with such ballads as 'Old Pardon, the Son of Reprieve', 'Clancy of the Overflow' and 'The Man from Snowy River'. They presented a glamorous view of life in the bush, substituting deeds of story-book heroism for the hard grind depicted by Lawson. Lawson's idea was that the two mock antagonists ought to be 'able to get in three or four sets of verses each before they stop us'. Lawson began in July 1892 with a poem subsequently entitled 'Up the Country', expressing affected outrage at the disparity between the sunlit plains and shining rivers in the poems of such writers as Paterson and the actual 'burning wastes of barren soil and sand'. Paterson responded with 'In Defence of the Bush', suggesting that Lawson went 'up the country' in the wrong season and met the wrong people, and ending with the advice, 'the bush will never suit you, and you'll never suit the bush'. Lawson's 'The City Bushman' was followed by Paterson's 'An Answer to Various Bards', in which he all but admits that the Australia he is writing of is that conjured up in memory by a countryman now confined to the city, taken back 'in fancy . . . To a sound of other voices and a thought of other years'.

This is certainly the mood of 'Clancy of the Overflow', where the speaker says he is 'sitting in my dingy little office', entertaining the 'fancy' that 'I'd like to change with Clancy'. 'The Man from Snowy River', a poem still recited and admired by tens of thousands of Australians, is a tale of the underdog, the 'stripling on a small and weedy beast' who is almost excluded from the attempt to bring back the errant thoroughbred horse from the mob of 'wild bush horses'. But he proves more resolute and daring than 'all the cracks', and singlehandedly performs the desired feat. That, at any rate, is the way the poem is mostly read – as a ballad of mateship and bush egalitarianism or as celebrating the triumph of the underdog. The chief emphasis has, however, been on the quality of the stripling's horse rather than of the stripling himself. In the end it is the horse whose 'pluck was still undaunted, and his courage fiery hot'. And there is certainly no mention of monetary reward for the Man from Snowy River, no suggestion that he will ever be wealthy enough to own a wayward horse 'worth a thousand pound'. The emphasis is on taming nature, on returning the rebellious to the fold.

If that seems like reading later social prejudices back into Paterson's work, it should be realized that he had a great love of horses and an unrivalled knowledge of them. He loved horse-racing and the lore that went into the breeding of champions. He did in fact write a compendious and astute book, *Racehorses and Racing in Australia*, which remained unpublished till the appearance of his *Complete Works* in two volumes in 1983 – the publishers of which are reported to have sold out the edition of 50,000 copies in a week.

Paterson is a master of the easy-going ballad of action. He does not suffer from the inanition that sometimes defeats Lawson's narrative or the introspection that delays Lawson's action. Some of his best ballads, such as 'The Man from Ironbark' and the 'Saltbush Bill' sequence, achieve humour at the expense of several familiar butts – the countryman in town, the new chum, bush logic, for instance – but do so with undented good humour.

Paterson was an admirer and collector of bush songs and ballads. In 1905 he published his collection *Old Bush Songs, Composed and Sung in the Bushranging, Digging and Overlanding Days*, and in 1930 a revised edition. Most of the songs, some dating back to at least the 1820s, were anonymous. They covered both the depressed and the defiant style of convict ballads and bushranging ballads, wry songs about the problems of settling on the land, gold-digger songs, and songs of life as a jackeroo, squatter, small farmer, shearer, bullock-drover or swagman. While the narrative models, verse forms, and tune outlines are sometimes derived from English, Scottish, American or most commonly Irish sources, the great majority of these songs are based on bitter experience, often humorously recalled. This is especially true of the songs derived not from transportation, felony and anti-British sentiment, but from the time of extensive land settlement. Even so, many of the settlers' songs seem directed to an audience in the homeland, as the earlier dissident Irish songs had been. One version of 'The Settler's Lament', for instance, begins with the words

All you on emigration bent
With home and England discontent
Come listen to this my sad lament
About the bush of Australia.

Paterson himself added, in a more self-consciously literary way, to this tradition of songs and ballads. His best-known song, 'Waltzing Matilda', the tale of a swagman pursued by policemen and a squatter for the theft of a sheep and escaping from them only by drowning himself in the waterhole or billabong, preserves the anti-establishment tone of the tradition. Paterson based the song on a bush story from Queensland.

Some writers for children

A. G. Stephens and other critics believed that the *Bulletin* 'school' included such writers for children as Ethel Turner (1872–1958) Mary Grant Bruce (1878–1958), and Jeannie (Mrs Aeneas) Gunn (1870–1961). Although Ethel Turner attempted serious adult fiction for much of her writing life, she never achieved as much fame as she did with her first work of fiction, *Seven Little Australians* (London, 1894). Most of her children's fiction has a city or suburban setting, and *The Little Larrikin* (1896) offers an important early depiction of the city street urchin. She often presents parents who are perceived to be inadequate in some way. Judy in *Seven Little Australians*, for instance, is rebellious against adult restrictions, though courageous and self-sacrificing in a crisis.

Mary Grant Bruce's world is more idealized. Her first novel was *A Little Bush Maid* (London, 1910). It and subsequent books relate the adventures of the two children of David Linton, owner of Billabong station. The bush children lead a vigorous physical life, but the world of Billabong is rather romanticized.

Mrs Gunn's *The Little Black Princess* (1905) and *We of the Never-Never* (1908) were derived from her experiences on the Roper River cattle station Elsey, where her husband was manager. They present an idealized account of black–white relations, a paternalistic attitude to Aborigines, and a misunderstanding of Aboriginal culture. The whimsical charm, unalloyed cheerfulness and patent exoticism of these works, however, made them popular.

A more imaginative and humane work was *Dot and the Kangaroo* (1899) by Ethel Pedley (?1860–98), combining adventure story and fairy tale with realistic observation. Dot is a girl who lives with, is protected by and talks to bush animals. Satire and farce are mingled in the witty conversation of the animals, whose opinions of human beings are less than flattering.

Ethel Pedley borrowed some of her ideas, situations and linguistic exchanges from Lewis Carroll. May Gibbs (1877–1969) was equally original in her observation of the Australian bushland but more inventive and entirely underivative in her creation of characters. She began her career as a freelance journalist and artist in Perth and England. Returning to Australia in 1913 she settled in Sydney. Her various freelance work included the design of covers for the *Sydney Mail* and the *Lone Hand*. For the *Lone Hand* issues of January and September 1914 and December 1915 she designed accurately drawn gum leaves inhabited by naked gumnut babies – that is, chubby putti with hats like the nuts of gum trees and long eyelashes like the fronds of gum blossoms. These creatures were then used to illustrate a series of booklets about life in the bush, beginning with *Gumnut Babies* (1916). In 1918 they were developed into engaging and far from insipid characters in the illustrated story book *Snugglepot and Cuddlepie*, a book which astonished the publishers by rapidly selling 17,000 copies. May Gibbs writes a simple, almost biblical narrative (reminiscent of Helen Bannerman's prose style in *Little Black Sambo*). The naughtiness and mischief of the bush babies is clearly distinguished from the irredeemable evil of wicked Mrs Snake and the predatory Banksia men. These and other characters were also used in a long-running children's comic strip, *Bib and Bub*, which appeared in Sydney papers from 1924 to 1967.

Dorothy Wall (1894–1942), author of *Blinky Bill, the Quaint Little Australian* (1933) and subsequent adventures of the same character, seems more limited, deliberately charming, and verbose in her creation of talking animals which are largely anthropoid.

Joseph Furphy

The most gifted novelist cultivated by Stephens and the *Bulletin* was Joseph Furphy (1843–1912). He began to contribute paragraphs and poems from 1893 onwards, using the name 'Tom Collins' – a bushman's term for a rumour-monger in the Riverina district. Furphy was the son of Irish immigrants. He had first worked as a farm hand, miner, selector (a farmer buying a small block of Crown land by instalments) and bullocky, but then went to work for his brother in his iron foundry and farm-implement works at Shepparton in Victoria. (His brother's most successful invention was a water tank on a cart, a device much used by the Australian army in the 1914–18 war. Because the drivers of these carts were prone to rumour-mongering, the name of the manufacturer, Furphy, prominently displayed on the tanks, came into use to mean idle rumour.)

At the beginning of April 1897 Furphy wrote from Shepparton to Stephens to ask his advice about the appropriate publisher for 'a full-sized novel: title, *Such is Life*; scene, Riverina and northern Vic[toria]; temper, democratic; bias, offensively Australian'. At Stephens's suggestion, Furphy sent the 1125 pages of the manuscript to him, accompanied by a 'fee' of five shillings (also suggested by Stephens). Stephens thought it was 'good', 'fitted to become an Australian classic, or semi-classic', but not likely to find 'a quick sale, or an extensive sale'. He considered it would cost £400 to print 1000 copies of 550 pages in Australia, perhaps £300 in England; that the price should not be above five or six shillings; and that 'there are only three Australian publishers worth treating with, and they are all small men'. On receiving Furphy's admission that he could not afford to subsidize or share in the publication expenses, Stephens replied that 'There is practically only one firm to deal with – Angus & Robertson – who are Scotch and canny'.

In the end – and it was 1903 by then – the only publisher prepared to accept this prolix novel was the *Bulletin* itself, and even then the text had been substantially shortened in 1901.

Such is Life: Being Certain Extracts from the Diary of Tom Collins purports to be an account by Collins of his life in the years 1883–4, prompted by randomly selected diary entries. His account of himself is in the form of a series of masquerades:

rake, in order to deter the amorous advances of Maud Beaudesart; Scotsman, in order to satirize a nationality he despises; *faux-naïf* to the magistrate Mr Q—, in order to recover his kangaroo dog and avoid detection as a haystack-burner. It is significant that, although he announces himself as Collins, his name is never retained by Mr Q—, who metamorphoses it, in the space of one conversation, into Connell, O'Connell, O'Connor, Connor, Connelly, Conway, Connellan and Collingwood. One masquerade leads to another, needed to avoid detection for the first. It may also lead to the false conviction of an innocent man, for Collins's insouciant and self-protective conversation with Q— leads Q— to believe that he can identify the incendiarist as the deaf swagman Andrew Glover; Glover is sentenced to three months' imprisonment.

Collins is a former bullocky, somewhat distrusted by the other bullockies now he is 'a Government official, of the ninth class'. Dixon thinks he is 'Too thick with the (adj.) squatters for my fancy. A man never knows what that bloke's up to'. To the bullockies he seems a bit too well educated, over-didactic, too fond of philosophizing.

This is, in part, a way of forestalling the reader's criticism too. But it is a set of traits integrated into the telling of the tale, for it is Collins's tendency to absorb himself in speculation that makes him prone to distort the facts, fail to relate them coherently, or overlook vital clues. The narration is full of Tom's speculations on determinism, Christianity, socialism and Australian nationalism. Two philosophical problems keep recurring: that of determinism and free will and that of the characteristics of knowledge. Almost all events in the novel can be linked to one or both of these problems. Tom believes that there are two kinds of knowledge. One is derived from the Old World; it subsumes facts into ideal categories; it is civilized, effeminate and contemptible. The other is Australian or 'barbarian'; it empirically recognizes the individuality and intransigence of facts and things; it is down-to-earth and solid.

Tom's manner of conducting his own life fails, ironically, to support his belief in the superiority of first-hand knowledge. He persistently fails both to identify and to classify correctly. He is deficient in both kinds of knowledge, but constantly, if inadvertently, provides evidence of his need for both. He mistakes as beneficial, in both an economic and scenic way, the effect of sheep hooves and sheep eating-habits on the Australian landscape; he mistakes the identity of Chinamen; he fails to recognize a swagman under a tree as being on the point of death; he fails to recognize that Rudolph Winterbottom constantly blocks his advancement in official service.

There are also, however, two major narratives intersecting with his own life that he completely fails to identify. So in fact did Furphy's readers until the 1940s. One is the identity and biography of the boundary-rider 'Nosey' Alf Jones. Alf's hut is neater than average, he is shy, irascible and sullen, and obviously sensitive about the disfigured nose and eye resulting from an accident with a horse. Collins notices that his face is 'More beautiful, otherwise, than a man's face is justified in being', that 'His lithe, graceful movements had at first led me to mark him down as a mere lad', that he is beardless, and in bodily shape is 'tapering the wrong way, if I might so put it without shocking the double-refined reader'. Collins, in his usual garrulous way, talks to the boundary-rider about matters that are clearly upsetting – but Collins never notices. He talks about Warrigal Alf Morris, who works as a carrier, and is surprised at Nosey Alf's curiosity. Later in the conversation he suggests that Alf should play his violin in public performance, regardless of his facial disfigurement: 'It's pure effeminacy to brood over such things, for that's just where we have the advantage of women. "A woman's first duty", says the proverb, "is to be beautiful." ' Collins continues to talk while Alf sobs. Though Collins never realizes it, Alf is in fact a woman. As Molly Cooper she was engaged to Alf Morris, who broke off the engagement when she was disfigured. She had spent ten years of her life following Alf in disguise.

The second major narrative concealed from Collins is that of the deaf swagman Andrew Glover. At the end of the book, Collins has a 'vaguely-fancied recognition of the man'. But he fails to recognize his own part in saving his own skin at the expense of putting another man in gaol for the hay-burning incident.

Despite all his advocacy of the values of the working man, Collins is himself a snob. Talking to Nosey Alf he professes to be descended from the eighteenth-century poet William Collins.

'But Collins was never married', interposed Alf.
'True,' I replied pleasantly. 'But our family is aristocratic, and a baton-sinister only sets us off.'

This kind of inconsistency, self-protectiveness, and cavalier attitude to truth is characteristic of the narrator.

He professes however, to be an opponent of the popular romance mode of fiction and the melodrama. In *The Buln-Buln and the Brolga* (rewritten from the discarded chapter 5 of *Such is Life*, but not published until 1948) Collins defends his pedantic, ornamented and tangential style as 'far less reprehensible than the converse impropriety of writing for grown people in the painfully simple manner so often affected in literature intended for the "masses" '. *Such is Life* is the converse of such despised modes as nineteenth-century servants' romances, which so often had the purpose of making their readers contented with their lot and obedient to their temporal and spiritual masters. Furphy's book is democratic and radical in spirit, didactic like servants' literature, but didactic as a difficult game is didactic. It avoids romantic clichés (except when Collins is being obtuse or amorous), and often draws attention to its avoidance. Dixon, the foul-mouthed bullocky, is introduced in this way:

> He was a magnificent specimen of crude humanity; strong, lithe, graceful, and not too big – just such a man as your novelist would picture as the nurse-swapped offspring of some rotund or rickety aristocrat. But being, for my own part, as I plainly stated at the outset, incapable of such romancing, I must register Dixon as one whose ignoble blood had crept through scoundrels since the Flood.

Rigby's Romance was rewritten from the original chapter 2 of *Such is Life*, serialized in the *Barrier Truth* (Broken Hill) in 1905–6, published in a truncated book version in 1921, and in full form in 1946. It carries over the characters and much of the style of its original parent, but Tom as narrator is less prominent and Jefferson Rigby, the socialist philosopher, occupies the centre of attention. *The Buln-Buln and the Brolga*, like *Rigby's Romance*, is largely occupied with the question of the relations between life and its fictional representation and Tom is, once again, mistaken about the consequences of his own actions and of his own profession of adherence to truth.

Collins is in all three works a zig-zagging, tangential

narrator, ever ready to introduce anecdotes, biblical and literary references and philosophical disquisitions. It all comes out like a learned bushman's interminable tale, told with all the time in the world, in a tone of false ingenuousness somewhat akin to Sterne's in *Tristram Shandy*. Like Lawson's, his plots are discontinuous, with unexplained lacunae, and like Lawson's, but more overtly and systematically, they raise the question of what is truth and what is fiction.

A writer of less inverted and self-aware fiction, 'Steele Rudd' (Arthur Hoey Davis, 1868–1935), had his yarns of life on a small selection appear in the *Bulletin* from 1895. They were subsequently gathered into two *Bulletin* collections, *On Our Selection* (1899) and *Our New Selection* (1903), the first also being turned into a successful play. Rudd writes comic sketches of the disasters that befall Dad, Mum and their son Dave at Shingle Hut on the Darling Downs in Queensland. The disasters may be trivial, such as the attempt to install a window blind, or major, as in a crop failure, but the comedy invariably arises from Dad's cranky optimism, Dave's naïve dim-wittedness, and the anarchistic turmoil created among human beings, horses, cows, pigs and dogs by one initial mistake. The oft-stated moral that bush-learning is always superior to book-learning is constantly belied by the action.

Rudd's formula of hope yielding to comic failure recommended itself to film-makers and radio serialists, though both media turned Dad and Dave into mere caricatures, a buffoon and a dolt. Rudd himself was as unsuccessful financially and socially as his creations. *Steele Rudd's Magazine*, which ran intermittently between 1903 and 1927, was always on if not over the brink of insolvency, and Rudd was an indifferent farmer.

Miles Franklin

Before Furphy's first novel was published, Miles Franklin (1879–1954), who greatly admired his work and subsequently wrote an account of it and of their friendship, had produced *My Brilliant Career* (Edinburgh, 1901). A. G. Stephens said it was 'the very first Australian novel to be published. There is not one of the others that might not have been written by a stranger or sojourner'. Miles Franklin grew up in the Monaro district, near Tumut, NSW, part of the countryside that Tom Collins roams over and the setting of the novels she later wrote under the pseudonym 'Brent of Bin Bin'. *My Brilliant Career*, originally written when she was sixteen, is an autobiographical novel, with an outlook on life and fiction not dissimilar to Furphy's. The narrator, Sybylla Melvyn, begins by averring that 'This is not a romance' and that it lacks 'such trash as descriptions of beautiful sunsets and whisperings of wind', for 'We (999 out of every 1000) can see nought in sunsets save as signs and tokens whether we may expect rain on the morrow or the contrary.' Sybylla, thinking of herself as 'so very plain' and hence 'not a valuable article in the marriage market', finds that the only respectable careers open to her, marriage and teaching, are both oppressive. What she seeks is some occupation of independence rather than 'the degradation of marriage'.

The style of *My Brilliant Career* is melodramatic, the central character, though eloquent, unable to express her distinctive principles to her suitors. *My Career Goes Bung: Purporting to be the Autobiography of Sybylla Penelope Melvyn* was written about 1903, but not published until 1946. It admits that the earlier work was a kind of parody of the popular autobiography and offers a true recension. But the reader is deliberately left in doubt about whether this is yet another spoof.

Miles Franklin worked as a journalist in Sydney until 1906, when she went to Chicago. As an ardent socialist and feminist she worked for the National Women's Trade Union League, contributing to its journal, *Life and Labor*. She found such involvement, and disappointing personal relationships that she established, another kind of oppressive and degrading trap. *On Dearborn Street*, written at the time with a Chicago setting, but not published until 1981, lacks both liveliness and passion. In 1915 she went to London and had published another novel with a Chicago setting, *The Net of Circumstance*. Published by Mills and Boon, it has a liberated New Woman, Constance Roberts, as the central character. She makes a tenuous living as a writer, lives frugally in a hostel, falls ill, recovers, and marries a man who is prepared to accept and even admire her independent spirit.

Franklin served as an orderly in Macedonia with the Scottish Women's Hospitals in 1917, then lived in Bloomsbury until

1933, when she returned to Sydney. The best of her novels after *My Brilliant Career* is *All That Swagger* (1936), a saga novel covering the period from the 1830s to the 1930s, based in part on the experiences of her paternal grandfather. It begins with Fearless Danny Delacy in Ireland, and goes on to relate his arrival with his young bride in Sydney, and the attempt to set up a squatting dynasty. The setting is the Murrumbidgee and the Monaro. It is full of pioneering incident, but is loosely linked and clumsily narrated. Despite Franklin's claims to the avoidance of romance, it is a tale of chivalry on horseback that loses life when its main larger-than-life character, Danny, dies three-quarters of the way through the book. His role for several chapters previously had been reduced to the muttering of prophecies of woe in a heavy Irish accent.

Franklin set six other novels in the Monaro, though she refused to acknowledge authorship, persistently but falsely denying until shortly before her death that she was 'Brent of Bin Bin'. As her friend Marjorie Barnard said later, Franklin 'was a curious woman. She *hid* things. And she liked to hide from people. It was just a little quirk.' Although never rich, Franklin managed to leave £9800 in her will for the establishment of an annual award for a novel of 'the highest literary merit . . . which must necessarily present Australian life in any of its phases'. It is a much-sought-after award, won by many of Australia's best contemporary fiction-writers.

Christopher Brennan

The connection of Christopher Brennan (1870–1932) with the *Bulletin* was more extensive than that of Franklin, but his work is not of the nationalistic strain that became dominant from the early years of the twentieth century. The eldest of a large Irish Catholic family, living in Sydney, Christopher Brennan was a brilliant student at St Ignatius' College, Riverview, and the University of Sydney, from which he graduated with honours in classics and philosophy. A travelling scholarship took him to Berlin for two years. He became immersed in the French symbolist movement and began to write poetry. Returning to Sydney at a time of depression, he found work as a cataloguer in the Public Library of New South Wales. His first printed volume of poetry, *XXI Poems: Towards the Source*, appeared in 1897, the year in which he also married his German fiancée.

These poems were incorporated in Brennan's collected volume *Poems* (1913 for 1914). This volume, consisting largely of poems written in the 1890s, is a symbolist dramatic narrative in which the speaker assumes different roles and attitudes. The general subject is the common symbolist one of the infusion of matter by the soul and the struggle towards reconciliation of the discordant elements. Several of the poems create a sense of being adrift in an indifferent, featureless universe.

Brennan's preoccupation with the past, his sense of a lost Eden, the notion of spiritual drifting, and his struggle towards understanding and harmony can be seen as common features of 1890s writing, whether Australian or English. Brennan's imagery is different from the outback of Lawson, for instance, but both writers are concerned with a feeling of emptiness and hopelessness metonymically represented by the landscape surrounding and pressing in on the speaker.

The first section of the book, 'Towards the Source', creates a sense of infinitely extended silence and aloneness, both in a timeless land- and seascape and in a tenantless city. The heart aches both for the beloved and for the lost Eden.

In 'The Forest of Night', the second and perhaps most powerful section, the central figure is Night, personified as Lilith, the demon bride of Hebrew mythology. She opposes man's struggle to regain Eden, she is an irresistible lover, holding Adam back from Eve. Adam's only hope of defeating her is by increased self-knowledge, from either divine or earthly sources:

> if no divine
> revealment star me with the diadem
> hermetic, magian, alchemic gem,
> shall I not feel the earth with firmer tread
> if abdicating to the viewless dead
> the invaluable round of nothingness?
> Kingdom awaits me . . .
> to rule and mould
> in mine own shape the gods that shall be old.

The remainder of the poem is filled with symbols of this search. In the next two sections, 'The Wanderer' and 'Pauca

Mea', the speaker's self-pity, sentimentality, self-melodramatization and bardic display are recognized as illusions which he must cast off as impediments to his quest. In these sections, the landscape is chiefly mental.

The poem ends with two poems forming section v, 'Epilogues'. The second of them is dated 1908, the year Brennan returned to the University of Sydney as a temporary lecturer in French to evening students. It is the journey to the University from the Public Library on a writer's evening that is described. The 'four-turreted tower of the University' stands for one path to Eden, 'The lucid diamond-probe of thought'. The 'plain obtruncate chancel' of St Benedict's Church, where he had once been an altar-server, had previously offered a comforting way, but it had been rejected as requiring hell as well as heaven, neither really appropriate to 'this mid-world'. In any case, the search for Eden continues. Eden is harmony of soul and body, sexual fulfilment, poetic creativity and its perfect product, intellectual consistency, and a life that can be rationally defended.

Brennan's own life never achieved such a harmony. He was appointed Associate Professor of German and Comparative Literature in 1920, but was dismissed from the University in 1925 following evidence of his infidelity given in Mrs Brennan's proceedings for divorce. He spent the years up to his death in considerable wretchedness and intermittent poverty.

As with many symbolist poets, Brennan's life runs parallel to his poetry. He had many glimpses of opportunity, tried to pursue them, but failed every time: his academic career, his marriage, his relations with his children, his friends and his mistress all ended in failure. He was a wanderer, restlessly searching, eternally unsatisfied. What he was able to achieve was a body of poetry that expressed the aching quality of such a life. But because the chain by which he derived his symbols was attenuated and because his surroundings were unrelated to the European milieu in which he tried to work, his expressions of alienation can seem confused and obscure.

4
National self-definition

Suburban life

THE second of Christopher Brennan's 'Epilogues' depicts an inner-suburb scene of 'the twisting shabby street', lit garishly by orange or 'ghastly blue' light, with 'niggard homes' and the 'gin-shops's ochrous flare'. Ameliorate the tone of depression and remove the symbolic intent and you have the suburban landscape of *Jonah* (1911) by Louis Stone (1871–1935). Stone, a social-realist writer, offers a tough-minded look at the slums of Sydney and the struggle for survival. At the centre of the novel is Jonah, a hunchback who grows up among the larrikin pushes of Cardigan Street. But he gives up his larrikin friends when he marries. He learns a trade, prospers, and comes to feel superior to his origins. He has risen by cunning and duplicity, supplanting the old man who taught him his trade. But he is in fear of being overthrown by the larrikins of the push (the band of young hooligans). Stone's novel (published originally in England) served to create the larrikin figure in prose (as C. J. Dennis did for the Melbourne larrikin in verse). Norman Lindsay said that in *Jonah* 'There, for the first time, types idiosyncratically Australian moved through Sydney streets, and those streets were brilliantly alive with crowds of people.'

There is another side, however, to Stone's depiction. It is in part an idealized portrait of exuberant, rumbustious working-class life. The tendency to sentimentality can be seen, for instance, in the portrait of Mrs Yabsley, the wise old confidante of Cardigan Street:

> Yet the women took their secret troubles to her. For this unwieldy jester, with the jolly red face and rough tongue, could touch the heart with a word when she was in the humour. Then she spoke so wisely and kindly that the tears gathered in stubborn eyes, and the poor fools went home comforted.

The Melbourne larrikin push of Bill, Ginger Mick and others depicted by C. J. Dennis (1876–1938) in *The Songs of a Sentimental Bloke* (1915) and later works is weaker in reality, stronger in humour and sentiment. Dennis's characters speak in an argot closer to stage Cockney than street Australian.

Theatre

Stage Cockney was a theatrical language used in much of the comedy and melodrama presented in Australian theatres in the nineteenth century. Mixed playbills of farce, nautical drama, Shakespeare, recitations, operetta songs and variety acts were the staple of the Australian as of the English theatre. Some of the material was imported, some drew on the local experience of convictism, bushranging and the gold rushes for its melodramatic material. The convict writer Edward Geoghegan (1813 – after 1852), for instance, wrote nine or ten plays for the Royal Victoria Theatre in Sydney during the 1840s. They included *The Currency Lass* (1844), a sentimental farce, and *The Hibernian Father* (1844), a historical melodrama set in Galway.

Professional theatre had begun in Sydney with the opening of Barnett Levey's Theatre Royal in 1833. Levey's plans had earlier been delayed by Governor Darling, who considered that the theatre could be an instrument of anti-government agitation and a consorting-place for criminals. Before long, the other main settlements had regular performances in permanent playhouses. Hobart's Theatre Royal opened in 1837, to be followed by the Queen's Theatre Royal in Melbourne and the Queen's Theatre in Adelaide. The names given to the theatres indicate their proprietors' desire to appear loyal subjects, unlikely to offer to the Chief Secretary for his approval any plays of a subversive spirit. By the early 1890s there were five large theatres in each of Sydney and Melbourne, three in Brisbane, two in Adelaide and two in Tasmania, as well as many smaller semi-professional and amateur theatres. Between 1834 and 1914 over 600 Australian plays are known to have been performed. Texts have survived for little more than 100 of them, but in any case it should be realized that Australian plays formed only a small fraction of the plays presented, most of which were English or American, performed either by local actors or by touring English or American troupes.

In 1908 a writer in the *Lone Hand* expressed the opinions that

Many of us are almost in despair when we see how little relation the theatre in Australia has to the national life of the country. There is no Australian dramatist earning his livelihood by writing for the Australian stage. No one for that matter, can name any Australian play that has ever had any pretension to being considered seriously as drama.

The example advocated by the writer was that of the Irish national theatre, which, he believed, had successfully weakened the commercial monopolies of the theatre and introduced a national alternative to imported English plays.

The most talented of the playwrights who sought to follow his prescription was Louis Esson (1878–1943). With the writer of the article in the *Lone Hand*, Leon Brodzky (later known as Spencer Brodney, 1883–1973), he had met J. M. Synge in Dublin and heard him advocate the creation of a national theatre in Australia. Synge thought that 'all those shepherds going mad in lonely huts' was the very stuff of drama. From 1910 Esson turned aside from the pieces he had been writing for the *Bulletin*, feeling that it was now neither a very national nor a very original paper. He wrote three one-acters for performance in Melbourne. Then came his first full-length play, *The Time is not yet Ripe*, a political comedy. In it, Esson indicates a contemptuous dismissal of party politics and a cynical distrust of politicians' language and promises. The main butt for satire is the conservative Prime Minister Sir Joseph Quiverton, a pompous equivocator. His only definite policy decision is to express support for an American entrepreneur. Asked if he will support a national theatre, he temporizes. Contrasted with his drab, vacillating, unprincipled character is that of his political opponent, Sydney Barrett, an enthusiastic idealist. His view is that 'Australia doesn't need workers – it needs idlers – it needs Egyptologists, and biblical critics, metaphysicians and Italian tenors, and it needs them very badly.' In some ways this may seem as alien as the presumptuous and boorish demands of the American entrepreneur, John K. Hill, but Barrett is treated more sympathetically and redeems his faults by eschewing politics for marriage.

After returning from four years in the United States and England in 1921, Esson established, with Vance Palmer and Stewart Macky, a writers' theatre in Melbourne known as the Pioneer Players. The first production was Esson's *The Battler, or Digger's Rest* (1922) and succeeding plays were provided by the three principals, Katharine Susannah Prichard, the New Zealand writer Alan Mulgan, Furnley Maurice, and others. But after two seasons Pioneer Players came to an end, the victim of poor management, inadequate capital, poor publicity and Melbourne apathy.

The best of Esson's plays is probably his one-acter *The Drovers* (published in his *Dead Timber, and Other Plays*, London, 1920). Its central character is a dying drover, fatally injured in a stampede. His mates offer many off-handed attempts at sympathy and philosophy ranging from 'hard luck' to a consideration of fatalism, tragedy, human absurdity and isolation. It is more important as a philosophical play than an 'outback' one, for Esson's strength is with the brisk exchange of ideas rather than with outback detail. The best detail in his plays is, in fact, usually urban. Here, however, his dramatic skill has found a denouement that represents the loneliness of both the bush and human existence. The drover is left by his old mate to die on the track, because the cattle must be driven on to water.

'Henry Handel Richardson'

'Henry Handel Richardson' (Ethel Florence Lindesay Robertson, 1870–1946) was the daughter of an Irish doctor, whose experiences on the Ballarat goldfields and subsequent mental deterioration provided material for his daughter's impressive trilogy, *The Fortunes of Richard Mahony*. It was her own more immediate experiences, however, that formed the substance of her first two novels, *Maurice Guest* (1908) and *The Getting of Wisdom* (1910). Richardson's experiences as a music student in Leipzig, where at the age of seventeen she had been taken by her mother to continue her piano studies, forms the background to *Maurice Guest*. The novel, begun in 1897, concerns the enthusiasm for music and for life of a romantic and rather priggish English piano student. Gauche and lonely, suffering from bad teaching in the past, he is overcome by the beauty of an indolent, passionate and rich Australian girl, Louise Dufrayer. She is, however, engaged in an affair with a brilliant Polish violinist, Schilsky, a fact which causes Maurice intense mortification. Schilsky, a roué, disengages himself from Louise, who remains in love with him. Maurice, incapable of expressing his love except in foolish and unappreciated ways, and unable to acknowledge either to her or to himself the sexual nature of his attraction, becomes her devoted companion and dogged slave. Just when he has come to the realization that this is futile and that he must leave her to continue his studies, she entangles him further by seducing him. After a few days of happiness, his jealous and puritanical nature reasserts itself. He makes himself insufferable to Louise, even beating her when in a drunken frenzy. She leaves him, marries the highly successful Schilsky, and Maurice, insanely jealous and beset by monetary problems, commits suicide.

Maurice Guest is a book set within the closed hothouse atmosphere of a conservatorium – a place of exile for most of the students. The students range in temperament from the intensity of Maurice to the heartlessness of Schilsky, from the quiet devotion of Madeleine Wade (who gradually falls in love with Maurice) to the passionate directness of Louise. There are no permanent or genuinely reciprocal relationships: inexperience, ignorance of the self, egotism or the pursuit of a musical career intervene. A musical career can be a success; a career in life and music never. Richardson's conduct of the story is inexperienced and clumsy. She alternates theatrically effective scenes with long passages of authorial psychological analysis.

The Getting of Wisdom is much lighter in tone. Richardson called it 'a merry little book', though it has its episodes of bitter disappointment and frustration. Based on her own experiences at Presbyterian Ladies' College, Melbourne, it was begun before *Maurice Guest* was finished. Laura Rambotham at the age of twelve is sent by her widowed mother living in the country to a city boarding-school. Mrs Rambotham has a decided, if meretricious, notion of what clothes are suitable for Laura, and spends a great deal of time making them. Laura knows them to be wrong, but imagines that her school companions will overlook them in consideration of her beauty and deportment.

In fact her cousin describes her hat as apparently designed so that 'you shouldn't get lost as long as you wore it' and making Laura look 'just like a great big double dahlia'. A teacher describes her clothes as 'fit for a Punch and Judy show'. Gradually, however, and painfully, she learns to curb her spontaneity and effusiveness. This is another enclosed, oppressive world, but treated more satirically and humorously. The girls' imaginations and hopes are centred on matrimony, though Laura privately casts doubt on 'one single event, which though it saved you from derision, would put an end, for ever, to all possible, exciting contingencies'. To satisfy the gossip-mongers of the school and to attract attention Laura invents a circumstantially detailed account of her flirtation with a married curate. When the truth of the curate's opinion of Laura ('a nice little girl. But very young for her age') emerges, Laura is humiliated and sent to Coventry.

Laura is like Maurice in that she does not care for the person who admires her – she 'had not cared two straws for Chinky', a girl who is dismissed for theft. Like Maurice she adores someone who is unattainable – the older girl Evelyn – and fails in her studies as a result. Where she differs from Maurice is in her ability to suppress or distort her own instincts without undue psychological damage. She learns to conform, to damp her exuberance. But she is still the least conforming of all the girls, still full of dreams, even if they promise to have little substance.

She is like Maurice in one other major respect, lack of knowledge of when to stop. Like him she tends to excess (emblematized by her mother's outrageously trimmed clothes). At the school Literary Society, for example, gratified at the invitation to join, she presents a twenty-page account of 'A Day at School', tedious in its detail and boringly veracious.

The Fortunes of Richard Mahony is a saga of some twenty years beginning in 1852. For much of its fabric Richardson draws on material in her own life earlier than the material that supported her two earlier novels. She returned to Australia only once after her studies in Leipzig. While at the Conservatorium she met a Scottish student, J. G. Robertson, who became the first Professor of German Language and Literature at the University of London in 1903. They married and lived in Europe. Henry Handel Richardson made a six-week visit to

Australia in 1912 'to test my memories' by visiting the places of her childhood. During this visit she was refused entry to her old school and had to gaze in from the gates.

The Fortunes of Richard Mahony consists of three books originally published separately: *Australia Felix* (1917), *The Way Home* (1925) and *Ultima Thule* (1929). *Australia Felix* opens in Richardson's characteristic way with a theatrically vivid scene. It is, in fact, two scenes, one of the death of a luckless miner when an imperfectly slabbed shaft caves in, the next of the arrival of the licensing-commissioner and troops to inspect miner's licences. The store-keeper, Richard Townshend-Mahony, goes bail for a young miner, Purdy, arrested in the course of distracting attention from the dead miner's chief mate. Mahony is an Irish doctor who, unsuccessful in his search for quick riches on the goldfields, has turned store-keeper. He is, and remains, like Maurice and Laura, an outsider in his society. It is the period just before the Eureka Stockade, when feelings against goldfields' inspectors and police ran high. Mahony addresses a meeting of rebels with 'Mr Chairman! Gentlemen!' and offers three cheers for the British flag and an exhortation to law and order, gentlemanly conduct and legal reform. He is shouldered aside by Purdy, who begins with 'Brother diggers!' and launches into a vehement attack on the licence-tax system.

Mahony brings his new bride, Polly, back to the diggings. The 'loneliness of the bush' closes round them, it is wet, they sink down in the mud, oaths emanate from the grogshops, and Polly is appalled at the primitiveness of the smelly 'half a tent and half a log-hut' that is to be her home. Mahony's opposition to the Reform League leads to something of a boycott on his store. This, with his wife's importunacy, leads him to return to his profession as a doctor in Ballarat. His own preference is to return to practice in England, but he is weak willed and chooses the line of least resistance.

The disagreement about the relative values of England and Australia explicit in Mahony's dealings with the rebel diggers and with his wife continues through the book. Polly, now called 'Mary' to avoid confusion with her slap-dash sister-in-law, is accommodating and generous, but she comes to have 'a faint, ever so faint a doubt of Richard's wisdom'. Unlike him she 'was not a creature of moods, did not change her mental envelope a dozen times a day'. As he anticipates, she raises many objections to his ill-considered romantic idea of going to England. She defends Ballarat against his description of it as a 'God-forsaken hole', but comes to regard Richard's decision as irrevocable.

The Way Home presents Mahony equally dissatisfied with England. He is irritated by the rapacity that cheats him over his purchases of medical practices, irritated by being treated as a colonial, and irritated by the narrowness and provinciality he encounters. Almost at the end of his money, he returns to Australia, to find that he is a rich man through the unexpected success of some mining shares. He buys a substantial Melbourne house, 'Ultima Thule', but remains restless and dissatisfied. Precipitately he sells the house and arranges another visit to England. Mary, used to 'this Irish fluidity', once again has her 'wishes and feelings . . . trampled on'. But the visit is cut short when Mahony's financial agent absconds, an action Mahony had dreamt of but put from his mind.

Ultima Thule begins with the words, 'When, for the third time, Richard Mahony set foot in Australia, it was to find that the fortune with which that country but some six years back had so airily invested him no longer existed.' He feels 'doubly alien', unable to appreciate any of the natural beauties of a country he constantly belittles. Melbourne society seems a small world, 'a narrow clique' that excludes him. In part he is right. The novelist is critical both of Mahony's dismissiveness and of the oppressively sterile society that he dismisses. He sets up again as a physician, first in Melbourne, then in an isolated town called Barambogie. One of the children dies, Mahony's mind disintegrates, he feels himself going mad, and he has to be put into an institution. Mary takes a job as a country postmistress, releases Richard from literal bondage in the institution, and brings him home to die. In this volume, the Australian landscape is presented at its driest and least fertile. It reflects and in part causes the disintegration of Richard's mind into dust.

The opposition of values in Richard and Mary represents a tension in Richardson herself. Her values are grounded in European art and thought; her literary models are Flaubert, Tolstoy and Dostoevsky. But Mary is consistently presented as having the more rational side of the argument in favour of

Australia. It is the Bishop, with his vacuous and unctuous speech extolling 'the splendid tale of Australia's progress', who is the object of satire, not Mary. Richard and Mary also represent the two sides of an opposition between idealism and pragmatism, changeableness and constancy, defeat and endurance. Mary is the hero, Richard the pathetic rather than tragic failure. He is a person who keeps trying to break out of the straightjacket of conformity or sameness. Whereas Maurice Guest was obsessed by a single unattainable ideal, Richard Mahony is obsessed by his own chimerical nature, which imposes its will inevitably – a word Mary often uses – on his wife. His is the dark side of the mercurial nature of Laura Rambotham.

Richardson wrote one other novel, *The Young Cosima* (1939). It concerns Franz Liszt's daughter, Cosima, who left her husband, von Bülow, to become Wagner's mistress and, later, second wife. It is another novel in which the protagonists sacrifice life for musical fame, and to that extent it seems dry and factitious.

Richardson has a grim outlook on life and a dour and sometimes awkward style. Her special ability is in the depiction of the fraught Byronic hero, never satisfied, hovering on the brink of inevitable disintegration, failure, and decay. These are characters who have romantic aspirations but lack the strength to bring them to fruition.

By contrast with the anti-romantic cast of Richardson's narration, the novels of William Gosse Hay (1875–1945) offer melodramatic sensationalism. His first three novels concern the early convict days of Australia, mingling brutal horror with sentimental love. His fourth novel, *The Escape of the Notorious Sir William Heans (and the Mystery of Mr Daunt): A Romance of Tasmania* (1918), tells the story of a wrongly convicted aristocrat who eventually escapes from custody in Tasmania at his third attempt. Hay said it was 'a summing up in one three-volume novel of all the more polite romance and tragedy of the late 1830s in Hobart'. Seeking for 'a crime that I could bear in a man for a hero', Hay made Heans's alleged crime that of the abduction of an aristocratic beauty. The mesmeric, Meredithian prose and deftly conveyed atmosphere fail to conceal the hollow artifice and triviality of the events in this costume novel.

Nationalism and internationalism: Mary Gilmore and the Norman Lindsay coterie

An Australian nationalist who has continued to have an influence is Mary Gilmore (1865–1962). After working as a schoolteacher she went with William Lane's group to found a socialist community in Paraguay, the New Australian settlement Cosme. The venture failed and she returned to Australia with most of the other settlers. In 1908 she began a twenty-three-year stint editing the woman's page of the *Worker*, a Labor Party newspaper in Sydney. In the retirement years of her long life she contributed to a Communist paper, *Tribune*, finding no incongruity between that and her royalist beliefs (she had been created a Dame Commander of the Order of the British Empire in 1937).

Mary Gilmore's poetry has a gnomic quality; it deals with elemental features of the landscape and corresponding general ideas. Much is in ballad and hymn metre, a choice that later seems to have influenced Kath Walker.

Her first volume, *Marri'd and Other Verses* (1910), is largely composed of poems on domestic themes. *The Passionate Heart* (1918) relates motherhood to the loss of young men in warfare. Two of her volumes of the early 1930s, *The Wild Swan* (1930) and *Under The Wilgas* (1932), sympathetically introduce Aboriginal material. In 'The Lament of the Lubra', 'The Myall in Prison' and 'The Waradgery Tribe', for instance, she expresses the plangent cries of dispossession and persecution. In 'The Waradgery Tribe' the emphasis is as much on the land as on its former inhabitants: 'Emptied of us the land'. But the people too can cry,

> We are the lost who went
>   Like the cranes, crying;
> Hunted, lonely, and spent,
>   Broken and dying.

In these volumes she also laments the encroachment of cities on the countryside, and the loss of bird life in such poems as 'A Song of Swans', 'The Birds', and 'I saw the beauty go'. These too are preoccupations of later poets, notably Judith Wright and Kath Walker.

Mary Gilmore was known and admired by generations of writers in Australia. She knew Henry Lawson well, was perhaps unofficially engaged to him in the early 1890s, and, probably rather fancifully, she laid claim to having helped his career. With the poet Roderic Quinn she helped to found the Fellowship of Australian Writers in 1928.

R. D. Fitzgerald edited a selection of her verse in 1948. But it was Hugh McCrae (1876–1958) whom she admired most and who returned her affection and respect. He was a member of the pagan bohemian coterie of Norman Lindsay, who persuaded him to come to Sydney from Melbourne. His varied and precarious career included acting (including the leading role of Adam Lindsay Gordon in a silent film, despite his inability to ride well), and periods as a theatre critic and editor, and as a black-and-white artist. Like Lindsay in his paintings and drawings, McCrae peopled an imaginery landscape with mythical rather than realistic figures: fauns, satyrs, nymphs, unicorns, centaurs, colombines, harlequins and pierrots.

His first book, *Satyrs and Sunlight* (1909), was published with 'decorations' by Norman Lindsay. Lindsay also illustrated later volumes. McCrae's world of imagination has many suggestions of lasciviousness and bacchanalia. In 'I Blow my Pipes', 'The sweaty centaur', it is said, 'leaps the trees'; in 'Ambuscade', the 'moving eyes' of 'the black centaurs' are said to 'devour the snuffling mares'; in 'Colombine' the 'long eyes and pointed chin' of Colombine engage in a game of temptation with Harlequin. It is the tension between this sexuality and the surface appearance of harmless play-acting and image-making that raises McCrae's work above the level of *fin-de-siècle* period pieces.

Although slightly younger than McCrae, Norman Lindsay (1879–1969) was a great influence on him, as he was subsequently on Kenneth Slessor and Douglas Stewart. Lindsay was the fifth of ten children of Dr Robert Lindsay, an Irish Protestant of Scottish descent, and Jane Williams, the daughter of a Wesleyan missionary in Fiji. Six of the children had prominent careers in the arts, Percy, Lionel, Norman, Ruby and Daryl being artists and illustrators, Joan (along with Lionel and Norman) a writer.

Norman Lindsay made his career chiefly as a cartoonist, graphic artist, and painter. From 1901 until 1958 he worked, with only two breaks, as resident cartoonist and illustrator for the Sydney *Bulletin*, his salary (then £800) being withdrawn in 1958 because of the financial difficulties of the magazine and Lindsay's lessening output. His drawings, etchings and paintings frequently ran into problems of censorship because of his fondness for amply proportioned, menacingly seductive nudes. One of his novels, *Redheap*, was, almost unaccountably, banned in Australia until 1959.

Norman's elder brother, Lionel, introduced him to the works of Nietzsche, which, in a simplified and personal form, became a large part of the gospel that he subsequently preached. Lindsay's Nietzscheanism is vitalism, earth glorification, the joy of living, the joyousness of sex, and the central value of art. Although scornful of nationalism in art, he believed that in the Australian climate a new classicism might flourish, and the values of the fringe or province displace those of the centre. His heroes were Shakespeare, Beethoven, Byron and Browning; he admired Swinburne, the *Yellow Book* and Oscar Wilde; his favourite artists included Dürer, Rubens, the Pre-Raphaelites and the Australian *plein-air* (or Heidelberg) school. At the big stone house in Springwood, to the west of Sydney, where he lived in later life, he liked to read and be read to from Petronius, Rabelais, Cervantes, Scott, Dickens, Balzac, Conrad and Louis Stone.

The 1914–18 war, in which he was vehemently anti-German but horrified by the carnage and human waste, shattered part of his philosophy of earth glorification. He turned to a kind of neo-Platonism, based on a hierarchy of levels of existence and a strong anti-materialism. These later views of Lindsay on life and art are incorporated in *Creative Effort: An Essay in Imagination* (1920), as well as in two fictional works, *Hyperborea: Two Fantastic Travel Essays* (1928) and *Madam Life's Lovers: A Human Narrative Embodying a Philosophy of the Artist in Dialogue Form* (1929). They are also to be found, filtered through his son Jack, in the four issues of *Vision: A Literary Quarterly*, edited by Jack, Frank C. Johnson and Kenneth Slessor in 1923.

Jack said later that novel-writing was for his father 'a peripheral activity', but he wrote twelve novels and two children's books, as well as many stories. Many of his stories stayed in manuscript for years, even decades, because he liked to read from them to friends and revise them as a consequence.

They are artificial comedies, for though he preached the zest of living for the moment he was temperamentally detached from the life of his own time. He vehemently opposed modernist tendencies in art and literature and he was highly selective in what he saw, being unaware, for instance, of the wild flowers in the grounds of his home at Springwood until Douglas Stewart wrote about them. His world in literature and art was that of the radiant imaginary country of Atlantis or Hyperborea.

His first novel, *A Curate in Bohemia*, was written in 1904–5, but not published until 1913. It is a light-hearted account of his art-student days in Melbourne in the later 1890s. Lindsay is Partridge; the Australian artist and later art-teacher Max Meldrum is MacQuibble; the innocently eager young clergyman is the first of his many humorous anti-clerical portraits.

The Magic Pudding: Being the Adventures of Bunyip Bluegum and his Friends, Bill Barnacle and Sam Sawnoff (1918) is the account of the efforts of three bush friends to protect their magic pudding from the dastardly assaults on it of two professional pudding thieves. The importance of the pudding is that it is a companion as well as an inexhaustible source of delicious meals. The zany, sometimes verbose humour can seem a bit academic to modern children, but the book is still widely admired as *the* classic Australian children's story.

Redheap, written near the end of the 1914–18 war, when Lindsay was in some distress, revising his ideas about life and art, was published in 1930 by Faber in London. Robert Piper is nineteen, growing up in a devout family in the country town Redheap, but passionately attracted by the forbidden items of sex and beer. The book tells of his sexual pursuit of the parson's daughter, Millie Kneebone, his success, her pregnancy and discovery by her costive father. The Revd Mr Kneebone's moral outrage is punctured by the words of Robert's drunken tutor: ' "Well, I'm damned!" said Mr Bandparts. "You are an invention of cheap fiction after all" ', and by the gin-sodden Mrs Kneebone's uncharacteristically energetic response, 'Go to the devil, you sulky hound!' Millie is taken by her mother to Melbourne for an abortion; Robert goes off cheerfully to the University.

The Cautious Amorist (1932) is a tale of three males and one female shipwrecked on an island. Lindsay said it was a realistic rebuttal of the falsity of De Vere Stackpool's romance *Blue Lagoon*, which he read while convalescing from a period of ill-health.

Saturdee (1933) is a collection of small-boy stories. It is derived from his own childhood recollections, supplemented by a few more up-to-date details such as motor cars and pianolas. The boys are tough and unsentimental, fascinated by matters (like sex) that they boast of understanding but do not, and having about them the same predatory, selfish air evident in Robert Piper, with little even of the mateship that exists between Piper and Bandparts.

People without responsibilities, not required to stand alone, supported by a prevailing ethos and some sense of mateship, lie at the heart of all Lindsay's novels. Boys and adolescents are perhaps the best possible exemplars of such a code of behaviour, and that may explain the success of *Redheap* and *Saturdee*. In the adult books, love represents a fearful surrender of the self to another person and to vulnerability. Woman is powerful, intimidating, and masterly. In the world of children and adolescents, however, she poses less of a threat.

Norman's son Jack (1900–) established himself as the most prolific of all Australian authors, writing or editing close to 200 works. Among them were over forty novels, many volumes of poetry and over 100 works of translation, history, literary history, art history and Marxist political commentary. As editor with P. R. Stephensen of the *London Aphrodite* (1928–9) he was responsible for publishing in England the work of his father, his brother Philip, Brian Penton, Hugh McCrae and Kenneth Slessor. His autobiographical trilogy, *Life Rarely Tells* (1958), *The Roaring Twenties* (1960) and *Fanfrolico and After* (1962), provides a graphic account of his life in Brisbane, Sydney and London.

Some social realists: Prichard, Palmer and others

Katharine Susannah Prichard (1883–1969), though born in Fiji, was brought up in Melbourne and Launceston, her Launceston experiences forming the basis for the autobiographical children's story *The Wild Oats of Han* (written 1908, published 1928). At the age of nineteen, needing to support her ailing parents, she took a job as a governess in South Gippsland. These experiences later formed the background to *The Pioneers* (1915), a novel which won for her the prize in the Australian section of the Hodder and Stoughton All-Empire Novel Competition.

The Pioneers, the story of the hard-working settlers Donald and Mary Cameron, the Irish political convict Dan Farrell, and the children of both families, is a romance of pioneering in the bush. Escaped convicts, cattle-duffers, murder and corruption are pitted against determination, endurance and sheer hard work. The work of rugged Australians, assisted by their domestic animals, is a recurring theme in her work. The aged Mary Cameron, an emancipated convict, tells her grandson at the end, 'This country has been the redeemer and blotted out all the old stains. . . . You will be a pioneer, too, . . . a pioneer of paths that will make the world a better, happier place for everybody to live in.' The apocalyptic vision is also typical of her work; later it was to take a distinctively Communist cast.

In all, Katharine Susannah Prichard wrote eleven novels, many short stories, at least twelve plays, two volumes of poetry, an account of a visit to Russia, and a great many political pamphlets and articles. Her early novels deal with romantic infatuation, beautiful women and handsome lovers, but from *The Black Opal* (1921) onwards fashionableness and 'style' become insignia of spiritual emptiness.

During the 1914–18 war she reported as a journalist on Australian military hospitals in France. What she saw of warfare horrified her and strengthened her growing humanitarian philosophy. Back in Australia, she married in 1919 Captain Hugo Throssell, VC, the son of a former Premier of Western Australia. Shortly afterwards, in 1920, she became a founding member of the Australian Communist Party.

From 1917 onwards, Katharine Susannah Prichard was working on her fourth novel, *The Black Opal*, published in 1921. She had begun to gather material for this novel while working as a governess on a station not far from the White Cliffs and Lightning Ridge opalfields beyond Broken Hill. *The Black Opal* presents the independent opal-miners at Fallen Star Ridge, led by Michael Brady, as oppressed both by station-owners and by an interloping American investor, Armitage, who wants to consolidate the mines and pay wages. Brady has a romantic Lawsonian idea of the mateship of the miners, allied to a sense of the necessity of individual initiative and the importance of working in harmony with the earth. In Brady's scheme, 'the Ridge idea' is one where 'every man was the proprietor of his own energies, worked as long as he liked, and was entitled to the full benefit of his labour'. The romantic interest in the book comes from Sophie Rouminof, who becomes a Broadway star, returns to the Ridge, rejects the immensely wealthy Arthur Henty (who commits suicide) and Armitage, and ends up with Potch, the humble opal-gouger, with whom she looks forward to a lifetime of 'faith and loving-service'.

Working Bullocks (1926) is a less sentimental and philosophically tangled book. This time the community is that of the bush workers in the karri forests of Western Australia, struggling against the brutality and danger of the work and the heartlessness of the employers. The real hero is Mary Ann Colburn, the first of Prichard's strong, mature, sexless women characters. She has borne eighteen children, 'worked like a bullock herself; . . . taught her children to work like that too, to help themselves and each other', and held the home together in spite of having an inadequate, improvident husband who 'liked his beer'. Her daughter, Deb, falls in love with Red Burke, a virile bullock-teamster, full of courage and audacity. The mother's advice is 'don't go stuffin' your head full of love and that sort of thing. . . . don't take Red on till he's showed he can go straight . . . keep off the drink and save a bit.' Red does neither of these, but it is Deb not her mother who begins to see a deficiency in his values compared with those of the idealist Mark Smith, who alerts the timber-workers to the supineness of their union-organizers and calls a strike, taunting the men with being 'working bullocks' who will go 'crawling back to work tomorrow when the whips are cracking'. As Mark predicts, the strike collapses, his own sexual attractiveness fades, and Deb goes back to Red. In the last scene Red and Deb go off with a bullock team to become working bullocks themselves, to breed, and to continue life in the forest 'with its silences, whisper of leaves, murmur of small birds, flung through by the laughter of a butcher-bird, melodious and cruel'.

Coonardoo: The Well in the Shadow (1929) tied for first place in the first *Bulletin* novel contest. Set in the north-west of Western

Australia on the cattle station Wytaliba, it is the first novel with
a major Aboriginal character; her name and its meaning give
the book its title. Katharine Susannah Prichard gained much of
her knowledge of Aborigines from K. Langloh Parker's
Australian Legendary Tales (1896–8), but also from months of
living on an outback station. On Wytaliba the Aborigines call
Mrs Bessie Watt, the widow who runs the station, 'Mumae',
that is, 'father', because she is both father and mother to her son
Hugh. Hugh is brought up with Coonardoo, who is intended by
Mrs Watt to be his house-keeper on the station after she dies.
But, to the neurotically repressed Hugh, Coonardoo in some
way takes the place of his mother and is thus sexually
untouchable. He fails to understand her spiritual affinity with
him and with the land on which Wytaliba operates; he fails to
understand her sexual devotion to him. Hugh sublimates his
own sexuality into devotion to Wytaliba. His neglect of
Coonardoo (except for one night when she finds him lost in the
bush) is one factor in her being forcibly seduced, experiencing
fascination as well as horror, by the neighbouring station-
owner, Geary. Hugh, in jealous anger, banishes her from the
house, she sinks into degradation ('rotten with disease') as
Wytaliba sinks into drought and debt. Hugh, repressed and
depressed, has lost her, his shallow, fashionable wife Mollie,
and a prosperous station. Mrs Watt and Coonardoo are the
strongest characters; Hugh is inadequate and basically
inhumane – as a woman character says of him at the end, 'his
repressions have rotted in him'.

Some of the same human material and certainly the location
of *Coonardoo* were used in Katharine Susannah Prichard's
three-act play *Brumby Innes*. Its central character is similar to
Geary in *Coonardoo*. The play was written in 1927, but not
published until 1940. Another writer who used the same
location and a rather similar situation was Mary Durack
(1913–). Her novel, *Keep Him My Country* (1955), concerns a
young station-owner, Stan Rolt, who renounces Dalgerie, the
Aboriginal companion of his childhood and adolescence, in
order to preserve his European heritage. He comes to realize,
however, that in renouncing her he also renounced the land, so
he seeks her out, though she is by this time dying, and they are
reconciled.

Haxby's Circus: The Lightest, Brightest Little Show on Earth

(1930; published in New York in 1931 as *Fay's Circus*), like all of
Katharine Susannah Prichard's novels, began from personal
experience. She had seen her brother, a doctor, treat a circus
rider who had broken her back in a fall, and some years later, in
1927, she spent several months touring with Wirth's Circus in
Western Australia.

Once again Prichard chooses a self-contained group united
by common working-interests. Haxby's daughter, Gina, falls
during a circus riding-act and, now a cripple, becomes
alienated from circus life. The hunchback dwarfish clown
Rocca, who has mutely loved her, leaves her money in his will.
With it she returns to the circus, restores its fortunes, and
eventually takes Rocca's place as a clown who uses a deformity
to make people laugh. She 'seemed happiest, really, when, in
her clown's dress, made-up with plastered face and rouged
mouth, she waddled into the ring and tumbled about, making
herself grotesque and hideous, to get the brittle, crashing
merriment of the crowd that could hurt her no more, in whose
laughter she could join, at the order and harmony of a world to
which the circus held the dim surface of its mirror'.

Intimate Strangers (1937) is a novel dealing with a suburban
married couple, Greg and Elodie Blackwood, their opacity to
each other, the near break-up of the marriage, and their
salvation through commitment to socialism. The novel was
completed in draft in 1933. Katharine Susannah Prichard then
travelled overseas, to the USSR and elsewhere. While she was
away, her husband committed suicide. After a lapse of some
time, she returned to the novel and altered the original ending,
in which Greg Blackwood, having gambled away all their
assets, committed suicide. In the revised form he was
discovered in his suicide attempt and prevented. Prichard's
novels, with their frequent suicides, may be seen as reflecting
her own inevitable obsession with a reality in which both her
father and husband committed suicide. *Intimate Strangers* is,
however, the first of her novels to accept city life as natural,
instead of representing a fall from a rural Eden. Both Greg and
Elodie feel trapped by economic need, unable to express their
artistic personalities.

Katharine Susannah Prichard returned to her formula of life
in a closed working community with her trilogy on the Western
Australian goldfields, *The Roaring Nineties* (1946), *Golden Miles*

(1948) and *Winged Seeds* (1950). She had gathered material in visits to the goldfields during the Depression of the 1930s. Militant unionists concerned with the exploitation of workers and conscious of the need to educate them about the evils of capitalism are prominent in the fabric of these works.

Vance Palmer (1885–1959) has already been mentioned in connection with the Pioneer Players. He is, however, better known as a novelist, short-story writer and essayist than as a dramatist. From the second decade of the century he and his wife Nettie Palmer (1885–1964) made a precarious living by their pens, keeping up a world-wide correspondence with writers, socialists, and members of the peace movement, and frequently travelling abroad.

Vance Palmer's first published article was 'An Australian National Art', which appeared when he was nineteen in *Steele Rudd's Magazine* (1905). In it he offered the opinion that, 'until the Australian writer can attune his ear to catch the various undertones of our national life, our art must be false and unenduring'. The lives of both Vance and Nettie Palmer were devoted to that creed. They continued into the 1950s some of A. G. Stephens's interests and ideas. Vance's critical book *The Legend of the Nineties* (1954) offers a view of the Australianness of Australian literature as conveyed by its egalitarian, democratic and social-reformist character – a good description of Palmer's own books but not necessarily of many other Australian works.

Vance Palmer wrote several romantic novels with island and bush settings (some under a pseudonym) before his first substantial work, *The Outpost* (1924; revised as *Hurricane*, 1935). In it he introduces what was to be his essential theme: a man physically and psychologically strong engaged in a contest with fate. In *The Outpost* Faulkner, a resident magistrate in Papua, delays taking action to suppress an indigenous uprising because of his romantic interest in a girl; the results are disastrous. In *The Man Hamilton* (1928) a station-owner suppresses his desire for Nina Byrne, governess on a neighbouring station, out of consideration for his half-Aboriginal wife and their son. In *Men are Human* (1930) Roger McCurdie and his soldier-hero son, Boyd, are both strong in body and in will, but both are fated not to achieve their will: Boyd is fatally thrown by a horse; Roger, unable to run the station alone, returns to his second wife, who insists on living in the city. In this novel, too, there is a choice to be made between an Aboriginal and a white woman: Boyd fathers a child by Josie, the daughter of his father's Aboriginal stockman, but wants to marry a white woman, Barbara. *The Passage* (1930) concerns another strong man who makes sacrifices. Lew Callaway becomes responsible for supporting the family by fishing when his father is taken by a shark. He carries the problems of near-insolvency, a drunken, useless younger brother, and a disastrous marriage. One acquaintance says, 'Lew never had no luck'; his mother regrets that 'she had put too much weight on those broad shoulders of his when the family was struggling'.

Palmer provides excellent depictions of small rural communities, mostly made up of humble, unassuming people. There is a strong sense of personal and communal morality, symbolized by small enterprises such as a fishing-business or the protective relationships within a family or a sense of mateship. The texture of his novels is much less highly coloured than that of Katharine Susannah Prichard's: there are many more ordinary, decent people and few melodramatic incidents. His chief characters tend to be emotionally reticent, even inhibited, wary of doing anything that might leave them open to sarcasm or mockery. His novels lack almost entirely the open passion of Katharine Susannah Prichard's. What they are particularly good at – and this is true also of his short stories – is conveying the awakening of the adolescent mind to adult consciousness. The novels also excel in presenting the encroachment of 'civilization', in the form of roads, houses and shops, into isolated rural communities.

Palmer wrote several other novels, the most notable being the Macy Donovan trilogy, *Golconda* (1948), *Seedtime* (1957) and *The Big Fellow* (1959). Golconda is an inland Queensland mining-town, modelled on the silver–lead–copper mine of Mount Isa. Donovan begins as a brash union-organizer, but becomes a Labor member of Parliament and ultimately Premier, sceptical of whether the workers are much better off under such a government. Like all Palmer's heroes he is slightly detached from those around him, enjoying male company more than female, and rather humourless and dogged in his espousal of political principle.

Life in the outback, but less socialistically conscious life, is the material of Frank Dalby Davison (1893–1970). Leaving school at fourteen, he worked as a farm boy, printer, sailor, estate agent, unemployed dole recipient, writer, public servant and farmer. *Man-Shy* (1931), which he tried to sell from door to door, became a publishing success when it won the gold medal of the Australian Literature Society as the best novel of the year. It attempts to see life from the point of view of a red heifer who loses her mother soon after birth. She and the other cattle experience fear, bewilderment, pain and hunger. She witnesses rivalry between the two bulls and the excitement of a breakout from the stockyard. It is a sustained exercise in point of view, with moments of pathos and terror, but Davison's trailing descriptive sentences are incapable of concealing the paucity of dialogue.

Dusty: The Story of a Sheep Dog (1946) is the story of a dog which is the product of the mating of a dingo with a red kelpie. The wild and the tame sides of his nature are at war: he wins prizes as a sheepdog, but kills the sheep at night. With the death of Old Tom, the man who has raised him, Dusty 'goes bush', mating with a dingo and evading capture and death at the hands of several men until, inquisitively watching a police trooper make camp, he is killed by a falling tree branch. Davison told a television interviewer that 'every man is a cross between a kelpie and a dingo, and so is every woman'.

Davison's last novel, the immensely long *The White Thorntree* (1968), was one he had worked on for over thirty years. It presents a boringly clinical treatment of many kinds of sexual inhibition and practice in carefully inoffensive language. Pursuit of the romantic ideal is shown to be destructive – often ending in murder or suicide; ordinary people are shown to have a wide range of sexual instincts; and both points are repetitively made in leaden prose, only fitfully relieved by humour or satire.

A broader canvas than Davison's but a similar commitment to mimesis was adopted by Marjorie Barnard (1897–) and Flora Eldershaw (1897–1956). The two women met as undergraduates at the University of Sydney and, although pursuing independent careers, managed to collaborate successfully in several books under the pseudonym 'M. Barnard Eldershaw'. Marjorie Barnard said in 1983 that in their collaboration

We'd go for long walks together and talk and talk about the book we were going to write until it was worked out thoroughly. After that it didn't really matter who wrote it. Flora had a better brain than I had but I was probably the better writer. I'd write a chapter and she would criticise it and then I'd rewrite.

Marjorie Barnard by herself also produced a volume of short stories, *The Persimmon Tree, and Other Stories* (1943), and several Australian historical works.

M. Barnard Eldershaw's first collaborative work, and their best known, was *A House is Built* (1929), which shared first place with *Coonardoo* in the first *Bulletin* novel competition. Serialized in the *Bulletin* as *The Quartermaster*, it is the saga of a retired navy quartermaster's establishment in Sydney in 1839 of a waterfront store, its rise into a prosperous business, and its decline forty years later in the hands of the founder's timid grandson. *A House is Built* is a briskly written book, full of vivid action and epigrammatic prose. One of its attractions is that it provides painlessly a good outline of New South Wales economic and social history in the middle of the nineteenth century.

Barnard Eldershaw's last novel was the work published, after some post-wartime censorship, as *Tomorrow and Tomorrow* in 1947. It was written almost entirely by Marjorie Barnard, Flora Eldershaw being out of sympathy with the ideas of the book. In its fully restored text and title, as *Tomorrow and Tomorrow and Tomorrow*, its publication by Virago in 1983 occurred in the same year as that in which Marjorie Barnard, the surviving joint author, won the Patrick White Award. It is set 400 years in the future. Knarf, a novelist and historian (named after Marjorie Barnard's close friend, Frank Dalby Davison), writes a historical novel beginning in the Depression years and passing through the 1939–45 war. At its centre is Harry Munster, a 'brooding Anzac' representing a sense of national awareness and the possibility of the people's control of destiny and justice. After a Third World War, a middle-class leftist peace movement comes to power in Sydney. International intervention overthrows them; in retaliation they burn Sydney as 'a symbol of greed and profit', but are unable to prevent the triumph of the right wing. Knarf's world, by contrast, is one of peace and prosperity, if over-regimentation. State socialism has succeeded the collapse of twentieth-century

Australian society. Knarf lives in the Tenth Commune, that is, the Riverina, where his son Ren seeks to organize the gradual return of individual freedom. *Tomorrow and Tomorrow and Tomorrow* has vivid and moving scenes set in Sydney in the 1930s and 1940s. It scenes of the future are vague, both in visual detail and in intellectual ideas.

A more overt socialist in all her writings, but a clumsier stylist, was Jean Devanny (1894–1962). Born in New Zealand, she set her early novels in that country. The first of them, *The Butcher Shop* (1926), had the distinction of being banned in New Zealand, Australia, Boston (Mass.) and (later) Germany, for a variety of reasons: its unflattering account of farming conditions in New Zealand, its detailed account of how sheep are crutched, its feminism and its Communism. In 1929 Devanny and her husband moved to Australia, where they continued to support the Communist Party. Many of her subsequent novels were pot-boilers, but *Sugar Heaven* (1936), set in the north-Queensland canefields, has more substance. Devanny gathered material for it during the time of a protracted strike against the danger of being required to cut green cane: 'Burnt cane is the issue with us, the fight for life', because of the risk of contracting the fatal Weil's disease from green cane. In the end the strike is lost and the men vote to return to work: 'We have been defeated by political factors. . . . Our fight is to democratize our union: to take it out of the control of the boss! . . . Every fight of the workers is actually a winning fight. . . . Our time will come.' Devanny's novel is also an interesting study of the relations between women's sexual interests, inhibitions and prejudices, and effective political power.

Political power, personal conflict and Australian history are also the interests of Eleanor Dark (1901–), though her political position is less overt than that of Marjorie Barnard or Jean Devanny. Dark, the daughter of a minor short-story writer and poet, Dowell O'Reilly (1865–1923), wrote two groups of novels, the first six contemporary, the final three set in the early days of white settlement. The early works, with their thriller-like plots and long excursions into the remembered past, can seem awkwardly contrived, but they are more experimental in narrative technique and more concerned with psychoanalysis than other Australian works of their time.

In *Prelude to Christopher* (1934) the past is re-created through the delirious memory of Dr Nigel Hendon as he lies injured in hospital after a motor accident. He had discovered that his wife Linda came from a family in which madness existed. Because of his eugenicist beliefs, he gave up hope of a child, turning his efforts into the establishment of a colony based on his social and medical ideals, but Linda disrupted it. All of this comes to the reader through the fragmentary recollections of Nigel. In *Return to Coolami* (1936) the past is again re-created through flashbacks. They occur during a two-day car trip in which Bret Maclean, his new bride Susan and her parents recall and interpret the past. Bret's brother, Jim, had previously had an affair with Susan, but had died in a car crash. Bret, fulfilling his promise to marry his brother's pregnant lover, is also a catalyst in getting his mother-in-law to express to her husband her dissatisfaction with the sheltered conventional life he has provided for her.

Three of Eleanor Dark's later novels are careful, historically accurate works of fiction set in the first quarter-century of European settlement. They focus on what she takes to be the Aboriginal sense of timelessness and the impact on it of the European sense of history. *The Timeless Land* (1941) begins with the Aboriginal memory of Cook's visit to Botany Bay – a 'magic boat', capable of 'folding its wings like a seagull' when it came to rest. Then in 1788 Phillip arrives. He and the Aboriginal leader each consider the other 'incredibly ugly', but at first there is good will on both sides. The novel goes on to tell of the misunderstandings between blacks and whites, reprisals, Phillip's fatal experiment in socializing Arabanoo to white customs, the opposition of other officials to the just rule of the Governor, the sullenness of the convicts, and the hardships of the little white colony. Attention is divided between the point of view of the whites and the blacks, the chief black character being the young man Bennilong.

More than half way through the book the Second Fleet arrives, bringing with it the Mannion family to settle from Ireland. The newcomers' impressions are conveyed through the eyes of their six-year-old son, Patrick, an important character in the second and third novels of the trilogy. He hears his father ask Captain Tench of the Marines, 'you have hunting here, Captain, no doubt? Is the sport good?', and Tench reply tersely, 'We have hunted only for food, sir, and then it has been too serious to be amusing.'

Patrick learns a great deal from Johnny Prentice, a convict boy whose mother becomes first a wet-nurse for Patrick's baby brother, and later a house servant and mistress to Patrick's father. Johnny runs away and makes a rebel life among Aborigines. Bennilong, another of Phillip's socializing-experiments, succumbs to liquor, learns hubris from the white men, and knows that he has 'forgotten how to be at peace'.

Dark manages to maintain interest in the heroic character of Phillip; the Aboriginal sense of wonderment and dismay at the intrusion of aliens to subvert their land, way of life and beliefs; and the various fictional characters, notably Patrick and Johnny. In *Storm of Time* (1948) the fictional characters and the historical characters draw apart, as the colony expands and the common interest in sheer survival no longer exists. The central historical figures are now Governor Bligh and his implacable enemy, John Macarthur. Bligh is a perceptive and inquisitive newcomer to the colony, bellicose and choleric, but indefatigably energetic. 'Rogues have cooed at me before now', he tells King, his predecessor, 'and I have known them for rogues.' His first meeting with Macarthur is stormy: 'Are you to have such flocks of sheep and such herds of cattle as no man ever heard of before. *NO*, Sir!' But Bligh's support of the small settlers against the large landowners, monopolists, military and officials leads to armed insurrection against him, fomented by Macarthur. He is deposed and arrested.

The lives of the fictional characters intermittently engage with the official events. Patrick's father takes a new Irish wife, Conor, who comes to the colony, like Bligh, with her own curiosity and values, superior to and bound to come into conflict with those prevailing in the colony. Johnny Prentice becomes a hunted man, who comes to regard Mannion senior as his bitter enemy.

No Barrier (1953) begins with the murder of Stephen Mannion, a revenge actually accomplished by Johnny, but one for which Ellen Prentice, his mother, takes the blame and is executed. The official story, covering the early years of Governor Macquarie's rule, now fades into secondary importance. There is a good deal of laborious detail about the crossing of the Blue Mountains and the building of a road through to the fertile slopes beyond. Some attempt is made to identify this as an intrusion into Johnny's territory and to suggest the inevitable ending of the outlaw's life as settlement expands. Patrick, always an observer rather than an initiator, is murdered and robbed in the end, shortly before being due to embark for Ireland. All strands of the plot, then, meander inconsequentially. The reader is left, though, with a sense of the various groups that are laying claim to the land: the Aborigines, who are being forced off it; the outlaws, who see it with a wild territorial romanticism; the settlers, who have visions of progress and wealth; the convicts, who remain depressed, sullen and rebellious; and the Governor's party, concerned with good administration. But now the sense of excitement has been succeeded by the sense of inevitability. The Aborigines no longer wonder; they know what the white men are like. And Johnny is a doomed outlaw, who will one day fall victim to official vengeance. Dark's merit is that, notably in *The Timeless Land*, she has provided the best account of the early years of the white colony, and, until the work of Xavier Herbert and Colin Johnson, the best fictional account of Aborigines in early contact with whites.

The historical novels of Brian Penton (1904–51), written in the 1930s, deal with a later period of white settlement and a different colony. They concern the period of settlement in Queensland from the early 1840s to near the end of the century. The two novels completed, *Landtakers* (1934) and *Inheritors* (1936; published in the same year in London as *Giant's Stride*), are centred on Derek Cabell, a young Englishman who comes to Australia to make his fortune and return, but finds he has been won over, grudgingly, by the land. His 'Perhaps I was always meant to stay' echoes the words of Hugh Watt in *Coonardoo* and anticipate those of Stan Rolt in Mary Durack's *Keep Him My Country*. Penton is unremitting in his depiction of the brutality, degradation, opportunism and self-interest of the settler; the romantic portrait of heroism and respectability is created, falsely, by Cabell's son only in retrospect. Cabell thinks he is escaping from the brutality and oppression of his father and older brothers, but the colony is peopled by convicts, gaolers and adventurers whose obsessiveness borders on the insane. Gradually he remakes himself in their mould. He becomes a pastoralist who faces flood, fire, plague and his own emotions with little respect for the rights of others. The two novels are saturated with melodramatic violence, such as when the evil McGovern is blinded by the already blind Cabell, killed with an axe by Cabell's ex-convict wife, Emma, then burnt in a fire that destroys the homestead. By this time Cabell has become a 'battered old relic out of the past', consumed by avarice, driven by an indomitable will. Penton's portrait is unremittingly anti-romantic, except in its depiction of the landscape. There is hardly a human being in either novel who is not venal and brutal or brutalized. To that extent, Penton's thesis is that white Australian society has never escaped its convict origins, its early struggle for existence, its incapacity for morality or altruism.

5
New reputations of the 1920s and 1930s

John Shaw Neilson and Kenneth Slessor

WHERE Christopher Brennan used once to be regarded by modern Australian poets as the finest of their precursors, that position is now more often occupied by Kenneth Slessor or, less frequently, John Shaw Neilson (1872–1942). Neilson, greatly admired as a lyrist by James McAuley and Judith Wright, grew up on his parents' impoverished farm near the Victorian–South Australian border and later worked as an itinerant farm labourer, harvesting, droving, fencing, fruit-picking, clearing, road-making, shearing and so on. Never very strong physically, he found that his eyesight began to fail to the point where he could no longer see to write, and he had to ask astonished and sometimes unsympathetic workmates to write down what he had composed while labouring. Despite having less than three years' formal schooling, Neilson was well read in English poetry. His father and uncle were also poets and they encouraged him to read and write. Neilson was familiar with the work of the English Romantics and major Victorians; English, Irish, Scottish, and American songs and ballads; and the Australian bush balladists.

His first publications were in the local newspaper at Nhill in Victoria and in the Melbourne paper the *Australian* in the early 1890s. Later on, he sent his work to A. G. Stephens for advice and publication, finding that it often appeared with substantial editorial emendation. Stephens accepted work from Neilson for the *Bulletin* and the *Bookfellow*, which he edited. He also arranged the publication of his first volume, *Heart of Spring* (1919), and the subsequent volumes *Ballad and Lyrical Poems*

(1923) and *New Poems* (1927). There is still no complete edition of Shaw Neilson's works, though *The Poems of John Shaw Neilson*, edited by A. R. Chisholm (1965), *Witnesses of Spring*, edited by Judith Wright, Val Vallis and Ruth Harrison (1970), and *Green Days and Cherries: The Early Verses*, edited by Hugh Anderson and Les Blake (1981), provide a good foundation.

Comparisons in style have been made between Neilson's work and the unaffected directness of Blake, William Barnes and John Clare. Comparisons in vision have been made with Traherne and Blake, for there is something of the possessed mystic at times in Neilson. The circular movement of his poems, the way in which they dwell on a few related images and then return to the original cause of inspiration, strengthens this impression.

Although A. R. Chisholm believed that 'Shaw Neilson's work is practically timeless; there are no "periods of development" in his career', it is possible to detect a movement from innocence to experience and disillusion in his work. Until about 1910 he writes about an idealistic world in which childhood and youth are immortal and the deity beneficent. In 'Heart of Spring', an early poem flawed by rhetorical phraseology, spring, conceived of as 'Youth's emblem', suffers 'dim death' but not pain, and is exhorted to die quietly in the knowledge that 'The Sun shall raise thee up again'. 'Green Singer' offers an even more exuberant image for spring and love, a divine 'singer' and 'player' entirely devoid of 'shadows'.

The poems of 1910–11, such as 'My Love is Like a Violin' and 'As Far as my Heart Can Go', suggest a more physical, less idealistic experience of woman's love. Woman, rather than spring, youth, or the colour green, now seems to permeate the universe, though these earlier images are still used and incorporated in the altered vision. In 'My Love is Like a Violin', he associates his loved one with music, rest, 'green joy', 'honey-cells', 'an opening flower', various water images, and the ethereality of blue. But it is a mystic as well as a physical love, for she is associated with 'All children and all womenkind' and she has warmed his heart

> Ere ever the red earth was formed,
> Or a pale soul with love was stormed,
> Ere ever the round earth could spin . . . .

'As Far as my Heart Can Go' presents a more intimate portrayal of love – 'The little flower in the firelight is as far as my heart can go' – but again in terms of symbolic redness, this time represented by firelight and lips.

Neilson's best-known poem, 'The Orange Tree' (finished about 1919, though he had been working on it for some time), represents a further stage in his development. He still clings to the divine notion of love, but is now anxious to understand its nature and its effect on the young girl who experiences it. The worldly wise, literary and romantic poet questions the girl about all kinds of possibility. Sometimes his suggestions have the magic of poetry about them, when he suggests that the girl's mystical illumination may be due to

> The heartbeat of a luminous boy
> Who with his faltering flute confessed
> Only the edges of his joy.

Sometimes they are romantic stereotypes ('a fluttering heart that gave / Too willingly and was reviled'). But the speaker's attempts to define and limit the experience are received with increasing impatience by the girl, who eventually commands his silence so that she may perceive the light in the orange tree and also listen to a call that speaks through the tree and to which the tree itself is listening. The orange tree has, then, been transformed by a power beyond itself into which the willing listener can be drawn. The defining power, even the poetic defining power, is a hindrance in experiencing this power, but a hindrance that cannot be discarded.

Two earlier poems, written in 1913, explicitly state the association of sexual love with rivalry, sorrow and death. They are 'Petticoat Green' and 'The Wedding in September', which Neilson said were 'twins in spirit. They ramble about the influence of colour and sound on the human being'. In 'Petticoat Green' the poet asks a painter to 'Paint me lilies and summer maids / And skeletons'. In 'The Wedding in September' a fiddler plays magic music about God, and spring, and love, and death.

Neilson writes breathtakingly about such subjects. He says that the effect of his Calvinist Presbyterian mother was to make him believe as a boy that God was 'terrible and thunder-blue'

('The Gentle Water Bird'). Through his poetry, however, he came to believe that God could be understood only by inference from nature, not by defining and limiting creeds. In 'The Poor Can Feed the Birds', he says that the God of the poor is 'too dim' to be spoken of much. All they can do is emulate his benevolence by feeding the birds.

Neilson's ballads have in their ancestry both Scottish border ballads and Australian bush ballads. 'The Moon was Seven Days Down', for instance, has a Scottish sense of doom achieved through incrementally repeated lines of dialogue between husband and wife, but an Australian locale and situation. Peter is obsessed by his crops and livestock; his wife – whom he always addresses as 'Woman' – dies slowly of neglect and hard work. Matter-of-factly he speaks to his neighbour first of his hopes for a good crop of wheat and then of his need for a coffin.

Neilson also had some talent for satire. At times it was mockingly light-hearted, as in 'The Sundowner', a satire against Lawson's romanticizing of the swagman, 'With his shrewd, sable billy-can / And his unwashed Democracy'. At times it was solemn and bitter, as in the anti-war poem 'The Soldier is Home', a moving generalized portrait of the man whose enjoyment of life has been atrophied by his experience of war. The 1914–18 war and later the depression of the 1930s seem to have had their effect in moving his poetry away from the green freshness and joy he had expressed beforehand more towards a sense of disillusion. But the conflict of innocence and experience in him preceded the war.

A poet of small output, Kenneth Slessor (1901–71) has a substantial reputation as a writer who managed to combine Australian and international poetic influences and to write with understanding of past and present, the imaginary and the immediate. He has a separate reputation as a bohemian newspaper-editor, writer of light verse, and club raconteur. He spent almost his whole professional career as a reporter and editor, working for daily and weekly papers in Sydney and Melbourne. From 1927 to 1939 he worked on the satirical and often scandalous *Smith's Weekly* in Sydney, rising to become editor-in-chief. These were perhaps the greatest days of this irreverent paper. Its comic writers included Slessor, Ronald McCuaig (a poet of both serious and light ability) and the prose writers Lennie Lower, Ross Campbell, Bernard Hesling and Alexander Macdonald. More extraordinarily, the paper retained more black-and-white artists on its permanent staff than *Punch* or the *New Yorker*. They included Stan Cross, Joe Jonsson, Virgil Reilly (who illustrated Slessor's volume of light verse, *Darlinghurst Nights*, 1933) and George Finey. It was Cross who produced the famous sketch of two men hanging precariously from a construction site, the second having pulled down the pants of the first, with the caption, 'For gorsake stop laughing – this is serious!'

In 1940 the Australian War Cabinet appointed Slessor a war correspondent. He served in Greece, the Middle East and New Guinea, writing dispatches of great perception and humanity, some of them later assembled by his friend Douglas Stewart in the volume of occasional prose entitled *Bread and Wine* (1970), all of them collected in Slessor's *War Diaries*, edited by Clement Semmler (1985). In 1944 he was publicly criticized by the Australian Prime Minister John Curtin for his reporting of the war in New Guinea, particularly his attitude to the Australian Commander-in-Chief, General Thomas Blamey. Slessor resigned, disgusted with the heroics of war, the posturing of commanding officers, and the neglected sufferings of the troops. His poem 'An Inscription for Dog River' is bitterly anti-Blamey.

Slessor himself divided his serious poetry into three chronological groups, 1919–26, 1927–32 and 1933–9. In the first period he was strongly influenced in choice of subject and attitude by Norman Lindsay and Hugh McCrae, with whom he continued to be friendly. It is poetry with a romantic interest in the grotesque, the exotic and the literary, a depiction of a pagan world inhabited by classical gods, swashbuckling lovers and adventurers, and vulnerable sprites. The statues, stone, fountains and bubbles of Lindsay's and McCrae's imagery are found here too; indeed they persist in Slessor's work and may account in part for the cold, distant, impersonal impression that Judith Wright and Vincent Buckley find in his work. These early poems are often like poems for paintings; they have a highly developed visual sense, an affectation of the theatrical (as in Lindsay and McCrae); but they lack the determined fleshliness of his mentors, and give the impression that Slessor was a rather muted carouser.

Vision, the short-lived magazine produced by Jack Lindsay, Slessor and Frank Johnson in 1923–4, was vehemently opposed to modernism in the arts. Slessor himself said that 'It was not until 1927 that I first came into contact with any of Eliot's major work, in the second edition of *Poems 1909–1925*. Until then, all I had known of Eliot was a few rather bleak anthology pieces, such as "La Figlia che Piange" and "Sweeney Erect", which I heartily disliked'. In the period beginning in 1927 Slessor assimilated influences from Eliot and Pound, as well as from Wilfred Owen and Edith Sitwell (who had been cruelly satirized in *Vision*). What he derived was a tone of elegant weariness; certain imagery (for example, clouds or fog scraping against the window occur in 'Heine in Paris' and 'Captain Dobbin' as in Eliot's 'The Love Song of J. Alfred Prufrock'); a fascination (also as in Eliot) with time (particularly noticeable in the 'Out of Time' sequence and in 'Five Bells'); and the unapologetic treatment of the city and suburbs as material for poetry. While there is some tendency towards surreal association, Slessor's poetry never departs from urbanity and control; form and syntax remain orderly and conventional; and diction is experimental within historic standard limits, as in such images as 'flap-dark', 'quince-bright' and 'Crow-countries graped with dung'.

Although born in the New South Wales country town of Orange, Slessor was very much, in the words chosen by Douglas Stewart for the title of his 1977 memoir, *A Man of Sydney*. He went to preparatory and grammar school in Sydney, had his first work published in the *Bulletin* when he was still at school, and took his first job on the Sydney *Sun*. The city of Sydney, particularly its harbour, provides the sense of place for much of his best work. His very first published poem, 'Goin'', concerns soldiers at Gallipoli remembering with tenderness the harbour they have left behind. 'Captain Dobbin', from the second period, is also a poem about memory spreading over seascape, recalled in this instance through the medium of old books and charts, as well as instruments and photographs. It is a poem full of nautical lore – the names of shipping-firms, strange sea creatures and navigational aids, for instance. It also has a number of epigrammatic descriptions: mementos as 'a lock of the sea's hair', 'a chest of mummied waves', and 'his little cemetery of sweet essences'; or drawing-room landlubbers as 'lap-dogs in clean shirts'. There is also an eerie sense of lost companions which Slessor was to evoke many times later. Here it is expressed in the imagery of an ocean graveyard, with some reminiscence of Eliot's subaqueous imagery in *The Waste Land* and perhaps a touch of Hart Crane's *The Bridge*:

> Flowers rocked far down
> And white, dead bodies that were anchored there
> In marshes of spent light.
> Blue Funnel, Red Funnel,
> The ships went over them, and bells in engine-rooms
> Cried to their bowels of flaring oil . . . .

The bells and the sense of the dead as also encompassing the living (here the hell-contained stokers) were to be used again in 'Five Bells'.

A second major poem from Slessor's middle period, 'Five Visions of Captain Cook', has been immensely influential. Its combination of memory, time and the history of discovery has inspired comparable work by R. D. Fitzgerald, Douglas Stewart and Francis Webb. Its excited tone is rather forced, and its attempts at onomatopoeia, though clever, can seem a little childish, but it is memorable for some much-quoted epigrammatic lines and for its more reflective fifth vision. The first vision, after more of Slessor's mariner-*manqué* technical details, ends with the choice Cook made in 1770 to sail west across the Coral Sea instead of north to the Dutch East Indies:

> So Cook made choice, sailed westabout,
> So men write poems in Australia.

The next three visions concern the exploration of the east coast of Australia, the near-wrecking of *Endeavour* on the coral of the Barrier Reef, and Cook's navigational aids and methods of charting. The last vision is of the retired Captain Alexander Home and his memories of adventuring with Cook. He sees in the mind's eye – he is physically blind – the death of Cook, an accident set off by one of 'the trumpery springs of fate'. Returning to 'The vague ancestral darknesses of home', purblind, he finds that all he can see is 'Dim fog-shapes, ghosted like the ribs of trees', which, even before they disappear entirely, are far less vivid than the remembered 'blazing waters and blue air'. It is a symbol both of the central reality of Australia for an Australian writer and of Slessor's own introspective reliance on memory rather than current fact.

Slessor's duties as editor of *Smith's Weekly* seem to have interfered with his writing of serious poetry. At any rate, the number of poems he produced slackened somewhat in the 1930s before the complete cessation of the early 1940s. It is the final few poems that have generally been regarded as his best. 'Five Bells', written between 1935 and 1937, is in part an elegy for Joe Lynch, a black-and-white artist whom Slessor knew from both Melbourne *Punch* and *Smith's Weekly*. In 1927, on his way to a Saturday-evening party, he toppled from the rail of a crowded harbour ferry and drowned. The title of the poem, apart from Slessor's unexplained fondness for five, presumably refers to the approximate time of Lynch's death, 6.30 p.m., as he and a friend, their pockets filled with bottles from a hotel that closed at 6 p.m., were on their way to the party. Thirty years after writing the poem, Slessor spoke of the time of his own meditation as the subsequent five bells (that is, 10.30 p.m.) but such a fact – if it was a fact – should not obliterate the alternative meanings. Slessor, with his love of sea-faring lore, would have been aware that in the British navy, after the mutiny of the Nore in 1797, five bells at 6.30 p.m. (the mutineer's signal) was replaced by a single bell. Thus, five bells never strikes, mutiny never begins, the regular progress of measured clock time is displaced by an ideological memory. This is highly relevant in a poem influenced by Henri Bergson's process philosophy of psychological time, a poem in which Slessor tries to privilege memory, 'the flood that does not flow', above 'Time that is moved by little fidget wheels', 'the bumpkin calculus of Time'. It is an attempt that in the end fails. 'Five bells' keeps sounding through the poem, interrupting the poet's memories of the dead man, but indicating the richness and speed of memory that can occur while a single ship's time is being rung. Joe has gone where

> The tide goes over, the waves ride over you
> And let their shadows down like shining hair

says Slessor, using an image that speaks directly to anyone who has swum under the bright waves that cast their shadows on the sand below. But he finds no purpose in life or death. Memory and the search for meaning dissolve; what he heard as he looked through the window of his home out over the harbour

> Was a boat's whistle and the scraping squeal
> Of seabirds' voices far away, and bells,
> Five bells. Five bells coldly ringing out.

'Five Bells' was the first poem in the volume of that title (1939) and the last in Slessor's *One Hundred Poems, 1919–1939* (1944), a collected volume that included two-thirds of the poems in *Earth-Visitors* (1926) and all of those in *Cuckooz Contrey* (1932) and *Five Bells*.

Slessor preserved only three later serious poems; they were added to the collection in his *Poems* (1957). Slessor's first wife, Noela, died in 1945. His last poem, 'Polarities', a disillusioned love poem, grew out of an affair he had with a blonde-haired woman some time after this. Its movement between two opposing attitudes is an appropriate symbolic coda to his work. 'An Inscription for Dog River' is a bitter satire against General Blamey for his hubris in adding his army's inscription to those of Ashur-Bani-Pal's, Nebuchadnezzar's and Caesar's on the cliffs above Dog River. 'Beach Burial', the poem placed last in *Poems*, is set on the Mediterranean coast near El Alamein, during the battles against Rommel's German army in 1942. Once more death and water are associated. The bodies of drowned sailors 'sway and wander in the waters far under', then are washed up on the shore. The soldiers find time to bury them in shallow sandy 'burrows', marked briefly by a cross of driftwood, nameless, unidentified as friend, enemy, or neutral. Slessor's humanity and his confession of helplessness in the face of questions about any purpose in life and death are once more unself-consciously expressed.

Slessor's awareness of international movements in twentieth-century poetry, his close-packed richly associative lines, his easily grasped ideas, and his reputation as a bohemian *bon-vivant* and raconteur appealed to many Australian poets in the 1950s, 1960s and 1970s. More philosophical or academic poets, including Judith Wright and Vincent Buckley, found his work thin.

Martin Boyd

Martin Boyd (1893–1972) is rather a cult figure among some Australian academic critics, perhaps because he can be safely acclaimed as an entertainer and romancer who is undeniably intelligent, perhaps because he holds social and political views that can be described as radical conservative. Boyd's parents were both painters; one of his brothers (Merric) was a potter who produced five distinguished artist children, including Arthur (1920–), Guy (1923–), and David (1924–); another brother (Penleigh) was a painter, whose son Robin (1919–71) was a distinguished architect and art critic, best known for his book *The Australian Ugliness* (1960).

The Boyds were landed gentry in Victoria from before the goldrush period, and lived on inherited income. Martin Boyd went to England in 1915 to join first the infantry, and later the Royal Flying Corps, and after that spent most of his time in England and Italy, returning to Australia for a few years just after the First World War and again in 1948. Needing to supplement the small income provided by his parents, and finding that he had no vocation as an Anglican Franciscan, he determined on a career as a novelist. The first of his novels, *Love Gods*, published in 1925 under the pseudonym 'Martin Mills', is based on the six months he spent at Batcombe, Dorset, among the Franciscans, and it presages the fact that most of his novels have a theme or sub-theme of religious quest. He was intensely Anglo-Catholic in his thirties and forties, a convert to Roman Catholicism at the end of his life, but his beliefs and practice tended to be personal, poetic and even sceptical, rather than conformist. He was eventually attracted to Italian Catholicism because it is the form of Christianity that builds on Mediterranean classicism rather than on the barbarism of northern Europe, but for Boyd religion was in any case more a means of adapting man's imperfect nature to this life than a preparation for a life to come. He believed in a constant warfare between absolute good and absolute evil and considered that human beings should search for the God within themselves, seek a balance between spiritual and physical needs, and learn to appreciate the goodness of the things of the earth and the pleasures of the senses.

The Montforts (1928), his third novel, was also published

under the pseudonym 'Martin Mills'. It won the first gold medal awarded by the Australian Literature Society, in 1929, and, like many of his other works, it was later revised, appearing in its altered form in 1963. *The Montforts* offers a record and exposition, in barely disguised form, of the history in Australia of the Boyds and the à Becketts (his mother's family) from about 1830 to 1921. This material is reworked and expanded in the Langton tetralogy, *The Cardboard Crown* (1952, revised 1964), *A Difficult Young Man* (1955), *Outbreak of Love* (1957) and *When Blackbirds Sing* (1962).

Before that series, though, Boyd wrote what he regarded as his best book, *Lucinda Brayford* (1946, revised 1954). In Boyd's words, it 'ridiculed savagely the Establishment, the great war leaders, the bishops, the business men, in fact everything except the landed gentry, the creative artist and the Christian religion, all in decline at the moment'. The novel has an immense time scale, beginning in the middle of the nineteenth century with two young men sent from Cambridge to Melbourne, one for reasons of honour, the other for reasons of health. After one-third of the book the scene moves back to England, when Lucinda Brayford, granddaughter of both the Cambridge men, returns with her English husband. Lucinda's son, Stephen, dies in the middle of the 1939–45 war, worn out by the wickedness of the world and the beatings he has received as a conscientious objector in a military prison. His mother thinks back on him as a schoolboy, 'a nice, affectionate duffer' – a fair appraisal of several of Boyd's heroes.

The first of the Langton novels, *The Cardboard Crown*, is the story of Alice Langton, who, like Richard Mahony, is torn between the milieu of Europe and that of middle-class Australia. In her personal life she is also torn between loyalty to her husband, Austin, and her children, and her love for Aubrey Tunstall, a distant relative. Austin is attached to his estate in Australia, Aubrey to the milieu of Europe. Austin has been, and there is substantial suspicion that Aubrey also is, attracted by her money. Experiencing personal and cultural conflicts, she confides in tiny writing to her secret diary, 'Je dois être deux femmes, pouvante habiter deux mondes'. The interpreter of the diaries is the narrator, Guy Langton, Alice's grandson. One of his first explorations of the diary is to find the date of his birth – in 1893, the year of Martin Boyd's birth. He is ostensibly writing a novel about his grandparents, not a history, so both he and the reader are aware that his judgement and interpretation may be faulty. As he says at one stage in his account, 'Again I come to the falsification of history which can come from putting events in the wrong sequence.'

Although aware of the social and political events of the twentieth century and using them in his novels, Boyd never emancipated himself from a certain social ambience, a style and diction redolent of George du Maurier's *Trilby* (a book he admired) or the more dynastically laden parts of Trollope's Palliser novels. In *The Cardboard Crown*, Guy Langton reacts to his cousin's suggestion that he should write a novel about his grandparents with the words 'It wouldn't be decent. . . . I should be cut by everyone.' When Aubrey introduces himself to Alice on the railway station at Pisa, the conversation begins

> 'Surely you must be one of the Langtons of Waterpark?'
> 'My husband is a cousin of Mr Thomas Langton's', said Alice. 'We are Australians.'
> 'Are you Mrs Austin Langton?' he asked.
> 'Yes,' said Alice, 'but how do you know my name?'
> 'I am Aubrey Tunstall. My sister Damaris married your brother-in-law.'

A Difficult Young Man was considered by even Boyd himself to be 'very snobbish'. It continues the family saga through to Guy Langton's own generation, with particular reference to Guy's older brother, the moody and unstable Dominic. His experiences in the 1914–18 war are the focus of *When Blackbirds Sing*. In the final scene Dominic flings his Military Cross, just arrived by post, into the pond, considering that it had been awarded 'for what to him was the worst thing he had ever done, when he had violated his own nature at its deepest level'.

Despite the many passages and situations in his novels that depend on a relative judgement of the merits of Australia and Europe, Boyd himself did not regard his work as dealing with something analogous to the 'Jamesian theme', the relation between a parent culture and its more vigorous and honourable offspring. He objected to being described as the victim of 'double alienation' – that is, both from Australia and from England – believing that 'My inner division, if I have one, is the age-long one of the European, between the Mediterranean and the north, the Classic and the Gothic worlds.' Yet, whether the sources of indecision are internally European or extend also to Australia, it is justifiable to see in his own life and in the lives of many of his characters a sense of religious and social questing that never finds the right milieu. He and his characters often have a self-assured discontent, as if aristocracy, democracy, the establishment, culture and religion have all deviated from the Boyd way of righteousness. As a novelist he is, in fact, at his best with misfits: the lonely, the unwanted, the elderly, the unmarried. Romantic love and the commitment it entails are important to him neither as plot situations nor as symbols of any deeper values in life. He depicts sensitive and intelligent loners, moved by affection but rarely by passion. He is essentially a literary entertainer, dealing with serious but unresolved ideas. He is impatient of cant, pomposity and vulgarity (though sometimes, like Henry James, succumbing to them himself). In many ways, his most entertaining writing is in his two autobiographies, *A Single Flame* (1939) and *Days of My Delight* (1965), where he can be himself without feeling that he has to follow novelistic conventions.

Christina Stead

Christina Stead (1902–83) was, like Boyd, an expatriate writer, but, unlike Boyd, a materialist in her philosophy. She was the daughter of David G. Stead, a naturalist and conservationist who subsequently married another person of similar interests and talents, Thistle Y. Harris (1902–), a prolific writer on Australian flora. Christina Stead trained as a schoolteacher, but because of a weak voice was assigned to psychological testing and correspondence teaching more than classroom teaching. In 1928 she left Sydney for London. Subsequently she lived in Paris and the United States. After her marriage to an American businessman and novelist she spent some time in Switzerland and Holland, before settling first in the United States and later in England.

Her first novel, *Seven Poor Men of Sydney* (1934), was written shortly after her arrival in Paris. It is in stark contrast to the social-realist novels of Prichard, Palmer, Devanny or Penton in that its concentration is inward rather then outward, its prose

poetic rather than directly mimetic. With Seaforth
Mackenzie's *The Young Desire It* (1937) it marks a new stage in
the history of the Australian novel.

Seven Poor Men of Sydney, the only one of Christina Stead's
thirteen works of fiction set wholly in Australia, concerns seven
friends whose lives intersect not for causal reasons but for the
author's thematic reasons. The most memorable of the seven
are Michael Baguenault, 'a beachcomber – spiritually', and his
paralysed friend Kol Blount, who says, 'Michael is like me,
paralysed, armless, a brother'. Michael's half-sister Catherine
is a socialist activist, or, as one of the other 'poor men', Tom
Withers, describes her, 'a nun in reverse. It's not religion but
irreligion that drives her mad'. Michael is doomed to suicide
from the beginning; indeed Blount, who has characterized him
as a brother, goes on, rather mysteriously, to say, 'Who does
not wish to spend his life in communion with himself? What is
stranger, more painful, richer, like the three white nights before
suicide?' This kind of enigmatic language characterizes the
central figures in the book. It is a novel that avoids almost all
expectations: of construction, relationships and language.
Michael and Catherine love each other, but shrink from a
physical relationship; both are swept by 'Strange cross-
currents and maelstroms in a mind'; both experience 'an inner
struggle to union with [one]self'. Michael, a deserter in the war,
himself deserted in love and thwarted in his love for Catherine,
throws himself into the sea from the Gap, a precipice in
suburban Sydney. Catherine, his *alter ego*, unsatisfied by her
missionary fervour for international socialism, commits herself
to an asylum. Yet these two misfits are counterpointed by their
cousin Joseph, a printer, 'a letter of ordinary script' as he
describes himself, one who is neither a missionary nor an
intellectual, an ordinary and orthodox believer for whom
'History is at a standstill'. Communism, Christianity,
evolutionary theory, the nature of humanity, the nature of
knowing and of action, the 'bitter genius' of Australia that
needs to work out its own destiny, and the essential aloneness of
the individual are constantly discussed in this intensely
intellectual and expressionistic work.

Christina Stead's publisher in London, Peter Davies, offered
to publish the work if she would give him something more
conventional first. Drawing on her experiences of six weeks

spent in 1931 in Salzburg listening to Mozart, she wrote the fifty interconnected stories of *The Salzburg Tales*, including a few remembered from an earlier unpublished manuscript. This volume was published in 1934, nine months before *Seven Poor Men of Sydney*. The motley collection of stories, fantastic, extravagant, idealistic and cynical, is supposed to be related over seven days during the Festival, somewhat in the style of the *Decameron* or *The Canterbury Tales*. In the Prologue, the city of Salzburg in August is described, with witty, satirical portraits of those gathered there. They include the music critic who can 'describe his state of mind at a concert in such sympathetic terms that the majority of people imagined he had heard the music', and the Viennese conductor who 'sometimes took shorter steps and sometimes longer as if to show that in him the passion of rhythm was constant but tidal' and who 'was a wonderful actor of concertos'. The stories are rounded off each day by the Centenarist, a magus-like character with a penchant for the supernatural. Some of the other tales are also supernatural, but others are retellings of legendary stories, some are in the style of nineteenth-century romances, some are satires of social types and of literary styles.

House of All Nations, Christina Stead's longest book, was written in a matter of weeks about the time of the beginning of the Spanish Civil War. It was published in New York in 1938 and in the same year by Peter Davies in London (under the title *The Revolving Hive*). It is an account of the dealings of a foreign bank, the Banque Mercure, in Paris. Christina Stead's father was a socialist, her husband was strongly attracted by Marxism, and she had contributed articles during the 1930s to *Left Review* and *New Masses*. In all her books money and economic imperatives are central.

Much of the material for *House of All Nations* was gathered during the five years she spent as secretary and courier to a Paris bank between 1929 and 1935, and from her husband's business connections and interests. The theme of the novel is the self-interested pursuit of money, an aim that affects almost every character. Unlike Dickens's *Our Mutual Friend*, with its similar theme, *House of All Nations* eschews the cunning merger of plots apparently separate at first in favour of Christina Stead's characteristic expressionistic technique. What general plot there is is very simple. Jules Bertillon, owner with his brother William of the Banque Mercure, is fascinated by the craft of making money. He gambles on the stock exchange with the bank's money, gradually falling into a trap that his arch-enemy Jacques Carrière lays. But in the end he flees with all the cash he can collect, leaving his brother and the bank's honourable economist, Alphendéry, to face disaster. His betrayal of both his commercial trust and his own dependants seems not at all untoward in this mercurial, insubstantial world of finance. His explanation of the bank's closure is airily dismissive: 'Oh, I should just say it closed from absence of liquidity; a not uncommon weakness with banks nowadays.' There is in the novel a sense that the money-making process goes on (like the trade of the brothel after which the novel is named) irrespective of politics, social change or revolution. Alphendéry is a Marxist in beliefs, but he does not see why he should not enjoy the money-making intrigue that a capitalist system fosters.

Stead's next two novels, *The Man who Loved Children* (1940) and *For Love Alone* (1945), concern the growing into adolescence and young adulthood of a girl who bears a close resemblance to the author. In the first of these fictionalized autobiographies the setting is deliberately transferred from Watson's Bay (the Fisherman's Bay of *Seven Poor Men*) and the University of Sydney to four American sites: Baltimore, Georgetown, central Washington, DC, and Annapolis. The novel concerns Sam and Henny Pollit, Sam's daughter Louisa (the Teresa figure of *For Love Alone*) and the six younger Pollit children. The change of locale, according to Stead, was 'to shield the family', for otherwise it would have been 'a bit too naked'.

The two parents live in their own separate worlds (like so many of Stead's characters), Sam's one of generalized abstract optimism, a universal good will neglectful of any individual's actual needs, Henny's a world of self-victimization and resentfulness. The children receive oratorical affection, promises and organization, but never warmth. Sam and Henny are entirely ill matched and they engage in reciprocated vituperation within the family. Sam is feckless, improvident and inconsistent; Henny enslaved by marriage, practical and persistently gloomy. When Henny fails to carry out her threat to kill herself and the whole family, Louisa determines to rescue the children from their impossible parents by murdering them both. At the last moment, however, she bungles. Henny, quickly grasping Louisa's intended plan, deliberately drinks the poisoned cup of tea. Louisa is terrified by what has happened and readily accepts Sam's imperceptive verdict of suicide. After the inquest she tells him the truth and leaves.

The Man who Loved Children is a subtle study of family relationships, with a tragically inevitable outcome. Its characters, whether exploiters, such as Sam, or victims, such as the children, are self-contained egotists who try to seize love rather than to give it. Each lives in an internalized counterpart of the outer economic world, relying on fantasies of sexuality, power, pain and punishment to sustain them.

In *For Love Alone*, attention is centred on Teresa Hawkins, a young schoolteacher in Sydney, living in a harbourside house, who feels the need for love as an escape from drabness. She falls in love with Jonathan Crow, the leader of a discussion group. When he leaves for London on a university travelling-scholarship, she determines to impose every manageable economy and privation in order to follow him. Although he has encouraged her to follow him, when she arrives after four years of near-starvation he brutally tells her she means nothing to him, indicating that he has never opened some of her letters. His self-absorption, his incapacity to love anyone but himself, is something that Teresa takes time to accept. Then in her disillusion she finds that her employer, the American businessman James Quick, offers her a warm love. Gratefully she acknowledges, 'you've restored me to life'.

There is, however, the suggestion that this is no conventional fairy-tale ending, no just recompense for the unhappiness Teresa has suffered. She becomes unsatisfied with romantic monogamy, and has a passionate affair with one of Quick's companions. Though she returns to Quick, she is wary and cautiously ambitious to find an outlet for her intellectual and sexual energy.

The question of any choice needing to be made between colonial and imperial values does not matter to Christina Stead (by contrast with a New Zealand novel having a somewhat similar plot to hers, *The Godwits Fly* by Robin Hyde, 1938). Although place and atmosphere can be richly created, place as such means little in her novels. Teresa is not fleeing from Sydney or Australia; she is fleeing from the restriction of family, occupation and acquaintances, and she is seeking intellectual liberation not the imposition of a European set of values.

Christina Stead's three New York novels, *Letty Fox, Her Luck* (1946), *A Little Tea, a Little Chat* (1948), and *The People with the Dogs* (1952), lack something of the intellectual and verbal incisiveness of her best work. *Letty Fox* is a first-person narrative, from childhood to marriage, of a dispossessed, alienated woman. Her parents and their relatives have unsuccessful marriages and sexual experiences, she is aware of the economic and political turmoil of the 1930s, and she becomes active in leftist politics. After several unsuccessful affairs, including an abortion, she gratefully sinks into marriage with a millionaire's son, who is promptly disinherited. *Letty Fox* was vehemently criticized as a slur on American womanhood and banned for some years in Australia. More recently it has been regarded, equally oddly, as a feminist manifesto. This is to mistake the essentially unevangelical nature of Stead's satiric exposures.

A Little Tea, a Little Chat has another of Christina Stead's male egoists in Robbie Grant, a cotton millionaire, but he has less superficial charm and more vileness than her other examples. *The People with the Dogs* is a more genial book, sharp in its satire but also comic, a book in which Edward Massine represents the human face of capitalism. The commercial 'creative sloth' of his relatives and dependants during their summer vacation at his home in the Catskills is paralleled by the easy community of his New York tenants. In New York, however, Professor and Mrs Barbour are dissidents; they object to Massine's capitalist comfort and spend their time 'getting up petitions, and sending around typed circulars'. And, in a return to her best comic satire, Stead describes Mrs Barbour as 'an energetic body-snatcher' who wrote 'passionate biographies of the fashionable extinct, such as Henry James, Tchaikovsky, Chopin, Freud, Baudelaire and Tolstoy, and dealt with popular resurrection at the rate of not less than one a year'.

After a long silence, Christina Stead produced her next novel, *Dark Places of the Heart*, in 1966. (The London publication of the following year reverted to her preferred title, *Cotters' England*.) It is set in the 1950s, among working-class and middle-class characters. It shifts from the Tyne–Tees area to the East End of London, dealing with Stead's favourite material, family tensions. Set in Switzerland just after the 1939–45 war, *The Little Hotel* (1973) concerns the obsession with money, madness and suicide, and family relationships, all conveyed with devastating black comedy. *Miss Herbert (The Suburban Wife)* (1976) is like a less dark and fraught reworking of *Letty Fox*. Eleanor Herbert has ambitions of liberation like Teresa and she tries to realize them in the literary world of London. It is her unimposed choice in the end to adopt marriage and have children.

In an interview late in her life Christina Stead said that at high school she knew Nietzsche's *Thus Spake Zarathustra* by heart, and years later in Switzerland, finding an edition in German, realized that she still remembered it. What she disclaimed, however, was any particular interest in Nietzsche's philosophy. It was 'his words, his poetry, the way everything was a chant' that captivated her. Yet there is something of Nietzsche's ideology as well as his impassioned ecstatic language in her work. She constantly uses a technique of thesis and antithesis to question all the basic social institutions, including marriage, the family, patriarchy, capitalism, socialism and liberal humanism. She is fascinated by the sources and the manipulation of psychological power. And she is, morever, always opposed to theistic interpretations of life. But Stead is never nihilistic. Her characters believe in love, which she presents as a substitute religion, sustaining whether in delusion, hope or reality. Most importantly, perhaps, her sense of there being no other sustaining force, and love itself operating only intermittently, leads her to her expressionistic construction, her de-emphasis on plot, and her poetic interweaving of lives and themes.

Xavier Herbert

Xavier Herbert (1901–84) is a novelist who bears comparison with Patrick White and Christina Stead but, unlike them, has lived almost all his life in Australia and writes solely about Australia. It would be a mistake, however, to compare him with such social realists as Vance Palmer or Katharine Susannah Prichard, for, although he expresses a love for Australia as a land, his vision of what it should be as a nation and his disappointment at the gulf between that vision and the reality causes him to express contempt for white Australians as 'lousy bastards', 'lousy Aussies', 'colonialist bastards' and 'expatriates in their own country'. The British and the Americans are almost as vehemently reviled for their commercial and cultural incursions in Australia. Herbert is, in fact, contemptuous of most nationalities except Jews; his wife, Sadie, was a Jew and Herbert always speaks affectionately of Jews and their way of life. Even the land of Australia is not something he approaches unequivocally. 'You have to hate this country to love it', he said. 'You have to fling yourself into the wilderness time and time again saying "Well, kill me you bastard, if I don't belong." '

Herbert's rebelliousness and resentment of authority began in his boyhood. His own parents were rebels too, rejecting the authority of the Catholic Church and expressing prejudices against many institutions and people. Herbert resented his mother's preference for an older half-brother and her domination of his father. He did nevertheless use the name of her spurious French aristocratic ancestors, the de Laceys, for the hero of *Poor Fellow my Country*, Jeremy Delacy.

Herbert was born to unmarried parents on the north-west cape of Western Australia. He grew up among Aboriginal children and nursemaids and subsequently celebrated the glory and the tragedy of Aborigines in his two great novels *Capricornia* (1938) and *Poor Fellow my Country* (1975). After becoming a qualified pharmacist in Perth, Herbert lost interest in the profession (though he always found it a useful source of income when in need) and enrolled in the first year of medicine at the University of Melbourne. By the end of the first year he had abandoned interest in that career too and had determined to be a writer. Some of his stories, written under the pseudonym 'Herbert Astor', had by this time been accepted by the Melbourne *Australian Journal*, the staple of which was romantic fiction for women readers. Herbert then spent some four years roaming the northern parts of Australia, working as a drover, railway-fettler, pearl-diver and prison-overseer before departing by ship from Darwin to London in 1930. On the ship was Sadie Norden, a young Jewish milliner returning to England after the failure of her marriage to a man whom she had come to Australia to marry. Herbert 'cut her out from the mob' on his first night, and then wooed her for the rest of the voyage. He had just finished his first novel, *Black Velvet*, and was hoping to attract a London publisher. *Black Velvet*, an account of white men's sexual use of black women (black velvet) in the Northern Territory, was a raw and provocative book. Sadie did not like it; neither did London publishers, one of whom, dressed, according to Herbert, in a frock coat, dismissed him with the words, 'It deals with relations between black women and white men. Good day sir!' Almost starving, and having pawned his typewriter, Herbert encountered Sadie in the street. She found him a garret to live in, redeemed his typewriter, and persuaded him to 'write the way you talk'. The result was *Capricornia*, written feverishly at the beginning of 1931 in six weeks. The novel ran to half a million words and was rejected by Jonathan Cape as being over-long. Herbert returned to Australia in 1932, followed shortly afterwards by Sadie. In Sydney, Herbert took the typescript to P. R. ('Inky') Stephensen, who had been associated with the Lindsays in the Fanfrolico Press. He agreed to publish the work, provided Herbert agreed to co-operate in shortening and making other changes in the text. Then the novel was set in type. At that point, the badly undercapitalized P. R. Stephensen and Co. went into voluntary liquidation, the large established firm of Angus and Robertson refused to take over the publication, and the type was melted down after the pulling of galley proofs. Hebert 'went bush' to north Queensland and the Northern Territory, eventually becoming Superintendent of Aborigines in Darwin for a time. Meanwhile Stephensen had found a source of capital in the Sydney solicitor and businessman W. J. Miles, who provided the money for a journal, the *Publicist*, and a small associated publishing company. He set about publishing *Capricornia* again, producing one advance copy just before the close of 1937 in order to comply with the conditions of the Sesquicentennial Commonwealth Prize for 'the best novel published, or accepted for publication in Australia in 1937'. Stephensen formally published the work on 26 January 1938, Australia Day, the 150th anniversary of white settlement. It was also the day which Stephensen helped organize as an Aboriginal Day of Mourning and Protest. *Capricornia* won the £250 Sesquicentennial Prize and publication was taken over by Angus and Robertson.

Capricornia is about the northern part of Australia between 1904 and the late 1930s, about the appalling treatment of Aborigines by whites, about the land that the whites abuse but the blacks love, and about the pretentiousness, snobbery, and social distinctions of the whites. The white Government grants grazing-leases, the introduced cattle drive away the native game, the Aborigines starve, kill the cattle, or work for the white man. 'Most Aborigines who had been born in freedom preferred to do their starving in the bush. And all the while the Nation was boasting to the world of its Freedom and Manliness and Honesty. Australia Felix!' is Herbert's acidulous comment.

Norman Shillingsworth is the son of Mark Shillingsworth and an Aboriginal woman; he is regarded as a 'half-caste brat', or 'yeller-feller', a disgrace to his father and his uncle and foster father, Oscar. Heir to both white and black cultural traditions, Norman is the focus for both cultural and psychological conflict in the book. He is never properly instructed into or accepted by white or black society and drifts into and out of both and into and out of the territory of Capricornia.

Connie Differ is another half-caste, the daughter of Peter Differ, who loves her and intends 'to take her South out of this colour-mad hole'. Before he can do so, however, he dies, pleading with Oscar to save Connie from 'The Compound, humiliation, prostitution, at last a place by the camp-fire in the bush, and always the unutterable debasement of being coloured and an outcast'. Oscar declines. Connie comes into the care of a missionary, Humbolt Lace, is seduced by him, and, when she is pregnant, is married off to another half-caste, Peter Pan. Her baby, Tocky, is brought up by Tim O'Cannon with compassion, the intention being that she should have a white education and marry respectably. Tim, a fettler, is killed by a railway engine and Tocky finds herself in the prison-like Gospel Mission. Escaping from it she makes camp in the bush and is found there by Norman. But Norman tires of her amorousness, fears that he may be in trouble with the law for 'consorting' with her, and eventually sees her taken into custody by Trooper O'Crimnell to be returned to the Compound. Escaping again, and now pregnant with Norman's child, she continues to run from the police and other predatory men. At the end of the novel Norman finds her body and that of her baby rotting in a water tank.

Capricornia is a novel of a land criss-crossed by the futile and sometimes tragic wanderings of whites and of blacks harried by whites. There are dangerous railways bringing sudden death to unsuspecting workers, police trails leading to the apprehension of murderers and suspects, wanderings that lead to the discovery of decaying bones. The plot is picaresque, but the episodes are held together by contiguity of parallel happenings and by the brooding sense of the land. Mark's discovery of Tocky's bones, for instance, is immediately preceded by the courtroom scene of his own trial for murder, in which his counsel rearranges the contents of a bag of human bones to explain a theory. The land itself is the main character, in the way it is in much European fiction about India (by Kipling, Forster and Paul Scott, for instance). Its moods provide rhythm to the plot and symbolism to the theme in so far as the recurring Wet Season never fails to show how ill equipped the whites are to cope with the land or with their own intellectual rationalism or passions. The Wet Season destroys the grand railway project, resulting in eight deaths and, indirectly, a murder. The pastoral industry and officialdom, with its office rules, police action and legal system, can operate efficiently only in the Dry Season. Throughout the novel there is a continuing symbolic collocation of day, the Dry Season, fire and redness around the whites' rationality and collaborative endeavours. By contrast night, the Wet Season, black and silver surround the physical side of humanity (birth, coition, death) and the sense of Aboriginality.

Capricornia is a novel that Herbert later characterized as something he detested, 'my bastard son that keeps following me around', 'a botch, the work of a boy . . . a work written by an amateur'. It is true that the writing is flawed and that the author's comments about the country are often intrusive, but it is also true that those comments, particularly about the treatment of Aborigines, the fallacy of believing that they were a dying race, and the crassness of the whites' fear of Asian immigration expressed far-sighted and prophetic views.

During the 1939–45 war Herbert served as a soldier (lowering his age to enlist), and after the war settled in the rain-forest country of north Queensland (a place, he said, more like Ceylon than the common notion of Australia). Between 1942 and 1959 he published nothing. Then came *Seven Emus* (1959), a novella set on a cattle station in north-west Australia, centred once more on a character of mixed descent. It is burdened, however, by a verbose style and an idiosyncratic experimental system of punctuation which sit oddly with the tall-tale nature of the plot.

The unfavourable critical reception of *Seven Emus* caused Herbert to revise substantially the long work he had earlier written in the same style, *Soldiers' Women*, which was published in 1961. It is the only one of his major works not set in the north of Australia, the only one not dealing with the land and Aborigines. Its subject is a wartime city (for the most part identifiable as Sydney) and the exploits, mainly sexual, of its women. Its concerns are male aggressiveness, female sexuality and the nature of destiny. Rape, unintended and unwanted pregnancies, abortion, lesbianism, and whoredom permeate the novel. Against them, Herbert as an author upholds standards of faithfulness in marriage and respect for motherhood as unrealized ideals. The novel is riddled with authorial homily and a sense of fastidious distaste for promiscuity, female or male. The large cast of characters is handled with skill; the counterpointing of characters and incidents is much used (as in *Capricornia*), though here with more attention to opposites than to similarities; and there is a vivid sense of the social entertainment available in a wartime city away from the front line. But the novel is overloaded with repeated clichés and emblems and with empty rage, tears and reproach. Herbert himself later said that it was 'purely synthetic, through and through'.

Herbert's somewhat fictionalized autobiography, *Disturbing Element* (1963), tells the story of his life from boyhood until his departure from Melbourne for Sydney in 1925. The title is derived from the name his father 'roared at me in times of household upset in which I was involved'. *Disturbing Element* is an eloquent and fascinating book, honest in its self-appraisal, and sharply pointed in its dialogue. It is not to be relied on, however, as a source of factual biographical event. Herbert incorporated into it parts of a semi-biographical novel, *The Little Widow*, which he had come to consider unpublishable, and he is, in any case, a person who prizes a good story more than actuality. There is also in him a little of the interest in mystifying the self to others that is more fully developed in Mary Gilmore and Miles Franklin.

Herbert's short stories, *Larger than Life*, were published in the same year (1963). His story-telling technique hardly changed from the time when he was writing for the *Australian Journal*. He needed a plot in the Maupassant or O. Henry mode; he told it in the relaxed tone of a familiar yarn-spinner; and he avoided moral comment, relying on the plot to make his point. The twenty stories are all set in northern Australia, many are concerned with the nature of destiny, and tricks or duplicity frequently occur in the plots. But none of them are as well told as some of the episodes in *Disturbing Element*.

Herbert spent nine years writing his next novel, *Poor Fellow my Country*, which was finished in October 1973 and published in 1975. It is a work written during protracted periods of self-imposed isolation, avoiding all human contact. Its territory is again the northern part of Australia; its period that from the accession of Edward VIII in 1936 to the turn in the fortunes of the Pacific War just after the battle of the Coral Sea in 1942, with a brief coda set in the 1970s. It is a very long novel – some 850,000 words – published with substantial fanfare by William Collins, and selling 14,000 copies in two days.

Poor Fellow my Country is a compendium and manifesto of Herbert's ideas about Australia; it is an epic lament for the despoliation of the land by its white inhabitants and their failure to make use of the many opportunities available; and it reviews only to deride the many faiths and myths that whites have brought to Australia, judging them by the standards of Aboriginal myth and religion which are entirely in tune with the land itself. Herbert's construction and presentation of the myth of what might have been, his vision of a Terra Australis del Espiritu Santo respected by its inhabitants and expressing the magical spirit of the land, is the great achievement of this book. It provides the tragic quality in his presentation of the ignorance, carelessness, hollowness and cupidity of the white invaders.

One of the central characters in the book is Prindy, a quarter Aboriginal in descent, the son of the white station-manager, Martin Delacy, and a half-Aboriginal girl, Nellyerri. The scenes in which he comes to realize and identify with this

Aboriginal heritage are brilliantly managed. In the opening scene, as a boy of eight, he is intently fishing in a waterhole when an Aboriginal man of high degree (a *koornung, pookarakka* or witch doctor) seems to materialize from the earth. In the man's emaciated left arm he holds a bundle of spears; in his claw-like right hand he holds a spear-thrower or womera. Both he and Prindy remain absolutely still. 'The spell was broken by slight movement of the claw holding the womera – raising of the index finger. In common sign-language that meant "Who are you?" ' Prindy knows that the proper response to a senior is not his personal name but the sign for his *Skin*, his place in the totemic system of relationships. But thinking that the apparition may be a '*Moomboo* or Devil-devil, wanting to know your Skin only to judge the propriety of eating you', he is too fearful to reply. To win the boy's confidence the *koornung* sings a magic song that entices a fish to the pool and onto the boy's spear and then Prindy reveals that he is of the same totem.

Prindy's brutal treatment by whites, particularly by police, is a symbol for the mishandling of the land by white settlers. Like Norman in *Capricornia* he is heir to two cultural inheritances, though his experiences of both are wider and more complex than Norman's. Near the end of the novel he is initiated by Bobwirridirridi, the *pookarakka*, but the ceremony is ritually violated by the intrusion of Savitra, his young lover, an Indian girl. She is brutally mutilated and killed by the Aborigines; Prindy is sentenced to a trial by ordeal. It is on this trial, where he defends himself against spears when armed only with a boomerang, that his white grandfather, Jeremy Delacy, intrudes. As a result, Prindy is fatally wounded, an outcome that Bobwirridirridi says would not have occurred had his magic not been vitiated by the intrusion of the white man's rifle.

Jeremy Delacy, the 'Scrub Bull', is the main white character in the novel. A conservationist and agnostic, he carries many of the author's ideas about Australia as a nation and its proper relationship to other nations. He leases a property, Lily Lagoons, on which he cares for injured native animals and tries to mend the scars of past mining activity. His two sons, Martin and Clancy, manage properties for Lord Vaisey, the absentee British landowner who is the subject of some of the sharpest invective in the novel. Jeremy's ex-wife, Rhoda Eaton, is now married to another of Vaisey's managers. In his search for an acceptable spiritual vision, Jeremy turns first towards a nationalistic fascist organization, clearly based on the Australia First movement of the 1930s and early 1940s. The 'mouthpiece' of the organization is 'the Bloke', who is 'reputed to be a genius . . . an opportunist, renegade Communist . . . an erudite wrangler'. The portrait is unflatteringly recognizable as one view of 'Inky' Stephensen. Later he finds consolation in some of the rituals of Judaism, as expounded to him by Rifkah, his beautiful Jewish lover. When Jeremy is impercipient Herbert does not hesitate to offer his own authorial opinions. The weakness of the book is, in fact, its garrulous opinionation and the vehemence of its condemnation, by both Delacy and Herbert, of almost every aspect of non-Aboriginal society. They detest any kind of officialdom or authority, whether petty or grand in scale, British landlords and imperial laws, American businessman, every kind of European immigrant to Australia, most Indians and Chinese, all politicians and all cities. They – and Rifkah, who also carries a number of Herbert's ideas – are contemptuous of white Australians, a contempt that reaches the height of its expression in the third section, 'Day of Shame', which recounts the flight from Darwin (Palmerston in the novel) when it was threatened by Japanese invasion. (Herbert had treated the episode in one of the stories of *Larger than Life*, also called 'Day of Shame'.)

As in *Capricornia*, comings and goings and annual celebrations give shape to the kaleidoscope of incident. Christmas and New Year celebrations, Anzac Day and the annual Beatrice River races each provide recurring opportunities for Herbert to symbolize his attitudes to religion, nationalism, politicians and apathy. If he has a solution for white Australia – and the novel is a lament for what might have been, not a vision of what might be – it is revolution. The reason, as one character tells Jeremy, is 'To inspire people . . . to revolution, if necessary. We're the only people on God's earth who've never had a revolution.'

As a lyrical but embittered elegy for a potential nation, *Poor Fellow my Country* has no equal in Australian literature. As a portrayal of Aboriginal ways of behaviour – though not necessarily thinking – it is also unexampled, at least by white writers. And for its set of still, magical scenes at waterholes it ranks as a great poetic novel.

6
Major new voices of the 1930s and 1940s

R. D. FitzGerald

R. D. FITZGERALD (1902–), a surveyor by profession, and the son and grandson of surveyors, grew up in Sydney in a family that valued its Irish ancestry. In the early 1920s he associated with Jack Lindsay, Kenneth Slessor and others in the group that produced *Vision* (1923) and its associated anthology, *Poetry in Australia* (1923). He contributed poems to both publications. His humanist, 'vitalist' ideas seem, however, to have been acquired independently before he began this association.

His first separate publication, *The Greater Apollo: Seven Metaphysical Songs* (1927), introduces his lifelong concern with the nature of time. He writes about the ubiquity of transience and decay, but finds comfort in the assurance of recurrence in situations, life and beauty.

Time, death and beauty are the subjects of the long meditative poem 'The Hidden Bole' of 1934. In language owing something at times to Shakespeare's sonnets and with a central cluster of images drawn from W. B. Yeats's 'Among School Children', it offers both a muted elegy on the death of Pavlova and a grave combating of the notion that beauty might die like individual human life. Its form, both outwardly in the complex rhymed pattern of twelve-line stanzas and also in the varying lengths of the syntactical units, is an analogue both of the steps of the dance and of the jets and pauses of thought. Its philosophical system of existence in space and time as an organic process is derived from A. N. Whitehead's *Science and the Modern World*, a work which he regarded as offering a philosophical interpretation of his own poetic vision of the world.

FitzGerald's volume *Moonlight Acre* (1938) won for him the gold medal of the Australian Literature Society for the best book of verse by an Australian author in that year. Among its contents was another long poem, 'Essay on Memory', which won the Sesquicentenary Prize Poem competition conducted in association with the 150th anniversary of white settlement in 1938. The impermanence of human deeds and of human life is said to be retrieved by the creative power of memory. Memory 'is the past itself', re-created by 'the wind's voice in the crevice'. Its nature and form are described as something mysterious and awesome: 'darkness it is and talons of the rain'. It is not something over which we have control, for it is inhabited by the dead and by past history, which determine our lives and our memories: 'we are storm-carried, storm-shed, / battered by streaming multitudes of these dead'. Memory, paradoxically then, is controlled by the past but also re-creates the past for us; it is both 'behind flower-growth' and 'the flower'. Towards the end of the poem FitzGerald seems to have felt the need for some kind of tonic uplift appropriate to cultural celebration. Turning aside from the primeval rain image that has dominated the poem, he offers a vapid Browningesque optimism in a more insistent rhyme scheme: 'Whatever the task, it lies in front; we must / build upward though we guess not to what skies'.

FitzGerald returned to the question of organic process in a 1944 poem, 'The Face of the Waters', which, he said, was 'conceived as a foot-note to lines occurring in "The Hidden Bole" ' in which he touched on the nature of nothingness and its relationship to concepts of the Ultimate. In 'The Face of the Waters' he develops the notion of nothingness as 'a placeless dot enclosing nothing', lacking all possibilities, and therefore being constantly invaded by possibilities which 'shatter and return to it'. Materiality and mind are not on different planes for FitzGerald: mind creates the notion of the material, the material is re-created in memory. Mind contains both the notion of an agent generating the existing processes of life and the notion that no such agent exists or is needed by the processes: the notion of God and of no God. Organic process can be described in vitalist language or in phenomenological language:

You may say hills live,
or life's the imperfect aspect of a flowing
that sorts itself as hills . . . .

In the 1940s FitzGerald's major poems were written in a
dramatic-narrative rather than a philosophical mode, though
his central characters are thinkers who espouse FitzGerald's
philosophical ideas. 'Heemskerck Shoals', published in 1944, is
based on an account in G. C. Henderson's *Discoverers of Fiji* of
the near-shipwreck of Abel Tasman in 1643. Caught by the
wind perilously close to a reef in the Fijian islands, Tasman
escaped by sailing his ships directly across the reef where he
judged the waters to be deepest. The poem is his interior
monologue after the event. In style it is colloquial, owing
something to Eliot's and Pound's adaptation of Browning's
dramatic monologue style to create the impression of a mind
communing with itself rather than with a listener. Tasman
begins with a complaint against the formality and rigidity with
which the voyage was administered, his own language being by
contrast informal and loose:

Too many councils and committees, too many
making decisions beforehand – that was no way
to run an expedition.

He goes on to complain of the cupidity of his backers by
contrast with his own love of discovery, his desire to fill the
oceans of the cartographers with 'better than spouting
dolphins'. He confesses his obsession with 'the problem of New
Holland', a country he had never seen because it had been
written off by his backers as barren and worthless. He is
obsessed too with the difficulties of reckoning longitude at sea
and the insolubility of the problem 'unless you carried time
round in your pocket'. 'Heemskerck Shoals' is in many ways a
commentary on Slessor's 'Five Visions of Captain Cook', which
deals with Cook's chronometers. FitzGerald also represents
Tasman as worried by 'these Englishmen everywhere', who
would 'rediscover, then claim for themselves' and as a person
who envisages the possibility of 'acquisitive settlement' in New
Holland. The poem also points forward to such other 'voyager
poems' (Douglas Stewart's term) as Francis Webb's *A Drum for
Ben Boyd* and *Leichhardt in Theatre*, Stewart's 'Worsley

Enchanted' and James McAuley's *Captain Quiros*. In all of them a narrative with mythical possibilities is used as a means of philosophizing: the myth is reinterpreted in the poet's own image. It is a process that A. D. Hope aptly described in 'An Epistle from Holofernes':

> It is the meaning of the poet's trade
> To re-create the fables and revive
> In men the energies by which they live . . . .

A much longer poem of this kind is FitzGerald's *Between Two Tides*, on which he had been working since 1940. It was published in 1952 with a frontispiece by Norman Lindsay. Like 'Heemskerck Shoals' it is based on material that he became interested in while working as a surveyor in Fiji before the war. This time the source was John Martin's *An Account of the Natives of the Tonga Islands* (2nd edn, 1818). Martin reported the adventures of Will Mariner, ship's boy on the privateer *Port au Prince* which was captured and burnt by Tongans in 1805. Mariner survived the massacre of the crew and was taken under the protection of the Tongan chief Finau, in whose household he lived for four years. Eventually he returned to England, living a routine existence as 'the sound stockbroker, the reliable agent'.

The interest of the poem is not in the narrative or the passages of dialogue but in the reflections of Will Mariner and of those on the periphery, particularly the author, Dr Martin, and the poet himself. Their reflections continue the interests of FitzGerald's non-narrative philosophical poems. Will, for instance, leaving Tonga, leaving part of his life behind, considers that 'And at this moment like death the dead too were near / as any of the living'. He knows that in England as in Tonga 'there would be something missing never to be attained'. Years later, at the end of his life, he recognizes that, though his buccaneering and Fijian experiences have been overlaid and supplanted by his English ones, they are still within memory's recall. The 'brown girl' who gave him a gold buckle at Tola in Spanish South America is still the subject of a recapturing quest, a memory 'of a firm throat and shoulder and a dark head / bent over a buckle on a shoe'. FitzGerald exemplifies in this poem his revised belief that human beings have a limited choice of action available to them. It is a belief adopted partly because of a rereading of Browning's *The Ring and the Book* in preparation for writing his own poem. It certainly has the effect of allowing him to develop individuality in characters and to open up not only the question of what choice an individual should make but also the more general question of how far choice is constrained by past history and character.

FitzGerald's shorter poems from the 1940s, including 'Heemskerck Shoals' and 'The Face of the Waters', were collected in the volume *The Night's Orbit* (1953), probably the richest of all FitzGerald's individual volumes. The long gap in full-sized book publication between 1938 and 1952 (when *Between Two Tides* was published) had allowed him to accumulate a valuable set of poems, mostly written in his newer, more colloquial style.

'The Wind at your Door', published in the *Bulletin* in 1958, won for him the 1960 Grace Leven Prize for poetry. He had earlier shown an interest in his family's Irish ancestry with the ballad 'Legend', concerning his great-grandmother, Mary Ann Bell, daughter of Dr Bell of Trinity College, Dublin. 'The Wind at your Door' concerns another kinsman on his mother's side, the surgeon Dr Martin Mason, who attended the flogging of Irish convicts suspected of plotting an insurrection in the early nineteenth century. One of those punished was Maurice FitzGerald, with whom the poet feels more kinship in spirit than with his own heartless ancestor:

> could I announce
> that Maurice as my kin I say aloud
> I'd take his irons as heraldry, and be proud.

The poet finds the need of 'some star / of courage from his firmament, a bar / against surrenders: faith'. He finds something of himself in the convict, probably more in the conscientious Mason. The wind that blew blood and sinew from the backs of the convicts onto the faces of the bystanders is used as an image of the wind of history, blowing savagery, a sense of duty and courage onto those who now inhabit the same land.

'The Wind at your Door' was collected in *Southmost Twelve* (1962). A retrospective selection, *Forty Years' Poems*, appeared in 1965, winning for FitzGerald, jointly with A. D. Hope, The Britannica Australia Award for Literature in that year. It was not, however, a volume that excited unrelieved praise. James McAuley, while praising the later short poems, found the general effect of FitzGerald's work 'toneless and unmusical', with 'phonetic textures' that were 'coarse and abrasive'. But FitzGerald himself had always recognized that although he wanted to be a lyrical poet he was unlikely to be considered one.

FitzGerald's last volume, *Product* (1978, though dated 1977), contains a number of mellow poems, with a tendency to garrulity. In style the graceless knotty quality of which McAuley complained is still there, but the tone is more relaxed. What also remains is the sense of a probing mind, concerned with exact statement, with the qualifications necessary for precision. Everything is set down bluntly, with assurance and conviction, in homely images.

FitzGerald's poetry offers a constant struggling criticism of life; it is stubborn, honest and gritty. He is concerned to use the concepts of physics and metaphysics to explore the notions of time, memory, nothingness, chaos and process, not in an abstract and impersonal way but by fleshing out abstractions in imagery and in human personality. His influence has been widespread, notably on Thomas Shapcott and Les Murray, whose tone of voice is often close to FitzGerald's.

Christina Stead and Xavier Herbert introduced into 1930s Australian fiction a strain at great variance from the social-recording conscience evident in Vance Palmer, Katharine Susannah Prichard and Marjorie Barnard. It was a strain of poetic symbolism that is also found in the novels of Kenneth Mackenzie (1913–55) who published two volumes of poetry under that name and (to avoid confusion with another writer) four novels under the name 'Seaforth Mackenzie'.

His first novel, *The Young Desire It* (1937), won the gold medal of the Australian Literature Society. Set in a large boarding-school outside Perth, recognizable as Guildford Grammar School, where he himself had been an insecure and introspective student, it is a story of two love affairs. One is a chaste adolescent love by the fifteen-year-old Charles Fox for a girl he meets while on holiday in the Western Australian wheatfields. The other is that of the repressed homosexual classics master, Penworth, for Charles. Penworth seems to the boys 'a stranger who talked of Home and meant that shape on their maps which they recognized as England, a place in which they believed, without imagery or emotion, and which few of them would ever see'. Both he and Charles feel alienated from the boorish, conformist school environment.

Chosen People (1938) is a sequel, written at the same time. Its setting is some ten years later. The 'chosen people' are a Jewish family in Perth, the Elisons, who are encountered by Richard Mawley, a concealed narrator in *The Young Desire It*. The Elisons are isolated by their culture from their neighbours and acquaintances. Ruth Elison has been the lover of Michael Levey, who is now her daughter's fiancée and, later, husband. It is a novel in which Richard, caught up in the tensions and power play of the Elisons, finds that his own relationship with Marjorie Allardice is threatened. In the end he remains puzzled by the passions and the actions that he has witnessed.

Mackenzie served in the 1939–45 war as a conscripted soldier. He was assigned, with the rank of sergeant, to the prisoner-of-war camp at Cowra, in New South Wales. In 1944 he witnessed a good many of the incidents in an attempted uprising by 1100 Japanese prisoners – men considered 'dead' in Japanese thinking because they had been captured instead of dying in battle. The Japanese prisoners, inspirited by illicit home-made *sake*, stormed the barbed-wire fence, their leaders making a ramp with their bodies over the wire. 234 prisoners died, some shot by guards, some committing suicide. Rigid censorship was immediately applied, and Mackenzie's novel based on the events, *Dead Men Rising* (1951), was for many years not published or distributed in Australia, apparently from fear of attracting a defamation action. Mackenzie's name for Cowra is Shotley. In this novel the misfits are both the guards and the prisoners, Italians, Japanese and Koreans. The narrative centres on Corporal Sargent, the observer–narrator. Blind in one eye, he is lonely and alienated from the camp environment, but aware of the growing sense of menace as the uprising is secretly planned.

Mackenzie's last novel, *The Refuge* (1954), concerns another alienated central character, Irma Martins, a Lithuanian refugee in Australia who claims to be Dutch. She marries an Australian crime-reporter, a widower, but also sleeps with his son, to whom the father has a strong sexual attachment.

Mackenzie is reworking, with the sexes reversed, the Elison ménage from *Chosen People* and the novel is forced and melodramatic. Mackenzie himself, a victim of alcoholism, who drowned on his farm in the following year, included conventional melodramatic plots in his second and fourth novels, though he had no great talent for describing action. His forte was in the growing awareness of love and in reworkings of his childhood and youthful experiences and fears. Suicide always fascinated him – the headmaster in *The Young Desire It* commits it – as did love across generations, incest and drunkenness. His central characters are always uneasy in and threatened by their environment, which they find uncouth, hostile or insupportable.

A. D. Hope

A dialectical poet like FitzGerald, A. D. Hope (1907–) was born in the same year as W. H. Auden, a poet to whom he bears some resemblance. Both have well-stocked, inquiring minds; both are satirists who delight in disappointing the expectations of readers; both profess an eighteenth-century common sense and appreciation of absurdity; and both are highly competent with occasional poems. There is, for instance, an unmistakable Audenesque tone (close to that of 'In Praise of Limestone') in 'The Wandering Islands', where Hope speaks of the islands as

> Incurious whether the whales swim around or under,
> Investing no fear in ultimate forgiveness.
> If they clap together, it is only casual thunder.

A. D. Hope's boyhood was spent amid Scottish settlers in the Campbelltown district of Tasmania, where his father was the Presbyterian minister. Until he was eleven he attended school for only one month a year, the month when shearing was done in the district and a school was set up for the shearers' children. For the rest of his education he depended on his mother, a former schoolteacher, and, for Latin, his father. Although he began writing poetry at about the age of eight, he felt that poetry was a private occupation. Other than in university magazines and one poem in the *Bulletin* he published nothing until he was well into his thirties, and his first book, *The Wandering Islands* (1955), came about only through the request of a small, quality publisher in Sydney. By then he was Professor of English at the Australian National University, having previously been an industrial psychologist and a lecturer in English in Sydney and Melbourne.

Hope's literary credo has always been one of respect for traditional forms and scepticism towards experimentalism and fashionable ideas. He regrets the loss of the great traditional forms such as the epic, the philosophical poem, verse tragedy, satire and the ode. He regrets the Romantic move towards poetic autobiography as the material for poetry. He blames the first two decades of the *Bulletin* for establishing two 'myths', one that 'the scenery, the land itself in some mysterious way generates a peculiar sort of poetry impossible in any other setting', the second, following from it, that 'only poetry generated in this way is genuine Australian poetry', the rest being derivative and second rate. By contrast, his own view is set out defiantly in his *Current Affairs Bulletin* essay 'Standards in Australian Literature', of 1956. It is a vigorous rebuttal of such chauvinistic assertions, particularly as expressed by the Jindyworobak movement of the 1930s and 1940s. He recalls that British literature is based not on Teutonic myths, but on two traditions alien to the Anglo-Saxons, the Judaeo-Christian and the Graeco-Roman. Hope's view is that the European literary tradition derived from these sources is still a single tradition and that Australian literature 'grows directly from it as a branch of English literature'. Hope was not hostile to the notion of Australian literature or to its study; he was, in fact, largely responsible for instituting the first full-year course in the subject anywhere in Australia (at Canberra). What he objected to was a limited view of its antecedents and of its appropriate subjects and the notion that Australian cultural manifestations could not be objects of satire. His own practice (akin to that of Coleridge) has always been to use wide and curious reading as a means of jolting his imagination. His work is full of overt and glancing references to classical and biblical myth and many of the great British and European poets. Evan Jones aptly called him a 'Polyglot motley puzzle-minded man' and a 'Scholar of monsters, sciences and magic, / lore of the folk and nit-wit nursery rhyme'.

Hope's earliest published poems record many attitudes that were to remain in his work. The problem of male loneliness, only partially abated by treating women as goddesses, sex objects or works of art, is conveyed in such poems as 'The End of a Journey', 'The Damnation of Byron', and 'Massacre of the Innocents'. In 'The End of a Journey', a meditative lyric conceived as a more realistic and less heroic account of Ulysses on his return home than Tennyson's poem, Ulysses and Penelope tire of each other on the first night of his return. Ulysses passes on to express Hope's characteristic horror of ordered domesticity and to hear himself mocked by the Sirens, whose promises and lures he evaded. 'The Damnation of Byron' presents Byron in Hell as sickened and maddened by a surfeit of sexual contact in which he knows himself to be quite alone. Ultimately 'even his own society' becomes 'a loneliness he cannot bear'. It is a poem notable among other things for the Byronesque triumph of the phrase 'the tender dislocation of her walk'. In 'Massacre of the Innocents' there are more of the overblown pneumatic Norman Lindsayish women, this time, as in Cornelis van Haarlem's painting, watching their offspring massacred by representatives of 'the bull male' in their 'contraceptive hate'.

The question of amelioration for human solitude is taken up again in 'The Wandering Islands', a rebuttal of Donne's 'No man is an island'. For Hope, human beings are like uncharted, unsought, wandering islands. Love – or rather 'the sudden ravages of love' – may seize them, but it will be like 'acts of God', which they can neither resist nor control. Their isolation is broken, however, only for an instant; their emotional and mental contact is momentary.

Love and domesticity are more significant in one of Hope's most admired poems, 'The Death of the Bird', in which love, instinct, and the repetition of social functions exist for several seasons, only to be ultimately snuffed out by the inevitability and unfathomability of death. The image of the bird migrating between summer and winter stations, enjoying one and remembering the other, can also be interpreted as symbolizing the poet's oscillation between domesticity and adventure or between writing and exploring through reading.

'Imperial Adam', on the other hand, expresses Hope's scepticism about domesticity and his sense of the power of womanhood. Its retelling of Adam's first finding Eve ends with another of his surprises on the reader. The sexual act, entered with joy by Adam and a cry of triumph by Eve, produces a child; Adam and the beasts watch to see

> Between her legs a pigmy face appear,
> And the first murderer lay upon the earth.

Hope's cultural attitudes were expressed in poems such as 'Standardization' (which mocks the popular romantic cult of individuality by reference to the standardization and mass production of nature), 'Australia' and 'The Return from the Freudian Islands'. 'Australia' presents the same ambiguous attitude to the country and some of the same arguments as Adam Lindsay Gordon presented in 'A Dedication'. It characterizes the place, with a testiness later disavowed, as 'A Nation of trees', peopled by 'monotonous tribes' of 'immense stupidity'. With no culture of their own, Australians constitute

> a vast parasite robber-state
> Where second-hand Europeans pullulate
> Timidly on the edge of alien shores.

But Hope, ever impishly disabusing the reader of preconceptions, goes on faintly to praise Australia for its intellectual dullness. At least, he says, some 'savage and scarlet' spirit, alien to the cultivated intellectual fields of Europe, may emerge. It is, in a sense, a later manifestation of Norman Lindsay's vitalism, expressed in Hope's typically brutal imagery.

'The Return from the Freudian Islands' is a satire of single-minded views of human behaviour. Freud's psychoanalysis is ridiculed by having it represented as leading, by logical extension, to the stripping-away of all flesh and the consequent death of the patient. The first sceptic to cease adoration of the new religious leader is a poet.

Hope's satires are often expressed in ballad quatrains, a form that he returned to late in life. Often they are comic, though sexual fierceness and horror make them less light-hearted than the comic ballads of John Manifold. Hope's 'Conquistador' and 'The Martyrdom of St Teresa', for instance, are in the style of Auden's 'Miss Gee' or John Crowe Ransom's 'Captain Carpenter'. 'Conquistador' is a surrealistic comedy of deflated sexual fantasy in which the suburban conformist ventures into the 'grisly jaws' of an escapade with a large prostitute. After their sexual contact she rolls over, squashes him flat, and thereafter uses him as a bedside mat.

Towards the end of the 1950s, Hope began to write a set of complex meditative poems, somewhat in the style of Keats's odes, full of arcane reference and ingenious thought. Mostly they are focused on a book, an incident, or a painting, sometimes mythological, sometimes scientific. The set includes 'Soledades of the Sun and the Moon', 'The Double Looking Glass', 'Moschus Moschiferus' and 'On an Engraving by Casserius'. Many of them concern the vision and task of the poet, frequently conceived of in contrastive terms. In 'Soledades of the Sun and the Moon', dedicated to the Canadian poet P. K. Page, Hope uses a series of opposites to convey the complementary sides of the poet's nature as 'raving sibyl' and 'lucid seer' which are combined in 'The life of poetry, this enchanted motion'. 'The Double Looking Glass' presents from many possible points of view the story of Susannah seized and accused by the elders. The poet imagines himself watching the naked Susannah, he imagines himself sometimes as innocent, unaroused observer, sometimes as representative of humanity, sometimes as an admiring young man, sometimes as lascivious like the elders. He imagines himself imagining this. And he imagines what the elders might be thinking. And he imagines Susannah, vaguely aware of danger, imagining for herself a desperate and besotted young lover – a dream that she excuses on the ground that she may end it when she pleases. She allows the imaginary lover to mount her, as she both enjoys and observes the whole scene. This is Hope's most complex poem of the workings of the imagination, the power of dreams and words. It expresses an attitude quite remote from Hope's early vitalism or from FitzGerald's belief in the power of work.

'Moschus Moschiferus: A Song for St Cecilia's Day' is centred on the musk deer, a diminishing species, which is sought with ever 'new means, more exquisite and refined' because its musk pods are used for the making of perfume. The hunters include a flute-player whose task it is, Circe-like, to lure the deer to the archers. The deer is shot, the music 'soars to a delicious peak' and continues on to lure the next victim. At dusk 'the little glands that hold the musk' are cut out and the carcasses left to rot. The multiple ironies of the poem are characteristic of Hope. It is a song dedicated to the patron saint of music, but it is about music perverted to cruel, profit-motivated destruction. The beauty of language expressing the beauty of the music and of the deer assorts oddly with the vicious cunning of the circumstances. The moment of death corresponds to the most exultant movement of the music. The music continues after each death, but the continual killing will shortly make the deer extinct and the music redundant. Unlike FitzGerald, who is more explicit and discursive in his use of myth, Hope leaves the story to speak for itself. Such wise reticence is rare in Australian poetry.

'On an Engraving by Casserius', after discoursing on the relations between science and art and the elevation of humble material into art, offers two opposed views of art and science. They both 'show the mask beyond the mask beyond the mask', as a skilled anatomist penetrates deeper and deeper, but they also reveal the limits of knowledge, the supersession of certainty by doubt and the knowledge of ignorance.

The long dramatic poem 'Vivaldi, Bird and Angel: or Il Cardellino' focuses Hope's common images of earthly music, celestial music and love on the dramatic scene of Vivaldi's rehearsal and direction of his 'bird concerto', *Il Cardellino*, in which the solo flute is played by a beautiful and talented orphan, Julia. Vivaldi finds himself lifted up, by music and female beauty, into a realm of paradisal music, 'A mutual ecstasy of consenting love'. The poet and a companion, experiencing the music, find it a symbol of their love and a means of entry into the 'divine Rage of a cosmos'. Yet – and the scepticism of contrariety is typical of Hope – the lovers know 'this music is not ours' and that their rapture in it is temporary.

After *The Wandering Islands* and *Poems* (1960), Hope gathered his poems into *Collected Poems: 1930–1965* (1966). A second edition of this volume, entitled *Collected Poems: 1930–1970* (1972) also incorporated an intermediate volume, *New Poems: 1965–1969* (1969). The poems of the 1960s often have a substantial length, which is sometimes uncontrolled by narrative, movement of thought, or poetic shape. Although constantly intelligent, each stanza can seem to begin with a fresh heave of thought, connected only loosely to the original impulse or theme. *A Late Picking* (1975) contains a number of garrulous poems (some of them surrealistic or bizarre in their iconography) together with a few indications, notably in 'Hay Fever', that Hope might be moving away from his rigid versification. Later work, however, reverts to very formal measures, generally comic or light in tone. *The Drifting Continent, and Other Poems* (1979), illustrated by Arthur Boyd for a limited edition, contains several comic bush songs, as well as a serious landscape poem of the countryside near Canberra, 'Beyond Khancoban'. *Antechinus: Poems 1975–1980* (1981) gathers these and other poems.

From *The Cave and the Spring* (1966) onwards, Hope has published several volumes of reviews and extended articles and lectures, some about Australian literature, some about European work. They include *Native Companions* (1974), *The Pack of Autolycus* (1978), and *The New Cratylus* (1979). In them he parades his *bêtes noires* for execution: 'free verse', modernism, academic thesis-spinning, and the notion that language is merely a signalling-device. Often he adopts a more-in-sorrow-than-in-anger tone, an expression of wishful thinking that modern excesses will vanish and enlightened sanity prevail. But he also offers notable insights into the work of medieval and Renaissance poets and twentieth-century Russians, for instance. He reprints his devastating review of Max Harris's novel *The Vegetative Eye* (1943) and his infamous review of Patrick White's *The Tree of Man* (1955). Hope, antipathetic to the experimental and the pretentious, referred waspishly to White's 'pretentious and illiterate verbal sludge'. The phrase has been remembered, long after the measured praise that Hope accorded the novel has been forgotten.

Hope's poetry, satiric, erotic, mythological and erudite, once seemed the apogee of Australian poetry. Its scepticism about easy solutions, its sinewy dialectics, its robust treatment of sex, and its deft versification raised Hope above his contemporaries. More recently, his mind has been accused of being well-stocked but trivial (a criticism the English poet Roy Fuller made in 1966), his attitude to women has been condemned as redolent of a smoke-filled clubroom, and his attitudes to verse form have come to seem stubbornly antiquated. Some of these criticisms, however, are over-solemn; they fail to take account of Hope's impish satire, his delight in misleading the reader, and the modesty and confessions of ignorance in many of the poems. They mistake the doctrinaire and acerbic prose-writer for the much subtler poet.

Judith Wright

It is conventional to consider Hope in association with James McAuley, his friend, fellow excoriator of modernism, fellow professor, and fellow devotee of classicism. In many ways, though, it is more appropriate to consider first another dialectician, Judith Wright (1915–). She grew up in the New England tableland area of New South Wales and has lived most of her life in the countryside, at first in open grazing-country, but for the second half of her life in forest country in Queensland and New South Wales.

Although she had had poems published in children's papers from the age of ten, it was not until the early 1940s, when she was living in Brisbane and associated with the magazine *Meanjin Papers* that she felt she had completed her apprenticeship. Poems such as 'Bullocky', 'The Company of Lovers' and 'South of my Days' excited interest when they were published in magazines such as *Meanjin*, *Southerly* and the *Bulletin*, and her first volume, *The Moving Image* (1946), was an immediate and continuing success. In these poems she set about her lifelong quest to define Australia as a land, a nation and a metaphysical entity, in language that showed awareness of contemporary overseas writing in English but also recognized the unique environment and society of Australia.

'Bullocky' is a good example of Wright's passage from scene to myth-making, from physicality to metaphysics. The bullocky plodding the 'long solitary tracks' comes to believe that he is Moses and – in some confusion of the biblical details – the bullock team his slaves whom he is driving to the Promised Land. This is the kind of sea-change that European mythology commonly makes in Wright's work. This Moses, with his nightly 'shouted prayers and prophecies' that none heard (except the poet), is dead, but his inflamed vision has been transmuted still further into the poet's prayer and assertion that the Promised Land has now covered the countryside where the bullocky used to work.

The inevitable passage of time, the glamour of the stories and myths that solitary men make, and the harshness of the land encountered by pioneer white settlers are also conveyed in 'South of my Days'. Living in Brisbane, the poet looks south from her present 'days' circle' to the New England tableland country of her youth and in particular to the tales of 'old Dan', a drover, stockman and coach-driver for Cobb and Co.

'The Company of Lovers' is the first of her major love poems, relating the poet's love relationship to that of all lovers throughout the world (a 'company' in the collective sense) who think the world well lost for the 'company' (in a more intimate sense) that the grave will soon enough destroy. The same sense of time leaching away both individual and collective accomplishment is to be found in 'Bora Ring', one of Wright's many poems about Aborigines. Its opening clause, 'The song is gone', may have suggested the well-known poem 'We are Going' to Wright's friend and fellow poet, the Aboriginal writer Kath Walker. Wright herself is well aware of the reason why 'The song is gone' and 'The hunter is gone': it is because of the curse of Cain, the murder and extermination brought by white settlers.

The title poem, 'The Moving Image', refers to the Platonic quotation that provides an epigraph for the volume, 'Time is a moving image of eternity'. In it there is the sense of celestial time never suiting the human rhythm of the blood, but also the sense that 'both time and fear' are a creation of the poet, who must resist both her creatures, otherwise she will die. Despite the oppressiveness of time and death, life and desire are to be found in nature, visionary madness, and love. Despite the immensity of the dark and the silence, there is both music and light:

> It is the corn rising when winter is done.
> It is the madmen singing, the lovers, the blind;
> the cry of Tom of Bedlam, naked under the sun.

In the mid 1940s Judith Wright met her future husband, Jack McKinney, a philosopher who also wrote at least one well-constructed comic play. Her love for McKinney and her sensations and thought when she was carrying their child form the substance of the opening poems of her next volume, *Woman to Man* (1949). 'Woman to Man', 'Woman's Song' and 'Woman to Child' are solemn, ceremonial lyrics, written in the knowledge of the love poetry of Dylan Thomas and W. B. Yeats but full of Judith Wright's own supple movement of thought. Love and procreation are seen as profound mysteries, shaded by the thought of death. They are expressible in complementaries and antinomies: the foetus, for instance, is to its parents 'our hunter and our chase', 'the maker and the made', 'the question and reply'; in its birth it 'shall escape and not escape'. These three poems, celebrating love, fecundity, and the quickening of the child, seemed to most readers thoroughly original poems about subjects rarely touched on. They have been very influential in encouraging other women writers, particularly in the 1970s and later, to write about procreation and childbirth.

Woman to Man also contains some pure lyrics in short lines, notably 'Stars', 'The Old Prison', and 'Wonga Vine'. 'Stars' and 'Wonga Vine' are almost Blake-like in their sense of an infinite world impinging on innocent and beautiful life. The 'swarm of honey-bees' and the flower of the wonga vine are symbols of the childlike quest for eternity. 'The Old Prison' presents a song of experience to balance the two songs of innocence. The decaying and deserted prison becomes a symbol of man's loneliness enunciated by the hollow fluting of the wind among the ruins.

'The Cycads' more overtly raises the question of time once more. The ancient fern trees seem as if they have been forgotten by time and change, for they endure changelessly. Because of this they can provide a means of entry for the poet, moving through and beyond their nature in the fashion of Wordsworth, to that 'unthinkable, unfathomed edge / beyond which man remembers only sleep'.

In her first two volumes, Judith Wright enunciates the three chief concerns of her work. The first is the nature of time, the notion of flux or change, and the resoluteness that the poet must conjure, mostly through love, to defeat her fear of time. The second is the attempt to resolve into a harmony or a creative paradox the basic antinomies of human existence – man and the environment, person and person, past and present, soul and flesh. The third is the Australian landscape and its appropriate expression and sublimation in language. This third matter, with its related concerns for the preservation of the natural environment and for the Aborigines, the original protectors of the land, flows over into her later political activities, especially as President of the Wildlife Preservation Society of Queensland.

Wright's third volume, *The Gateway* (1953), disappointed some critics. They found some of the poems too abstract, too philosophical, too factitiously symbolic. Such criticism is perhaps best seen as a belated reaction to the rapturous reception of *The Moving Image* than as a substantive comment on the poems of *The Gateway*. Among them are poems of the poet's response to the magic of landscape, such as 'Train Journey'. Travelling at night through the New England district she wakes to find the trees transfigured into a symbol of determination, durability and essential life. They imaginately blossom within and by means of the poem into 'flowers more lovely than the white moon'.

'Our Love is so Natural' is another poem of the transfiguration of the actual into the realm of the ideal, with no loss of the sense of the real. 'Our Love' is described in images of a fairy landscape with honey bees, shores on which wild animals become tame, and a star living in a tree. But the human impression is what is asserted: 'Our love is so natural'.

'Two Songs for the World's End' presages Wright's later anti-war poems. The first part is addressed to herself, with a sense of self-recrimination and responsibility for bringing a child into a world of hatred and fear. The second is addressed to her child, urging the privacy and strength of love to combat fear and, maybe, death.

'The Gateway' introduces a new strain to the argument about life and death. It seems to depend on a Jungian sense (perhaps a Buddhist sense) of the dissolution of the self in 'the depth of nothing'. The collective unconscious is the abode of both death and life, for from it emanates 'the bright smoke' that is 'the flowing and furious world'.

The Two Fires (1955) contains a number of poems, including the title poem, written at the time of the Korean War, when the world's destruction by atomic warfare seemed distinctly possible. Images of fire and burning permeate 'The Two Fires', the destructive fire being opposed by the resistance of 'rock and the waters'. The original fire (a concept from Heraclitus) yielded to the generation of nature; now, in the apocalyptic fire, 'time has caught on fire' (a phraseology that gave Thomas Shapcott a title for one of his volumes). Wright finds it unnerving in 'West Wind', 'to love in a time of hate and to live in a time of death'.

A more personal image of the same fear is expressed in 'The Harp and the King'. The old king Saul, isolated and fearful, deserted by God and terrified of eternity, asks David to sing of time and mortality. The song ranges over decay and creation, betrayal and affirmation, but ultimately proclaims that time cannot comfort the soul, which can be renewed only by metamorphosis.

In some poems, notably the song lyric 'Nameless Flower' and 'Gum-trees Stripping', Wright privileges nature above language in a manner that was to become increasingly common as she became committed to the conservation and environmental movement. In 'Nameless Flower' she says that words are incapable of trapping the essence of beauty. They are 'white as a stone is white / carved for a grave', but the flower, symbolizing love, 'blooms in immortal light'. In 'Gum-trees Stripping' she resists the temptation to engage in the pathetic fallacy when confronted by gum trees shedding their bark; she recognizes instead that 'Words are not meanings for a tree'.

After a lapse of several years, Judith Wright produced a set of poems on the birds of Tamborine Mountain, where she was living. Written for her daughter, Meredith, a few were published, with illustrations by Clifton Pugh, in *Australian Letters* and then the full set in *Birds* (1962). In these poems most of the earlier bardic qualities give way to a personal and intimate delight in the creatures she describes. Sometimes she sees them in anthropomorphic terms (the magpies walk along the road 'with hands in pockets'); sometimes she uses them as reflections of her own mood (as when she tells the brown bird, 'I am thirsty for love').

Five Senses (1963) is a retrospective selection, with many new poems. The more relaxed, personal mood continues, though the old images of light, bone and depths continue, and so does the emphasis on time's flux, death and fear. 'For my Daughter' speaks about the separation of an adolescent daughter from her mother's ways and the mother's need to recognize the change and to retame the lion of her emotions. *The Other Half* (1966) continues with the strain of personal poems. It includes 'Turning Fifty', in which she reflects on 'having met time and love' and on living in a world where 'we've polluted / even this air I breathe'.

Jack McKinney's death in 1966 is reflected in many of the poems in the final section, 'Shadow', of Judith Wright's *Collected Poems: 1942–1970* (1971). Her love continues with resolution and fortitude. Though alone, she overcomes disconsolateness in 'This Time Alone', 'Love Song in Absence', and 'The Vision'. In 'The Vision' she goes close to explaining why some of her earlier metaphysical poems might seem sterile or over-insistent. She admits her envy of her husband's devotion to philosophy, while she lacked his concentration and whole-heartedness.

The first poem of 'Shadows', modestly entitled 'Two Sides of a Story', is perhaps the best of all the explorer poems of the 1940s, 1950s and 1960s. It concerns Edward Kennedy and his Aboriginal guide, called Jacky-Jacky, who engaged on an expedition to the dense rain forests of Cape York Peninsula in northern Queensland. The poem suggests the complexity and contradictoriness of each man, both in himself and in his relationship to the other. It is particularly understanding of the Aboriginal's confusion of identity: the poet asks whether he was Galmahra, a songman, or the white man's servant, Jacky-Jacky.

There are also poems on the environment, revealing a new stridency of declamation. They include 'At a Poetry Conference, Expo '67' and 'The City'. They are related to the bitter satires on the Vietnam War, 'Fire Sermon', with its emphasis on chemical rain, and 'Christmas Ballad', with its portrayal of a psychologically destroyed veteran.

Judith Wright's later volumes, *Alive: Poems: 1971–72* (1973) and *Fourth Quarter, and Other Poems* (1976), and her contributions to *Journeys* (1982), edited by Fay Zwicky, continue and extend these interests. *Alive* is one of her best volumes. Its topics are limited to those associated with her home on Tamborine: her house, birds and trees; the contrast with them of city streets and their incidents; Australia and its history; her parents; Jack McKinney; poets, dreams and poetry; personal sickness; and the iniquities of businessmen and politicians. She is grave and gay by turn, righteously indignant and helplessly uncertain, vibrantly alive and almost despairingly half-dead. 'Houses' mingles in her characteristic way 'thinginess' ('crockery bits, smashed bottles, / iron bolts, shoesoles, / lost toys') and personal revelation ('when I'm alone / it creaks like footsteps'). 'Two Dreamtimes' addresses Kath Walker as 'My shadow sister', expressing a sense of implication in the wrongs done to the plundered black tribes of Australia.

Fourth Quarter is less successful. Its strident protest poems are often querulous and nagging, shrill and abstract. She borrows images from her earlier poems and inserts them intrusively and distractingly. It is in the more personal poems, about her move from Queensland to near Canberra, about growing old and about memories of childhood, that she writes best, though even these poems are often vitiated by incursion into flabby, undisciplined free verse.

Judith Wright has been a prolific writer apart from her poetry. She has written school plays for the Australian Broadcasting Commission, children's books, short stories, literary criticism, and history. The best of her literary criticism is to be found in *Preoccupations in Australian Poetry* (1965), a series of perceptive essays on some major Australian poets. *The Generations of Men* (1959) is an account of her family's association with settlement in the Hunter Valley, New England, and central Queensland districts. *The Cry for the Dead* (1981) tells the story of the settlement of the Burnett and Dawson River district of central Queensland. It is also a story of her family, for her grandfather, Albert Wright, was one of the squatters and she again uses his diaries from 1867–1890 as part of her material. But his book tells less of the official story than of the disastrous neglect of proper land-management procedures and the story of the brutal extermination of Aborigines. It describes too the prickly-pear infestation, when families fled from the land before the advancing 'impenetrable walls of green, taller than a man'.

Judith Wright, in both poetry and prose, presents a wide panorama of the interests of the socially conscious present-day Australian. Unlike Xavier Herbert she does not despair for her country, for the movement of her thought is always inwards to the human resources of fortitude and love and to the sense of eternity that together provide the will to continue. Her constant quest has been, in the words of the early poem 'Waiting', that we should be made 'whole in man and time, who build eternity', and that, in the words of another early poem, 'Nigger's Leap, New England', 'all men are one man at last'. It is a quest for unity and wholeness analogous to Christopher Brennan's, but conducted through a quite different and solider landscape.

James McAuley

A professor of English like Hope and with similarly conservative views about versification, James McAuley (1917–76) was also, like both Hope and Wright, a major critic of Australian poetry. Although he lost his Anglican faith at the age of fifteen through reading *The Golden Bough*, was influenced by the secularist anti-metaphysical philosophy of Professor John Anderson at the University of Sydney, and was converted to Roman Catholicism in 1952, McAuley was a religious poet throughout his career, and in attitude a remarkably consistent one. He is fascinated by a mood close to despair and a sense of futility: he does not succumb to it, but he considers what it would be like to despair, estimates how close he is to total despair, and contrasts his despair with the hope he longs to have. If the fairly late poem 'Childhood Morning – Homebush' is autobiographical – and several of McAuley's later poems seem to be – the proclivity to solemn melancholy verging on, but rejecting, despair dates from childhood. The poem ends with the lines

> I don't know what there is to know.
> I hear that every answer's No,
> But can't believe it can be so.

His education, his wartime service in New Guinea, his later occupations as teacher and lecturer, his conversion to Catholicism, and his experiments with a variety of forms and modes in poetry all fail to affect his basic mood. Even when he celebrates the joyfulness of God's grace he does so in a sombre, measured style. Even when he essays humour he often achieves an atmosphere of ceremonious, even heavy-footed playfulness.

McAuley came to a position of traditionalism and conservatism in politics, religion and poetic history. Early in his career he used his sense of poetic tradition to attack two movements in Australian verse. The first was the Jindyworobak movement, an Adelaide-based group of Rex Ingamells, Flexmore Hudson, Ian Mudie, William Hart-Smith, Roland Robinson and others. It was an anti-European cultural movement concerned with locating and turning towards what Ingamells considered the 'primaeval' traditions of Australia, the land itself and its magical guardians and talismans. In *Conditional Culture* (1938) by Ingamells and Ian Tilbrook, the authors draw heavily on P. R. Stephensen's then-recent book, *The Foundations of Culture in Australia: An Essay towards National Self-Respect* (1936). Ingamells announced that the transplanted English culture must be rejected in favour of the unique local one: 'From Aboriginal art and song we must learn much of our new technique; from Aboriginal legend, sublimated through our thought, we must achieve something of a pristine outlook on life'. 'Jindyworobak' was one of a number of Aboriginal words discovered by Ingamells in James Devaney's volume of stories *The Vanished Tribes*, and the collection of tales by 'Catherine Stow' (Mrs K. Langloh Parker). 'Jindyworobak' means 'to annex' or 'join', and Ingamells adapted it as a convenient symbol for 'distinctive Australian quality in literature'. The movement objected to such English descriptive words as 'vale' and 'dale' as inappropriate to the Australian landscape – through this very attitude goes back well into the nineteenth century. Many of the poets were inclined to include Aboriginal words indiscriminately, a procedure that could produce a bizarre or even incomprehensible effect. Nevertheless, the movement, lasting from the mid 1930s to the early 1950s, did publish a substantial number of important poems in its *Jindyworobak Anthologies* (1938–53). McAuley's 'Jindyworobaksheesh' indicated his satiric opposition to the factitiousness, populism, and mandatory chauvinism of the movement.

McAuley made himself even more unpopular with his spoof against another and very different Adelaide movement, Angry Penguins. Its often uncritical admiration for international modernism in general and for the work of Dylan Thomas and other members of the New Apocalypse in particular aroused the hostility of McAuley, who felt that the movement was deleterious to the preservation of standards. He was particularly irritated by the iconoclasm and strident experimentalism of Max Harris, who, with John Reed, edited the journal *Angry Penguins* from 1941 to 1946. After deliberating on the matter for some time (and perhaps discussing it with A. D. Hope), McAuley and another poet, Harold Stewart, spent an afternoon concocting a set of verses that they considered so nonsensical as to be likely to appeal to Max Harris. They sent to Harris a covering letter, purporting to be written by Miss Ethel Malley of Sydney, who had been surprised to discover that her deceased brother Ern had left behind a sheaf of poems. In a subsequent letter she described Ernest Lalor Malley as a former garage mechanic who had died at the age of twenty-five. Harris felt that 'here was a poet of tremendous power, working through a disciplined and restrained kind of statement into the deepest wells of human experience'. The poetic sequence 'The Darkening Ecliptic', accompanied by Harris's extravagant praise, appeared in *Angry Penguins*. Amid the parodies of pretentiousness, surrealism and radicalism were some memorable epigrams and phrases. Two have subsequently been used as book titles, for Chris Wallace-Crabbe's *The Emotions are not Skilled Workers* (1980) and Humphrey McQueen's *The Black Swan of Trespass* (1979).

Once *Angry Penguins* appeared, McAuley and Stewart tipped off a Sydney newspaper-reporter. The sources used had been a dictionary of quotations, an army manual on hygiene, and a few other works selected at random. In the furore that raged following the disclosure, Harris was made to seem gullible and the perpetrators supporters of philistinism. Harris was even prosecuted for producing an obscene publication, the trial giving rise to a court exchange in which the prosecuting detective under cross-examination said, 'I don't know what "incestuous" means, but I think there is a suggestion of indecency about it'.

The damage done to *Angry Penguins* was to some extent damage done to the espousal of modernism in Australia. *Angry Penguins* had espoused the ideas of Freud and Marx, Sartre and Gertrude Stein; it had praised the work of Kafka, Rilke, Hölderlin and the Surrealists; it had shown awareness of contemporary poetic movements in England and America. It had also supported the work of young painters such as Sidney Nolan, Albert Tucker and Arthur Boyd, providing the earliest appreciation of their work. The whole affair gave great comfort to the traditionalists in literature and the visual arts, perhaps reinforcing the intensity of conservative protest when a mannerist portrait by William Dobell was awarded the Archibald Prize in the same year (1944). One other factor encouraging conservatism was Australia's engagement in the 1939–45 war. Like wartime governments everywhere, the Australian Government through its propaganda and its support of publication by servicemen and servicewomen encouraged the illusion of realism. It was a sanitized and devulgarized realism, but, whatever its accuracy, it was in a mode antipathetic to modernism. The war was also, of course, responsible for the deaths of some promising, experimental young writers, resulting in something of a lost generation.

McAuley's first volume, *Under Aldebaran* (1946), was, with Judith Wright's *The Moving Image*, the most admired volume of its year. The early love poems, consisting of short-breathed statements in lines of two and three stresses, typically depend on a worrying, unresolved dualism between mind and body. 'When shall the fair' and 'Envoi' represent well the solemn melancholy in these poems. 'Monologue' deals with the 'loneliness' and the 'unknown' quality of the 'self' that one speaks of 'giving' in love. 'Tears' are frequently said to be attendant on love. The dichotomy of mind and body is a constant subject: in 'Gnostic Prelude' it is said to lead to discontent, pain, and nightmare.

A set of poems touching on Australia and how it is to be understood includes 'Envoi', 'Terra Australis', 'Henry the Navigator' and 'The True Discovery of Australia'. 'Terra Australis' introduces McAuley's interest in the Portuguese Captain Pedro Fernandez de Quiros, which he was later to develop in a major poem. 'The True Discovery of Australia', continuing the interest in voyages of navigation, now uses it for a scathing satire on Max Harris and *Angry Penguins*, said to be an ambience without true standards of judgement, in which 'Th' egregious penguin, amorously blind, / Confuses oft a man with penguin-kind'.

The poems of the next ten years, collected in *A Vision of*

Ceremony (1956), include many that overtly celebrate Christian joy. The joy is, however, often less vivid than the nightmares and the fears. After McAuley's conversion the most terrifying fear is that of falling from grace, expressed in such poems as 'Exploit', a prayer to 'Lady of the Maze' for grace to cope with 'formless fear'. 'A Letter to John Dryden' provides a good conspectus of McAuley's political, cultural and religious ideas. It is a diatribe against liberalism and 'progressive' ideas in all three areas, some of the *bêtes noires* being identified as Marx, the United Nations, 'democratism', Malthus, state secularism, and lack of poetic standards. McAuley had been substantially involved in trying to preserve Catholic influence in the trades unions and the Australian Labor Party, but when this influence was denounced by the parliamentary leader of the party, Dr H. V. Evatt, McAuley threw his energies behind the splinter group the Democratic Labor Party.

Because of his staunch anti-Communism, McAuley was asked to edit a new quarterly magazine for the Australian Commitee for Cultural Freedom. It was to be both polemical and broadly cultural. *Quadrant* appeared at the end of 1956, its first issue containing poems by Hope, Wright, Vincent Buckley, Rosemary Dobson and Roland Robinson, its articles including Hope's defence of 'The Discursive Mode'.

Captain Quiros (1964), a poem celebrating the Creator and justifying the unshakable hope of a godly and visionary man, Quiros, is almost free from McAuley's personal despondency, though the story told is grim enough. The voyage of General Mendaña to the Solomons, in which Quiros was pilot and later Mendaña's deputy, is marked by mutiny, senseless murder, bad management and ill health. In the second part, Quiros seeks to establish a religious community in the New Hebrides (now Vanuatu), but is thwarted by human malevolence and unbelief. The third part looks forward to Quiros's death in Panama and to his vision of the South Land dedicated to the Holy Spirit. McAuley's handling of causality and motive is often rather glib, perhaps because of his belief in unredeemed man's depravity. He contents himself with statements such as 'disorder spread under Mendaña's moody vacillations', 'The angry natives jeopardized their hold', or 'Insatiate for mischief, Prado went sowing his hints'.

Surprises of the Sun (1969) marks a return not only to the

short-line, short-period stanzas of McAuley's earliest
published work, but also to his overt personal fascination with
despair. In 'Time out of Mind' he confesses that his joys are
those that lie 'closest to despair'. The confessional note in this
volume, the bitterly honest facing-up to the extent of his
near-despair, is even stronger than before. 'Self-Portrait,
Newcastle 1942' presents a mood of almost suicidal 'guilt,
tension, or outrage' experienced when he was a young
schoolteacher. 'Because', a depiction of his relationship with
his parents, speaks of them being 'all closed in the same defeat'.
'Anonymous Message' speaks of himself as 'a native of the
country of despair', though one who advocates never giving up
hope.

Throughout his career, McAuley's persistent fearfulness and
misery finds both expression and refuge in nature, especially in
trees and birdsong. The early poem 'Envoi' begins with a
passage of *paysage moralisé* in which he almost blames nature for
his own disappointment, for producing 'the faint sterility that
disheartens and derides'. Thirty years later, in 'At Rushy
Lagoon', he speaks of the meadows, cattle, sheep, ducks and
children as making up a way of life that is 'a world of sense and
use'. In 'The Garden' he contrasts his own spiritual restlessness
with the calm voice of nature and prays that nature may 'Be a
grace against despair'.

McAuley's later poetry, gathered in *Collected Poems: 1936–
1970* (1971), *Music Late at Night: Poems 1970–1973* (1976) and the
posthumous collection *A World of its Own* (1977), is delicate,
graceful and less doctrinaire than much of his earlier work. He
knew for some years that he was dying of cancer; he spoke of it
with sombre resignation in his poems and he celebrated the joys
of nature. The distancing that he applies in his earlier poems,
the sense of classical detachment applied even to experiences of
love, has passed. The prudence, restraint and decent reticence
have been discarded in favour of a more spontaneous, more
personal voice that is confident enough not to need over-
assertion.

Of McAuley's six books of literary criticism, the most
comprehensive is *The Grammar of the Real: Selected Prose
1959–1974* (1975). It enunciates the virtues of restraint, order,
and decorum, deploring what McAuley speaks of as 'the
Magian heresy', that is, the error of late-nineteenth- and

twentieth-century poets in seeking to become magi or sages, a role usurped from religion. McAuley discusses a number of Australian writers whom he respects (including Shaw Neilson, Kenneth Slessor, Judith Wright and Rosemary Dobson) as well as Spenser, Dryden, Milton, George Eliot and Solzhenitsyn. With predictable consistency he praises respect for tradition and convention, sanity, moderation and religious faith.

7
The last decades of
the 'old' *Bulletin*

Douglas Stewart

Douglas Stewart (1913–85), literary editor of the *Bulletin* from 1940 until 1961, was, like Hope and McAuley, a practitioner and encourager of formal verse. Stewart was born in New Zealand, but his father was an Australian and Stewart made several visits to Sydney before settling there in 1938 to assist Cecil Mann, the editor of the Red Page of the *Bulletin*. By then, his first volume of poetry, *The Green Lions* (1936), had already appeared. Even it omitted most of the poems he had written between the ages of fifteen and nineteen, some of which had appeared in the *Australian Woman's Mirror*, published by the *Bulletin* company.

Stewart's *Springtime in Taranaki: An Autobiography of Youth* (1983) is a more genial account of life in Eltham, a country town in the province of Taranaki, than is suggested in *Green Lions*. The poems, as Stewart, admitted, convey 'a constant state of fury, and a kind of black exaltation', as if he were taking out his displeasure by fighting the climate and the landscape. Amid the naïve colour symbolism of *The White Cry* (1939), a few poems, including the title one, convey a sense of vast meaninglessness that the helpless poet observes. In 'The White Cry' a newborn lamb, 'So frail against the breath of ice', is reduced to 'A Dream, a white cry'.

Two small books, *Elegy for an Airman* (1940) and *Sonnets to the Unknown Soldier* (1941), contain few memorable poems. 'Heritage', however, adverts to Stewart's Scottish ancestry, in which, as in his understanding of country life and ecology, he took pride. The images of storm, and of black and of the whiteness of snow are used again as representatives of the harshness of the Scottish and New Zealand terrain and climate. Against them stands out 'the red rowan', symbol of the pride, rage and faith that he finds in his ancestor, even when faced with personal and clan disaster.

The Dosser in Springtime (1946) is the first of Stewart's volumes to indicate his acceptance of the Australian countryside and the end of his poetic apprenticeship. It indicates too his acceptance of two poetic kinds new in his work, but engrained in the history of Australian poetry as represented by the *Bulletin*: the ballad or narrative and the whimsical speculation. Stewart says that he turned to narrative because he was also writing verse plays and was unattracted by poetry exploring 'the author's own state of mind'. There are poems about a bunyip (the legendary swamp-dwelling monster), a lizard, a magpie and so on; ballads about the prosecutable Bill Posters and a fey-like convict who jumps up to the moon. 'Child and Lion' is another fantasy ballad, but this time with a sense of the wilfulness of adolescence and the accompanying parental sense of loss. 'Rock Carving' is a more solemn poem altogether, in which the poet, fishing in an inlet near Sydney, finds Aboriginal stone carvings at night and feels a communion in fishing and in artistry with the long-dead carver. 'We cut our thought into stone as best we can', says Stewart; 'Maybe it's all for nothing' or 'maybe for us the distant candles dance'.

Glencoe (1947) is a ballad sequence on the subject of the massacre in 1692 of the MacDonalds of Glencoe by the Campbells. Stewart's ancestors, the Stewarts of Appin, gave refuge to the surviving MacDonalds. Once again the imagery of redness against snow and dark provides a visual refrain for poems which, as Stewart said, are a contemporary 'protest against barbarity, cruelty and violence'.

Sun Orchids (1952) is the first of the volumes containing substantial numbers of the meditative nature poems for which he is best known. They are highly visual poems – perhaps it is significant that Stewart married the painter Margaret Coen – and full of a sense of the mysterious duality of the universe. The studies of 'A Robin', 'Mare and Foal', 'The Moths', 'Helmet Orchid', 'The Green Centipede', 'The Bees', 'Sun Orchids', 'Flying Ants', 'The Fireflies' and others lightly hold a symbolized human relevance as well as a metaphysical sense of the unearthly within the earthly. 'Terra Australis' is a light-hearted fantasy ballad of an imaginary meeting in the Pacific between Captain Quiros sailing west to found paradise in the New Hebrides and William Lane sailing east to found a utopian New Australia in Paraguay in 1893.

'Worsley Enchanted' is a longer narrative sequence, more serious but by no means solemn, about Shackleton's Antarctic expedition of 1914. Commander Worsley was a New Zealander who captained Shackleton's ship, *Endurance*. It was trapped and crushed by pack ice. Shackleton, Worsley, Crean and three other men set out in a ship's boat 900 miles to South Georgia to bring help. Many sections of the poem are in long five-stress lines organized into stanzas with an unobtrusive pattern of rhyme and half-rhyme. It is a form more deliberate than in Stewart's plays, capable both of dramatic thrust and retrospective savouring. Shackleton is presented as an heroic figure, responsible for his men, dogged by disaster, having a strong sense of the theatrical excitement of their adventure and a belief that he is united with the power that carries them onward. By contrast, Worsley is phlegmatic and Crean a 'saturnine bear'.

Clearly observed and reflective nature poems continue in *The Birdsville Track* (1955), some from the desert country of the title, some from the snow country of the Southern Alps, some from Stewart's haunts around and west of Sydney. Stewart's bold colour imagery, now handled without self-consciousness, runs through these poems. In 'Brindabella', for instance, the magpie listens to the echo of his song, 'Watching that white whisper fill his green world'. In 'The Snow-Gum', too, bold colours are worked into a shimmering impressionist delicacy, this time to describe 'the silver light like ecstasy' flowing 'where the green tree perfectly / Curves to its perfect shadow'.

Rutherford (1962), the most admired of all Stewart's volumes, contains masterpieces such as 'The Silkworms' and 'The Garden of Ships', as well as more impish poems such as 'Sarcophilus FitzGeraldi' and linguistic dances such as 'A Country Song'. 'The Silkworms' concerns the limit of human ambition and venturing; the magical transmutation that occurs with love; and the frailty of the whole endeavour. And all of this is conveyed with a naturalist's precise concentration on the life of silkworms. 'The Garden of Ships' is a fantasy based on an episode in Marco Polo's *Travels* telling of ships being driven far inland. In the poem, lost travellers light on a paradise where bridges and gardens have covered the ships and they shelter 'people of all the nations living in peace together untouched by the world'. The travellers are refreshed, but in the end they know they must return to the world. Stewart's sense of heroic endurance always denies the possibility of endless delight.

'Rutherford' is another narrative of exploration and questioning, this time concerned with the New Zealander (also from Taranaki) Lord Rutherford, 'The great sea-farer of science'. In his Cambridge study he ponders on what else he might have been – a farmer, Prime Minister of New Zealand, perhaps – what the origin of energy in the atom and the universe is, and whether knowledge can lead to evil. Much is conveyed in the recurring image of the wheel: his father's waterwheel; the universe, 'Full of black space, the huge wheel slowly spinning'; and in the atom the race of electrons 'Circling that radiant centre'.

Stewart's *Collected Poems: 1936–1967* (1967) begins with what were then his most recent poems. 'The Flowering Place', a narrative and reflective poem about the naturalist Kingdon Ward, who, gathering rhododendron seed in the Himalayas, found himself overlooking 'the naked edge of the world'. The image of beauty and extinction, glory and fear is one that runs through many of Stewart's nature poems. 'One Yard of Earth' applies Darwin's method of minute observation over a measured extent to provide a means of understanding the world. The migration of seeds from one continent to another, Darwin discovered, was not the result of 'some quite incredible fluke' or a strange divine fiat, but 'all was due to the most useful duck', whose muddy feet carried the seeds. Similarly, in 'B Flat', the Revd Henry White, brother of the naturalist Gilbert White of Selborne, is celebrated as 'The most harmless, the most innocent of mankind' for thinking of recording that the barn owl hoots in B flat.

At the height of his poetic powers, Stewart found his production slacken. It took him over seventeen years to collect the material for another volume, to be published posthumously.

As literary editor of the *Bulletin*, Stewart had a profound influence on the publishing of Australian poetry in the 1940s and early 1950s. More eclectic than he is often given credit for, he did have a distaste for rhetoric and declamation and a preference for the Audenesque air of jaunty reasonableness. Closely associated with Norman Lindsay, he was sceptical about large religious affirmation, but receptive to vitalistic liveliness. Under his literary editorship, the *Bulletin* drew attention to the work of a great number of young poets, including Judith Wright, Francis Webb, David Campbell, Jack Blight, David Rowbotham, Rosemary Dobson, Roland Robinson, Randolph Stow, Chris Wallace-Crabbe and Vivian Smith.

Stewart has another major claim to attention, as the most workmanlike and imaginative of Australian radio dramatists and of verse dramatists for the stage. Into his plays he transferred his early interest in violence, while his non-dramatic poems became genial. His plays are for the most part heroic tragedies in which, as he said in 1956, the 'significant crime against divinity and society' that characterizes Greek tragedy is replaced by its modern, more humanistic equivalent, 'mutiny on sea or land, which still has a smack of something sacrilegious about it; [in] the rebellion of the bushrangers against society; [in] the dispossession of the aborigines; perhaps, thinking of the convicts and completely reversing the theme, [in] the State's crime against humanity'. The first of his plays was *The Fire on the Snow*, broadcast nationally by the Australian Broadcasting Commission in 1941. Stewart had read the journal of Captain Robert Scott when a boy and had always been fascinated by the snow and ice of the Antarctic. He had tried for some years to deal with the story of Scott's 1911–12 expedition as a narrative poem, but suddenly found the key by reading Archibald MacLeish's verse play *The Fall of the City*, in which the announcer is used as a chorus. Using this device, Stewart found he could write his play.

His acceptance with the listening audience was so great that the Australian Broadcasting Commission began a verse-play competition, won in 1943 by Stewart with *The Golden Lover*. By then he had also written *Ned Kelly*, perhaps the best of his plays. *Ned Kelly* presents a conflict between the values of rebellion and conformity, typified by two sets of characters. Rebellion is represented by Ned and Joe Byrne. Ned is a Nietzschean striver after power and fame, a person who overemphasizes his own importance. He identifies himself with his bushranging gang, but believes they are unworthy of his leadership and wishes to outstrip them in ambition and achievement. Those who oppose him are a social force – 'they', 'traps' – who victimize and persecute him. Joe Byrne is more glamorous than Ned, perhaps because less is known about him historically and Stewart could invent more freely. He is intelligent, a successful philanderer, an idealist who realizes the emptiness of his own life and who has a passion for freedom for its own sake. Where Ned's language is simple in diction and more abrupt in rhythm, Joe's language is studded with vivid images, even when, disillusioned, he refuses to join Ned in a final shoot-out, saying, 'There's death in our breath, / We poison sunlight and lamplight'.

The Golden Lover is neither heroic nor tragic. It is a romantic comedy about a young woman's desire for a legendary lover whom she can never retain. Stewart revised *Ned Kelly* for the stage (published 1943) and wrote another stage play, *Shipwreck* (published 1947).

Shipwreck is the most gruesome in mood of Stewart's tragic plays. No character rises to heroism, though Cornelius, the supercargo who becomes captain-general of the mutineers, and Pastor Sebastian recognize what heroism is. The history covered by the play concerns the wreck of the Dutch ship *Batavia* off the Western Australian coast in 1629 and the subsequent descent into rebellion and bestiality of some of the survivors. It is a play full of brutality, rape, murder and torture. The subject is the lust for power, the weakness of those in command, and the unjust commercial and judicial power of the company that instituted the ill-fated voyage. There is so much vehement invective that the play, though full of fine poetry, lacks the relief of changes of pace.

Stewart's literary essays are for the most part less important than his briefer reviews and his editorial work. An exception is the percipient analysis in 'The Playwright in Australia', contained in the Australian Elizabethan Theatre Trust publication, *The First Year* (1956). Of his edited works the most useful are his two volumes based on Paterson's work in which he collaborated with Nancy Keesing, *Australian Bush Ballads* (1955) and *Old Bush Songs and Rhymes of Colonial Times* (1957).

Other poets

One of the many young poets whom Stewart encouraged in the *Bulletin* was Francis Webb (1925–73). Although their theological beliefs were far apart, they shared with Norman Lindsay an interest in Nietzschean power. Like Stewart, Webb was interested in the corrupting, corrosive effect of power on the gifted individual, a theme that he worked out in long narrative poems. Stewart's heroic failures – Scott, Ned Kelly, and some characters in *Shipwreck* – have their counterpart in Webb's doomed heroes: Ben Boyd, Ludwig Leichhardt and Edward John Eyre. Like Stewart, too, Webb wrote radio plays, including *Birthday* (1953), about the last days of Hitler, and *The Ghost of the Cock* (1964), a post-nuclear-holocaust fantasy.

Webb was influenced in various ways by Hopkins, Yeats, Pound, Eliot, Dylan Thomas, and Robert Lowell and by several Australian poets a little his senior, including FitzGerald, Slessor, and Stewart. He was also greatly interested in painting and in the music of Mahler, Bruckner and Vaughan Williams. These interests reflect an obsession with emotional crisis, with a sense of being driven and living on the edge of sanity, and with the theatrical expression of inner tension.

Webb, born in Adelaide, lost his mother when he was two and was brought up in Sydney by fond grandparents. He came to love the south coast of New South Wales, which provided the background material for such poems as 'A Drum for Ben Boyd' and 'Disaster Bay'. After demobilization from wartime service as a wireless air gunner in Canada, Webb attended the University of Sydney for half a year in 1946; he continued his athletic achievements by winning the University mile. In 1947 he returned to Canada, working first on a farm, then as a publisher's reader and editor. In England in 1949 he had his first mental breakdown, which forced him to return to Australia. He returned to England in 1953, living in Norfolk on and off for six years. Much of his best poetry, including 'Eyre All Alone', was written during this time, although he spent several periods in psychiatric hospitals. His last years, in Australia, were spent mostly in psychiatric care, as is indicated in the unblinking honest horror of such poems as 'Ward Two'.

'A Drum for Ben Boyd' is the title poem of Webb's first volume, published in 1948 with illustrations by Norman

Lindsay. It is a commentary on the ambition and achievement of a merchant adventurer, Webb's concern being largely with how authenticity can be achieved in the face of informants who are 'Dramatizing themselves right to the asylum-gates' and the fact that 'truth itself is a mass of stops and gaps' (the averted cliché and the concealed pun on 'stop-gaps' being a fair sample of Webb's linguistic subtlety).

'Leichhardt in Theatre', the title poem of his second collection (1952), uses the image of theatre rather than of the reporter to reflect the difficulty of obtaining a true picture. Leichhardt is as elusive as Ben Boyd, though we see him more in close-up. After a ludicrously unsuccessful second expedition in which 'The intrepid Doctor is kicked by several mules' alternates with 'The Doctor makes a speech', he experiences a sense of self-confrontation in a room, which yields to a desert as 'The walls slope out, / Space bunts at the doorway'. In a sense, as Webb points out, Leichhardt had died after his first and only successful journey, a crossing of the continent from south to north.

'Eyre All Alone' is the major poem of Webb's fourth volume, *Socrates and Other Verses* (1961). Edward John Eyre, the explorer who found a route from South Australia to Western Australia, is more solidly present in the poem than either Boyd or Leichhardt were. The question of the relationship between the real and the imagined does not so much concern the author's view of him as his view of his Aboriginal companion, Wylie, with his 'boomerang-shaped smile' and his 'Mistrust, hate, and a dark gargantuan sorrow'. Like Webb's other heroes, Eyre suffers both from pride and from the knowledge that he is hallucinating and basically alone.

Webb's long historical poems, in their concerns, their stanzaic versification, and their colloquial diction, have much in common with Stewart's. In their emotional tension they are more akin to Stewart's plays and Robert Lowell's poems. His shorter poems are less derivative. 'Five Days Old' is both a Christmas meditation and a personal cry of gratitude for the trust implied by parents who, aware of his mental disorder, gave him a young baby to hold. In 'The Yellowhammer', 'the footfall of the yellowhammer' and 'the grey rat nibbling at the soul' are metonyms for mental disorder and spiritual disorientation. 'A Death at Winson Green' and 'Hospital

Nightfall' are untheatrical, unself-pitying accounts of fear, matter-of-factness and aspiration in mental hospitals. 'Around Costessey' is a meditation on agony and salvation, mental, artistic and spiritual; the places from which the meditation arises are all close together in Norfolk, mostly near water.

Webb's agonized struggle towards mental, artistic and spiritual salvation is the theme of almost all his poetry. Through pain and sacrifice (including the sacrifice of the Mass), through the contemplation of small, insignificant and ordinary things (as Stewart does), and through confrontation with the elusive nature of truth, he aspires to a world of certainty and assurance, a world of greenness and stars. He is a religious poet less self-melodramatic than Hopkins, more closely textured than the later Robert Lowell.

John Blight (1913–) was one of the young *Bulletin* poets of the 1940s who particularly impressed Kenneth Slessor. Slessor referred to the 'spiky brilliance, like that of the banksia or the bottlebrush' in Blight's work, its quality of being 'utterly individual', its 'gnarled and knobbly surface, its apparent gruffness'. Blight has always been a poetic iconoclast, accepting international modernism before his contemporaries, accepting no limits to his poetic subjects or his poetic self-exposure, contemptuous of traditional limitations on rhythm or conventions about the appropriate parts of speech to end lines or poems with.

Although born in a suburb of Adelaide, Blight has spent most of his life in Queensland. Growing up on his parents' 800-acre property outside Brisbane, he had access to an extensive home library, and at the age of about seventeen, when he had already had his first rejection from the *Bulletin*, he began to read everything he could find, including Shakespeare, Milton, Wordsworth and Dickens. It took him years, he said, to 'disgorge the influence of the English poets' from his own writing.

The Depression years of the 1930s, with no jobs available, caused him to go 'on the track', wandering (with a notebook) from town to town on the dole, picking up odd jobs ring-barking (a means of killing trees in order to clear land for farming) and mining. In 'Old Wound' he speaks of having 'fence wire for a button', a 'garment patched in squares'. Along the way he qualified as a cost accountant. Subsequently he

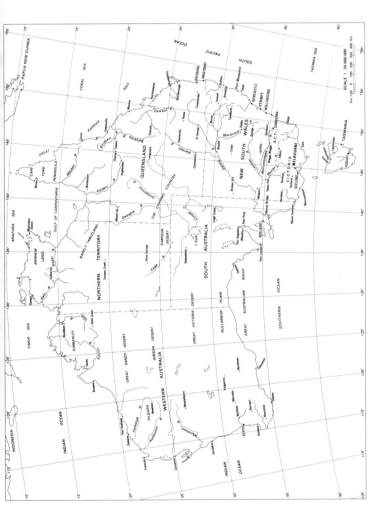

1. Map of Australia

2. Landing at Botany Bay, 1786, engraving by John Boyne

3. *The Kangooroo,* drawing by Arthur Bowes (Smyth) in his *A Journal of a Voyage from Portsmouth to New South Wales . . 1787–1789.*

4. *Attacking the Mail,* lithograph, from *The Australian Sketchbook,* 1865, of Samuel Thomas Gill.

5. *Death of Constable Scanlon,* 1946, enamel on composition board by Sidney Nolan.

6. A shopkeeper in the gold-mining town of Gulgong, 145 miles north-west of Sydney, 1872.

A CURIOSITY IN HER OWN COUNTRY.

7. *A Curiosity in Her Own Country*, cartoon by Phil May in *The Bulletin*, 3 March 1888.

8. *Bourke Street* (Melbourne), 1885–6, oil painting by Tom Roberts.

9. *Shearing the Rams,* 1890, oil painting by Tom Roberts.

10. Cover design of *The Lone Hand,* 1914, by May Gibbs, using the gumnut babies later developed as characters for her children's stories.

11. Aerial picture of Sydney harbour from the north shore, 1982.

13. Cartoon of Henry Lawson (1867–1922), drawn in 1922, by David Low.

MARCUS CLARKE

IN 1866 AT 20

12. Photograph of Marcus Clarke (1846–81), when aged 20.

14. Photograph of Miles Franklin (1879–1954).

15. Portrait of Patrick White (1912–) by Brett Whiteley.

worked in the public service, served as a member of the Timber Industry Inquiry Commission in 1949–50, and became a partner in a group of sawmills.

Blight's notion of poetry is derived from Goethe, that it is 'a criticism of life'. An avid reader of newspapers, he makes poems from any chance discovery or acquaintance. His sea sonnets, for instance, in *A Beachcomber's Diary* (1963) and *My Beachcombing Days* (1968), begin with flotsam, the creatures of the sea and the rock pools, mud, or the human characters of the sea. From them he finds material to fantasize, feel, and think about. In the much-anthologized 'Death of a Whale', for instance, he notes that, 'When the mouse died, there was a sort of pity' and we experience sorrow at the death of a child, but the death of a whale draws 'an excited multitude' of spectators not mourners and 'at the immolation of a race who cries?'

After *My Beachcombing Days* it was some years before Blight published *Hart* (1975), followed shortly afterwards by his *Selected Poems: 1939–1975* (1976). He had experienced a new burst of creativity in 1973 when he was able to resign from the public service to take one of the first Senior Writers' Fellowships offered by the new Literature Board. The new poems, somewhat freer and more experimental in form, contained more quizzical and quirky speculations, more intimate revelations, more metaphysical leaps from the springboard of a single word. He wonders whether the crown of a waterlily might have dandruff, he literalizes the metaphor in 'train of thought' (a process perhaps learned from Bruce Dawe), he thinks of a paling-fence as a lipless row of teeth, he wants to hang up the leaves of poems in trees chosen appropriately to mood.

These poems, ranging in subject from the meaning of life to a casual fancy and in style from Browning to Ashbery, won for Blight in 1976 three major awards: the Patrick White Literary Award, the National Book Council Award and the Grace Leven Prize. Blight's material was obviously coming to reflect his urban environment, and, indeed, he went on to produce a collection called *The New City Poems* (1980). It is an impressive volume, reflecting on his life, the disappointments and accommodations of growing old, the sense of a changed and changing world that must be accepted and not deplored, considering the merits of the religion of nature and the religion of theology, and wryly commenting on some of his critics. He recognizes that times have changed from 'the old gold-leaf days' importance of my father's name on windows'; now he feels menaced and robbed of his inheritance by the city buildings that 'blink like the glasses of anonymous men'. In 'Empire –' he refers to past days with a different view of their relative predatoriness and oppressiveness, the days of the British Empire when 'our blood [was] the wine of profiteers'. Blight is, in fact, neither nostalgic nor iconoclastic; for him the essential values are those of nature and the individual. Real isolation, as he says in 'Leichhardt as Voss', is to lack a context or a past, the tragic fate that Leichhardt and Voss found in a topography and mental landscape in which 'tyranny lies in all absence of direction'.

David Campbell (1915–79), a member of a family that pioneered the settlement of the Monaro region around Canberra, was another *Bulletin* poet of the 1940s encouraged by Stewart. They had much in common, for Campbell loved the landscape, its birds and animals, fishing, and working the land. Campbell's mode is lyric, pastoral and celebratory; his subjects are nature, work and love; his language is an educated vernacular; his poems at their best are witty, playful miniatures.

In the late 1960s he departed from his Australian version of the Elizabethan lyric, particularly in the volume *The Branch of Dodona and Other Poems, 1969–1970* (1970). He developed into autobiography in such poems as 'Starting from Central Station', mythology in such poems as 'The Branch of Dodona', and a mild surrealism in such poems as 'Rock Carvings'. John Blight's modernism may have been an influence; so too may the younger poets of the late 1960s. What he managed to preserve was an easy-going acquaintance with the life of the country, a humanity stirred by the feel of animals or grain, a genuine understanding of issues such as pollution and damage to the environment by contrast with the factitious howls of some of his younger contemporaries. What he did not quite excise were touches of obsolete slang, a sense of general rather than specific good will, and an abstract quality in his expressed interest in time and illusion. There remains something old-worldly about Campbell's poetry by comparison with the work of contemplative nature poets such as Shaw Neilson, Stewart, Blight, Roland Robinson and Les Murray.

Rosemary Dobson (1920–1985), a miniaturist like Campbell and a collaborator with him in two volumes of Russian translations, also draws much on European civilization (particularly myth and painting). Her verse is made up of gracious, quiet-toned reflections, and she is even more impersonal in tone than Campbell.

In sharp contrast to David Campbell's and Rosemary Dobson's European culture lies the Jindyworobak background of Roland Robinson (1912–). An Irish immigrant, he has always advocated a fusion of natural, Aboriginal, and white Australian themes as the appropriate material for poetry, and an organic, sculpturesque form as the appropriate appearance. Like other Jindyworobaks he turned to the centre of Australia and to Arnhem Land in the north for understanding, listened receptively to Aboriginal story-tellers, and learnt how Aboriginal myth breathes through all the land and through every tree, animal and bird. His poems, collected from various publications in *Deep Well* (1962), *Altjeringa, and Other Aboriginal Poems* (1970), *Selected Poems* (1971) and the quite different *Selected Poems (1944–1982)* (1983) are sometimes retellings of Aboriginal tales, sometimes his own Wordsworth-like responses to the landscape. His vivid palette for the interior is reminiscent of the paintings of Albert Namatjira, though like Namatjira he can be repetitive and inconsequential in his description.

Robinson has made several prose collections of Aboriginal legends, published a volume of short stories and three volumes of autobiography, and been instrumental in organizing the publishing co-operative Lyre-bird Writers, and in the preservation for a time of *Poetry Magazine* from the hands of various factions in the Poetry Society. Robinson was not able, however, to fend off the *Putsch* of young poets, headed by Robert Adamson, who took over both society and magazine (turning it into *New Poetry*) at the end of 1969.

John Manifold (1915–85), like David Campbell in coming from a wealthy family on the land and in being a Cambridge graduate, is unlike him in having been a Communist since his university days. While his love lyrics have a similar

Elizabethan quality to those of Campbell, he writes with a more
vigorous, romantic, swashbuckling quality. He has also written
a good deal of social and political satire.

Manifold is also a musician and musical historian. A fine
recorder-player, he has edited recorder music, produced in *The
Amorous Flute* (1948) a treatise for amateur players, taught
hundreds of children and adults how to play the recorder, lute,
cittern and various bush instruments, made many instruments
and taught others how to do so, and, in *The Music in Elizabethan
Drama* (1956), written a major work of reference. From the
1950s he collected, edited and performed the songs and ballads
of bush and other workers, producing two notable anthologies
of words and tunes in *The Queensland Centenary Songbook* (1959)
and *The Penguin Australian Songbook* (1964). *Who Wrote the
Ballads?* (1964) is a contentious but knowledgeable and
plausible account of how ballads come to be composed and
transmitted within communities.

Of Manifold's lyrics, the best-known is probably his elegy in
terza rima, 'The Tomb of Lt John Learmonth, AIF', which is, he
says, 'A cairn of words over a silent man', a fellow poet killed in
Crete. He praises Learmonth for his courage, unadulterated by
'sacrifice or duty or career', and for his 'panache . . . True to no
crown nor presidential sash / Nor flag nor fame'. By contrast
with this sense of sturdy affection, Manifold's love lyrics can
seem too assertively and theatrically masculinist. His greatest
achievement is, in any case, his narrative poems, in the
tradition of Paterson and often surpassing Paterson in his
combination of raciness with drollery, wit or bawdiness.
Sometimes they simultaneously satirize, mock-heroically
extend and utilize the bush-ballad tradition, as in the
brilliantly paced comic ballad 'Incognito'.

An under-rated writer of the *Bulletin* school of the 1940s,
David Rowbotham (1924–) is a follower of no school or
fashion. After some early sunny, but slight, nature pieces he
became more introverted, edgy and ill-at-ease with life in his
third volume, *All the Room* (1964). In this and his next two
volumes he seemed constantly struggling with his rigid forms,
alternately compressing and attenuating his meaning. He was
out of humour with much of his recent experience and the
irritability was not always subsumed into art. *The Pen of Feathers*
(1971) revealed the value of his protracted and dedicated

struggle with himself and his art. He was still restless in manner, but his thought was more concentrated than before and often of daring metaphysical imagination. Now there was a full-toned resonance as he transcended his self-absorption and considered the wider issues of creativity, war, colonialism, the variety of love from the hopeful to the doomed and from the enticing to the domestic, and the possibilities of the youthful generation. A recurring image is of the poet as lover, adventurous, determined and stoic.

Rowbotham's *Selected Poems* (1975) and *Maydays* (1980) contain a number of later poems drawn from experiences and meetings arising out of international travel. He continues to be solemn, uncompromising, even intransigent, but always toughly intelligent. He is often in a reminiscing mood, honestly confessing his preference for the not-too-distant past and his sense of the shoddiness and distastefulness of the present in poems such as 'Hymn to Mary Maria' and 'The Avant-Garde in Market Street, Brisbane'.

Short-story writers

The three periods in which the short story has flourished most have been the 1890s (and early 1900s), the 1940s (and 1950s), and the end of the 1960s (into the 1970s). The *Bulletin* of the 1890s imposed on its writers a preferred formula (as rigid as but quite different from the *Blackwood's* formula, to which Conrad adhered). Short sketches, with some anecdotal narrative interest (often inconclusive), no words wasted in description or dialogue, no long speeches, a characterized story-teller, a setting among bush workers, and some humour or sentimentality is a formula that covers a good many of the *Bulletin* stories.

The stories of the 1920s and 1930s are more varied in form, though sometimes more earnestly uniform in social outlook. Katharine Susannah Prichard, Vance and Nettie Palmer, Frank Dalby Davison, Cecil Mann and Marjorie Barnard were no longer constrained by length. The *Bulletin* (of which Mann was literary editor) accepted much longer stories at this time and Australian writers often sought overseas publication anyway. But the notion of the story as just a yarn – entertaining or depressing – that might or might not be true had given way to a stronger sense of the author's social responsibility to document and expose.

At least two circumstances at the beginning of the 1940s correspond to those of the 1890s. First, it was again a time of national re-examination and assertiveness, the stimulus this time being the threat to national security by war rather than the possibility of federal nationhood as it was in the 1890s. (The resemblance is more to the national questioning generated by the Vietnam War at the end of the 1960s, the beginning of another creative period of the short story.) Secondly, the number of outlets for stories increased, as *Southerly* began in 1939, *Meanjin* in 1940, *Angry Penguins* in 1941, and, most importantly of all, *Coast to Coast* in 1941. Beatrice Davis and Douglas Stewart established *Coast to Coast* as an annual (later a biennial) anthology of Australian short stories. Published by Angus and Robertson with a changing editorship, it was the most prestigious outlet for stories in the 1940s and 1950s, commonly attracting 300–500 submissions. Daily and weekly newspapers, working with united journalistic resources during the war, also welcomed stories.

Gavin Casey (1907–64) grew up in the Western Australian gold-mining town of Kalgoorlie. At various times a car salesman and competitive motorcyclist, he often found himself out of work during the Depression of the 1930s. He turned his hand to writing for newspapers, becoming both a greatly admired journalist and story-writer. Following the old *Bulletin*'s advice, he wrote out of his own experience, often about economic insecurity and loneliness, the experience of finding life becoming oppressive and rushing off for a few beers. His narrative is unobtrusive, realistic and sustained in mode, and tinged with humour that is sometimes melancholy. Most of his stories are set in goldfields towns.

Casey's early stories, many first published in the *Bulletin*, were collected in *It's Harder for Girls* (1942; republished as *Short-Shift Saturday, and Other Stories* in 1974) and *Birds of a Feather* (1943). Of Casey's six novels *Snowball* (1958) has some interest in so far as it offers a sympathetic study of Aborigines.

Casey's narrators – often they seem to merge into a single narrator – tend to be loners, even when among their mates. In 'Miners' Holiday', for instance, the narrator keeps wanting to extricate himself and his mate from their chance drinking-companions. Sometimes they are barely aware that their wives and children are even more alienated than they themselves, typically through being neglected in favour of drinking-companions, as in 'The Last Night'. 'It's Harder for Girls' and 'Short-Shift Saturday' are good examples of the estrangement between the sexes that Casey handles so well. As the narrator says at the end of 'Short-Shift Saturday',

> I wanted the old times back but I couldn't get them. I wanted to touch her, to make some sort of contact with her that might help the words to come. But there was so much time between now and the last time I'd spoken that I knew I could never fill it in. I'd grown new ways of thinking, and so had she.

Casey is also master of another mode of short story, the Australian tall tale, represented by 'The Men from Hannigan's Halt' and 'The Irish Oafs from Ugly Gully'. It is a mode found occasionally in Alan Marshall (in 'They were Tough Men on the Speewah', for example) and developed into an art form by Dal Stivens with his Ironbark Bill and by Frank Hardy with his Benson's Valley and Billy Borker yarns.

Another writer of social-realist stories, John Morrison (1904–), is as well known for his wharfside stories as Casey is for his goldfields ones. Morrison came to Australia from Britain in 1923, subsequently working as a jackeroo, milker, wool-presser, wharf labourer, and gardener, as well as having periods as a swagman. His stories are largely based on his experiences of working as a wharfie and gardener, his experience of unions, and his encounters travelling to work. He has a humane sense of the complexity of life, a militantly anti-capitalist outlook, and a strong belief in the oppression of the individual by institutions.

His first volume of short stories, *Sailors Belong Ships* (1947), his third, *Twenty-three* (1962), and a retrospective collection, *North Wind* (1982), contain the best of his work. He also published two novels.

Morrison has the enviable ability to create expectation and suspense without sacrificing the subtlety of his characters to the exigencies of the plot. In 'Going Through' the suspense centres on whether Colin Lamond will be admitted to the Waterside Workers' Federation of Australia or lynched as a scab worker. The narrator, a young man applying for a union ticket, finds that his sympathies are divided between respect for the solidarity and ceremony of the union (and its ticket to better wages) and doubts about the long, bitter memories and the clan bestiality and persecution that can erupt as the older men protect what little power they have. In 'To Margaret', the narrator, a middle-aged gardener, mistrusts his employer, a successful barrister, on sight, and finds on experience that he is tyrannical and obsessive, feared and detested by his wife and daughter. The suspense lies in how the barrister will react to his daughter's flight from home and subsequent actions by his wife. When the wife also leaves, however, the gardener experiences pity for a man who is troubled and disturbed. But that does not prevent his playing a harmless trick on the man when he is dismissed. A similar ambiguity and concern for the intricacy of character and life mark 'Black Night in Collingwood', where a thoughtless, football-obsessed husband's response to his wife is self-defensive and guilt-ridden.

Alan Marshall (1902–84) wrote both stories and travel documentaries. Marshall, growing up in the Victorian countryside, contracted infantile paralysis at the age of six and almost lost his life. He learned to become mobile on crutches – hence the title of his best-selling autobiography of childhood, *I Can Jump Puddles* (1955) – and later travelled a great deal in the outback by caravan.

Marshall won the short-story prize of the Australian Literature Society in 1933, but his first volume, *Tell us about the Turkey, Jo* was not published until 1946. His *Complete Stories*, collecting the work of this and three subsequent books, was published in 1977. He has been a singularly successful author, with over 4 million copies of his books sold, including translations into over forty languages.

Marshall continues the casual yarn in the style of Lawson, with inconsequential beginnings and endings, but a good deal more optimism and sentimentality than Lawson. His work is full of victims who survive by an effort of will and of those who need reassurance or acceptance. 'The Three-legged Bitch' is an example of courage and persistence on the part of the rogue dingo and the need for acceptance by the retired dogger (dingo hunter) who is asked to bring in her scalp. 'Tell Us About the Turkey, Jo' is one of Marshall's many stories about childhood told by a child narrator. It concerns a child's desperate if amusing need for reassurance.

The stories of Peter Cowan (1914–) present a much bleaker world than those of Alan Marshall. His style, which has remained almost constant since he began writing in 1939, is spare in narrative, concentrated in focus, and avowedly influenced by Hemingway. His hallmarks are short sentences, unnamed characters (who are often lost, trapped or stranded) and unidentified locales. Many of the early stories are set in the Depression years in Western Australia, apparently in the wheat belt or in outer suburbs. It is a grey, monotonous world that he presents, one that has to be accepted despite the nearness of despair.

In his five collections of stories, beginning with *Drift* (1944), Cowan often writes about inconsequentiality, inaction or timidity. In 'Living' the farmer is trapped on an unprofitable farm, deserted by his wife and fearful of madness. In 'Night', the serviceman on leave, attracted by a girl whose boyfriend is away at the war, asks himself, 'who am I to destroy his memories and what perhaps keeps him for life in the unbelievable and the insanity, and he said I cannot destroy them for there is nothing now, and I destroy my own'. In 'The Voice' a male schoolteacher seems about to reveal or commit himself to a fellow teacher in a situation similar to that of many of Joyce's stories. In the end, however, 'he thought perhaps his feeling had been imagination, that he had somehow, on the verge of making a humiliating revelation, been reprieved'. The air of hopelessness and inanition is typical of Cowan's work.

Hal Porter

Although Hal Porter (1911–84) published short stories in the 1940s, including the privately printed volume entitled *Short Stories* (1942), he is unlike any other writer of that period and was, in fact, much more productive in the 1960s and 1970s. He grew up in the Gippsland town of Bairnsdale, a locale re-created in the first volume of his autobiography, *The Watcher on the Cast-iron Balcony* (1963), in many stories, and, with his own line drawings, in *Bairnsdale: Portrait of an Australian Country Town* (1977). He was a secondary-school teacher for many years (including a period in Japan, where he taught the children of the occupation forces) and an actor and country librarian before becoming a full-time writer at the age of fifty.

Beginning with his novel *A Handful of Pennies* (1958, revised 1980) and his stories *A Bachelor's Children* (1962), Porter has published three novels, five major collections of stories, three volumes of autobiography, three volumes of poetry, and three plays. His mannered style, unsaleable in the 1940s and for much of the 1950s, is extravagant, painstakingly graphic, acerbic, and persistent to the point of pain. He affects a ninetyish aestheticism, a fastidious withdrawal from other people's vulgarity and foibles. Return and recognition, the re-creation of an event or a character through memory, is a recurring theme. As a narrator he often poses puzzles for the reader: how will this person's career work out? What are this person's motives? And at the end the narrator often confesses himself puzzled by the puzzles he has set, defeated in the attempt to account for human behaviour.

A Bachelor's Children contains revised versions of almost all Porter's earlier stories published in *Short Stories* and subsequently in journals (mostly the *Bulletin*) in the 1950s. As A. A. Phillips said in 1962, 'seemingly the Australian reader has belatedly acquired a taste for pickled cucumber'. The tartness is most obvious in the stories of school, such as 'Revenge' and 'Fiend and Friend', where there is a strong sense of the struggle for linguistic mastery. Porter has a gift for both the one-liner and the sustained put-down. In 'Fiend and Friend', for instance, the Head, 'distant behind railway novels' most of the time, listens to the disciplinary problems of the new young master, Perrot, making them seem trivial and even self-imposed. 'Cynical bastard' is what Perrot thinks, but what he says is 'I'll learn to cope'. ' "Cope?" said the Head as though Perrot had used four-letter obscenity', and Perrot is forced to correct his choice of diction to 'Manage . . . that is, handle the situation, sir.'

In 'Revenge', a thirteen-year-old schoolboy travelling home for the holidays administers a series of devastating ripostes to a patronizing actress who shares his compartment. He explains to her, having realized that 'Barbara Cartland was her literary Everest', that the author of his book is a nineteenth-century Frenchman. Her response is to feel belittled and valueless: 'she felt icy vermin race in her sheaf of flesh; her scent cheapened; her dress-poppies rusted; her fur coat, she remembered, was torn at the arm-pit. Thank God! she thought stupidly, I have on my new undies.'

Yet, though the boy misses no opportunity to be dismissive, Porter as narrator does not leave him in command of the field. He wins constantly against Miss Morrison, even taunting her with the name of her lover at the end as he shouts with devastating clarity, 'Good night, Mrs Paget. Goodnight, Mrs Pag-et.' But he himself is exposed to the author's ridicule with the schoolboy modishness of his language (particularly his favourite adjective, 'awesome') and the crass vulgarity of his mother's party to meet him on the station.

The train journey in 'Revenge', the enclosed compartment that forces people's lives against each other, is a device that Porter uses more than once, notably in his story 'Brett', from *Fredo Fuss Love Life* (1974). The significance for Porter of the chance meetings that punctuate a lifetime is very evident in 'Fiend and Friend' and particularly in 'Otto Ruff', another early story that is made up entirely of encounters between the narrator and his former school friend Otto Ruff. At one point the narrator speculates that the relationships between their two lives are such that 'no one but I travelled beside him, a useless portmanteau, to every station of his haunted journey'.

Ruff's assumptions of role after role, jazz-age youth, aesthete, rural poet, gambler and derelict, are simply more highly coloured examples of the tendency of Porter's characters to pose, to affect a style, outrageous, intimidating or simpering, but always compelling. Often there is a savouring of faded detail from the Edwardian and Georgian eras, as in the witty refrain of references to *Peter Pan* in 'Fiend and Friend'.

Porter's characters and Porter as narrator can sometimes seem witty to the point of heartlessness. His stories are full of throwaways such as 'he chewed at the edges of his repugnant hotel luncheon' or 'a singlet abandoned like an after-birth'. (Porter's witty horror at the expense of bad food is equalled, incidentally, only by Thea Astley and the Canadian novelist Margaret Atwood.) But Porter is not heartless. He encompasses tragedy and tragi-comedy. Death is, in fact, one of his commonest subjects. Sometimes it seems as if it might be portrayed from the point of view of the Victorian narrative and

pictorial cliché 'Too Late', but always horror or sympathy
drives out sentimentality. In 'Miss Rodda' physical death is
averted, for Miss Rodda is unsuccessful in her suicide attempt,
but there is death of the spirit evident when Miss Rodda is
glimpsed ten years later. The narrator had once been a music
pupil of hers and he became agitated at her concern over the
non-payment of fees by his mother. When he eventually brings
the cheque he is told by Mr Rodda, the teacher's father, 'My
daughter . . . is, they tell me, seriously unwell. She cut her
throat early this morning.' 'Act One, Scene One' deals with a
boy's response to actual death, the death of his mother
accompanied by the death of innocence and an awareness of the
aging of the world. 'On the Ridge' is an account, with gothic
trappings of horror skilfully used to enhance the sense of
mystery, of the murder of a tempting boy by a schoolmaster, his
marriage to the boy's slatternly mother, and his own death.
The order of telling is reversed to heighten the suspense and to
create a tension between three adult views of death – those of
the dead man, his wife and his former friend – and between
those views and the sense of satanism attributed to the boy.

Porter said on more than one occasion that 'most of the short
stories *happen*' to him, at least as initial, generating incidents. In
many cases, 'any mortar of guesswork was minimal' he says
about a list of sixteen stories offered as a typical list of stories
that 'really happened'. 'House-Girl' from *A Bachelor's Children* is
not one of those on the list, but, as Porter appears in the story as
himself, Porter-san, being looked after by an ugly Japanese
house girl who infuriates him with her solicitude and
persistence, but also excites his sympathy, this could well be
added to the list.

Porter's next short-story volume, *The Cats of Venice* (1965),
also contains stories clearly based on his own life. In 'Party
Forty-two and Mrs Brewer' he appears as 'Hal-pal' in the role
of both 'toreador' and 'terrified spinster'. Two of the finest
stories, the uproariously macabre 'Great-aunt Fanny's Picnic'
and the school story 'Say to me Ronald', are vouched for by
Porter as true. 'Say to me Ronald' in fact reintroduces the
hapless schoolmaster Perrot from 'Fiend and Friend'.

Porter's *Selected Stories* (1971) provides a good sampling of
both these two major volumes. *Mr Butterfry, and Other Tales of
New Japan* (1970) contains only seven stories, all longish, and all

but one originally published in the *Bulletin*. Perrot appears again in 'The House on the Hill', now an artist and unconnected with any former schoolmastering he might have done in the past except that he is the victim of late-adolescent spite and trickery. He is the victim of a Potiphar's wife-type of accusation by a Japanese *au-pair* girl whose wild life he had tried to reprove. Each of the stories explores at least one character in some detail, moving easily in a milieu of expatriate Australians in post-war Japan.

Fredo Fuss Love Life (1974) consists of nine stories, again in his more expansive mode. In some, his irritable prejudices seem rather extensively on display, but others, notably 'Brett', present a delicate, nervy portrait of a complex personality responding to a worrying set of circumstances. 'Brett Something-or-Other' is a chance acquaintance made in a train compartment. She is irresponsible, bitchy, and prejudiced, self-pitying and calculating. But in the end she is revealed as insecure and frightened, by no means in command of herself or the situation.

The Clairvoyant Goat, and Other Stories (1981) continues his revelation of prejudices, fascination with jewelled detail, and fastidious (and sometimes fastidiously offensive) taste. By now, the well-rounded incidents that form the backbone of the earlier stories have given way to circumambulations into, around, and out from an incident, with beguiling casual openings and endings.

Porter's three novels, *A Handful of Pennies* (1958, revised 1980 as part of the Portable Australian Authors *Hal Porter*), *The Tilted Cross* (1961) and *The Right Thing* (1971), have the same scintillating texture as the short stories, but in striving for thematic depth he often sacrifices the integrity of both narrative and characters. *A Handful of Pennies*, set in Japan at the time of the post-war military occupation, is intended to counterpoint the insensitivity and indelicacy of the imposed 'democratic' regime (often as represented by boorish Australians) against the insight and understanding of the underlying feudal Japanese attitude. It is a very satirical and sarcastic depiction of the delusions of the occupying forces.

The Tilted Cross is set in another milieu of occupation and cultural dominance, the convict settlement of Hobart in the 1840s. The historical convict Thomas Griffiths Wainewright is transformed fictionally into the artist, Judas Griffin Vaneleigh. He is befriended by a Christ-surrogate, the handsome Cockney Queeley Shiell, who dominates the foreground of the novel. The notion of inherent evil and the possibility of salvation – a frequently occurring theme in Porter – is, however, overshadowed by his painstaking fascination for the details of colonial Hobart, particularly in its contrast between a civilized veneer and a corrupt reality.

The Right Thing again explores the contrast between appearances that are kept up and emotions that are pent up. It is a confusingly presented account by many narrators of a wealthy family that is dehumanized by clinging to outworn conventions. Its most noticeable example of Porter's tendency to push detail to the threshold of pain is its maddening repetition of the phrase 'the right thing'.

Porter's plays enjoyed only moderate success. Their gothic exuberance and melodrama are too concentrated and unremitting. In fiction such a tone can be placed by an authorial voice that is impossible to present on the stage. The most popular is *The Tower*, based on some of the same Hobart convict material that Porter used for *The Tilted Cross*.

The first of Porter's three volumes of autobiography, *The Watcher on the Cast-iron Balcony* (1963), enunciates, amid brilliant narrative and comic technique, his concern for time, change, chance and memory and their relationship to the elusive, perhaps unknowable, nature of truth. In one of many animadversions on this theme he says that 'I began to hear time running away in sumless various fashions; it dawns on me, a startling revelation, that each sound I hear is one sound fewer to hear in my destined total of sounds to hear.' The reference to savoured sensation is typical. *Watcher* covers the time from his birth to the death of his mother. Sights, smells, sounds, and tastes of suburb and country town are re-created. The dense network of relatives and friends is brought to life. The symbols of culture and convention are recalled and examined. The legend of Anzac was generated when Porter was a boy; he speaks of it as 'a sarsaparilla-like creeper twining its way through the undergrowth of earlier less nationally glorious legends about convicts, coach-robberies, bushrangers, Captain Moonlight, gold and aborigines'.

Other fiction-writers

Kylie Tennant (1912–) is a prolific novelist specializing in social-realist works bulging with incident and minor characters, based on working life, and offering a cheerful, even jolly, interpretation of vitalism. Her first novel, *Tiburon*, appeared in the *Bulletin* in 1935, drawing murmurs of recognition from the inhabitants of Canowindra, the small New South Wales country town in which it is set. It concerns impoverished families subsisting on the dole during the Depression. For later novels she lived and worked in slum suburbs of Sydney, travelled with itinerant workers, and worked with ship-builders and bee-keepers.

Preparing to write *The Battlers* (1941) involved travelling in men's trousers and coat on the roads in a horse and cart, seeking itinerant work and mingling with those who were forced to do this to exist. The result is a novel of the comradeship – a cheerful mateship – of the poor. In this novel, and others such as *Ride On, Stranger* (1943) and *Time Enough Later* (1943), she espoused the values of the country as inherently superior to those of the city – a late manifestation of part of the legend of the 1890s. For Kylie Tennant, consciously heir to the inheritance of the social-realist writers of earlier decades, the city is decadent, corrupting and full of social injustice. *Ride On, Stranger* combines comic satire of charlatanry, especially religious charlatanry, rather in the style of Sinclair Lewis with a more serious left-wing treatment of political and unionist organizing and lightly sketched romantic interest. At the end of this amusing picaresque novel, Shannon, the high-spirited and rebellious heroine, retreats to the country for a kind of spiritual refreshment. Kylie Tennant's last novel, *Tantavallon* (1983), keeps up a similar hectic pace, and profusion of modes. It includes Vietnamese migrants mining uranium, a churchwarden attempting suicide in Sydney Harbour, a fire, a suburban street battle, a spectacular car accident, and a cancer scare. It illustrates well her belief that life in general is 'a thin layer of ice over a raging human volcano', full of 'absurdity and chaos'. But there is always vigour, entertainment, and comedy in her depiction.

Dal Stivens (1911–) represents two strands of Australian story-telling, the tall tale, which has its origins in the nineteenth century, and the more recent strand of fantasy and fabulism. Stivens's first volume, *The Tramp, and Other Stories* (1936) was, however, of a different kind again. It was social-realist in tone, but the manner of telling was more concise and pointed, in the manner of American stories of the 1920s. Its material – alienated out-of-work men who grubbed for food, grabbed rides on goods trains and avoided the police – was gathered from his experiences while growing up in West Wyalong in the central west of New South Wales. It was with his second and more especially his third volumes, *The Courtship of Uncle Henry* (1946) and *The Gambling Ghost, and Other Tales* (1953), that he began to draw on his fund of outback tall stories. They continued in *Ironbark Bill* (1955) – mostly written to be read aloud to his children – and *The Scholarly Mouse, and Other Tales* (1957). These volumes contain tales of outlandish characters such as Ironbark Bill and Cabbage Tree Ned, of various ghosts, and of remarkable creatures such as the cockerel that learns to understand human language. Stivens is also noted for his tall tales about cricket, which are collected in *The Demon Bowler, and Other Cricket Stories* (1979). 'The Man who Bowled Victor Trumper', an early example, contains not only the claim enunciated in the title but also a claim to have fought Les Darcy, and to have owned a kelpie bitch so intelligent she could dip her tail in a milk bucket in order to feed her litter.

Stivens's third novel, *A Horse of Air* (1970), indicated his commitment to fantasy and surrealism. It concerns the search by Henry Craddock in central Australia for the rare Night Parrot. But the narrative status of Craddock's account is ambiguous: it is written for his psychiatrist, and contains many indications of doubt about the boundary between truth and fiction. It is this kind of concern with narrative games that relates Stivens to such younger writers as Peter Carey and David Ireland. The novel also touches on a number of Stivens's political concerns, such as his opposition to nuclear warfare, conscription and the Vietnam War.

Stivens's political and organizational interests were for some years turned towards the Australian Society of Authors. He was the foundation President in 1963, and it was partly owing to his efforts and those of Colin Simpson that a scheme of public-lending right was established in 1975.

Judah Waten (1911–) is a writer of unvarnished social-realist stories and novels. Of Russian Jewish background, he has been a member of the Communist Party for most of his life, viewed with revulsion and prejudice by committed capitalists and more recently to derision by members of the more anarchist side of the New Left. He is a straight-forward writer, sceptical of the narrative puzzles of Pynchon and Barthelme and their Australian followers, and inclined to believe that such writers 'have a fear of politics and take refuge in cynicism'.

After a brief writing-career in England in the early 1930s, Waten returned to Australia in 1933 and devoted himself to the political struggle. In the 1940s he turned to writing stories again. 'After several false starts', he says, 'I finally decided on a new course. I would write about people I knew, real people as it were, not changing them into other people.' So he wrote about his parents, his boyhood, and his parents' relatives and friends. These stories, collected in *Alien Son* (1952), form a kind of discontinuous narrative of a Jewish boy and his parents. The boy is persecuted at school and in his suburb because of his Jewishness, but he finds the religion and customs of some of the older members of his parents rather alien too.

Beginning with *The Unbending* (1954), Waten wrote seven novels. *Time of Conflict* (1961), set in the Depression, tells how Mick Anderson becomes a Communist as a result of having his labour exploited. *Distant Land* (1964) deals with the Depression period too, but also with the anti-conscription campaign in Australia during the 1914–18 war and the special problems migrants had adjusting to life in Australia. *Scenes of Conflict* (1982) is a fictionalized autobiography, at least in substantial parts. Its hero, Tom Graves, is dedicated to the Communist movement, desires to be a writer, and has a marked tendency to fall in love. He is presented as a romantic idealist, deficient in common sense, easily duped, and sentimental towards older women, but eventually he gains experience and resignation. The autobiographical element is present inasmuch as Tom Graves's life intertwines with several actual events of historical political importance. Like Waten in 1932, Graves participates in the third of the great hunger marches from England and Scotland that converged on Clerkenwell Green and later Hyde Park. At Clerkenwell Green, like Waten, he steps forward to make a speech pleading with the police not to draw their batons if ordered to. Like Waten, he is arrested, tried, found guilty, and sentenced to three months in Wormwood Scrubs.

Waten's work provides a chronicle of European migrant life in Australia from before the 1914–18 war until the 1970s. He is the inaugurator of a strand of migrant writing that became especially prominent in the 1970s and 1980s, and he initiates it with an attitude of understanding and compassion that is not afraid to appear naïve or sentimental.

Olaf Ruhen (1911–), a New Zealander by birth, is Australia's most prolific writer about the South Pacific. In his varied life he has been a gold-digger, fisherman, timber-mill worker, bomber pilot, adventurer and writer. His published works include novels, historical accounts, short stories, poems and articles.

Something of his boyhood in Dunedin and some of his Pacific travels are recounted in *Tangaroa's Godchild* (1962). *Minerva Reef* (1963) tells the true story of the wreck in 1962 of the Tongan cutter, *Tuaikaepau*, on the South Minerva reef. Her crew survived for 102 days on the inhospitable reef, built a boat, and then sailed 220 miles until it too was wrecked on a reef off one of the Fijian islands. Ruhen's great affection for the people of Tonga was recognized by the conferral on him of a Tongan title, Manusiu Oe Pasifik – Frigate Bird of the Pacific.

Ruhen's novels include *Naked under Capricorn* (1958) and *The Flockmaster* (1963), both of them concerned with taming and husbanding the resources of central Australia.

8
Symbolic and social-realist fiction

Patrick White as novelist

The eleven published novels of Patrick White (1912–)
constitute the most impressive oeuvre in Australian fiction, a
judgement verified by his being the only Australian writer
awarded the Nobel Prize (in 1973). White's symbolic novels,
with their sometimes slow openings, their many new starts,
their frequent time and place shifts, their fastidious fascination
with bodily functions and oddities, and their homiletic
passages, took some time to gain acceptance, though White's
many statements about a uniformly hostile reception in
Australia for *The Aunt's Story* and *The Tree of Man* are
unsupported by the facts. From the beginning, partly because
of his familiarity with twentieth-century French and German
experimental writing, he was in a different mould from the
social-realist writers of the 1930s, though he was not without
interest in some of their concerns. In the 1970s, for instance, he
became involved in public demonstrations and speeches on
such matters as urban conservation and republicanism. His
novels tend to move from outer reality into the disturbed or
fragmented mind (a process influenced in later works to some
extent by his reading of Jung), and, for a few central characters,
the unsuccessfully resisted impulse to spiritual understanding.
Despite the jerkiness of parts of the narrative, the thematic
construction is always carefully moulded, sometimes seeming
to be imposed on the characters irrespective of their natures.
   White's paternal ancestors founded several extensive and
beautiful pastoral properties in the Upper Hunter Valley of
New South Wales. These included Edinglassie (near

Muswellbrook) and Belltrees (near Scone). Although White's parents gave up their interest in Belltrees shortly after his birth, the property forms the basis for the Kudjeri homestead in *The Eye of the Storm*. White grew up in Sydney, where his parents had a flat in Phillip Street in the city and later a large house, Lulworth, in the near-city suburb of Darlinghurst, which forms a background for the family home of the Bonners in *Voss* and for the Courtney house in *The Vivisector*. Later the family owned a summer house, Withycombe, at Mount Wilson in the Blue Mountains to the west of Sydney; this area is the setting for the play *Night on Bald Mountain*.

White's early schooling was mostly at Tudor House School, Moss Vale, to the south-west of Sydney. It appears as Sorrel Vale in *The Aunt's Story*. At the age of thirteen he was sent to Cheltenham College in the Cotswolds, which he found regimented and farcical. Some of the poems of *Thirteen Poems* (1929 or 1930) were presumably written there.

In 1930 and 1931 White worked as a jackeroo in the Monaro district – later to be the background for *Happy Valley* and *The Twyborn Affair* – and in the dry north-west of New South Wales at Walgett, but he found the work lonely and without stimulus. He returned to England in 1932 to read modern languages at King's College, Cambridge. While there he continued writing, producing a volume of poetry, *The Ploughman, and Other Poems* (1935), and having two plays produced back in Sydney at Bryant's Playhouse, Darlinghurst.

After graduation, White lived in London, meeting the Australian painter Roy de Maistre who, with Sidney Nolan, provides pàrt of the model for the portrait of Hurtle Duffield, the artist, in *The Vivisector*. He wrote satirical theatre sketches, but found he could not sell his serious plays and novels.

The fourth novel, *Happy Valley* (1939), was, however, accepted. The ironic title refers to the frozen landscapes of an isolated mountain community in the Monaro, a symbol of isolation. White went to the United States in 1939, where he partly wrote – very hastily because of his intention of enlisting for war service – another novel of isolation, *The Living and the Dead* (1941). Set in the Pimlico district of London, it is the only one of his novels with a non-Australian setting. Despite his own opinion of it as premature and 'wretched', its publication drew from reviewers some comparisons with Joyce, Lawrence and Woolf.

White was an intelligence officer in the RAF during the war, serving in Africa, the Middle East and Greece. During this time he formed an attachment that was to be life-long with Manoly Lascaris, an English-speaking lieutenant in the Greek Sacred Regiment, who later came to Australia to live with White. At the end of the war he wrote *The Aunt's Story* (1948), the story of a middle-aged woman who grows up in Australia but subsequently travels in Europe and the United States. In the earlier novels, the central character is engaged in a quest for self-knowledge. Theodora Goodman in *The Aunt's Story* is, however, engaged less in a quest for personal identity than in one for the nature of being itself. The ego is now seen as imprisoning the spiritual sense in much the same way as materialism can do. The minor characters in the novel are nevertheless presented as engaged in the search for self-identity; they live a pragmatic existence unimpelled by the necessity to seek meaning.

In Part Two of *The Aunt's Story* Theodora develops a fantasy life which White represents by dreams and visions, a merging of memory, creative memory and the present. Within this soft-edged, shifting pattern, however, some symbolic objects stand out boldly, as when Theodora tells General Sokolnikov, 'I believe in a pail of milk'. This faith in sacramental objects is a lasting feature of White's work. So too is the heavy reiteration of images, recurring like musical themes. In *The Aunt's Story* roses are used a symbols both of home and homeliness and of artificiality and falseness. Carved wood is used to suggest the solidity and soundness of Theodora in both her physical appearance and her personality. And among the many other images are black volcanic hills, fire, bones and knives.

White and Lascaris settled on a five-acre farmlet, Dogwoods, at Castle Hill, a semi-rural suburb to the north-west of Sydney, where they raised dogs and goats and tended an orchard. The house provides the background for both *The Tree of Man* and *The Solid Mandala*.

Over a four-year period, White wrote *The Tree of Man* (1955), an attempt, as he said, 'to discover the extraordinary behind the ordinary, the mystery and the poetry which alone could make bearable the lives of such people, and incidentally, my own life since my return'. In the same article he said he was 'determined to prove that the Australian novel is not necessarily the dreary, dun-coloured offspring of journalistic realism'.

The Tree of Man transformed the traditional Australian saga of the land. Stan and Amy Parker experience all the elemental rites of such sagas, but with an emphasis on the inward response, not the outward appearance. The novel deals with man against the wilderness, man and woman making a home, man against the four elements of nature (earth, wind, fire, and flood), parents and children, personal dishonour and national honour, suicide and murder, growing old, and redemption. Early in the novel it is explained that Stan

> had not learned to think far, and in what progress he had made had reached the conclusion he was a prisoner in his human mind, as in the mystery of the natural world. Only sometimes the touch of hands, the lifting of a silence, the sudden shape of a tree or the presence of a first star, hinted at eventual release.

Conceived and written in a D. H. Lawrence mode, Amy is absorbed in Stan: 'And the man consumed the woman. That was the difference.' Amy's quest is to 'learn about Stan perhaps in time'. His is to understand and accept the nature of Being, which he does, slowly and often reluctantly. He is Adam, naming features and events for Amy, coming to realize (in a repeated image) that they are ant-like, living in an ant world. His final epiphany is to find God in a gob of spittle, to express belief in a leaf, and then: 'I believe, he said, in the cracks in the path. On which ants were massing . . . . It was clear that One, and no other figure, is the answer to all sums.'

Stan as reluctant visionary and Stan as representative of the pragmatic and phlegmatic dailiness of life seem to some readers to be separate characters, but this is a plausible criticism only because one side of his nature has to be developed by sacramental image and sibylline language, whereas the other is developed by epic incident. The jumps from one side to the other, which White does not try to conceal, also give colour to this theory.

The novel also contains a good deal of dark comedy, slapstick, social satire and comically heightened narrative.

Much of this centres on the O'Dowds, a feckless down-at-heel Irish family, neighbours of the Parkers. In one Lawsonian scene O'Dowd pursues his wife with a cleaver around the house while Amy Parker hurries after him.

The conceptual origin of White's next novel, *Voss* (1957), lay in his reading of Eyre's journal in London during the war and his experiences in the Egyptian desert, when 'the perverse side of his nature' conceived the character at a time 'when all our lives were dominated by that greater German megalomaniac', Hitler. Later, in Australia, he read about Leichhardt and incorporated him into the vortex of ideas. Then, half drugged, in hospital, suffering from an acute attack of asthma, he 'became in turn Voss and his anima Laura Trevelyan'. While in hospital he sketched out the book he was going to write.

In *Voss* White continues to deal with some of the central Australian myths, including the attempt to conquer the unknown interior, authority and rebellion, and the contrast of Sydney and the bush – one redolent of tamed, soft corruption, the other wild, tough and irreducibly honest. Where earlier novels had dealt with the search for meaning, that search had been delayed and even vitiated by the concerns of society and the flesh. There were only glimpses of a vision rather than a steady illumination. In *Voss* White presented an obsessed visionary so that he could concentrate undistractedly on the process of illumination. Ulrich Voss, modelled on the explorer Ludwig Leichhardt, is a dreamer, with an egocentric wilful dream of exploring the continent. His inflexible will controls even the rebels in the party. Defeated by heat and thirst, they are guided to water by Aborigines, who interpret Voss as the Great Snake or ancestor spirit. Just before he dies, Voss has a luminous vision of himself and Laura, his psychic companion in the journey, now as husband and wife in a sacramental communion, travelling from Voss's cancelled coronation 'back in search of human status', with Voss, like Adam at the creation of a new world, naming and explaining the symbolic plants they encounter. It is a preparation for death. He is butchered by his young Aboriginal guide, Jackie, and for the Aborigines becomes part of the Dreaming, the creative power, the archetypal myth of creation. Laura puts it slightly differently: ' "Voss did not die", Miss Trevelyan replied. "He is there still, it is sand, in the country, and always will be. His legend will be written down, eventually, by those who have been troubled by it.'' '

Within the decorated prose style of *Voss*, psychic communion takes place wordlessly. Language is, in fact, a menace. For the society of Sydney it is a divisive social instrument; for Jackie a burden enveloping his psychic silence; for Voss an alien and alienating tongue. Even Laura, in Voss's final vision, is bored by his Adamic explanations. The novel, then, aspires to the condition and communion of silence, like Beethoven's last quartets or Eliot's *Four Quartets*.

By this stage of his career White could count himself a successful novelist. *The Tree of Man* was awarded the gold medal of the Australian Literature Society. *Voss* won the Miles Franklin Award (as did *Riders in the Chariot*) and the W. H. Smith Prize. *Riders in the Chariot* (1961) explores the minds of four characters who unwittingly aspire to the illumination of sainthood. They are social outcasts, 'burnt ones' in White's commonly used expression, who experience redemption (symbolized by a vision of the chariot) after suffering.

The character of Himmelfarb, the suffering Messiah who is tortured in a mock crucifixion by factory workers, was in part based on White's New York publisher, Ben Huebsch of the Viking Press – 'from the inherited psyche rather than the outer man', according to White. Alf Dubbo is alienated both by his Aboriginal inheritance and by the honesty of his painting. Mary Hare, owner of the decrepit mansion Xanadu, is alienated by solitude, repressed sexuality, and guilt about her father's death. Mrs Godbold is set apart by an unquenchable desire for vicarious motherhood. White had difficulty in intertwining the lives of these four and difficulty in extricating their interests from his sustained satire of society in the imaginary outer suburbs of Sydney 'Sarsaparilla' and 'Baranugli'.

White's own outer suburb of Castle Hill was becoming overrun by housing-development, and, as he was finding it inconvenient to travel between his home and the city, he and Lascaris moved in 1965 to a house bordering Centennial Park, in the near-eastern suburbs. The house appears in *The Eye of the Storm*. *The Solid Mandala* (1966), written about the time he became interested in Jung, is a study of two twin brothers, Waldo and Arthur Brown, who live all their lives in

Sarsaparilla. The central part of the book consists of an account of their lives, first from Waldo's and then from Arthur's point of view. Waldo is disappointed in love and in authorship and is increasingly resentful of his half-witted, incomprehensible brother. His sterile, jaundiced view of life is balanced by Arthur's. Confused and inarticulate, he nevertheless has a radiant goodness and insight that are represented by his four mandala-like marbles. He realizes that most of those around him cannot appreciate them or their meaning, that 'It was himself who was, and would remain, the keeper of the mandalas, who must guess their final secret through touch and light.' The struggle to guess their meaning is symbolized by the 'red gold disc of the sun', which he strives to hold, but also by icebergs that 'moaned and jostled one another, crunching and tinkling . . . to splinter into glass balls which he gathered in his protected hands'. The union of opposites, a distinctive feature of many of White's novels, here takes the image of androgyny, the attraction–repulsion relationship of the twins for each other. In the preceding novels the heterosexual couples Stan and Amy, and Voss and Laura, had been presented as seeking to merge into a primal unity.

The Vivisector (1970) and *The Eye of the Storm* (1973) are looked on by White as novels which 'belong to Sydney'. *The Vivisector* portrays both a painter, Hurtle Duffield (in part based on Roy de Maistre and Sidney Nolan), and a city. White says 'I wanted at the same time to paint a portrait of my city: wet, boiling, superficial, brash, beautiful, ugly Sydney, developing during my lifetime from a sunlit village into this present-day parvenu bastard, compound of San Francisco and Chicago.' This affection for a city is accompanied by fascination for the craft of painting (one of the careers White would have liked to follow). In this more relaxed, less intensely allegorical novel, there is a good deal of attention paid to the business of creativity.

Duffield, an arrogant, sensual man, is in many ways insufferable, but he has great integrity as an artist even when his vision drives him to derangement. Like most of White's heroes and visionaries he is tormented by his vision and by his humanity; like most of them his quest is for 'the mystery of pure being'. During his career he draws obsessional motivation from his encounters with women, for sex is more important in this novel than in the earlier ones. The women include his foster mother, Mrs Courtney, prim and suffocatingly genteel; his foster sister Rhoda, a hunchback; Nance Lightfoot, a vivacious and warm-hearted Sydney prostitute; Hero Pavloussi, the lustful wife of a respectable Greek ship-owner; and Kathy Volkov, whom Duffield regards as his spiritual child. All are related to Duffield through a semi-mystical vortex of sex and their response to his art.

This is a portrait of the artist as vivisector of experience, human beings and himself. When Duffield approaches his first sexual encounter with Hero Pavloussi, for instance, he wonders whether it will 'culminate on the operating table on a prearranged afternoon'. But there are other vivisectors in the novel. There is God the Vivisector and Artist, and there is Mrs Courtney, vivisecting her daughter Rhoda on her back-straightening board and vivisecting Duffield. And there are those who, like Rhoda, were 'born vivisected', destined to be always in pain.

White says that 'The Eye of the Storm came to me crossing Kensington High Street, London, after a visit to my mother at her flat in Marloes Road where she was lying bedridden, senile, almost blind, tended by a swarm of nurses and servants.' For the novel he transferred the site of Elizabeth Hunter's terminal sickness to Sydney. She lies, querulous and imperious, surrounded by nurses, arranging for her two middle-aged children to come and comfort her. After traumatic journeys, Sir Basil, an actor (White had wanted to be an actor as well as a painter) and Dorothy, Princesse de Lascabanes, arrive, but they are still too much in fear of their mother's powerful egocentricity to spend much time with her. Visiting the old family property of Kudjeri and imposing themselves shamelessly on the new owners, they feel afraid and lonely, and spend a night in bed together. 'What have we got unless each other? Aren't we, otherwise – bankrupt?' asks Dorothy.

This is a less compassionate treatment of artistry and family relations than in White's earlier books. There is more hatred and disgust, fewer redeeming transfigurations. It is also less baroque in style, more muted in its set pieces. There is nothing, for instance, like the florid satirical splendour of the pretentious society dinner party in The Vivisector.

A Fringe of Leaves (1976) compensates for these qualities. Its central character, Ellen Roxburgh, is the most immediately likable of White's middle-class heroines (though it should be noted that she rose from working-class origins through marriage, putting aside her speech mannerisms and pagan religion). This is a book in which iterative symbolism has ceased to be intrusive. The myth of redemption through suffering is this time worked out almost entirely through the narrative. The narrative has an historical basis, the wreck of the brig *Stirling Castle* off the Queensland coast in 1836, the survival of the captain's wife, Eliza Fraser, among a group of Aborigines, and her return to white culture after many privations. Inspired by and following the historically false account in Sidney Nolan's series of paintings on Mrs Fraser, White has his heroine guided to the Moreton Bay colony by a convict, who believes that she is about to denounce him. Some of the scenes, notably those in a lily pool and in a treetop, seem to be based on specific paintings by Nolan.

Mrs Roxburgh is married to the elderly invalid Austin Roxburgh. Having momentarily become the lover of his reprobate brother in Tasmania, Ellen fears that the baby to whom she gives birth after the wreck is his. When the longboat with the survivors lands on Fraser Island, the captain and Austin Roxburgh are speared by Aborigines, the others stripped, and the men marched away. Mrs Roxburgh, abandoned, makes herself a fringe of leaves from convolvulus. The Aboriginal women return, cut off her hair, paint her body, physically abuse her, often neglect to feed her, make her their slave and reduce her 'to an animal condition'. But she survives, partly by drawing on the hidden reserves of her past as the Cornish farm girl Ellen Gluyas – another example of White using the image of the double seeking unity.

Rescued by an escaped convict, Jack Chance, she sets out with him for Moreton Bay, becoming his lover along the way and releasing her repressed sexuality. Once back among white people, she experiences the need for healing. She associates with the guilty, the condemned, the punished and children. 'No one is to blame, and everyone for whatever happens', she says. Through understanding and identifying with sufferers she experiences the healing she sought, evidenced by the capacity to love.

White's last novel, *The Twyborn Affair* (1979), concentrates on the divided personality seeking unity. The androgynous central personality manifests itself as Eudoxia, Eddie and Eadith Twyborn, all of them 'astray in the general confusion of life'. It is a novel full of transvestism, sexual ambiguity, homosexuality and narcissism. The duality with which it deals is philosophical and theological as well as sexual. White raises the Manichean possibility that the world is an evil creation, antithetical to the goodness of God, and certainly the book rejects sensuousness as being deceptive and absurd. It consists of three parts, the outer two extravagantly Byzantine, the middle one matter-of-fact. In Part One, Eudoxia Vatatzes is married to an elderly Greek, Angelos Vatatzes, and living in France. In the course of the novel it is revealed that he knows his wife to be male. In Part Two, Eddie Twyborn tries 'coming to terms with a largely irrational nature' by working on a sheep station in the Monaro, working hard, even dispensing with sheets on his bed 'out of masochism or delusions of masculinity'. In Part Three, Mrs Eadith Trist flamboyantly runs a brothel in London during the 1939–45 war. But throughout Eudoxia/Eddie/Eadith experience difficulties with the sexuality of a female outlook in a man's body, what White sums up at the end as an 'interchangeable failure'. The novel is not, however, mawkish or self-pitying. It is quite matter-of-fact about the circumstances and their emotional effects.

White's stories and plays

White has published two collections of short stories, *The Burnt Ones* (1964) and *The Cockatoos* (1974). *The Burnt Ones*, stories written following *Riders in the Chariot*, contains eleven stories of 'the burnt ones' – that is, as the Greek phrase metaphorically means, 'the poor unfortunates'. Four are set in Greece, three in Sarsaparilla, and four elsewhere in Australia. These are stories of waste, misdirection, fantasizing, lust and panic. 'The Letters' (a story of waste and mental breakdown), 'A Cheery Soul' (a set of comic anecdotes centred on a dotty do-gooder, Miss Docker, in Sarsaparilla) and 'Down at the Dump' (another Sarsaparilla story) display White's range of satiric observation, comic inventiveness and undogmatic tenderness.

The Cockatoos: Shorter Novels and Stories, contains six works. Two of them, 'A Woman's Hand' and 'Sicilian Vespers', deal with middle-aged couples who excite White's satire and sympathy. 'The Night the Prowler' is about the connections of love and fear, conveyed largely in White's richly satiric vein of pretentious middle-class dialogue.

White's later plays have had at least moderate success on stage. The first of his mature plays, *The Ham Funeral*, written in London shortly after the war, is, like *The Aunt's Story* of about the same time, an expressionistic work. It is based on a story told to White by the painter William Dobell which also inspired Dobell's painting *The Dead Landlord*. From the story White created a symbolist play, influenced strongly by Strindberg and German expressionism. The Landlord dies of natural causes at the beginning of the play. Images of castration and killing dominate the Landlady's fantasies and the relatives' depiction of her. She tries to seduce the Young Man (a symbol of the search for self and creativity), but he brutally rejects her. She oscillates between remorse and acceptance, understanding neither.

The Ham Funeral was first performed in Adelaide in 1961 after having been turned down by the Elizabethan Theatre Trust and the Adelaide Festival on the grounds of its experimental nature and indecency. White's next three plays made more concessions to realism, two of them being set in fictional Sarsaparilla, one in the Blue Mountains. *The Season at Sarsaparilla* (written 1961, produced 1962) has at its centre the unfaithfulness of Nola Boyle to her husband Ern through her adultery with Rowley Masson. White satirically presents a society of snobbery and self-hate. As in *The Ham Funeral* he demands separate acting-areas on the one stage, in this case the kitchens of three adjacent houses.

A Cheery Soul (written 1962, produced 1963) reworks his story of the same name. Miss Docker through her unstoppable passion for good works disrupts the monotonous life of the middle-aged Custances. Even when put in an old women's home she is still rebellious, though the persecution is making her more and more isolated. White makes substantial use of a poetic chorus to comment on the action as well as, individually, to be part of it.

Night on Bald Mountain (written 1962, produced 1964) is a highly intellectual play, expressive of conflict between the earth (symbolized by the goat-keeper Miss Quodling) and human society (symbolized by Professor Hugo Sword). Miss Quodling envisages the destruction of the earth by humanity and then another beginning: 'The silence will breed again . . . in peace . . . a world of goats . . . perhaps even man!' White later wrote a script from this play for a film directed by Jim Sharman.

White wrote no more plays until the later 1970s, when he was stimulated by the new spirit of experimentalism in the theatre shown in the work of such directors as Sharman (whose direction of *The Season at Sarsaparilla* at the Sydney Opera House in 1976 seems to have encouraged White to return to writing for the theatre). *Big Toys* (produced 1977, published 1978), White's most political play, exposes the political power-brokers operating in Australian society: the representatives of multinational corporations and their local political, financial and legal contacts. It is a play written in satiric rage and dismay at the suppression of the Australian Labor Party's experiment with social-democratic government between 1972 and 1975. The baroque style does, however, tend to disguise the emptiness of the lives of the power-brokers, Mag and Ritchie Bosanquet, and to distract attention from the struggles for integrity of the unionist Terry Legge. The horrific nature of the Bosanquets' calm contemplation of nuclear disaster is thus diminished.

Signal Driver (produced 1982, published 1983) is more exciting. It is set at a suburban tram (later bus) stop. Theo and Ivy Vokes represent Australia's history from the 1914–18 war to the present in much the same way as the Landlord and Landlady represent the early part of this period. Both plays also make use of music-hall commentary on the action. Theo, like the Landlord, is withdrawn, contemplative and austere; Ivy, like the Landlady, is sensual but frustrated.

Netherwood (produced and published 1983) is closer to realism than *Signal Driver*. It presents the struggle between materialism (represented by Miss Jelbart's asylum, the police and the local farmers) and spiritual values (represented by Alice and Royce Best and their protégés at Netherwood). The first group are insensitive, selfish, brutal and dishonest; the second incompetent and anarchic. The denouement is a shoot-out, culminating in the Police Sergeant's words, 'Comical bastards, us humans. Seems like we sorter *choose* ter shoot it out . . . to find out who's the bigger dill.'

White's autobiography, *Flaws in the Glass* (1981), is a witheringly honest and cantankerous book. Recognizing its discontinuous character, which leaves many loose ends, White called it 'a self-portrait' rather than an autobiography, but it does reveal a good deal about many periods of his life. It also indicates his difficulty, at this stage of his life, of writing a flowing, sustained work – one reason why he turned back to drama.

White's corpus deals, in every style from farce to tragedy, with a small number of themes but a vast number of characters. He has conducted a continuous literary protest against materialism and the dullness of realism. His positive values are integration of the divided soul, receptiveness through genuine goodness to moments of illumination, and the struggle for creative forms capable of expressing these ideas. Novels, stories, and plays tend to alternate between identifiably placed social satire and commentary and more timeless and placeless settings. No other Australian writer has displayed such capacity to hate and to love humanity or such capacity to create comic and tragic character. He has always, as he says in *Flaws in the Glass*, been 'embarking on voyages of exploration which I hope may lead to discovery'.

Other novelists, including best-sellers

Eve Langley (1908–74) wrote two published novels, of which only the first, *The Pea Pickers* (1942), has excited much interest. Highly praised by Douglas Stewart and Hal Porter, it is based on a set of Furphy-like experiences Langley and her sister had in 1928. Dressing as young men they wandered through Gippsland and southern New South Wales as itinerant workers, picking apples, peas, hops and maize. In the novel the narrator reports that 'It was decided that my name should be Steve, because the comic literature of the Australian bush has always had a Steve in it.' Her sister is at first to be Jim, on the grounds that Lawson says 'There are a lot of good old mates named Jim, working around in the bush', but it is changed to Blue, after their night-soil man.

The Pea Pickers is full of gay insouciance, irreverence and vivacity. It is also a story of Steve's search for objects to love.

She delights in the earth and in work, but her search for reciprocated love is unsuccessful. A fellow worker, Macca, disappoints her romantic aspirations by forgetting or declining to use the term of endearment, *mia cara sposa*, that they have determined on. Like an earlier object of infatuation, Kelly, he fails to write, and Steve says she

> was forced to admit that I was unwanted and unthought of. In my bitterness, I became hard, masculine and truculent in manner, swore and blasphemed, became passionately fond of guns and bullets, killed every living thing I could see around me, and grew to love with a fierce mirthless joy, adventure and extravagant comedy.

The landscape, though equally indifferent to her, is the object of affectionate and accurate description throughout the book. Langley is particularly effective with her descriptions of starkness and isolation in the bush, especially by starlight – a poignant image of her own loneliness. In this landscape the androgynous youthful worker–poet finds that no permanent human relationships are to be made, and she is desolate.

Langley's later novel, *The White Topee* (1954), tries to continue the autobiographical novel, but the hilarity is forced and Steve is no longer so emotionally ambitious, so self-deluded, or so self-amused.

George Johnston (1912–70) is a novelist who wrote both serious works and journalistic pot-boilers, the serious works invariably being those closer to his own experience. A war correspondent in the 1939–45 war, he used the reporter-would-be-novelist as a character in several of his fictional works. In 1954 he gave up an eminent journalistic career to live on the Greek island of Hydra with his wife (Charmian Clift, also a writer) and family. He wrote at great speed to support his family, sometimes in association with Charmian Clift, sometimes independently. In 1964, knowing that he had incurable tuberculosis, he returned to Sydney, dying in hospital a year after his wife's suicide. It was in 1964 too that he had his first major success as a novelist, with *My Brother Jack*. Although there had been two previous novels in which David Meredith was a character, *Closer to the Sun* (1960) and *The Far Road* (1962), *My Brother Jack* was the first to base itself on the struggle for self-understanding of David Meredith himself, and the first to be so thoroughly autobiographical. With its successors, *Clean Straw for Nothing* (1969) and the unfinished *A Cartload of Clay* (1971), it constitutes an autobiographical trilogy exploring the self and the nature of Australia.

My Brother Jack, written on Hydra, is an ebullient chronicle of childhood and adolescence in Melbourne between the wars. David Meredith feels alienated from his family and surroundings and unable to win the approval of his less reflective but more popular brother, Jack. Jack represents an image of Australia, swaggering, boastful, hard-drinking and lustful, that both attracted and repelled Johnston. In the end, however, it is David who is the famous war correspondent, Jack the furtive, ashamed failure at home, anxious to gain what reflected glory he can.

Clean Straw for Nothing, without Jack as a nostalgic symbol of a past Australia, and set mostly in Europe, was less popular. Where *My Brother Jack* created a sense of the vast spaciousness of the Australian continent, the second novel creates a sense of the constraints of time. It moves backwards and forwards in slabs of time that gradually overlap with each other to build a composite picture of David and his second wife, Cressida Morley. Johnston creates a complex tension from David's ill health, sexual jealousy, monetary worries, sense of writing as a career, and concern about the alienation of the expatriate. In a rage at Cressida's confession of an affair, he reproaches her with

'It's your bloody obsession! These romantic idiotic dreams of yours! . . . You think you own some private bloody world of your own you don't have to give up for anyone. You talk about sharing. *You!* You won't share. You never have. You –'

A Cartload of Clay begins back in Sydney. David Meredith is in his late fifties, reviewing his earlier experiences and trying to cope with pain and the imminence of death. He is also trying, after a lifetime of alienation, to understand and relate to other people – to his daughter Miranda, now on the brink of marriage; to his son Julian, who whole-heartedly rejects the world; to his wife (including 'the haunting and terrible enigma' of her death); and to the occasionally encountered 'Ocker', with his fund of moral certainties ('Ocker' used to be a common Australian nickname as well as a common noun or adjective imputing uncouthness or unabashed boorishness, but the first of these usages is now obsolete). Once again Johnston has changed his style of narration. In *My Brother Jack* it was straightforward in chronology; in *Clean Straw for Nothing* it was in reordered blocks of time; in *A Cartload of Clay* it has a languid, dreamlike retrospection in which David simply goes for walks, thinks and talks.

A late pendant to the writing of Johnston and Clift was their volume of uncollected stories, *Strong Man from Piraeus and Other Stories* (1984), mixed in quality but redolent of their life together on Hydra.

While Ion Idriess (1899–1979), a prolific writer of popular documentaries such as *Lasseter's Last Ride* (1931) and *The Cattle King* (1936) as well as books of adolescent adventure such as *Drums of Mer* (1933) and *Headhunters of the Coral Sea* (1940), made his best-selling reputation mainly in Australia, a number of other writers made full-time writing-careers in the international fiction or documentary market. Arthur Upfield (1888–1964) is noted for his creation of the Aboriginal detective Napoleon Bonaparte or 'Bony', and for setting his mystery stories in central Australia. Frank Clune (1893–1971) and Colin Simpson (1908–83) mostly wrote travel documentaries. 'Carter Brown' (Alan Yates, 1923–85) wrote detective thrillers.

A popular novelist with a greater sense of style than any of these is Jon Cleary (1917–). The author of over thirty novels, he began his career as a short-story writer during his war-service years. When he became a professional writer in 1945 he already had good contacts with journals such as the *Saturday Evening Post*. His first novel, *You Can't See Round Corners* (1947), won second prize in the *Sydney Morning Herald*'s 1946 novel competition. Like most of Cleary's later works, it is full of adventure, rather in the old-fashioned style of Robert Louis Stevenson or John Buchan. It is the story of a Sydney larrikin, Frankie McCoy, an illegal bookmaker, army-deserter, thief and murderer. *The Sundowners* (1952) is a sprawling saga of the bush and its effect on the inhabitants; *The Climate of Courage* (1954; published as *Naked in the Night* in the United States) a New Guinea war novel counterpointed against a depiction of marital problems; and *The Country of Marriage* (1962) a close study of embattled but durable marriage. Many of his novels have as their central adventurer a man reluctant to make up his mind or take responsibility but forced by violent circumstances to do so. After *Remember Jack Hoxie* (1969) Cleary's work tends to be formulaic and deliberately popular and its sense of Australian life and dialogue grows weaker.

Morris West (1916–) is another highly successful cosmopolitan novelist. Like Cleary he served in the army during the 1939–45 war. Previously he had been a teacher with the Christian Brothers order, but after the war he became a radio producer and writer. Among his many adventure stories, written as entertainments to support himself and his family, are a number of novels that address the question of the moral life and the search for God's approval.

Children of the Sun (1957), a documentary account of Neapolitan street urchins, brought him to attention, but his first best-seller was *The Devil's Advocate* (1959). Within a Calabrian landscape and a brooding atmosphere suggestive of violence and revelation, Monsignor Blaise Meredith investigates as 'Devil's Advocate' the claims to sanctification of Giacomo Nerone. The circumstances surrounding the case – prostitution, illegitimacy, nymphomania and homosexuality – seem unconducive to the production of sanctity, but West and Meredith find real goodness and wisdom there. Some of the characters, including Nerone, who discovers his need of charity, find salvation.

The Shoes of the Fisherman (1963) continues West's preoccupation with the Roman Catholic Church and represents his own hopes for the post-Vatican II Church. A non-Italian pope, Kiril I, seeks to preserve the Church but modernize it. He engages in improbable secret diplomacy to avert a Third World War amid increasing loneliness and isolation. West's treatment of Father Telemond, a Jesuit scholar and scientist, is clearly modelled on Teilhard de Chardin, just as Kiril is modelled on John XXIII.

Like his books on the Catholic Church, West's political novels often had a prophetic timing that helped their sales. *The Ambassador* (1965) presented the moral considerations of the Vietnam War; *The Tower of Babel* (1968) presented a fictional account of Arab–Israeli hostilities at the time of the Six-day War.

This kind of timing, the ability to judge the newsworthy topics of the day, combined with serious intellectual skills of exposition, accounts for his best-seller status. Many of his books have sold over a million copies, several well over five million. The characters may be stereotypes, the description cliché-ridden, the dialogue flat and unmemorable, and the exposition of moral issues concentrated in blocks, but readers admire his carefully researched locales, his ability to keep narrative moving, and his studies of the delicate balance between principles and pragmatism.

The World is Made of Glass (1983), published about the time of his return to live in Australia, is of a higher order than any of his earlier works. It draws to some extent on his experiences of mind-control practices among the Christian Brothers and of his own nervous breakdown after leaving the order, a period in hospital when he was advised to but declined to have shock treatment. *The World is Made of Glass* is a fictional account of the psychoanalyst Carl Jung and one of his patients, given the name Magda by West. Jung's brief account of the episode that suggested the book is that a woman sought a single consultation with him in order to confess a murder. She had killed one of her closest friends in order to marry the woman's husband, but afterwards she felt that all humanity and nature turned against her. West's novel is a kind of detective story involving rape, sado-masochism, homosexuality and incest.

Both Magda and Jung dream in the novel, their dreams being in 'concord'. Magda dreams of a hunt, a horse-riding fall, and of being enclosed naked in a glass ball tumbling over blood-red sand; Jung of seas of blood, the thunder of hooves, the hunt, and of a young woman and a man. Both are doctors; both have led a 'hothouse life' involving incest or rape; both are currently engaged in difficult sexual encounters; both are, as Jung says, 'possessed by daemons – of rage, of destruction'. In seeking to cure Magda, Jung seeks to cure himself. He helps her to find a way out of a vortex of worries that are conditioned by a sense neither of God nor of sin. It is a change in her 'sense of direction' or 'myth pattern' and it involves a rebirth of hope and faith in a hospice for prostitutes. West's novel, though pompous at times, is a credible piece of fictional psychoanalysis expressed at times in concentrated epigrammatic prose.

Colleen McCullough (1937–) achieved an international best-seller with *The Thorn Birds* (1977), a family saga set on a large sheep station, Drogheda. When Mary Carson dies she wills the £13 million station not to her poor brother, Paddy Cleary, who has managed it on low wages for years, but to the Catholic Church, to be administered by the handsome local priest, Father Ralph de Bricassart. His ambition and machination lead him, not without some qualms of conscience, to becoming a cardinal in Rome. There, when in his seventies, he is visited by Meggie Cleary, Paddy's only daughter. Her son, a priest, has just died performing a heroic rescue in Crete. Meggie reveals to Ralph that the young man was his son too; she says, in the Hibernian melodramatic style that marks all but the first third of the book, 'we both stole, Ralph. We stole what you had vowed to God, and we've both had to pay.'

The Thorn Birds follows something of the history of Australia in the first seventy or so years of this century, though the historical background (including Prime Minister Robert Menzies's announcement of Australia's entry into war, and an account of the Battle of El Alamein) is never more than lightly sketched in to create an effect of national scope. Large-scale, if unsubtle and unexamined, emotions are at the heart of the book. Even the Clearys' and Ralph's love for Drogheda is stated rather than demonstrated. Colleen McCullough's talent is with a fast-moving narrative and with boldly drawn characters rather than with the national or international stage, and that is why her earlier novel, *Tim* (1974), a more modest study of a mentally retarded boy, is a less flawed work.

The success of *The Thorn Birds* in the United States was paralleled by the less spectacular success of *All the Rivers Run* (1978) by Nancy Cato (1917–), who had had her first novel published under this title in 1958. Rewritten, compressed, and accompanied by three sequels, it now forms the first part of a long saga of life along the Murray and Darling rivers in the late nineteenth and early twentieth century. Philadelphia (Delie) Gordon, a determined child and woman in the mould of Kylie Tennant's heroines, has an argumentative but tender married relationship with the resourceful but unlucky captain of a paddle steamer. The best of Nancy Cato's other historical novels is *Brown Sugar* (1974), a balanced but passionate account of blackbirding, the capture of Pacific islanders for the Queensland sugar industry towards the end of the nineteenth century. Like *All the Rivers Run* it has the merit of brisk narrative, understanding of the physical environment, and a deft handling of alternating attraction and repulsion between pairs of characters.

Another writer who struggled for many years to make a living, turning her hand to anything that paid, is Ruth Park (19??–), author of eight novels and over twenty children's books. Her first novel, *The Harp in the South* (1948), won the *Sydney Morning Herald* Literary Contest for 1947 and was serialized in that paper. It and its sequel, *Poor Man's Orange* (1949), centre on life in Surry Hills, the inner-city slum suburb of Sydney where Ruth Park lived with her husband, the novelist D'Arcy Niland (1919–67). Her eighth novel, *Swords and Crowns and Rings* (1977), winner of the Miles Franklin Award, was her first attempt to use a man as the central character. It concerns a dwarf, Jackie Hanna, living through difficult times and circumstances from early in the century to the Depression years of the 1930s. Like Nancy Cato, Ruth Park writes with vivid realism and a balance between sentimentality and anti-sentimental deflation.

Children's writers

Ruth Park's story for young children, *The Muddle-Headed Wombat* (1962), is in the succession of May Gibbs's *Snugglepot and Cuddlepie* and Dorothy Wall's *Blinky Bill* stories (1933–7) though her dialogue is less stiff than Wall's and her moralizing less overt. It was left to Jenny Wagner and her illustrator, Ron Brooks, in *John Brown, Rose and the Midnight Cat* (1977), to develop a style of story for young children as underivative and original as May Gibbs's had been. In their story none of the characters – an old woman, a dog and a cat – are youthful, but the emotions aroused are ones that children experience.

After the 1939–45 war, a substantial number of writers for adolescents gained success. They included Michael Noonan (1921–), Mavis Thorpe Clark (19??–), Ivan Southall (1921–), Joan Phipson (1912–), Patricia Wrightson (1921–), Colin Thiele (1920–) and Hesba Brinsmead (1922–). This group of writers naturalized the traditional English adolescent stories to make the settings, language and attitudes Australian. They extended their themes into the environment, multiracialism, physical handicap and family tension. South-all, having grown up admiring Ballantyne and the writers for the English comics *Champion*, the *Magnet* and the *Gem*, and having as an adolescent himself written adventure stories set in exotic places, began his career as a professional writer with a hero, Simon Black, who was an Australian, but an impossible super-hero, able to fly to Mars, the moon or Venus. Then, with *Hills End* (1962), his twenty-fifth book, he began to centre his stories on children, credible Australian children. At the request of Beatrice Davis, the formidable stylist who was editor-in-chief at Angus and Robertson, Southall cut 30,000 words from the script of *Hills End*, greatly improving its effect and laying the foundation for his later success. *Hills End*, set in Queensland on the Atherton Tableland, concerns seven children who cope with the aftermath of a cyclone without adult help. *Ash Road* (1965) concerns another horrifying experience, with children in a bush fire. *To the Wild Sky* (1967) shows Southall moving away from physical adventure into psychological adventure. With this book he began an international change in the nature of writing for adolescents, consolidating it in his best two books, *Bread and Honey* (1970) and *Josh* (1971), which deal with adolescent revolt engaging with conformist society. There is, however, a degree of psychological melodrama in these books: Southall's Simon Black persona still peeps through.

The other major innovator in writing for adolescents is Patricia Wrightson, who in *The Nargun and the Stars* (1974), *The Ice is Coming* (1977), *The Dark Bright Water* (1978) and *Behind the Wind* (1981) transmuted Aboriginal folklore into fantasy saga, in something of the way that J. R. R. Tolkien transmuted the world of Germanic folklore.

David Martin (1915– , earlier known as Ludwig Detsinyi), a Hungarian by birth, deals, as many migrant writers do, with the problems of intercommunal tension. His children's books deal with Aborigines and Chinese goldfields workers, but the prose is stiff and the narratives are awkward.

Novelists of social comment

The best of Martin's adult novels is probably *The Young Wife*

(1962), an account of the lives of post-war migrants in Melbourne, particularly Cypriots and Greeks. Yannis Joannides, a middle-aged fruiterer, gradually becomes vindictively suspicious of his beautiful and innocent young wife, Anna. Her increasingly difficult life with him, and her relationships with his brother and sister, the former terrorist Criton and Professor Barwing, a Greek scholar 'from the University', form the fabric of the novel. Barwing stages the *Alcestis* of Euripides and persuades Anna to take a small part. The plot of the play forms a near-tragic symbolic counterpart to her own life. Martin is also a short-story writer, poet, and political and social commentator.

While some writers in all genres have sought international audiences, others have believed that they have a particular duty to warn or instruct Australian society. The most outspoken of Australia's social and political novelists have been Xavier Herbert and Frank Hardy (1917–). Hardy's first novel, *Power without Glory* (1950), is an exposé of capitalism. John West rises from a poverty-stricken boyhood in a Melbourne suburb by setting up an illegal 'tote' for betting and later by entering into various dubious deals with the Catholic Church and Labor politicians. The family of the late John Wren, whose career had been somewhat similar to that of the fictional John West, unsuccessfully sued Hardy for libel in 1951. *Power without Glory* has the same kind of inner-suburban slum milieu as Louis Stone's *Jonah*, but with the added interest of large-scale political intrigue and marital infidelity.

The writing is inflated and cliché-ridden, the emotional pattern sentimental. Yet Hardy has an entirely different style in his yarns, which are plainly and idiomatically told, even when the substance is fantastic or extravagant. *The Man from Clinkapella, and Other Prize-Winning Stories* (1951) has some apprentice work, but *Legends from Benson's Valley* (1963; republished in an unexpurgated edition as *It's Moments like These*, 1972), *The Yarns of Billy Borker* (1965) and *Billy Borker Yarns Again* (1967) are comparable with the stories of Dal Stivens. They are the tales of smallholding farmers and itinerant workers.

Hardy's later novels use highly formal structures. *But the Dead are Many* (1975) uses a fugal structure to study the career of John Morel, an Australian Communist and ex-seminarian who eventually commits suicide. It covers the period of the ideological struggles within the Communist Party from the 1930s onwards and constitutes an exposé of Stalinist bureaucracy. *Who Shot George Kirkland?* (1981) is in the form of an unremitting game with reality and illusion, fact and fiction, autobiography and deception. In the second part a research worker steals a manuscript written by the deceased author Ross Franklyn and tries to find the key to Franklyn's political *roman-à-clef, Power Corrupts*. The stolen manuscript constitutes the first part of the novel.

Social commentary is also often an ingredient of Australian science fiction, which has gained some recognition in the international market, especially in the second half of the twentieth century. A. Bertram Chandler (1912–84), George Turner (1916–), Damien Broderick (1944–) and Lee Harding (1937–) all manage to combine a degree of social and philosophical curiosity in their imaginative leaps out into time and space.

9
Mid-century directions

Prose writers

THE most influential of the historians who have attempted to
analyse Australia as a land and a nation have been C. E. W.
Bean (1879–1968), Keith Hancock (1898–), C. M. H.
(Manning) Clark (1915–) and Geoffrey Blainey (1930–).
Bean, the editor and major author of *The Official History of
Australia in the War of 1914–18* (12 vols, 1921–42), tried to show
how the Australian people approached, survived and were
changed by the war. As a skilled journalist he decided to give a
first-hand account from soldiers' evidence, using 'about three
hundred volumes of diary, regimental records, and historical
notes' as his basis, together with his own observations and
reports made during the war. Bean characterizes the
Australian soldier as a bold romantic adventurer, a reliable
mate, a democrat sceptical of imposed authority and its forms
and proud of his nation, a kind of optimistic and resourceful
hero from one of A. B. Paterson's ballads. A novel by Frederic
Manning (1882–1935), *The Middle Parts of Fortune: Somme and
Ancre* (1929, 1978; published in an expurgated edition as *Her
Privates We* in 1930), offers a somewhat similar view of the loyal
but bewildered private soldier engaged in an extreme and
debilitating psychological and moral test. Bean's other major
works are *On the Wool Track* (1910) and *The Dreadnought of the
Darling* (1911), imaginative and impressionistic histories of the
wool trade and river commerce that provided both a stylistic
model for Blainey over forty years later and historical material
for Nancy Cato's *All the Rivers Run*.

Sir Keith Hancock's *Australia* (1930) is an economic history
that also attempts to characterize the national temperament of
white Australians. He emphasizes the urban origin of a

majority of the convicts, the disturbance by white settlement of the delicate balance of nature, the contribution of non-British migrants, the attempts of squatters to seize not only land but also political power, the resulting aspirations to democratic nationalism and egalitarianism, the easy-going unintellectual cast of mind, and the necessity from early days of state paternalism, later conceived of as state socialism. His view of Australia is one that has influenced most later social and cultural historians. His style, balanced, aphoristic, and illustrated by concise but telling examples, has had its effect on both Manning Clark (who, is, however, more hieratic and bardic) and Geoffrey Blainey (who is less tidy in sentence structure and less imaginative in imagery).

Manning Clark's *A History of Australia* is a multi-volumed work which began publication in 1962 and reached volume 5 in 1981. Clark's view of history is that it is a branch of art, that it should be dramatic and poetic. His models are Greek tragedy, the Old Testament prophets and Omar Khayyam; his philosophy a Manichean belief in the slight imbalance of evil over good in the world, the improbability of personal happiness, and some optimism for humanity as a whole; his method the imaginative reconstruction of significant incidents by indirect narrators who are either fairly major actors or chorus-like observers. His first major indirect narrator is the Cassandra-like chaplain to the Botany Bay colony, the Revd Richard Johnson. In volume 5 he uses Alfred Deakin, one of the architects of Federation and an early Prime Minister, and Henry Lawson. These two tragic figures in Clark's view have personal histories corresponding to the contemporary national tragedy of the outbreak of war with the resulting setback to the Labor movement and the futility of Gallipoli. The major influences that Clark sees throughout the white history of Australia are theological ones: the rationalism of the Enlightenment, the dry formal rectitude of Protestantism, and the emotional power of Catholicism.

Geoffrey Blainey's reputation rests on *The Tyranny of Distance* (1966), *Triumph of the Nomads* (1976) and *A Land Half Won* (1980). These works present a lively, impressionistic, and thematic study of the effect of large distances on Australian history, the ability of Aborigines to live in harmony with their environment, and the economic history of Australia to 1900.

On a scale of optimism, Blainey stands between Bean and Clark; politically he is somewhat to the right of Bean.

If many academic historians are suspicious of Blainey for the vigour, high coloration, and impressionistic quality of his work, they are even more suspicious of those writers who include more social comment and less verifiable fact. Since the 1939–45 war a number of seminal books seeking to identify the relationships between art, literature, culture and society have appeared. *The Australian Tradition* (1954) by A. A. Phillips (1900–), a regular contributor to *Meanjin*, helped to change critical opinion from mere platitudes about mateship to a study of the craftsmanship of Lawson and Furphy. The book is, however, most frequently remembered for its invention of the term 'the cultural cringe' to describe the attitude of mind that constantly seeks to make comparisons between Australian and English writers. *The Australian Legend* (1958) by Russel Ward (1914–) is an 'examination of the origins, growth and apotheosis of the national self-image' achieved by a concentration on materials transmitted by ordinary people – bush songs, stories, legends and diaries. His admiration is centred on qualities that he derives from convicts, emancipists and free settlers, not from colonial officials and military men: qualities of adventurousness, self-reliance, mateship, and scepticism about authority and its refined language. It is a view that Humphrey McQueen was later to characterize as romantic, chiefly on the ground that the oppressive conditions of convictism produced a scramble for status and hierarchy rather than mateship and that Ward's thesis gave too much weight to rural rather than urban life.

The Lucky Country (1964) by Donald Horne (1921–) is a journalistic rather than historical account of contemporary Australia, written by the editor of the *Bulletin* responsible in 1961 for its transformation into a news-commentary magazine. *The Lucky Country* is an acute criticism of the easy-going mindlessness of Australian society, governments and institutions. In a mood that has permeated Australian critical journalism since his time on the *Bulletin*, Horne carps at everything and everyone, even the profession of journalism. His summation is that 'Australia is a lucky country run mainly by second-rate people who share its luck. It lives on other people's ideas . . . .'

In *A New Britannia: An Argument concerning the Social Origins of Australian Radicalism and Nationalism* (1970), the Marxist critic Humphrey McQueen (1942–) rejects most of Russel Ward's 'frontier' thesis of the heroic, communally minded up-country worker in favour of an internationalist view that depicts Australia as 'a frontier of European capitalism in Asia', dominated by capitalists and aspirants to capitalism, mostly pro-British, conservative and anti-democratic. In his up-ending of conventional wisdom, he regards Lawson as a supporter of the middle classes, an admirer of popular dictatorship, a racist and a militarist. McQueen's later writings often sacrifice clarity of outline for excessive introspection, concern for ideological purity, and the struggle to master the dismal science of economics. A less scholarly New Left cultural historian is John Docker (1945–), whose *Australian Cultural Elites* (1974) and *In a Critical Condition* (1984) deal with the relationships between literature, literary criticism and social conditions.

A Million Wild Acres (1981) by Eric Rolls (1923–) offers a different, but equally contentious, kind of social history. Rolls has written the definitive history of the Pilliga forest or, more broadly, Liverpool Plains area to the north-west of Sydney. It is a study of Aboriginal land management, the pressure for white settlement, and the economic realities that have caused most of the land to be turned into state forests, national parks and nature reserves. Rolls's sense of the delicacy of human interaction with flora and fauna and of the constant adjustments occurring in nature is unequalled.

The renaissance of drama

The post-war years produced many significant works of social criticism and history, many new writers for children, and a major reshuffle of theatrical conditions. Already the establishment of radio in every city and large town and of cinemas in every suburb and moderate-sized town had affected professional theatre. Many theatres in the cities were turned over to film; the remaining theatres survived on vaudeville, musical comedy and imitations of overseas play productions. Amateur theatre, by contrast, flourished in most cities and towns; in Brisbane the Twelfth Night and Repertory Theatres, and later in Sydney the Independent, often excelled contemporary professional standards.

In the early 1950s a number of fundamental alterations occurred in the structure of Australian theatre. The University of Melbourne helped to found the Union Theatre Repertory Company in 1953 for the purpose of performing in repertory rather than in individual entrepreneurial productions. The same system was later applied in Perth and Sydney. A year later, the Elizabethan Theatre Trust was established, largely through the efforts of Dr H. C. Coombs, an economist and lover of the arts. The Trust was instrumental in promoting the idea of governmentally subsidized national theatre, opera and ballet companies, and these in turn encouraged the raising of professional standards of acting and direction.

The first post-war Australian stage play of merit was *Rusty Bugles* (1948) by Sumner Locke-Elliott (1917–), mounted at Sydney's Independent Theatre. It is an episodic work about the boredom of a group of soldiers at an ordnance depot in the Northern Territory. They resent the oppressive conditions of the outback, talk bawdily of the 'Big Smoke' and its comforts, and abuse each other affectionately. It was a socially controversial play in so far as there were official attempts to ban it because of the frequency of the (euphemistically modified) swearing.

Reedy River, an improvised play attributed to 'Dick Diamond' (published 1970), was performed by the New Theatre, a loose association of left-wing amateur organizations in most states, in 1954. The setting is the defeat of the shearers' strike of 1891, which sought to gain recognition for the Shearers' Union. The play expounds a sentimental view of collective workers' heroism through short scenes and the singing (with audience participation) of such work and protest songs of the late nineteenth century as 'Click Go the Shears', 'The Eumerella Shore', 'Flash Jack from Gundagai' and 'The Old Black Billy'.

The Melbourne Union Theatre (in 1954) and the Australian Elizabethan Theatre Trust (in 1955) had a box-office success with *Summer of the Seventeenth Doll* by Ray Lawler (1922–), himself director of the Union Theatre. It was a play that expressed, but in a critical fashion, the myth of the heroic outback worker, the myth of mateship, the myth of the great lover, and the myth of the 'decent' marriage. In realistic style, with an authentic, if heightened, colloquialism of dialogue, it moved from domestic comedy to romantic tragedy by a series of carefully contrived revelations. Dream after dream is shattered over a period of a few days. The cane-cutters Roo and Barney are down in Melbourne from north Queensland for the annual lay-off. For sixteen years, each symbolized by the gift of a kewpie doll, they have spent the lay-off with two Melbourne barmaids. But this year, the seventeenth, it is different. Nancy, Barney's partner, has married, so Olive, Roo's partner, introduces the wary Pearl as a possible replacement. Roo comes without money, allegedly because he hurt his back, but actually because his place as the head of the cane-cutting gang has been usurped by a newcomer, Johnny Dowd. Gradually all the illusions of the past are shattered: Barney is a rejected amorist, not the philanderer he claims to be; Olive has a romantically hyperbolic view of the lay-off; Roo and probably Barney are finished as cane-cutters. In the end Olive passionately rejects Roo's humiliating offer of marriage, and they all realize that seventeen years of their lives are at an end. The only myth that survives the turmoil is that of mateship. Roo and Barney leave Olive's house together, though their friendship has been strained and may never recover.

Lawler was not able to recapture the scope and intimacy of *The Doll* in later work. *Kid Stakes* (1975) and *Other Times* (1976) filled in the previous history of the same characters with the same movement from joy to nostalgia and sorrow. *The Piccadilly Bushman* (1959) treats the theme of the expatriate re-experiencing Australia. Many of Lawler's other scripts consist of excellent dialogue searching for a theme: *Godsend* (1983), for instance, trivializes the myth that surrounds Thomas à Becket into disputes over the importance of the Second Vatican Council.

Although a number of technically competent plays appeared in the 1950s, no play after *The Doll* excited widespread interest until *The One Day of the Year* by Alan Seymour (1927–). The Board of Governors of the Adelaide Festival rejected the recommendation of its drama panel to include the play in the 1960 Festival on the ground that it might prove offensive to the Returned Servicemen's League. It was nevertheless given an amateur performance in Adelaide after the Festival, and a professional Sydney production, supported by the Elizabethan Theatre Trust, in 1961. *The One Day of the Year* is another well-constructed realistic drama with authentic dialogue, and like *The Doll* it critically examines a myth, that of Anzac Day, Gallipoli and the notion of Australia's coming-of-age through military engagement. The older characters, Alf Cook and his mate Wacka and, to a modified degree, Alf's wife, Dot, associate Anzac Day with xenophobic nationalism and intoxicated celebration. The younger characters, Hughie Cook and his upper-class university girlfriend, Jan Castle, regard it as 'offensive', a debauched celebration of the 'bloody wastefulness' of the Gallipoli campaign. Hughie ends in confusion, torn between affection and pity for his father, doubtful of his girlfriend's and the university's values. Almost unconsciously, Seymour has turned the critical tactics back against the younger people, partly by making Jan so snobbish, condescending and pseudo-sophisticated. It is an imbalance in the sympathies of the play that he failed to correct in his revision of 1980 or in his novel version of 1967.

Peter Kenna (1930–) has also worked in the tradition of realism, but has introduced the shock tactics of extreme violence and a degree of theatrical self-consciousness. His plays explore the milieu of suburban Irish Catholicism on the fringes of crime. *The Slaughter of St Teresa's Day* (1959, published 1972) centres on Oola Maguire, who operates a thriving illegal betting-shop in Sydney in the 1950s. Her St Teresa's Day party is disrupted by the presence of two criminals recently released from gaol and her innocent convent-educated daughter. Oola's sentimental attachment to the past is shattered by the tensions produced by the concatenation of these opposed worlds. A knifing and a gun fight are the outward symbols of her own disturbance. *A Hard God* (1974, revised edition 1982), the first play of a trilogy set over twenty years between 1946 and 1966, introduces another Irish Catholic family, the Cassidys. The pressures of coping with time and change, love and sex, alienation and insecurity, faith and doubt are worked out in two generations.

All of these playwrights were theatre-directors. Opportunities for professional actors and directors were, of course, an essential condition for the growth of Australian drama and they continued to expand in the 1950s and 1960s.

The first professional training-school, the National Institute of Dramatic Art, was established in 1959; the Old Tote Theatre, a state professional company, in Sydney in 1963; Betty Burstall's coffee-house theatre, Café La Mama, in Melbourne in 1967; and the Australian Performing Group, which played at La Mama and the Pram Factory, in 1969. After a few years, every state had a state theatre company jointly funded by state and federal arts organizations; most had at least one other fully professional company and several semi-professional ones. The Australian Council for the Arts (later the Australia Council) supported the state companies and some others through its Theatre Board. That board, in conjunction with the Literature Board, also began in the 1970s to fund writers in residence for professional theatre companies, the National Playwrights' Conference, and various workshops and training-schemes.

In the 1960s and early 1970s, the centre of theatrical experimentation was in Melbourne. Barry Humphries 1934–) launched his one-man satirical shows in the mid 1950s, taking them around Australia and to London in the early 1960s. A selection of his scripts was published in 1981. His central character, Edna Everage, a self-confident opinionated suburban woman, has grown over the years into a complex character, able to laugh at and be laughed at by the audience, an extravagant follower, mimic and satirist of fashions, able to switch from naïvety to malicious satirical enjoyment. In Humphries's own words, she 'began life by winning the Lovely Mother Contest and ended up by imagining herself to be a cross between Barbra Streisand, Billy Graham and Sister Teresa'. Humphries has made her more right-wing politically and more intolerant of political or social change, just as he has made some of his characters who represent liberal social values more obviously phoney. He has also established a pattern for one-person shows, sometimes written by a playwright for a particular performer, sometimes assembled by an actor such as Reg Livermore or Robyn Archer for his or her own performance.

La Mama and the Australian Performing Group encouraged 'rough' scripts and performance, actor and spectator involvement, absurdism and satire. In the work of John Romeril and Jack Hibberd the satire often takes the form of political outrage at conformity, crassness, inactivity, and lack of compassion. It was an attitude common in Australia at the end of the 1960s as opposition to Australia's involvement in the Vietnam War mounted and exasperation with the conservative government led to the Labor Party revival under Gough Whitlam.

John Romeril (1945–) wrote a number of 'microplays' for La Mama and university theatre. His *The American Independence Hour* was an anti-American street-demonstration play for 4 July 1969. The expressionist plays *Chicago, Chicago* (published in *Four Australian Plays*, 1970), *I Don't Know Who to Feel Sorry For* (published 1973), *The Floating World* (1974) and *The Golden Holden Show* (1975) all expressed a generally pro-Labor, democratic, radical nationalism.

This was also the attitude of Jack Hibberd and Barry Oakley in Melbourne, of Michael Boddy and Bob Ellis in Sydney, and of Dorothy Hewett in Perth and Sydney. They frequently seek to reinterpret Australian history in these terms, using a mélange of styles and partly serious, partly satiric Australian vernacular language. Boddy and Ellis's *The Legend of King O'Malley* (1970, published 1974) is contemptuous, for instance, of Billy Hughes as a Prime Minister who became a Labor renegade, a collaborator with conservatives, and a pragmatist rather than an idealist.

Jack Hibberd (1940–) in the Introduction to his *Three Popular Plays* (1976), says that he seeks to establish a 'Popular Theatre', which he defines as 'a theatre of accessibility that is above all Australian in theme and substance, a theatre for the populace that deals with legendary figures and events, perennial and idiosyncratic rituals, mythically implanted in the nation's consciousness'. It is intended for the underprivileged and the theatrically disenfranchised. In style it is to contain 'facts, fibs, images, songs, occasions, jokes, straight lefts and inexplicable good temper . . . [and] good dramatic yarns'. This Brechtian programme was not accompanied by any call to political revolution, nor was it very successful in attracting the theatrically disenfranchised, who, for the most part, continued to content themselves with television and workers' club variety shows.

Hibberd's first full-length play, *White with Wire Wheels* (published in 1970), was performed at the Melbourne Union

Theatre in 1967. It treats four hard-drinking, randy, indistinguishable young men as analogous to the parts of a car, a juggernaut of mindless, uncaring, uncommunicative sexuality and drinking. It is bawdy, but the crudity of language is shaped and criticized by the young men's misplaced notion of propriety in speaking to their girlfriends and by the metaphor of the car.

Dimboola (1969, published 1974), an exposure of Australian behaviour at weddings, in which the audience are involved as the guests, is the one 'rough' play that has been a popular success, presumably because of its satiric accuracy. The same revue technique is applied in Hibberd's biographies of Australian folk heroes, *One of Nature's Gentlemen* (1968), *The Les Darcy Show* (1974) and *A Toast to Melba* (1976), published together in *Three Popular Plays*.

A Stretch of the Imagination (1971, published 1973) also balances affection and ridicule. Its central character, the eighty-year-old yarn-spinner Monk O'Neill, is an inveterate boaster. He claims to have met Les Darcy, the world middleweight champion, on the summit of Mount Kosciusko, to have shaken hands with Proust, to have had more beers and women than he can remember. All of it is related in an off-hand self-deprecating style, exciting alternate nostalgia and laughter.

Barry Oakley (1931–) has had two productive periods as a dramatist, one in the early 1970s in association with the Australian Performing Group, the other beginning in the late 1970s. Oakley is a zany, exuberant writer, skilled in depicting and celebrating the incompetent. Each of his heroes is a role-player of great facility and bizarre imagination. *Scanlan* (published in *The Great God Mogadon, and Other Plays*, 1980) is a one-actor play of great comedy and pathos, in which a middle-aged lecturer in English delivers a lecture on Henry Kendall to an audience containing a man who has ruined his life. *The Great God Mogadon*, a radio play, concerns an ailing Prime Minister and the obscure public servant who is chosen to impersonate him. Politics is the substance of the two later plays collected as *Marsupials and Politics* (1981). *Politics*, involving prime ministers and governments in Canberra, is a warning against the American invasion of Australia by 'Captain

Marvel, Colonel Sanders and General Motors'. *Marsupials* is a corresponding exposure of Australia's difficulties in emancipating itself from British influence.

Oakley's best-known play is another revisionary view of Australian history, *The Feet of Daniel Mannix* (1971, published 1975). Mannix, the Irish Catholic Archbishop of Melbourne from 1912 until 1963, was an associate of John Wren (the inspiration for Frank Hardy's novel), a bitter opponent of conscription in the 1914–18 war, and the prime instigator of the Catholic Action Movement in the trade unions and Labor Party after the 1939–45 war. The style is vaudeville. Mannix descends from the ceiling in a bosun's chair to bless the multitudes, shoots Billy Hughes, the pro-conscriptionist Prime Minister, with a shanghai (small catapult), and ends, a victim of disillusion and self-martyrdom, babbling from a wheelchair to a television crew on his birthday.

Oakley's three novels, *A Wild Ass of a Man* (1967), *A Salute to the Great McCarthy* (1970), and *Let's Hear it for Prendergast* (1970), were all written before he became committed to play-writing. They are picaresque in the manner of David Ireland and Peter Mathers, somewhat J. P. Donleavy-like in extravagant exuberance. All three centre on victims. Muldoon, the wild ass of a man with an insatiable desire to announce the end of the world, ends up addressing the crowds on St Kilda beach and is crucified on a ferris wheel for his pains. McCarthy is an Australian Rules footballer from the country who is torn apart after two seasons as a city star by the venality and callousness of his handlers. Prendergast, the tallest poet in the world, has a mission, like Muldoon. It is to be an iconoclast. In the end he converts the Shrine of Remembrance into an anti-war monument and burns down an elaborate exhibition of 200 years of national life in the Melbourne Exhibition Building. Like the other protagonists he is a humiliating failure, but only because of his excesses.

Oakley's volume of short stories, *Walking through Tigerland* (1977), is similarly surrealistic, witty and comic. 'The Late George Slipper' concerns an excessively boring writer-in-residence at a university who has an innocent penchant for causing trouble and confusion. 'Defending the Library' is a political story about independence coming to a Pacific-island country to the dismay of the expatriate academics. Almost all centre on inadequacy, stupidity, absurdity and exaggerated behaviour, but depicted with sympathy for courage and endurance.

Alex Buzo (1944–) locates most of his plays very specifically in the suburbs of Sydney, particularly the affluent suburbs inhabited by modish trend-setters. Like the contemporary Melbourne playwrights, he mingles music-hall routines, farce, surrealism and comedy of manners, but generally with an undercurrent of the sinister and the threatening bordering on nihilism.

Norm and Ahmed (1967, published in Buzo's *Three Plays*, 1973), counterpoints surface affability with an underlying suspicion and resentment that results in violence when Norm Gallagher, a hearty, matey Australian, attacks the Pakistani student Ahmed, punching him in the face and dismissing him with the final line, 'Fuckin' boong'. It was a line that resulted in a police prosecution for obscene language when first delivered publicly as written.

Rooted (1969) is another scarifying exposure of the illusion of mateship. Bentley, a young public servant, is a born loser, destroyed gradually by his own insecurity and by his coming-up against a Pinteresque power-broker, Simmo, who exists only in the dialogue, never quite on stage.

The Front Room Boys (1969) takes a similar group of men, this time a set of junior clerks in an office who are controlled like laboratory rats in a series of ritual experiments by the commercial bureaucratic system. In *Macquarie* (1971), a historical play, Buzo again shows a central character, Governor Macquarie, in a conflict between personal will and a bureaucratic system. He is also subject to a conflict, internal and external, between conservative and radical tendencies. The historical time is paralleled by action in the present, with actors playing both the historical part and its contemporary counterpart.

The interest in a single character is continued in *Coralie Lansdowne Says No* (1974), the study of a self-possessed feminist who exercises her wit against three suitors while struggling with the conflicts of her own emotions. But the surface wit of the dialogue and the sudden switches from vulnerability or self-revelation to satiric venom prevent the play from settling into comedy of manners or witty farce.

Martello Towers (1976) is equally ambiguous in mode, and even more coruscating in wit. Like *Coralie Lansdowne* it explores the nature of modern sexuality and marriage, but with less commitment to any of the characters. After *Makassar Reef* (1978), another essay in the ironic comedy of manners, Buzo returned to another historical setting for *Big River* (1980), and, surprisingly for such an urban playwright, to a rural landscape. The time is 1900, on the verge of Federation, the scene is the Murray River, the theme that of a new beginning in the nation and in the family of the widowed Adela Learmonth. It is a play that marks another stage in the development of Buzo's interests from nihilism to makeshift family relationships to national and regional concerns. His style began as surrealistic, added a somewhat Yeatsian imagism, then turned into a heightened realistic comedy of manners as a framework for farce and romance. His emphasis in the early, angry plays is on representative characters struggling as victims of a dehumanizing society, then it shifts to individual character studies, and later becomes centred on small family groups struggling to find a degree of honest satisfaction in life.

David Williamson

Although he began his work with the Australian Performing Group in 1970, David Williamson (1942–) soon became known for a smoother, more realistic style that appealed to much wider audiences than those of the experimental theatres. Only his first play, *The Coming of Stork* (1970), has the expressionistic structure of what was then the new style of satirical, vernacular comedy. It is a raucous exhibition of young male sexual competitiveness, reworked into a moderately successful film, *Stork*, in 1971. *The Removalists* (1971, published 1972) again deals with male rituals and insecurities, this time with a degree of on-stage violence that nauseated or outraged many theatre-goers. The prime removalists are Sergeant Simmonds and Constable Ross, who offer to help Fiona Carter move from her home before her violent husband Kenny returns. But Kenny comes home early, is pugnacious, and is systematically bashed by both policemen. When he dies, they rough each other up enough to give credibility to their concocted story of his dying while violently resisting arrest. As in most of Williamson's plays, sexuality, violence and power play are intricately connected; women are almost automatically regarded as objects to be mastered; male role-playing and psychological cruelty disguise insecurity.

With *Don's Party* (1971, published 1973), Williamson moves into a middle-class milieu, though it remains predominantly male and randy. The setting is election night, the expectation is of a Labor Party victory, the reality is that the party-goers are spiritually conservative and their political allegiances a kind of unexamined religious faith.

Jugglers Three (1972), *What if you Died Tomorrow* (1973), and *A Handful of Friends* (1976) all use middle-class well-educated groups of characters. They concern sexual ambition and frustration, suburban family claustrophobia (partly among the women characters), liberal ideals contrasting with self-satisfied lifestyles, professional success, and the place of the arts, including literature, in society. They are more psychologically slanted than the earlier plays, at times almost introspective. In structure they have the same restless, almost random, movement as *Don's Party*.

The Department (1974, published 1975) and *The Club* (1974, published 1975) mark a return to a more single-minded kind of narrative and to the more exclusively male rituals of the early plays. *The Department* is set in the engineering department of a tertiary college, *The Club* in the premises of an Australian Rules football club. Both are concerned with the struggle for power, one within a bureaucracy, the other within a commercial undertaking. Both use their settings as metaphors with considerable detail, the thermodynamics laboratory with its many mechanical and personal examples of inefficiency representing an impersonal, unexamined human system, the football club and its directorate representing varied notions of how the game of life might be played.

Travelling North (1979) takes an older group of characters, less well educated, but still concerned with sex, love, personal insecurity and an unattainable dream. Williamson tackles subjects rarely seen on the Australian stage: old people's sexuality and their fear of illness and death. *The Perfectionist* (1983) returns to his preoccupation with the tensions of the younger professional, this time with more sympathy for a woman character than he had previously achieved. Husband and wife are both exploiters; when they recognize this they agree to try to rub along in an unideal relationship.

Williamson's film scripts include a number of major box-office successes, such as *Eliza Fraser*, *Gallipoli* and *Phar Lap*; in addition he has written a number of television scripts. His own view of his work is that he is 'a storyteller with a slight edge of moralistic concern about the way Australians spend their lives'. He feels that it is essential 'to be faithful to your own home culture' by celebrating and satirizing it. And he is an unabashed proponent of realism, 'because it works and people respond to it. They want to have tales told to them which are particular to their own time and place.' In this respect he stands in opposition to most of the new dramatists and many of the new novelists and poets, who espouse disconnection, surrealism, and a mingling of styles.

Other playwrights

A good example of these tendencies is the work of Dorothy Hewett (1923–), though she adds to the common style an idiosyncratic infusion of fairy tale, romantic myth, and vitalism. Her exuberant plays make full use of mask, mime, dance, music-hall and popular song, vaudeville routine, oratory, soliloquy, literary allusion, satire, parody, farce and melodrama.

Her first play, *This Old Man Came Rolling Home* (1966, published 1976), is set in the Sydney working-class suburb of Redfern. An alcoholic mother and a Communist father, with their children struggling to make a satisfactory existence, are depicted in a realism akin to Sean O'Casey's. There is, however, a chorus of three old women and a derelict who comment on the action.

Later plays move from poetic realism to symbolic, expressionist use of an open stage. *The Chapel Perilous* (1971, published 1972) is a partially autobiographical study of a woman's struggle for personal identity against various pressures to conform. It is full of large poetic gestures and moments of temporary triumph. *Bon-Bons and Roses for Dolly* (1972, published 1976) and *The Golden Oldies* (1976) are musical fables of period nostalgia, each spanning three generations. *The Tatty Hollow Story* (1974, published 1976) has further elements of autobiography, though Hewett says that Tatty is 'much sillier than I ever was'. Tatty is the creation and catalyst of her various lovers, whose insecurity and aspiration are projected on to her.

The Man from Mukinupin (1979), commissioned for the sesquicentenary celebrations of Western Australia (the State in which Dorothy Hewett grew up and went to university), is the happiest of her plays and the most rigorously shaped. As she said about this time to an interviewer, one of her great difficulties is structure: 'That is why I was so keen on Communism. It structured the world for me. . . . you're continually caught in the moment and trying to make some existential sense of it. And the moment takes over and you lose the structure.' In *The Man from Mukinupin*, however, she seems to have been inspired by the prospect of reconciling herself to Western Australia and to the changes that had occurred in her ideology and view of life. The play is set in an imaginary wheat-belt town, 'east of the rabbit-proof fence', in the years 1912 to 1920, the years when her own parents were young. In it she draws on memories of her own childhood in the similar town of Wickepin, about 150 miles from Perth.

The Fields of Heaven (1983) is set in a similar place, spanning two generations, but without the same concentration of plot. With its similar amalgam of song, dance, poetry and story-telling it was, however, successful on stage.

Dorothy Hewett's four volumes of poetry, *Windmill Country* (1968), *Rapunzel in Suburbia* (1975), *Greenhouse* (1979) and *Alice in Wormland* (1985), are full of literary masks and melodrama, full of a sense of the larger-than-life personality of Dorothy Hewett in the act of balancing confession and play-acting. She is fascinated by metamorphosis, questing, religious ritual and Arthurianism, obsessed by the urgency of rewriting or transmuting the divided self. Hewett's one novel, *Bobbin' Up* (1959), is based on her experiences working in a spinning-mill, a kind of 'Alcatraz' in which she sought to make converts to Communism. In its sense of a warm human life managing to exist in spite of the brutalizing effect of a system it bears some relationship to the working-class novels of David Ireland.

The most intellectual of the younger playwrights is Louis

Nowra (1950–), who describes his work as 'emblematic theatre'. It works less by plot than by a succession of visual images, generally expressing some aspect of the struggle by a figure in a landscape to impose control over others through the acceptance of a coherent image of the world. *Inner Voices* (published 1977), Nowra's first major success, is set in Tsarist Russia towards the end of the eighteenth century. Ivan, a product of the Enlightenment, with an accepted rationalist education learnt by rote, proves to be an untamed adult. Part of his inner being is wild; he tortures his servants and, once he loses the restraint of his mentor, goes mad. This psychiatric study is really set in the country of the mind, for, as Nowra says, 'Because I have a Berkeleyan view of the world, that is, subjective, I essentially see my characters as mirror images of the world around them.'

Visions (1978, published 1979) has as its theme the inner nightmare as a reflection of imposed social conditions. The outside world depicted is nineteenth-century Paraguay, in the process of losing its independence; the inner nightmare is that of the peasant girl, Juana, who is blinded and brutalized. It is a play full of horrors, mutilations and victimization. The sketchy episodic plot is designed to avoid any temptation for the audience to be caught up in the literal meaning at the expense of the metaphorical. Nowra's intention is to have his characters detached from, almost alien to, the audience.

Visions has both a psychological meaning and a historical one. Like *Inside the Island* (1980, published 1981) it is an emblem of Australian history. In both plays self-styled European aristocrats seek to impose their notion of order and culture on a raw backward country, inhabited by 'savages' and 'exotic' animals. *Inside the Island* is set in north-western New South Wales in the summer of 1912. It is a play about cultural imperialism and the insanity of power, with Nowra's typical emblems of horror. A detachment of soldiers is given diseased flour from a mill owned by an ineffectual dipsomaniac and his imperious anglophile wife. In the madness that ensues from the soldiers eating contaminated food, both husband and daughter are killed and the mill and homestead set on fire. Lillian Dawson survives, however, and decides to sell up and go to England, dismissing the horror with the adage 'The strong forget, the weak remember.'

The Precious Woman (1980, published 1981), Nowra's most optimistic play, is in Brechtian short-scene form, with many songs for which the music was written by Sarah de Jong, Nowra's wife. Set in China in the 1920s, the play centres on the move from innocence and submission to knowledge and power by the Empress Su-ling. Her love for her husband and son is disabling and distorting, leading to their delusions and obsessions.

Sunrise (1983) is peopled by characters who are smug, well-insulated proponents of nuclear war. As in *Inside the Island*, the matter of Aboriginal dispossession is important. The Shelton family property is on what they say was once 'only a bald hill'. The fact is that it was an Aboriginal sacred site, 'where the honey ants dreamed of the dead'. The final judgement on the white settlers is 'How insular we are, here on this island, thinking we're so important.'

The first full-length play by Stephen Sewell (1953–), *The Father we Loved on a Beach by the Sea* (1978, published in *Three Political Plays*, ed. Alrene Sykes, 1980), and the fourth, *The Blind Giant is Dancing* (1983), deal with similar contemporary Australian matters. *The Father* is centred on a family that copes with unexpected economic recession and the Vietnam War. *The Blind Giant* is even more directly political, concerned with revolutionary theory and the ideological clash between right and left wings of a social-democratic party.

The two intervening plays, *Traitors* (1980, published 1983) and *Welcome the Bright World* (1982, published 1983), explore some of the international political theory and revolutionary events that bear on the present. *Traitors*, set in Leningrad in 1927, is an account of the betrayal of a revolution. *Welcome the Bright World*, set in present-day Germany, concerns the nexus between nuclear science and politics.

Both Sewell and Nowra are concerned with contemporary problems, Sewell being more directly political, Nowra more concerned with psychosis. Both use violence as a metonym for the worlds they depict. Both are sceptical about the insularity of the Australian plays of their immediate predecessors. One other playwright often linked with them is Steve J. Spears (1951–), best known for his one-man play *The Elocution of Benjamin Franklin* (1976, published 1977). Spears is a less intellectual writer than Nowra or Sewell, but perhaps has a better understanding of moment-to-moment entertaining.

Poets: Buckley, Harwood and others

Vincent Buckley (1925–) is as well known as a Catholic polemicist and Leavis-influenced literary critic as he is as a poet. All three professions are defended in his apologia or spiritual autobiography, *Cutting Green Hay* (1983). His two early volumes of poetry, *The World's Flesh* (1954) and *Masters in Israel* (1961), suffered from the prevalence of influence from poets admired by Leavis and the American New Critics. *Arcady and Other Places* (1966) is in freer verse, with more humanity and less cloistered rhetoric and obsession. The sequence 'Stroke' and the poem 'Parents' both deal with the question of psychological inheritance and with the range of moods that a son may experience for his parents. *Golden Builders, and Other Poems* (1976) has as its title poem a long work in twenty-seven sections. Even as late as this in Buckley's career the influences are still strong: this time from Blake's London poems, the London sections of T. S. Eliot's *The Waste Land*, Hart Crane's *The Bridge* and Robert Lowell's *Life Studies*. Using a variety of forms, including the self-aggrandizing monologue of the Irish pub story, Buckley depicts present-day and historical Melbourne. The sections are linked by the narrator's search for 'my Lord's grave'. The smells of trees and of poverty and want are counterpointed; the European migrants' hope of a promised land is set against the patient misery of their existence; university, Church and the Vietnam conflict provide recurring places and themes. Buckley is nostalgic but detached, as he is about all institutions, movements and ideologies. His concern is always to characterize in general and then distinguish his own position, emotional or intellectual, from that of the mass. His attitude is epitomized in the statement, 'I recognize Catholicism as a great religion with some claims on me, but not on my allegiance. That is, I don't owe allegiance to any organization.'

Buckley's grandfather migrated from Ireland, and he has always felt an affinity with what he melodramatically described in a 1979 interview as 'this despised minority I really come from'. Since his first visit to Ireland in 1955 he has felt that the IRA cause was just. In *The Pattern* (1979), as 'guest, foreigner, son', he meditates on the sea around Ireland and on Ireland's history, especially its phases of persecution by Britain. *Late Winter Child* (1979) concerns Buckley's second marriage and the belated birth of a child. Much of it is banal, but there is some self-criticism of his tendency 'to construct an angry, taut "I" '.

The cultivation and subjection of that individualistic, prickly, self-righteous 'I' is the topic of *Cutting Green Hay*, though it is more important for its insider reports on such controversialists as Archbishop Mannix, B. A. Santamaria and Frank Knopfelmacher, and such poets as A. D. Hope, James McAuley and Gwen Harwood. Buckley's literary criticism, gathered in *Essays in Poetry, Mainly Australian* (1957), *Poetry and Morality: Studies on the Criticism of Matthew Arnold, T. S. Eliot, and F. R. Leavis* (1959), and *Poetry and the Sacred* (1968), is magisterial in tone, with a tendency to prefer sharply defined dichotomies. Its attentive reading of texts combined with some flamboyant theories have made it influential in Australian universities.

Like FitzGerald and Wright (and the much younger Kevin Hart), Gwen Harwood (1920–) is a poet strongly influenced by European philosophy. Her affinity is with Ludwig Wittgenstein (1889–1951), whose interest in linguistic wordgames she shares. Wittgenstein's speculation in *Philosophical Investigations* (1953) that 'it isn't a game if there is some vagueness *in the rules*. But *does* this prevent its being a game?' is echoed in

> Language is not a perfect game
> and if it were, how could we play?

and his most famous dictum is echoed in Harwood's description in 'Wittgenstein and Engelmann' of the two friends humbly seeking

> the simple sources of that truth
>   whereof one cannot speak.

Some of her early poems in *Poems* (1963) are satirically witty, bizarre and paradoxical. They display a savage battleground of emotions disguised by a bland human exterior and a rigid form. In this volume and her next, *Poems/Volume Two* (1968), she writes frequently about situations where passions boiled but were not revealed, or where the poet was a silent and sardonic observer of others' venom. One of her major satiric targets is the pretentious, self-absorbed, essentially uncreative academic, a type distilled in the brilliant vignettes of the 'Professor Eisenbart' series.

Many of her poems are about the sense of entrapment experienced by women responsible for young children. The dowdily dressed woman of the sonnet 'In the Park' feels that 'They have eaten me alive'; the pianist in 'Suburban Sonnet' finds that because of her domestic duties 'a wave of nausea overpowers / subject and counter-subject'. Yet there is a vigorous spiritual courage that brings her characters through adversity and pain.

Poems/Volume Two opens with a long sequence on the dipsomaniac musician Professor Kröte, condemned by a philistine society to prostitute his art and exiled by hemisphere and language from his youth. Yet, despite the acerbity of some of the satire, it is often mingled with a romantic warmth and even respect for his devotion to art, an attachment represented in 'Flying Goddess' as aspiration to 'high transparent distances' and 'the charm of all that flows'.

The new poems of *Selected Poems* (1975) and *The Lion's Bride* (1981) offer a world that is less tortured, more relaxed and genial, more confident and personal, but still concerned with grief, pain, the loss of love and the musical and visual art that can transcend such grief and loss. There are Oyster Cove poems about meditation while fishing from a dinghy; Bruny Island elegies for the hunted, herded and exterminated Aborigines of Tasmania; and more Kröte poems, with Kröte now nostalgically and unashamedly confessing his faith in 'Music, my joy, my full-scale God'. Many poems have a sense, as she wrote in 1979, of 'the continuity of self through memory and through descendants; I felt myself to be part of an unbroken chain of women'.

Rodney Hall (1935–) is a poet of intense dramatization (often self-dramatization), political commitment, musicality, and, despite earlier disclaimers, confession and introspection. In a 1981 interview he said, 'I wanted to be an actor', and also that music constitutes 'half of my life almost'. From the beginning he has been romantically absorbed in the dramatized self, writing energetically about decisions, decisive events, and decisive gestures. Violence, controlled or barely controlled, lies close to the surface (as it does also in Thomas Shapcott). Suicide is contemplated in both an early poem such as 'The Climber' and the much later sequence 'The Owner of my Face' (in *Selected Poems*, 1975).

With his fourth and fifth collections, *The Autobiography of a Gorgon* (1968) and *The Law of Karma* (1968), he mastered the art of what he calls a 'progression' of poems, a sequence of short poems on a single theme, often a monodrama in many short snatches ending in a mood of self-pity. 'Romulus & Remus' (recorded, with music by Richard Mills, in 1971) is an exploration of the divided self and of sexual orientation that presages Shapcott's novel *The Birthday Gift* (1982).

Hall also has a substantial reputation as an editor and novelist. He was poetry editor of a national newspaper for over ten years, from 1967, and subsequently poetry editor for Angus and Robertson. In both positions he exercised an encouraging and eclectic influence.

Hall's first novel, *The Ship on the Coin* (1972), is a satiric allegory directed against American conformity, national aspirations and international manipulation. The ship representing America is a quinquereme into which Croesus Travel Inc. entices 322 paying passengers for a working holiday in the Mediterranean, escorted by a nuclear submarine. *A Place among People* (1975), set in a small bayside settlement near Brisbane, makes its moral point without satire. The unobtrusive, withdrawn Collocott buys a house there in the 1950s, but finds himself drawn into the bigotry and prejudice of the fishing community. Eventually he finds himself defending a despised Aboriginal woman, Daisy, against the vindictiveness of the whole town. In the process he characterizes his childhood and adolescence as a 'prolonged death' from which, through rejecting indolence and acquiescence, he now awakes.

The lovingly poetic description of small-town Australia is carried over into *Just Relations* (1982), set in the decayed mining town of Whitey's Fall, a community peopled by elderly eccentrics. This time the moral cause is one taken up by the whole town, as they protest about a bureaucratic decision to build a tourist road to the town. They have come into such a close relationship with the environment that they have become 'the first white Aboriginals', a notion often espoused by Les Murray. They remember their ancestral history in a religious ritualistic way while drinking at the Mountain Hotel, though not without some pale recollections of having dispossessed a more ancient culture. It is this brooding on place, ownership and affinity that has characterized Hall's second and third novels, though he still feels constrained to decorate them with classical fantasies and joking allusions.

Thomas Shapcott (1935–) began as a small-scale, almost suburban, lyrist, but soon developed into an inveterate experimentalist. *Time on Fire* (1961), his first volume, has poems about the impermenance of childhood, the operation of memory, the delights of nature, and the cycle of love, courtship, marriage and the birth of a child. Like so many Australian poets from the 1930s to the present day, he is awed by man's seeming subordination to time.

The Mankind Thing (1964), *A Taste of Salt Water* (1967), and *Inwards to the Sun* (1969) – to mention only his main volumes of the next few years – have one of their chief strengths in the historical poems, such as 'Macquarie as Father' and 'Portrait of Captain Logan'. Although they do not always avoid garrulity, they deftly combine sharply focused scenes with implied reflection. Scene is superimposed on scene to relate duty and childbirth, brutality and kindliness, civilization and nature. Oddly enough, considering Shapcott's own musicianship and his fruitful collaborations with the composer Colin Brumby, his poems directly about music and musicians tend to be so intense and palpable that their sense of form is endangered.

Begin with Walking (1972) and *Shabbytown Calendar* (1975) are quintessentially poems of place, particularly of New York, Brisbane and Ipswich (the town near Brisbane where Shapcott was born and brought up). They continue a line of poems of which 'Flying Fox' and 'Ceremony for Cedar, in an Old House' were earlier distinguished examples, poems in which experience is firmly located in place but not limited by it. 'Mango Weather', for instance, is an amusing Ipswich poem of the early 1970s meditating tangentially on the oppressive fecundity of nature.

Shapcott's *Selected Poems* (1978) presents a ruthless culling from his earlier volumes, together with a very varied set of experimental poems, none of them quite successful, some of them so inward-turning that they seem addressed solely to himself. *Welcome!* (1983) returns to his most successful mode of poems centred in the personal experience of place, of the vulnerable, self-amused self-celebrating existence in a specific locale. This is, after *Time on Fire*, the most unified of Shapcott's major volumes, one movement of emotion leading thematically to the next and reflecting back on others. What emerges is a very complex and intricate depiction of a person living in the suburbs of Brisbane. 'Half the world and life away' he can still feel impelled by childhood experiences: 'Somewhere we hoard the rush of stormwater gutters, toes direct spray/like punishment' ('Acknowledging Stormwater Gutters').

Shapcott has had a profound influence on contemporary Australian poetry, not only by his own experimentalism, but also through his prolific reviewing, editing and committee work. His anthologies *New Impulses in Australian Poetry* (1968, with Rodney Hall) and *Contemporary American and Australian Poetry* (1976) both identified major trends. His membership of the inaugural Literature Board in 1973 and his return to the Board as Director in 1983, together with his committee work for the Australian Society of Authors, brought him into contact with many writers, a good number of whom sought and profited from his advice.

In 1981 his first novel, *Flood Children*, was published. Its strength is in visual depiction rather than in narrative, but it is exciting enough as a book for young adolescents. *The Birthday Gift* (1982) takes up the concerns of such poems as 'Portrait of a Younger Twin'. Ben and Benno are twins growing up in Ipswich and subsequently living in Sydney and Tuscany. They are clearly delineated from each other, in itself a major achievement in view of Shapcott's desire to show that each can assume the basic character of the other at times. Their journey is the search for a unified personality and the discontinuous nature of the narrative has the dramatic advantage of delaying till near the end a crucial turning-point that occurred during the twins' compulsory military training.

White Stag of Exile (1984) is an even more experimental work. It is centred on the rise and fall of Károly Pulszky as Director of the Hungarian National Gallery of Art at the end of the nineteenth century. In a set of discontinuous narratives, dramatic monologues, and documents, it traces his arraignment on a charge of embezzlement, his breakdown in mental health, his self-imposed exile to Australia, and his suicide in a small settlement near Brisbane. It is a novel in which all interpretations of events are called in question, a novel where at the end one cannot judge Pulszky, his wife or his detractors. Poems, songs, dreams, anecdotes and fables are as important in evidence as court and parliamentary reports, newspaper-cuttings, diaries and letters. Pulszky, obsessed by a Sebastiano del Piombo portrait that he covets, comes to believe that it is of himself, and that consequently he is displaced both in time and place from his true home, Renaissance Italy. Shapcott also presents Pulszky in the role of Actaeon, the hunter whose presumption and hubris resulted in his being torn apart by his own hounds as he was metamorphosed into a stag. The menacing presage of the white stag exerts a brooding influence over the whole novel, as do the threat of Russian invasion, the notion of exile after hubris, the contrast of Europe and Australia, and the fear of dishonour and defeat. In this complex work, despite some attenuation of characterization and outward scene, Shapcott has written one of the most reverberating and intellectual of all the novels that seek to relate Australia to Europe.

Les A. Murray

More than any other Australian poet in the twentieth century, Les A. Murray (1938–) has argued for the pre-eminence of his own kind of poetry. In his two collections of prose pieces, *The Peasant Mandarin* (1978) and *Persistence in Folly* (1984), he espouses the importance of the Scottish bardic tradition; the Boeotian values of family life, respect for tradition (including religion) and personal endurance; the community of people with cattle and with the land; and the sense of independent nationhood. In a very early poem, 'Noonday Axeman', he says 'It will be centuries / before many men are truly at home in his country', and

Though I myself run to the cities, I will forever
be coming back here to walk, knee-deep in ferns,
up and away from this metropolitan century.

In Murray's view, the nation of Australia, its landscape and rural industries, its communities, its beliefs and its literature should all share certain qualities, the qualities that he metonymically describes as Boeotian. These values are rural, even provincial; directly related to the land; concerned with religion and its ritual rather than with the abstractions of philosophy; based on the family rather than the political unit, and egalitarian rather than rigidly democratic. In another of his memorable metonyms he describes himself as a supporter of the agrarian vernacular republic, though he accepts that this is as yet only a city of his mind.

His interest in communal rites of passage, the Catholic notion of sacrifice, and in particular the form and nature of initiation into manhood lead him to an almost obsessional interest in blood-letting as an important, authenticating male ceremony, manifested in war, hunting and other bellicose pursuits. Women are fringe-dwellers in many of Murray's poems, outsiders to be tolerated by males.

His first volume, *The Ilex Tree* (1965), was shared with his friend and former fellow undergraduate at the University of Sydney, Geoffrey Lehmann. The early poems, pleasantly descriptive but without much intellectual pressure, announce his interests in the country, in journeying and in the Aboriginal inheritance. *The Weatherboard Cathedral* (1969) contains much relaxed, self-confident concentration on himself as the source of values for the life and the people around him. It is a point of view not dissimilar to that of Wordsworth's *The Prelude*.

Poems against Economics (1972) is Murray's most defiantly Boeotian volume, and his most rhetorical. In his words, 'I set out to follow a cow . . . and I found a whole world, a spacious, town despising grassland where Celt and Zulu and Vedic Aryan and Queensland drover were one in their concerns.' Murray, tramping over furrows and climbing through fences, uses ambulation as a source of and metaphor for reflection. In the two major sequences, 'Seven Points for an Imperilled Star' and 'Walking to the Cattle Place', he combines a sense of rural self-sufficiency; national achievement through war, understanding the land, and the rejection of English values; the international fraternity of cattle people; and the certainty of being a poet naming and celebrating the sources of genuine human life.

Lunch and Counter Lunch (1974) contained fewer major poems, but applied Murray's ideas to a wide variety of subjects, including his ancestors, the University of Sydney, broad beans, aqualung diving, and police and their duties. There are bush anecdotes, lyrics, and extended conversation poems, but a single combative, proselytizing personality and tone of voice pervade them all.

In a publishing practice common in the 1970s, largely dictated by the school market, Murray's *Selected Poems: The Vernacular Republic* was published in 1976. His next volume, *Ethnic Radio* (1977), began with the new poems from *Selected Poems* and included Murray's long, prize-winning poem 'The Buladelah-Taree Holiday Song Cycle'. The song cycle was modelled, according to Murray, on the anthropologist Professor R. M. Berndt's translation of 'A Wonguri-Mandjikai Song Cycle of the Moon Bone'. Both cycles have thirteen songs, with Murray following the sequence of subjects and images in the Aboriginal work. Song 4 of the Aboriginal cycle, for instance, begins with 'The birds saw the people walking along'. Murray begins his fourth poem with 'The birds saw us wandering along'. The verse is not accentual or syllabic, but is based on a rhetorical pattern of two, three or four grammatical groupings to each line. It should not be thought, of course, that Berndt's renderings approximate in form to Aboriginal poetry. They are elevated literal renderings of the meaning, with no account taken of the taxingly complex cross-rhythms applied in Aboriginal performance. What Murray has done is find a useful, loose rhetorical form that he occupies with mostly triple-rhythmed verse. His poem celebrates the area near where he was born – the cental north coast of New South Wales – and the life of small farmers, itinerant workers and holiday-makers. His ideas about blood sacrifice, initiation, and joy in work are never far from the surface, but neither are his acute social observation, his wit and his good-natured banter.

The Boys who Stole the Funeral (1980) is a verse novel dealing with death, burial rituals, sexual hostility, male initiation, and the moral decency of rural values. It consists of 140 sonnets centred on two young men, Kevin Forbutt and Cameron Reeby. They remove the body of Kevin's great-uncle, Clarrie Dunn, from a suburban funeral parlour in Sydney in order to give it a decent – that is, rural – burial among Dunn's own people. Kevin is the main spokesman for Murray's ideas, the fourteenth line often being used for his final statement that wins the moral argument. He is initiated in the bush by legendary Aboriginals. They use the standard methods of the *karadji*, the 'clever man' or 'man of high degree', for initiating another man into privileged knowledge – that is, a ritual incision in the belly, the discovery in the body of a crystal 'that refracts Time', the insertion of a bag, education in customary lore, an ascent into the sky by cords, education in 'the blood-history of the continent', and the summoning of a spirit (Clarrie Dunn) temporarily from the dead. They eat from the Common Dish, representing both communality and ordinariness, knowledge that is both certain yet despised by many. Murray is also, of course, reinforcing the notion of a Christian accommodation with the ancient religion of the land.

A revised selected poems, *The Vernacular Republic: Poems 1961–1981*, appeared in 1982, containing 'all of the verse, apart from the novel sequence *The Boys who Stole the Funeral*, which the author wishes to preserve from his first twenty years' work'. Its final poems head Murray's next individual volume, *The People's Otherworld* (1983). In it he concentrates more on city settings, notably in a sequence 'The Sydney Highrise Variations' in which he speaks of Sydney, with its convict origins, as 'England's buried Gulag'. This is also the most overtly Christian of his volumes, with many glancing references to the richness of ritual, mystery and morality. In these poems the 'otherworld' is sometimes the despised one of 'media and action', sometimes the desired one of achieved justice; sometimes, in other words, hell, sometimes heaven.

Murray's poetic autobiography continues with 'Three Poems in Memory of my Mother', which come to terms with his mother's induced labour in giving birth to him and her death a few years later through a doctor's callous disregard of the urgency of her condition after a miscarriage. The rough justice of the ostracism of the doctor by the 'Clan' is not final, for 'Time cannot hold' equities of this ultimate kind that concern death: 'Justice is the people's otherworld'.

Murray continues his contumely against rationalists, humanists, agnostics and secularists, condemning them to a world of illogicality and deprivation, a world unable to explain death and justice. As usual, his ideas are based on the contemplation of solid objects and facts. The discourse is by turns playful, opinionated, anecdotal and obstinately assured. The lyrical voice of the early poems has almost been swallowed up by the meditative and button-holing voice.

Murray's range of subjects, his mingling of biography with opinion, and his declaratory style have been immensely influential. Poets as diverse in personality as Roger McDonald, Geoff Page, Robert Gray, Mark O'Connor, Alan Gould, Kevin Hart and Jamie Grant have learnt from him.

Geoffrey Lehmann (1940–) shared a first volume with Murray, but is distinctive in subjects, tone of voice and mode of poetry. He is above all else a monologuist, able to submerge himself, like Ezra Pound, from whose work he learnt the knack, entirely in the personality of an historical or contemporary figure. His first separate volume, *A Voyage of Lions, and Other Poems* (1968), includes the first of his longer sequences on the Roman Empire in its period of decadence, 'Meditations for Marcus Furius Camillus, Governor of Africa'. In this sequence he raises many of the concerns that characterize all his Roman pieces: the sense of cultural alienation; chafing for freedom of action and emotion against the constraints of administrative, legal and psychological bondage; fascination with the animal nature of mankind; casual acceptance of cruelty; and the debilitating effect of personal timidity, exemplified in such lines as

> Safer for me to quietly age
> Amongst familiar unrealities.

Amid the decadence, symbols of imagination, nature and purity are provided by dolphins, lions and water.

In this and in his later volumes *Conversation with a Rider* (1972) and *Nero's Poems* (1981) he pursues his Roman interests, concentrating on Marcus Furius Camillus and the Emperors Claudius and Nero. He is fascinated by corruption and decay, physical, political and moral. Physical corruption is used as an emblem both of political and moral corruption and of death and its horror. In his Nero sequence, subtitled 'Translations of the [imaginary] Public and Private Poems of the Emperor Nero', he offers his own interpretation of Nero, markedly different from those of Tacitus and Suetonius. Instead of being a monomaniacal monster, he is a mixture of lust and human concern, violence and considerateness, shrewdness and folly, but above all an artist who loved to recite his poetry in public and to play the lyre, the bagpipes and the water organ. He is a reformer of society, a town-planner and a conservationist. His brutal acts are mostly the result of fear, including fear at not understanding the world or the intricate machinations of his court. All is in sharp focus, intensely visual, intensely felt, heard and smelled. In this decadence there is a vitalism in sexual enjoyment and domination that seems to excuse minor injustices. Apart from the monologues, there are also lovely lyrical pieces, such as the two 'Aqueducts' poems and 'Gardens', in which the canker of fear is absent.

The earlier sequence *Ross' Poems* (1978) takes up another continuing strand in Lehmann's work, poems about the life of the Australian outback. It is based on the experiences of his first wife's father, Ross McInerney, living in the valley of the Lachlan River in central south-west New South Wales. These are imaginary dramatic monologues, like those of Nero, but their concerns are on a small scale. Ross is a man who has thought deeply about his life, and his agnostic faith, if simple, is also profound in its resonances. He has a companionable, sunny disposition, fond of a good yarn and a good joke. Like Lehmann himself he has the ability to imagine himself as someone else – even a horse or a cloud. And as in the Roman poems water is a symbol of the unchanging order of nature and of purity.

In a third group of poems Lehmann writes autobiographically of his own family and ancestors, somewhat in the mode of Robert Lowell. He writes of his maternal grandfather, William Rainer, a dipsomaniac doctor who died of an overdose of morphia; of his paternal grandfather, Johann Lehmann, a Saxon carpenter who built the first Anglican church in New Guinea and died shortly afterwards of yellow fever and malaria; of his father, a carpenter and unsuccessful inventor of systems for making money; of his Aunt Agnes (who asks in the overcrowded city, 'Where is the Milky Way gone?');

of lovers, friends and his wife. In these poems there is a deceptively simple flat quality, as if poetry is being made out of statement, but the vigour is in the verbs that almost invariably carry the colour, movement and resonating significance. Lehmann can be almost embarrassingly frank, but it is in his poetic nature to persist until he understands, to allow no doubtful shadows to smudge his dramatic tableaux, and to confront sexuality, brutality and self-interest as important facets of life.

Bruce Dawe

Like Les Murray, Bruce Dawe (1930–) has the distinction of bringing an individual tone of voice and an individual set of subjects into Australian poetry. Even more than Murray, however, he is a poet who is genuinely popular as well as literary, a poet of the spoken voice. He creates and writes about new Australian types, people who are not station hands, shearers, stockmen, lonely bush wives, city poets, exponents of alternative lifestyles, vagrant fishermen or exponents of the melodramatic self. His character portraits are of suburban and small-town dwellers, interested in cars, television, football, their families, hire-purchase debts, B-grade American movies, popular novels, magazines and songs, and, more recently, civil liberties, abortion, unemployment, autocracy, the treatment of Aborigines and the destruction of the environment. His point of view is that of what he calls the 'bottom dog', the Australian 'battler' who may be in part self-deluded but whose fantasies are less destructive than those of politicians and businessmen. Dawe records such people and their interests with understanding and sympathy rather than superiority and sarcasm.

He expresses their doubts and beliefs, their fears and hopes, and does not shrink from having them speculate on metaphysical and moral matters. In 'Homo Suburbiensis', for instance, he has a suburban man standing in his garden among the tomatoes, pumpkins, and compost-box, 'lost in a green confusion', meditating on

> Not much but as much as any man can offer
> – time, pain, love, hate, age, war, death, laughter, fever.

In ' "Some Village-Hampden . . ." ' he is content to end the poem with the potato farmer's confident self-justification for maltreating the schoolmaster:

'He beat my kid, so I beat him
– That's all there is to it.'

In 'Kid Stuff', a tribute to his older brother George, he risks an ending in which he recalls himself as a boy pleading with his brother to come out and play cricket in 'a nasal childhood whine / . . . the words pathetic / in both their hopelessness and their relentless love'.

Dawe's early poems often adopt the hardboiled tone derived from his early reading of schoolboy thrillers, Westerns, science fiction and mystery stories and from his later reading of the narrative poems of Edgar Lee Masters, Edwin Arlington Robinson and E. E. Cummings. From this training he evolved a style that is a metonym of his non-hierarchical view of the world, a style that incorporates imaginative, recondite and everyday language. Often he re-creates the dead metaphors of language, such as 'dry' applied to subject matter in 'Teaching the Syllabus', or 'getting it together' in the poem of that title.

His first book, *No Fixed Address* (1962), is in language less original and enterprising than his later work, more dependent on straining polysyllabic humour, more unctuous in its moral statements. It does, however, contain the brilliantly experimental poem 'Enter Without so Much as Knocking', influenced in subject and style by Kenneth Fearing's 'Dirge'. It offers a laconic, materialistic account of life between the maternity hospital and the casualty department and cemetery, all expressed in the superficial accompaniments of suburban life – neon signs, radio advertising, drive-in cinemas, competitiveness, drink, cars, and time payment. This volume also contains one of his most trenchantly observed portraits, that of the dead-beat moocher in 'The Flashing of Badges'.

A Need of Similar Name (1965) introduces a strong sense of political outrage, directed against the brutality and crassness of big business and politics. But there are also tender love poems to his wife. As in the earlier volume Dawe treats solemn historical and contemporary subjects in egalitarian vernacular language and exposes pomposity and heartlessness through the use of mock-heroic. 'And a Good Friday was Had by All' exemplifies his typical association of Christian faith with social justice. The centurion who is the speaker of this dramatic monologue believes that the death sentence is due to 'the big men who must have had it in for him'; a blind man is in tears; and Christ's arms are spread 'so it seemed over the whole damned creation'.

An Eye for a Tooth (1968) contains some of Dawe's funniest and most moving poems. 'The Not-So-Good Earth' is a dramatic monologue conveying an Australian family's off-handed efforts to interpret a television screening of a Pearl Buck movie. The speaker imagines that when Grandmother dies she was 'probably damn glad to be quit of the whole gang with their marvellous patience'. 'A Victorian Hangman Tells his Love' is a macabre and chilling dramatic monologue by a hangman in Victoria (the last Australian state to dispense with the rather Victorian punishment of hanging). Dawe concentrates on what he described later as 'the peculiar intimacy of the relationship of executioner and victim'.

Beyond the Subdivisions (1969) is notable for the finest Australian poetic response to the Vietnam War, 'Homecoming', an oratorical dirge in which the horror and tragedy are intensified by the impersonal language. Grief too personal and deep for pity is expressed also in 'The Raped Girl's Father'. By contrast, 'One Jump Ahead' is a fond portrait of feckless tenants, always on the move, always over-committing themselves to the hire purchase of unaffordable goods.

Selections from the previous volumes were collected, together with new poems, in *Condolences of the Season* (1971), a volume that established Dawe as a major poet. Among the new poems were the painfully cheerful 'Wood-Eye' and the mock-comic but intensely serious monologue 'Weapons Training'. By now Dawe was able to range within a single poem from comedy to wrenching sorrow, introducing the changes of mood with early hints followed by a gradual shift achieved by ambiguity of language. In 'Weapons Training', for instance, the drill sergeant begins by unleashing his repertoire of derisive banter on the recruits:

> And when I say eyes right I want to hear
> those eyeballs click and the gentle pitter-patter
> of falling dandruff . . . .

By the end of the lesson and the poem he has worked himself into a frenzy of imaginary combat in which his own fear is barely concealed

> they're on you and your tripes are round your neck
> you've copped the bloody lot just like I said
> and you know what you are? you're dead dead dead

Two later retrospective collections, *Sometimes Gladness: Collected Poems, 1954–1978* (1978) and *Sometimes Gladness: Collected Poems, 1954–1982* (1983), were published. Dawe's poetry over much of the 1970s seemed to falter. The topics and incidents that had earlier stimulated him seemed largely unavailable, though there were some light-hearted uproarious successes such as the mock elegy 'The Corn-Flake' and the monologue 'Pleasant Sunday Afternoon', in which an encyclopaedia salesman is reduced to ignominious, self-preserving flight. At the end of the 1970s, though, Dawe found a new political exasperation, expressing it in poems about particular issues and particular politicians. Living in the provincial city of Toowoomba he seemed sometimes to be chafing against its petty-mindedness and against the reactionary government of the State of Queensland. But he continued to find delight in the ratbag and circus element of Queensland politics, though, as he said to an interviewer, 'The disadvantages of ringside seats are of course obvious, too: tigers with toothache, elephants with the "trots" . . . .'

A number of his poems concern the uncaring and hostile attitudes of whites to Aborigines, the grand eccentricities of the Queensland Premier, the abhorrence Dawe feels towards abortion, and the injustice of the military regime in El Salvador. There are also poems of acute observation of suburbanites, including some particularly sympathetic portraits of women and girls.

Dawe once said, 'The world is a brutal, mysterious, beautiful, inexplicable affair.' To give it some kind of meaning he applies his moral and religious principles. In his world, people may at least try to be honourable and good, but

attempts to be heroic will be irrelevant. He also applies a
consistent sense of the importance of ritual. His poems draw
attention to the conventions and formulas of everyday life, as
evident to Dawe among milk-bar kids, bikies, football crowds
and housewives as among politicians and soldiers. He
celebrates, with amusement, satire and affection, the lives of
ordinary people, endowing their observances and habits with
the language and forms normally reserved for romance and
heroism. In his world comedy and tragedy, the ludicrous and
the solemn, are mingled. He has a masterly control of comic
effects, stemming from his extraordinary verbal range and his
ability to slide from one linguistic level to another.

His short stories, *Over Here, Harv! and Other Stories* (1983),
written early in his career, show less control of linguistic level,
but a comparable command of scene, significant detail, and
authentic kitchen and street dialogue.

Peter Porter (1929–) left Brisbane at the age of twenty-two
to live in London; he was twenty-eight before his first poem was
published, thirty-two before his first book. His memories of
childhood in Brisbane are radically different from those of
David Malouf; for Porter the memory is 'a private iconography
of hell'. His book publications have almost all been English; he
did not revisit Australia for twenty-three years; and his subjects
are largely English and European. He is, then, in a more
profound sense than Jack Lindsay, Christina Stead or
Randolph Stow, an expatriate writer.

His early volumes, *Once Bitten, Twice Bitten* (1961), *Poems
Ancient and Modern* (1964), *A Porter Folio* (1969) and *The Last of
England* (1970), offer coruscating satires, mostly in a single
speaking voice, sceptical of all achievement, sceptical of his
own scepticism. They are poems in which Porter engages in
constant debate with himself, ending each one not with the end
of the matter but with a neat lapidary line. The habitual mood is
of disillusion, malcontentment and gloom, though the texture is
witty and genial. A wide range of learning is lightly worn in this
often rather academic *vers de société*. Much is made of the
popular evanescence of fashionable clothes, cars, addresses and
music. Many poems depend on the mock-heroic, the invocation
of divine imagery upon trivial concerns. Phar Lap, the
racehorse preserved in a museum, for instance, is 'Australia's
Ark of the Covenant'. Or it can be reverse mock-heroic, as in

'Inspector Christopher Smart Calls', where the speaker says 'I can give you . . . Green Stamps for the furnishings of Heaven'; or in 'A Consumer's Report', where 'The name of the product I tested is *Life*'. At times the satire is mediated through so many stages as to become tenuous. One example is 'Elegy', an imitation of Ezra Pound's *Mauberley*, itself an imitation of *fin-de-siècle* poetry. Porter is so self-conscious that he calls all in doubt except, by implication, the virtues of intelligence, self-doubt and fortitude. If the references are recondite, the sentence structure is invariably in short snatches of meaning, like modish advertising-copy.

Preaching to the Converted (1972) continues the enthusiastic pursuit of disappointment through several European countries and periods, with rather more affected philistinism in language and outlook than before. *Living in a Calm Country* (1975) returns to the predictable social round of England. In those poems where he manages to slough off the spiral of self-consciousness, such as 'At the Castle Hotel, Taunton' and 'Anger', he indicates a new and promising direction for his verse.

The Cost of Seriousness (1978) has more fine poems than any other single volume. The pressure to be introspective, sceptical and jocular has relaxed; Porter is able to speak unironically with the assurance of over thirty years of writing behind him. Now the gaiety of self-deprecation is more fitful, the gloom more pervasive. 'Death', 'hell', 'nothing', 'nobody', 'non-existence', 'prison bars', and 'lies' are recurring words. The backgrounds are the familiar ones of paintings, sculpture, photographs, music, and the landscapes of Italy, England and Australia (which he revisited after the death of his wife in 1974). Many poems express or reflect his despair at the death of his wife, particularly 'An Exequy', 'The Delegate', 'A Lecture by my Books', 'The Cost of Seriousness', and 'Non Piangere, Liù'. Porter, the 'residual Christian', has become a theologian-*manqué*, practising 'A theology of self looking for precedents'. Poetry, at least in its guise of 'the lying art', seems incapable of providing either the expression of grief or any consolation for loss. It offers mere 'Inroads into rhetoric'.

English Subtitles (1981) continues this more solemn, less self-contorted mode in poems such as 'Good Ghost, Gaunt Ghost', 'What I Have Written, I Have Written', and 'Talking to You Afterwards'. These are, at times, intensely personal poems; Porter is still talking about himself, but no longer to himself. He is no longer seduced by the limitless possibilities of truth, but is more judicious and dignified.

Porter's *Collected Poems* (1983) drew together most of the work from his separate volumes, revealing a poet whose earlier work has affinities with that of Philip Larkin and Bruce Dawe, and whose later work is closer to Auden. But this volume also reveals Porter as a highly individual poet of dialectical self-criticism, a poet of the outer world in all its European cultural detail brought to bear on the inner world.

David Malouf

The early poetry of David Malouf (1935–) is reflective, reminiscent and autobiographical. He writes about his boyhood, home, parents, sister and friends, often with an air of wistfulness as if their possessions and their spaces were solid but his own were not, as if the personalities were secure but his own was peripheral to theirs. The past is more immediate to him than the present. 'Rome, two thousands years from here' is more vivid in the poem 'Reading Horace Outside Sydney: 1970' than his current surroundings, where 'Sydney glitters invisible' and all that remains of a 'plane overhead is that 'Its shadow dances in my palm'. In the personal stocktaking of 'Decade's End', all he finds is that he is 'growing accustomed to the dark'.

The two early volumes, *Bicycle, and Other Poems* (1970; republished in New York in 1979 as *The Year of the Foxes, and Other Poems*) and *Neighbours in a Thicket* (1974, revised 1980), were followed by a *Selected Poems* in 1981. It included a number of poems of reminiscence in a more hectic, over-wrought tone, mingled with meditation on life, death and political machination. They were denser in reference, less single-track in their narrative, written perhaps under some influence from the fashionable mode of New York poetry much acclaimed in Sydney in the 1970s.

The poems of *First Things Last* (1980) return for the most part to the less densely referential texture of the early poems. In a poem to his father, 'Elegy: The Absences', he epitomizes one of his own constant concerns:

You knew about absences. I am learning
slowly how much space they occupy
in any house I move to . . . .

This volume contains a number of longer meditative poems, notably 'Preludes', 'Deception Bay' and 'The Crab Feast', in which Malouf considers modulation and metamorphosis in nature and the individual, the assimilation of nature by the individual, the shadowy blue, crab-wise characteristics of the way we view the world, and the attempt to capture the Edenic state of childhood.

Malouf's first novel, *Johnno* (1975), evoked the dark under-the-house atmosphere of his Queensland poems about childhood. The narrator is a boy who grows into young manhood with an intermittent fascination for a more rebellious, adventurous, even scapegrace boy, Johnno. There is a wistful contrast between the orderly, decorous life of the narrator and the blustering energy of the anarchic, malcontented Johnno. The sense of boyhood in a war-threatened sub-tropical city is vividly conveyed; the scenes of an Australian exiled in Europe make less impact.

An Imaginary Life (1978) concerns the last ten years of the life of Ovid, exiled among the semi-barbarous Getae at Tomis on the western shore of the Black Sea. Malouf's sources were Ovid's account in the *Tristia* and Marguerite Yourcenar's *Memoirs of Hadrian*, but the theme is his own. It is of a 'glib fabulist' forced by a cruel edict to metamorphose himself into a creature of the diurnal world. He explores the walled village, learns the language of the inhabitants, even considers whether he might write in it. The final stage of the psychological escape from exile, the final loss of cynicism, comes through his acquaintance with a 'wild boy', said to live among wolves. The boy is captured and lives in Ovid's hut, but transmits a fever to the grandson of the village headman and is forced again out into the wilderness. Ovid accompanies him and begins to learn from him. He is surprised to find 'It is not as I had imagined. There are no wolves.' In the vast deserted plains, in a space that is boundless, timeless and void, Ovid finds that the 'footprints' of his life 'lead to this place and no other'. He dies ecstatically, content to see the boy preparing to step 'into his own distance', reassuring himself that 'I am three years old. I am sixty. I am six. I am there.'

Child's Play; with Eustace and The Prowler (1982) brings together a novella set in Italy and two short stories set in Australia. *Child's Play* has for its surface story the quest by a young terrorist to kill an elderly and admired author who specializes in the dualities of order and disorder, the decent and the disreputable, control and madness. But it is a book not about urban terrorism, but, metaphorically, about the act of writing. The terrorist is in some sense the creation of the elderly writer, the end to which writing aspires; so too is *Child's Play* itself, for it is the title of what the author is writing.

Fly away Peter (1982) is a short novel of the early decades of the century set in the hinterland of the south coast of Queensland. Jim Saddler, a naturalist, goes to the war and is killed. His dilettantish employer goes as an officer and returns. But it is the migratory birds observed by Jim that complete and repeat the only satisfying cycle of exile and return. By contrast each of the human lives is disrupted or broken. *Fly away Peter* is, like *Johnno*, a novel in which the European scenes are less convincing than the Queensland ones.

Harland's Half Acre (1984) is centred on the painter Frank Harland and his solicitor friend, Phil Vernon, who seeks to understand him and mediate between him and society. Double male characters, one reflecting the other, are found in all five of Malouf's major fictional works. As in *An Imaginary Life* and *Child's Play*, there is a creative artist of some eccentricity concerned with relating his work to the place in which he finds himself or to which he aspires. In *Harland's Half Acre*, though, there is the additional solidity of Frank's and Phil's families and the tactile descriptions of the houses they inhabit. By contrast, Harland is peripatetic, always seeking ambiguous spaces in various parts of south-east Queensland while having his mind set on buying back the family property in the town of Killarney. That space, so seemingly solid, is represented for him by the search embodied in his paintings, a search by a creator who, like Harland's idea of God, is always moving on. Once again, then, Malouf is concerned with the links and contrasts between the spaces of the imagination and the places of habitation, the incentives of memory, the theme of physical and psychical exile, the imaginative stimulus of invading alien worlds, and the sense of personal incompleteness and imperfect understanding.

10
The generation of the 1960s

Poets

IN the late 1960s a new generation of Australian poets and some middle-generation poets made a revelatory discovery of certain kinds of American poetry. *The New American Poetry*, edited by Donald Allen, had been published in 1960, but it trickled into Australia slowly because for some years it was construed as a prohibited import under the paternalistic Australian customs regulations. By the late 1960s, however, the Black Mountain Group centred on Charles Olson and including Robert Duncan and Robert Creeley and such New York poets as Frank O'Hara, John Ashbery and Kenneth Koch had caught the imagination of several Australians. Another substantial group, not included in Allen's anthology, simultaneously exercised an influence. They were the writers of confessional, post-confessional and 'life studies' work, such as Robert Lowell, Sylvia Plath and John Berryman. A third, less commonly acknowledged, American influence was that of Wallace Stevens, whose notion of 'poetry as the supreme fiction' was one inspiration of the New York school.

The enthusiasm for American poetry was often accompanied by disparagement of contemporary British poetry and of what was regarded as the poetic 'establishment' of A. D. Hope and James McAuley. It was accompanied also by antipathy to American (and Australian) foreign policy in Vietnam and a general sense of radical protest expressed in 'New Left' political opinions, civil disobedience, or drug-taking. In poetry the result was concern for poetry as process, as game and as lie. The much-used image of the fast car or powerful truck, with headlights raking the road or wheels slipping on greasy bends, perhaps symbolizes the sense of self-projection through life, the unpredictability, the nearness of death, and even a sense of being, if incompetently, in charge of one's own destiny.

Another, but unrelated, feature of poetry in this period is the frequency of poetic sequences, loose assemblages where one piece reverberates against another. The first notable sequence was Bruce Beaver's *Letters to Live Poets* (1969), sometimes regarded as the first large-scale open-field poem by an Australian writer. The example was followed by both radical and conservative poets, Michael Dransfield, Robert Adamson, John Tranter, Vincent Buckley, Rodney Hall, Thomas Shapcott, Les A. Murray and Geoffrey Lehmann.

Bruce Beaver (1928–) began with Slessor-like poems of Sydney and its harbour in his first volume, *Under the Bridge* (1961) and Francis Webb-like confessions of mental strain in his second, *Seawall and Shoreline* (1964). With *Open at Random* (1967), *Letters to Live Poets* (1969), *Lauds and Plaints* (1974) and *Odes and Days* (1975) he moved towards influences from several American proponents of open form, notably William Carlos Williams and Frank O'Hara. The result is a comfortably discursive poetry, constantly intelligent, often witty and amusing, full of vignettes and perceptive observations, and with occasional poetic rhetoric. Beaver is disarmingly self-deprecating, referring often to 'this prosaic kind of writing' or 'a paucity of themes', but he does not always avoid the danger of mere literary chat.

When he eschews the non-representational style of New York poetry (which, in any case, John Tranter imitates better), he can be very serious, as in his poems about Australia's involvement in the Vietnam War. In *Death's Directives* (1978), however, the large metaphysical issues, the fear of death and pain, the sense of evil and isolation, and gratitude for unexpected love can seem forced and artificially obtrusive. There is sometimes a self-conscious *fin-de-siècle* atmosphere in the blurrily depicted outlines.

Beaver was a major figure in the reintroduction of contemporary American poetry to Australia at the end of the 1960s. By contrast, his two novels of the mid 1960s made little impact. *As it was . . .* , an autobiography in poetry and prose, and his *Selected Poems*, both published in 1979, drew attention to his courageous struggle against mental illness and his vivid sense of place.

A thin stream of decadence runs through the last century and a half of poetry in English, paralleling a rather broader stream in French poetry. Australia had, in Christopher Brennan, one poet much influenced by both English and French decadents. In Michael Dransfield and Robert Adamson it gained two more.

Like Brennan, Dransfield (1948–73) used imagery of religious observance, silence, distant music, moonlight, the apocalypse, warfare, and the poet's role in war, but he was able to inject more of the contemporary world into this conventional storehouse and he was more epigrammatic. Where Brennan was troubled by the question of the appropriate life for a symbolist poet, Dransfield from precocious adolescence to his death at the age of twenty-four seems to have rejected all possible solutions except extinction.

His earliest poems, in *Streets of the Long Voyage* (1970) and the posthumous *Voyage into Solitude* (1978), contain most of his best work. The intense nervous pain of the drug-taker is represented with a wry, fatalistic amusement, lacking any trace of judgement against either society or addict, in such poems as 'Bums' Rush' and 'That which we Call a Rose'. Blithe insouciance characterizes such love poems as 'Chess' and 'For Hilary, her Birthday'. A love of blissful dreaming through romantic Australian landscape and ordered architecture is evident in the Courland Penders poems.

Dransfield is often weary, often aware of his own sense of *déjà vu* and of premonition, but he is never world-weary. He is always nervously alert and excited by his discoveries about himself and others. The experiences he writes about – drug-taking, the death of friends, pain, illness, waking in dismal beds or in gutters – are the substance of any decadent poetry, but Dransfield's self-inquisitiveness and strength of will prevent him from donning the comfortable pale-violet uniform of the 1890s. Thinness and inconsequentiality are, however, dangers that he does not always avoid in *The Inspector of Tides* (1972), *Drug Poems* (1972), *Memoirs of a Velvet Urinal* (1975) and *The Second Month of Spring* (1980).

Robert Adamson (1944–) has always been fascinated by metamorphosis involving change of shape, change of sex, change of human being into animal or bird, change of and ultimate dissolution of the self. This concept has probably been more central to his work than his espousal of poetry as the art of lying. He is the inventor and (as the 'I' of his poems) the invention of a chimerical, shifting world, shimmering with creation, play-acting, lying, and truth-telling.

His first volume, *Canticles on the Skin* (1970), established him as a poet drawing, in a playful surrealist mode, on his experiences of delinquency, gaol, drug-taking, delirium, bisexuality, fast cars and the lore of fishing. In it he plays the role of outlaw, tough guy and mischief-maker, and mythologizes the Hawkesbury River in a set of shimmering water poems. His influences were clearly the lyrics of Bob Dylan, Shelley, Rimbaud, and Ezra Pound. Later, he added Robert Duncan, notably in *The Rumour* and *Cross the Border*.

In *The Rumour* (1971) he managed to sort out some of his problems with syntax, but there were indications that his subject matter was increasingly concentrated on the process of writing. The title poem is an ambitious amalgam of nineteenth-century hieratic medievalism and open-form verse in a quest for the elusive rumoured muse. *Swamp Riddles* (1974) returns to the world of the Hawkesbury River. Its mangroves, mosquitoes, decaying jetties, kestrels, fish, prawns and butterflies become a complex symbol of the poet's search for wholeness and illumination in a tangled, puzzling world. The book also contains 'Sonnets to be Written from Prison', with their question

Surely there must be some way out of poetry other than
Mallarmé's: still-life with bars and shitcan.

Prison was also the subject of the semi-documentary novel, written in collaboration with Robert Hanford, that formed the major part of *Zimmer's Essay* (1974), one of the first books produced by the small 'alternative' press Wild and Woolley. It presents a brutal, violent world with its own rigid codes operating in defiance of the imposed orthodoxy.

Cross the Border (1977), like *Swamp Riddles*, combines a high bardic voice, a chatty confiding voice and what are almost random jottings. It also combines three kinds of poetry for three different audiences: river poems, self-referential poems and slight performance lyrics.

Selected Poems (1977) recognizes the variety of appeal of Adamson's poetry by dividing the poems not chronologically, but according to subject and style. There are sections on the poet as rebel, as poet and as river man, as well as the 'Grail Poems' inspired by Gary Shead's paintings.

Where I Come From (1979) consists of easily accessible, spare poems of biographical confession, less rhetorical and less romantically coloured than before. They rely for their effect on the shape of the line, the clarity of description, the nakedness of self-revelation, and the occasional hint of play-acting. There are poems of youthful delinquency on the Hawkesbury, of self-satisfied adolescent violence and vindictive trouble-making, of adult fears of aging and of declining sexual performance.

The Law at Heart's Desire (1982) continues Adamson's progress to honesty with himself. He confronts his own violent nature, his fear of death, and his capacity to love and be loved. His poetry is now less scintillating in texture, almost homely at times, the phrase-making has turned from cleverness to an almost runic quality, and the romanticism has accepted unironically the conventions of grand confession, the symbolic life and *paysage psychologique*. Adamson has been described as affecting the role of the *faux-naïf* in this volume and *Where I Come From*, but it is really the role of the Blakean innocent who has passed through experience back to innocence.

John Tranter (1943–) is a poet committed to experimentalism who has always been escaping from imitators and from his own dissatisfaction with the mode and achievement of his latest work. Within a general commitment to poetry of process and self-reference, twentieth-century modernism, structuralism, analogies with visual art and music, and the work of such American poets as Wallace Stevens, John Ashbery, Frank O'Hara and Peter Schjeldahl, Tranter has explored new techniques in each of his volumes. Like Michael Wilding, but without Wilding's Marxism, he is committed to the need for continuous aesthetic revolution. He has been influenced by aspects of Zen, especially the notion of putting two things together to achieve something different from either of them. His *Selected Poems* (1982) indicates his experimental trail. *Parallax, and Other Poems* (1970) is his most referential volume, full of brief narratives and vignettes set in slightly puzzling or menacing surroundings, constantly emphasizing the inevitable parallax error of perception. *Red Movie, and Other Poems* (1972) was notable for 'Conversations' and the title poem, one a poem of romantic decadence to illustrate the notion of writing a poem as 'an act of suicide', the other a less continuously referential mood poem in blue (rather than red), coiling round on itself, on the mind that made it and on experience to end with

> I think we are in winter again
> if you are ready
> we can begin

The Alphabet Murders (1976) was full of absurd similes, jokes, deliberate anarchy of value judgements – 'the page aflame with noise and verb geometry' – all designed to direct attention to the poetic process itself. *Crying in Early Infancy* (1977) was a sequence of 100 fourteen-line poems, surrealistically engaging in a dialogue between art and anti-art. The implication is that for Tranter place, solidity and reference are the stuff of anti-art.

Dazed in the Ladies Lounge (1979) is less tense, with more evidence of Tranter not taking himself so solemnly. It contains 'Rimbaud and the Modernist Heresy', addressed to Rimbaud with lines such as 'To follow you we must desert', 'I've loved and hated you for twenty long years', and 'that future under whose arrogant banner we have laboured for our own rewards'. The prevailing mood continues to be one of jaunty sombreness, but the aggressive hostility to referential poetry is fading.

Tranter is an intensely nervous, intellectual poet, doubting the existence of any discoverable reality, sceptical of all assertions (hence the proliferation of inverted commas and double negatives), fascinated by aesthetic pattern, and constantly seeking to slip away from any commitment to or typing by a style. He has been widely regarded as the leader of a Sydney 'mannerist' school that includes John Forbes, Nigel Roberts, Jennifer Maiden and Rae Desmond Jones. He has been contemptuous of gum-tree-laden poetry, poetry of assertion, and poetry that is not essentially about language and itself.

By contrast, an alternative group of younger poets may be seen as writing broadly in the rural tradition of Les Murray. Robert Gray (1945–), in *Creekwater Journal* (1974), *Grass Script* (1979) and *The Skylight* (1984), shows himself suspicious of formalism, whether conservative or modernist. Like William Carlos Williams he believes in the importance of things in the material world. He has for them a Buddhist or Taoist respect and a socialist's sense of their fundamental materialism. By contrast, the ego is an illusion. His contemplation of matter results in poetry of pure imagism.

Kevin Hart (1954–), influenced by another strain in Murray, writes in *The Departure* (1978), *Lines of the Hand* (1981), and *Your Shadow* (1984) as a mystical romantic, approaching the extrasensory world through accurate description of the visible world. His tone of meditative stillness seems to have been influenced by some Spanish mystical writers. Like Murray, he is a convert to Catholicism.

Thomas Keneally

Moral and metaphysical questions are central to the fiction of Thomas Keneally (1935–). In the twentieth century this is true also of Henry Handel Richardson, Patrick White, Randolph Stow and Christopher Koch, by contrast with a generally materialist line in Furphy, Katharine Susannah Prichard, Palmer, Thea Astley, David Ireland and David Foster. Keneally writes of a moral world inhabited and conditioned by guilt, suffering, sacrifice and atonement. The fleshly details of sex, violence and physical decay recur as metonyms for a morally corrupt world in which humanity is constantly vulnerable. Copulation, menstruation, abortion, madness, homosexuality, witchcraft, hanging and putrescence are described in detail; the womb is frequently presented as a source of life, female power, sin and decay, combining life, joy, blood, mystery and putrescence. The enclosed womblike settings for his novels are generally like the island of Mus, the setting for *Season in Purgatory* (1976), 'the place of blood sacrifice and wine, of love and the smell of gangrene. Above all, of near madness'.

Much of his work is concerned with the conflict between, on the one hand, authority and concepts of what is natural and right, and, on the other hand, the personal aspiration or need of simple, good-hearted, but bewildered individuals. Perhaps because of his early seminary training for the Catholic priesthood, Keneally very frequently depicts a rigid military or militaristic code crushing or muddling the individual. Sometimes it is the Catholic Church or powerful elements within it, as in Keneally's first novel, *The Place at Whitton* (1964), and in *The Fear* (1965), *Three Cheers for the Paraclete* (1968) and *Blood Red, Sister Rose* (1974) – the last of his obviously Catholic novels. Sometimes it is a military dictatorship or a country at war, as in *Bring Larks and Heroes* (1967), *Gossip from the Forest* (1975), *Season in Purgatory* (1976), *Confederates* (1979), *The Cut-rate Kingdom* (1980) or *Schindler's Ark* (1982). Sometimes it is the self-enclosed world of an Antarctic expedition, as in *The Survivor* (1969) and *A Victim of the Aurora* (1977).

Australia, contemporary or historical, is the setting for over half of Keneally's novels. It is presented as an indifferent continent, peopled by migrants whose hearts are elsewhere (especially Ireland) and by Aborigines for whom English is an alien and inadequate language. With *Blood Red, Sister Rose* Keneally turned for a few years to European and American history and to Antarctica for his settings, though his attempt to comprehend humanity remains constant.

Keneally's first mature novel, *Bring Larks and Heroes*, is set in an Australian penal colony (obviously Sydney) towards the end of the eighteenth century. The Irish convicts, incapable of generating redress or reform in any other way, plot the violent overthrow of the system. The ruling class, fearful of revolt, starvation and the unknown, suppresses the uprising with efficient brutality. Caught between the two forces is Corporal Phelim Halloran, a Wexford Catholic with a tender conscience who is pressed into the service of the Protestant Hanoverian king. He has to decide 'to what degree the true God, the transcendent *I am Who am*, was involved in the listless faith he kept with George R'. In the end, enlightened by bitter experience of the use of godly oaths as a means of consolidating civil power and by the perfidy of his superiors, he knows that the God he serves is 'a God who's owned by nobody'. But this is negative knowledge. As he is strangling in the noose, victim of an English Protestant notion of justice, his last thought is 'Am I perhaps *God*?'

The Chant of Jimmie Blacksmith (1972) is another historical novel, equally carefully researched. It is set a hundred years later than *Bring Larks and Heroes*. Its original was Jimmy Governor, the product of an Aboriginal mother and an Irish father. He was intelligent, literate, sober and industrious, but, marrying a white woman, was subject to ridicule and taunts. Under provocation he committed murder and became a bushranger. Keneally emphasizes his character's desire for racial revenge, introduces the illegitimacy of the child to whom his wife gives birth, and creates in Jimmie a craving for white flesh and for blood. Like Halloran, Jimmie comes to despise and resent the oppressive system that has made him submissive – in his case the self-interested self-righteous Methodism of the Newbys, who brought him up. To combat it, he has to surrender his innocence and even his humanity, a common outcome in the face of the world's ubiquitous violence in Keneally's subsequent novels.

Blood Red, Sister Rose, another historical novel, has as its setting fifteenth-century France and as its central character Joan of Arc, who had been mentioned in some of his earlier novels. Like Halloran and Blacksmith, she is fated from the beginning to be a blood sacrifice. Like Blacksmith she is surrounded by the ancestral 'presences' or voices of the land, and like him she is obsessive. She is presented as a visionary, a soldier and a revolutionary, preserving her innocence in a brutish and horrifying war. In this novel Keneally eschews some of his earlier grandiloquent atmospheric writing in favour of a plain workmanlike style that acts as an analogue to Joan's common sense and directness.

Gossip from the Forest is another European historical novel about war and politics. Though its setting is the railway coaches in which the 1918 Armistice was signed, the atmosphere of a civilization on the point of collapse, preyed on by self-interested politicians concerned to dominate the subsequent order, is similar to that of *Blood Red, Sister Rose*. The reluctant leader of the German negotiators is a vaguely socialist, vaguely pacifist parliamentarian, Erzberger, a peasant doomed, like Joan, to be sacrificed on behalf of the ordinary person. Like Joan he knows by experience and instinct things that the cognoscenti cannot and will not try to understand. As in *Blood Red, Sister Rose* much of the dialogue at moments of tension is written as if it were a play script or film script, with frequent changes of scene and focus. Keneally has in fact written plays, including some scripted from or based on the same material as his novels, but none have been very successful in the theatre.

Keneally had written an inventive fantasy novel in *A Dutiful Daughter* (1971), dealing with the fragility of conventional notions of human sociability. In *Passenger* (1979) he returned to fantasy with a novel narrated by a foetus. In the womb he experiences the blood vessels and nerve-endings of his mother, Sal, as the Tree of Knowledge. He becomes aware of all her thoughts as well as those of her doctor and her husband, Brian. He learns of Brian's wish that he should be aborted, for he fears the foetus – 'It's like God or something. An absent deity.' He experiences Brian's successful attempt to shut Sal up in a London lunatic asylum, and her escape to Australia, where she gives birth. And he sees the parallel of his own experiences to those of his convict ancestor Maurice Fitzpatrick, who had been transported at the end of the eighteenth century. The novel is in one sense a satire on domestic love and hate, in another a myth of the disorientation of values produced by colonialism, in a third sense a witty intertextual commentary on many of Keneally's earlier novels.

Confederates also involves a possible abortion, that of Ephie Bumpass, who feels miserably guilty at her infidelity to her peasant soldier husband away fighting in the army of North Virginia under General Stonewall Jackson. Illicit sex is for her like a disease, just as her husband, Usaph, finds war to be a tainting and morally debilitating disease. But again the characters act in a morally neutral or even perverse universe; the relation between moral deserts and fate is haphazard.

Keneally's Booker Prize-winning novel, *Schindler's Ark* (1982), is closer to actual happenings and to the present day than any of his other historical works. It is also the most optimistic, the most committed to the salvific effect of goodness. Oskar Schindler was the Catholic Sudeten-German factory-owner who saved some 1500 Jews in Cracow and later in

Brinnlitz, Czechoslovakia, from execution. He was charming, dishonest, licentious and hard-drinking, but was able to exploit these qualities to allay German suspicion of his compassionate mission. The Jewish judgement on Schindler, 'He was a god, but he was not a saint', represents Keneally's interpretation both of the best human characters and of the nature of the universe. With this novel he presents a character who is unlike his previous heroes and heroines. Schindler finds that his beliefs, prejudices and habits, far from disabling him in his attempt to cope with the imposed complexities of life, are in fact a positive advantage. He is able to exploit human greed and lust in order to express his own sense of human decency.

Novelists of poetic texture: Stow, Koch, McDonald

In the metaphysical world of Randolph Stow (1935–), a good deal of guidance is provided by the *Tao Te Ching*, which, he told an interviewer, 'provides for me a satisfactory model of the world'. The eternal Tao, or 'storehouse' of all things and of non-being, forbids action that has a personal purpose, on the ground that it will necessarily fail. Approved action must be spontaneous and in accord with nature. Force and the attempt to take possession or control of another person's life, whether by personality or dogma, is forbidden, because it too is ultimately futile. More positively, 'the highest excellence is like water', because it 'dashes against and overcomes the hardest'.

In Stow's novels, accordingly, when forceful characters employ force to achieve their ends the result is usually tragedy. In his third novel, *To the Islands* (1958, revised edition 1981), the elderly missionary Stephen Heriot comes to appreciate the futility of his attempt to rule the Aboriginal mission station by force. He leaves the station on a journey to the Aboriginal islands of death, achieving in the end a Taoist vision of a gull flying into the sun and the half-promise of islands. In *Tourmaline* (1963), the setting is a derelict goldrush town in Western Australia some time in the future. The narrator is an old former policeman, the Law, capable now only of impotent benevolence. Into the moribund town is brought a young man, Michael, who in his delirious half-dead state announces that he is a water-diviner. He discovers gold, and comes to be regarded by the whites as a saviour and by the Aborigines as Mongga, the creator and rain spirit. But he fails to locate water. The Law comes to consider him not as a Christ figure but as a glamorous Lucifer, perverting the town through the lure of gold, water and reconciliation with the divine. The Law's judgement is a Taoist one: 'There is no sin but cruelty. Only one. And that original sin, that began when a man first cried to another, in his matted hair: "Take charge of my life, I am close to breaking." '

The Merry-go-round in the Sea (1965) explores the cloistral power of the family over its members. Rick Maplestead, imprisoned by the Japanese in Changi during the 1939–45 war, finds that freedom is another kind of bondage to country, family, and friends. Eventually he casts off the new shackles:

> I don't want a family, I don't want a country. Families and countries are biological accidents. I've grown up and I'm on my own. . . . I can't stand . . . this arrogant mediocrity. The shoddiness and the wowserism and the smug wild-boyos in the bars. And the unspeakable bloody boredom of belonging to a country that keeps up a sort of chorus: 'Relax, mate, relax, don't make the pace too hot.'

His younger cousin, Rob Coram, also comes to understand that 'Australia had been a myth of his own mind, and he had been, all the time, an individual.' The *noli me tangere* effect is akin to a feeling often expressed by characters in Patrick White and Thea Astley.

Midnite: The Story of a Wild Colonial Boy (1967) continues the dissatisfaction with national stereotypes in a satiric children's book. Midnite is an innocent bushranger whose raids are masterminded by his gang, Major the cockatoo and Khat the cat. He is sentenced by a judge who finds him guilty of 'aiding, abetting, procuring and giggling at the bushranging of my wig'. The specific satiric targets are, of course, the eastern states' mythology of bushranging and the obfuscation of colonial justice.

After the intense, vibrant sombreness of his *A Counterfeit Silence: Selected Poems* (1969), Stow produced no further volumes until 1979. In that year *Visitants*, drawing on the experiences of the year he spent in the Milne Bay area of Papua New Guinea in 1959, was published. Alistair Cawdor, the patrol officer, is isolated from other human beings. His wife leaves him, he becomes ill and mentally unbalanced, and eventually commits suicide. But as a patrol officer he seemed to his assistant to be 'at the centre of the world' as he sat in the middle of the resthouse at Vilakota, with its square veranda surrounded by a circle of people and houses – the Taoist earth surrounded by heaven.

The Girl Green as Elderflower (1980), completed before *Visitants*, is a companion piece, tracing the recovery of Crispin Clare, an anthropologist, from a physical and mental breakdown, including a suicide attempt. As part of his cure he settles in a Suffolk village and undertakes the writing of three twelfth-century stories (from Ralph of Coggeshall's *Chronicon Anglicanum*). They all concern visitants from other worlds (like the mysterious UFOs and carriers of cargo reported in *Visitants*) who are unable to relate to the mortals that befriend them. The stories are reworked into a timeless present in which they are adapted to Clare's village contemporaries. The method is not dissimilar to that of Christopher Koch in his use of the *wayang* puppets in *The Year of Living Dangerously*.

The Suburbs of Hell (1984), set in an East Anglian fishing town, Old Tornwich, is a chilling murder mystery. The conventional patterns of life are fractured by the need to confront fear and death, a need that persists beyond the exposure and death of the murderer. Death is represented as the ultimate invader of privacy, the last unwanted voyeur, the final destroyer of individuality. As in *Visitants* and *The Girl Green as Elderflower*, Stow exercises his considerable talents in impressionistic atmosphere and in the representation of regional speech. These are metonyms of his belief in individuality both of place and of person. His fiction and poetry are properly seen as an exploration of the outward country in which one spends one's childhood and the inward country of adulthood. In these countries the Taoist values of reticence, withdrawal, and silence are achieved amid activity, madness, and fear.

Christopher Koch (1932–), although he had a few poems accepted by the *Bulletin* while he was still at school, determined quite early to be a novelist, albeit of a poetic kind, concentrating both on narrative and on extended organic metaphors. His first novel, the semi-autobiographical *The Boys in the Island* (1958, revised 1974), replaces the discarded Catholicism of Koch's upbringing with a rather assertive pantheism. Set in Tasmania, where he grew up, it presents a counterpoint between a boy's ideal inner world and the disappointing reality of his outer life.

Across the Sea Wall (1965, revised 1982) has as its metaphysical base the Tantric aspects of Hinduism. The group of Australians and Europeans who voyage to South-east Asia find their lives are reflecting the patterns of Indo-European myth. Koch's third novel, *The Year of Living Dangerously* (1978), makes similar use of the *wayang kulit* puppet theatre of Indonesia, which presages and parallels both the political struggle between Left and Right in Indonesia in 1965 and the lives of the two main representatives of Australia, the dwarfish Australian–Chinese cameraman Billy Kwan, and the half-English, half-Australian journalist Guy Hamilton. By dwarfdom and hybridization they provide metaphors for the colonial condition of Australia, which, more than Indonesia or its political turmoil, provides the focus of the novel. As in *Across the Sea Wall*, women are often treated with a disdainfully fastidious male rejection.

By the time he completed his third novel, Koch had reconverted to Catholicism, though the pattern assigned to the characters in the novel is derived from Hindu mythology. Hamilton is represented for Kwan by the puppet of Arjuna, who has first 'to master himself before he can master others'. The contrast with Stow's administration for withdrawal and reticence is striking.

The narrator of *The Year of Living Dangerously* is another Australian journalist, Cook – perhaps a bilingual pun on *Koch*. His flat reportorial sensibility and style are a useful defence against criticism of the novel, for its insistent moralizing, emphatic patterning and narrative clichés can be attributed to the narrator, not the author.

The two volumes of poetry by Roger McDonald (1941–) contain many of the interests developed in his first two novels. They indicate his concern for ordinary, unintellectual characters in moments of great pressure, for scenes of war and flying, and for judgements about the nature of defeat. *Citizens of Mist* (1968) and *Airship* (1975) contain a number of narrative poems, often with a dreamy, floating quality in them. They also contain a good deal of disturbing, sometimes menacing, surrealism, but this is not reflected in the novels. *Airship* contains the poem '1915', which gave its name to McDonald's first novel, published in 1979, as well as other poems of the First World War. It also contains several poems about the sensation of flying, which was later to be central to the novel *Slipstream* (1982).

In *1915*, through the lives of two country boys of contrasting character, Walter Gilchrist and Billy Mackenzie, McDonald confronts, in a generally approving way, the Australian myth of Anzac, a nation going to war and coming of age through courage, endurance and bloodshed. But it is a hollow achievement, gained at the expense of Billy's sanity, Walter's capture and an Australian retreat, each of them a metaphor for McDonald's sense of the madness, entrapment and defeat of much personal and national life. Hostility exists between almost every pair of characters: the two young men; their girls, Frances Reilly and Diana Benedetto; Frances and her mother; Frances and her admirers. Such bitterness reflects the large-scale conflicts between Turks and Australians; more notionally, between England and Germany; and, spiritually, between Christianity and materialism. Personal relationships are war in miniature; war is the magnification of personal hostility.

The rich clotted poetic texture of *1915* gave way in *Slipstream* to a thinner, more matter-of-fact medium, presumably to represent the taciturnity and inarticulateness of the principal character, Roy Hilman, a pioneer aviator. After an initial show of male assertiveness, his character pales in the presence of his wife, sister and mistress. Hilman is a man of action with an obsession but no inner life. He is seen through the eyes of his friends and associates, especially his devoted biographer, Claude McKechnie. Stunt flying, outback flying, trans-Pacific flying, and the formation of airline companies easily outweigh his interest in women and men. When he vanishes over Malaya there is the suspicion that his mechanic, with whose wife he is having an affair, may be responsible. The novel has a very large cast of characters – by contrast with the domestic scale of much of *1915* – most of them being only lightly sketched. The narrative is in a sense a revised version of Hilman's life, correcting and supplementing the superficial and heroic biography written by McKechnie. But as a whole it lacks the mythic unity and psychological plausibility of *1915*.

Novels written in the late 1970s and 1980s by writers who had first come to prominence as poets frequently have a static, mannered, picturesque air. It is as if the scenes were viewed through a picture frame or were stills from a slow-moving *plein-air* Australian film. McDonald is least subject to this predilection, Hall and Shapcott most, Malouf intermittently so.

Absurdist novelists: Ireland, Foster and others

Of the more sceptical and anti-metaphysical novelists, the most prolific has been David Ireland (1927–). An anti-heroic writer, he works by the accretion of small narrative segments concerning a large cast of loosely related characters to make points about the dangers of multinational corporations, the displacement of people by machines, and the wasteful use of natural resources in Australia. He is against all systems, including socialism, critical of the quiescence of ordinary workers, an anarchist who believes that oppressive systems will prevail. Pretension, wealth, commercial rapacity, industrial incompetence, bosses, the media, formal education, conformity, rationality and violence are all subject to his comic satire. His world view is bleak, ending in near-nihilistic despair. No metaphysical comfort is to be expected, for the universe is utterly indifferent.

His narrative method is fragmentary and disconnected, qualities contrived in the early novels by rearranging hundreds of cards containing short scenes into a significant order. Ireland considers the mosaic effect, derived originally from Laurence Sterne and the nineteenth-century Brazilian writer Machado de Assis, to be comparable to the effect of reading a newspaper or watching a montaged film.

His first novel, *The Chantic Bird* (1968), deals with a teenage delinquent who tries to find freedom from the social and commercial pressures to conform. His attempts to subvert the system by shock tactics are, however, failures, because workers are too quiescent and apathetic to be stirred even by horrendous events. In the end he is reduced to asking, 'If there is no other life, why is this one so lousy?'

The Unknown Industrial Prisoner (1971) concerns the factory-related lives of a large group of workers in an oil refinery, which is depicted like a penal colony. It is, in fact, located on Botany Bay, where Captain Cook 'first stepped ashore' in 1770. It is a rather despairing depiction of a male-dominated world in which hearty drinking, a limited code of mateship, story-telling, brawling and an off-handed acceptance of women for sexual purposes are standard behaviour. *The Flesheaters* (1972) continues the combination of absurdism and sickening reality in a confined setting. This time the prison is a 'home' where the rejects of a profit-oriented society, the poor, the unemployed and the elderly, are forced to live in sheds, trees or even a dog kennel.

Burn (1975) is Ireland's one realistic novel. Like his play *Image in the Clay* (1958, published 1964), it deals with fringe-dwelling Aborigines, whom Ireland sees as other rejects from the systems of white society. His general view of the depressing spiritlessness of white society is expressed in the statement by one character,

> the dead heart of Australia is . . . right back there in the cities. Not in the sand and the mulga and the stones burning hot under the sun and smoke going straight up into the sky like a spear at sunset. It's in the big blackness under the neon signs.

The Glass Canoe (1976) returns to the world of *The Unknown Industrial Prisoner*, though the setting this time is a Sydney suburban pub, the Southern Cross, located near an oil refinery. Bizarre stories, sexual deception and athleticism, and the urge to violence build up into a destructive denouement grander in scale and brutality than the assault on the brothel in *The Unknown Industrial Prisoner*. After a mammoth pub brawl, the society of pub-dwellers is dispersed disconsolately to less companionable waterholes.

Ireland's next two books, *A Woman of the Future* (1979) and *City of Women* (1981), are both centred on women. In the first, a female counterpart in some ways to *The Chantic Bird*, Alethea Hunt is a girl growing up in a Sydney suburb. She is a determined predator for all experiences; she lives for the moment, seeks sexual partners in great profusion and variety, and seems to represent Ireland's vision of a future feminist type that is physically strong, psychologically domineering, and triumphant in her power plays with men. She also represents Ireland's view of Australia as an adolescent society: 'The country is a virgin, as I feel I am essentially.' In the end she is metamorphosed into a leopard which flees into the Blue Mountains. Unlike the sterility, complacency and materialism of the society of the cities, Alethea has resilience and resourcefulness. She is an image of growth and fertility, which Ireland suggests may be found in the countryside, away from the cities, or may become available some time in the future. Alethea's story is fabricated from her notebooks, diaries and papers, in a manner akin to that of Peter Mathers in *The Wort Papers*.

City of Women is also centred on a woman, also set in Sydney, and also placed in the future. By this time, Sydney has been taken over by women. Men are allowed into the city on only one day of the year, for the Anzac Day march, though they are tolerated at night in order to provide sex shows for women. Billie Shockley is a retired woman engineer, tough but sentimental, experienced but innocent. She tells a succession of stories acquired as confidante or eavesdropper. The novel is, in fact, her long self-exploratory letter to her former lover, Bobbie, who has deserted her. This female world in which men are the marginal characters is, however, singularly like the eccentric, neurotic, perverse and diseased world of the male-dominated novels, and the violence is even more horrendous.

After this maelstrom of desolation, *Archimedes and the Seagle* (1984) took an entirely different turn. It lacks sex and violence, but retains Ireland's zany surrealism. Archimedes is a red setter who has taught himself to read. He regards human beings as listless and unenterprising, but he is fascinated by seagulls, to whom (unlike human beings) he can talk. In particular, he admires one seagull who remains apart from the others, soaring high over Sydney Harbour. Archimedes calls him Seagle. Archimedes' moral values are low-key and conventional. He believes in patience, gentleness, helpfulness, kindness, respect for nature and concern for the future. He advocates a democratic Australia for ordinary citizens, who should be tolerant, patient and affectionate, and be able to laugh at themselves. The novel, fragmentary in form, is a sensitively written fable, working on both the literal canine and the allegorical levels. Ireland has, this time, been more direct in his value judgements.

Peter Mathers (1931–) is another absurdist iconoclast who, like Ireland, uses short discrete blocks of narrative. Unlike Ireland, however, he is a painfully slow writer who has so far produced only two novels and a volume of short stories. *Trap* (1966) concerns a subversive, amoral forty-year-old man, Jack Trap, of mixed ancestry including Irish and Aboriginal, 'fermenting with ideas of anarchism, nihilism, Buddhism, allisms and wild, general revolt'. The satire is directed against conformity, hypocrisy, religion, and many of the other objects of Ireland's satire. Mathers also presents a view of Australian history through Trap's bizarre ancestry, a view that is subversive of conventional imported values and protective of the land and the Aborigines. The narrative, ranging from Tierra del Fuego, Hobart and Sydney in the early nineteenth century to Melbourne in the 1960s is also constantly being subverted, being taken out of the hands of the diarist, David David, by others.

The Wort Papers (1972) provides a satiric view of many aspects of the Great Australian Dream – the Englishman making good, the dream of wealth to be made in the outback, the epic journey, the family saga, xenophobia and colour prejudice, and many other staples of historical, literary and social documentation. Almost all is narrated through the Wort Papers, an anarchic collection of fragmentary notes by Percy Wort, the scapegrace brother of an executive in a communications firm.

Mathers' stories in *A Change for the Better* (1984) continue his surrealistic irreverence, this time in so condensed and concentrated a style that much of the reader's attention is inevitably directed to the pyrotechnic language rather than to the objects of Mathers' satire. As in the novels, the emphasis is on persecuted outsiders, who manage to maintain their freedom and independence amid a society in chaos.

David Foster (1944–) once described the qualities of his fiction as 'ambivalence, flippancy, obscurity, wit, gnosticism, guilt, schizophrenia, monomania, disgust and the struggle to emerge from all this ratiocination grown tired towards something better'. What sets him apart from Ireland and

Mathers are the obscure gnostic hymns to mystery and oddity that appear in his work.

Foster began writing after a career as a research scientist. His early fictional works, including his first novel, *The Pure Land* (1974), were conventional and literary in an antiquated way. Then he modernized and experimented with his style, introduced ambivalence, flippancy and self-reference. His second novel, *Moonlite* (1981), is a hilarious account of the spiritual desolation of colonialism. It is set in the Western Isles of Scotland, where an alcoholic chief, the MacIshmael, sells his birthright to the English. On an even remoter island, Hiphoray, an albino, Finbar MacDuffie, perhaps one of the Sidhe, is born. Both islands are clearly allegorical representations of Australia: the English dispossess the original inhabitants in the name of enlightenment, improvement, religion and commerce; a priest introduces rabbits; Finbar journeys to England for education, and later experiences the goldfields of the New West Highlands (Australia), where a drink-besotted population mindlessly brawls. Ultimately Finbar, saint and magician, dies in an Aboriginal ritual, wrestling with the Rainbow Fella before reappearing as pure spirit, rejecting his brief experience of humanity.

Plumbum (1983) is centred on a rock band – Foster himself having played modern jazz professionally. The first half, dealing with the birth of the Last Great Heavy Metal Rock Band of the Western World, moves slowly, perhaps in sympathy with the lead weight of the title. The second half, in which the band's fortunes expand internationally, accelerates into Foster's zaniest pace. The band, now rechristened Plumbum, struggles to survive in Calcutta ('The anti-Canberra: *totally* unplanned'), where each member conducts a bizarre disconnected life, Felix as a rickshaw wallah, Rollo as an entrepreneur on the black market, Pete as operator of a medical clinic, Sharon in Ananda Marga, Jason as a visionary. But Nick, the impresario, returns, brings them together again, and they triumph in a tour of Holland. *Plumbum* is a kind of paean to rock music, its practitioners, their lives and their adherents. Its Indian and Dutch scenes bear on the experiences of the Beatles, and its prose style approximates to the sense of dissociation often produced by hard rock or by hallucinogenic drugs. But the many references to Australia suggest also that in its dream of self-hypnosis and untold wealth the rock band is another symbol for Foster's own country.

Dog Rock: A Postal Pastoral (1984) is a witty satiric comedy directed at the postal service, railway system, trade unions, feminists, policemen, and doctors and lawyers pretending to be farmers as a means of avoiding tax. It is narrated by D'Arcy D'Oliveres, a full-time rural postman and part-time detective, who is a repository of arcane knowledge about rural and mechanical pursuits. He is also drolly self-aware and self-critical, with a comic inventiveness comparable to that of the characters of J. P. Donleavy or Flann O'Brien.

Satirical and domestic novelists

Almost all the novels of Thea Astley (1925–) deal with small-town philistinism, emotional selfishness, moral struggles, ritualized power relationships, and vindictive or retributive violence against outsiders. Her prose is tart and coruscating, reminiscent in its devastating wit of the novels of Margaret Atwood.

Girl with a Monkey (1958) begins Thea Astley's study of the emptiness and sterility of country towns and of many who live in them. As in later works, there are outsiders, Elsie (the girl escaping from her city admirer or 'monkey') and Laura, who provide a satiric point of view. In *A Descant for Gossips* (1960) the outsiders are the teachers in a small town, particularly Moller and Helen Striebel, who drift into an affair that arouses the lubricity of pupils, town gossips and the officious headmaster, Findlay. But the most sensitive character is a town girl, Vinny Lalor, whose loneliness is temporarily assuaged by Helen but who is mortified to find her gift left behind in the bottom drawer of Helen's hotel room. The girl's bitter recognition of her own limited worth even to one she admired as a friend is a common epiphany in Thea Astley's work; so is the violent outcome – in this instance her suicide.

The Well Dressed Explorer (1962) is set in the city, but its central character, George Brewster, experiences a similar sense of inconsequence, even in the eyes of the Catholic Church. This novel is unusual in being a single documented biography rather than a set of impressions of individuals. *The Slow Natives* (1965) returns to a more impressionistic mode, but continues the less floriated style of *The Well Dressed Explorer*. It continues also the interest in the way Catholicism deals with the permissive society.

A Boat Load of Home Folk (1968) balances satiric wit and affection for the aged. It manages to combine comedy and pathos in, for instance, the island boy's riposte to the aroused spinster, Miss Trumper: 'Oh no! You very ugly laydee.' *The Acolyte* (1972) is the account, in a bravura display of prose, of Paul Vesper's devotion as acolyte to the blind musician Jack Holberg. Holberg's effect on those around him is almost entirely destructive, and in the end Paul makes a violent ritual gesture of defiance against Holberg's sycophantic court. In this novel, as in earlier ones, the forms of Catholicism are used in the narrative as an ironic reflection of the lack of Christian substance in the characters themselves.

In *A Kindness Cup* (1974) and *An Item from the Late News* (1982) the return of a social alien to a brutal and vulgar country town is central to the plot. In the earlier novel it is Tom Dorahy, the schoolmaster; in the later, Gabby, an insignificant painter of the insignificances of life. In both there is a gentle Christ-like figure who is betrayed and sacrificed by male viciousness and 'mateship'. Thea Astley has great compassion for the outsider or misfit and fascination for the inadequacy of mateship and other myths to describe the self-assertive and brutal rituals of such males as Lieutenant Buckmaster in *A Kindness Cup* and the Vietnam veteran Moon in *An Item from the Late News*. She did in fact consider calling the later novel *Mythfits*.

Thea Astley's small towns are envisaged as epitomes of Australia, as are David Ireland's factories and pubs or David Foster's islands and rock band. Her most recent settings have been in the suspicious insular towns of north Queensland, where she has placed all eight of the stories in *Hunting the Wild Pineapple* (1979). In one story, 'A Man who is Tired of Swiper's Creek is Tired of Life', the narrator, Leverson, describes north Queensland as 'the place where anything screwball is normal and often where what is normal is horrible'. In this story a deaf old woman is dumped by her family in the 'stranger country' of Swiper's Creek, and it is certain she will meet with indifference if not hostility. The problem of gaining respect and value for human beings remains.

Elizabeth Harrower (1928–) is also a satirist of vulgarity and conventionality, but her characters, though more fully developed than Astley's, are themselves often conventional. Her style is also less acerbic and less subtle. The best of her novels is probably *The Watch Tower* (1966), which retains the air of menace of her earlier works but avoids injuring it by melodrama. As in the earlier novels, the prime interest is in modes of freedom. Stella, a widow, wants to free herself from responsibility for her two daughters and set off for England. One daughter, Laura, seeks to free herself from insecurity by marrying her employer. But he proves irascible to both Laura and her sister Clare, and generous only in his dealings with the younger men to whom he impulsively sells his business. Clare is the one character who comes to terms with the country and finds no need to escape.

The expatriate novelist Shirley Hazzard (1931–) writes of passion balanced by a sense of decorum or conformity, just as romance is balanced by satire and wit in her style. Her first volume, *Cliffs of Fall, and Other Stories* (1963), and her third, *People in Glass Houses* (1967), are ironically related stories frequently satirizing the inept and self-regarding bureaucracy of which she was once a part during her employment in the United Nations. They are more sharply focused than the often rather languid and mannered studies of love in the short novels *The Evening of the Holiday* (1966) and *The Bay of Noon* (1970), both set in Italy.

Shirley Hazzard's third novel, *The Transit of Venus* (1980), studies the progress of love in six main characters. It is a Jamesian work of studied nuance, occasional sententiousness and significant detail. Two Australian sisters, Caroline (Caro) and Grace Bell, come to England to learn about Europe. Their lives are, however, destined to be an exploration of love. The transit of Venus – a reference to Captain Cook's voyage, in which he both observed the transit and explored the east coast of Australia – is used as a recurring image for many events and situations, including travel, dislocation, disappointment in love, Caro herself and the discovery of Australia. Transits are both physical, between houses and countries, and emotional, between life and death and from love to love. As with Cook's scientists, so calculations about the transit of the emotional Venus are often hopelessly wrong: 'The years of preparation.

And then, from one hour to the next, all over.' This is said *à propos* Ted Tice, Caro's last lover, an astronomer who had loved her from his first sight of her thirty years earlier, but having finally gained her love was destined not to consummate it.

The Transit of Venus is a richly textured book that both uses complex patterns of symbolic imagery and denies that they are in any way foreordained or predictable. They are imposed by the author or narrator.

Barbara Hanrahan (1939–) is a novelist who began with two conventional, but minutely observed, novels and subsequently moved into gothic fabulism. *The Scent of Eucalyptus* (1973) is a semi-autobiographical first-person account of a girl growing up in Adelaide in the 1950s. The adolescent narrator is an inquisitive voyeur, privy to bizarre secrets and prepared to act out roles to disguise her real feelings. These qualities continue in later novels, though the events perceived become more bizarre. *Sea-green* (1974) follows another common pattern in the Australian novel, the rejection of domestic drabness in favour of experience in London, with the eventual finding of a satisfactory lover.

The Albatross Muff (1977), *Where the Queens All Strayed* (1978), *The Peach Groves* (1979) and *The Frangipani Gardens* (1980) are all set in the past, in England, Adelaide or New Zealand. They are period pieces of grotesquerie, full of physical and psychological deformity and unusual sexual appetites. All have at least part of the novel written from the point of view of a prying child or adolescent, sometimes in a rather cloying imitation of childish sentence patterns. Barbara Hanrahan said that she saw the novels as 'being concerned with contrasts, contradictions: beauty and horror, love and death, frivolity and menace; the precisely-detailed world of substance, the darker world of instinct, the queerness of mind split from body, the absurd fantasy of the "ordinary" '. The central characters generally find fulfilment in the discovery or mastery of an art-making power, capable of wounding and healing psychologically and socially. Only women achieve good art; men are either effete poseurs as artists or sexual manipulators of young girls.

In *Dove* (1982) Barbara Hanrahan returned to a more realistic mode and to a period shortly before her own experience, Adelaide in the early decades of this century. Once again, time seems suspended in favour of a detailed visual evocation of a mosaic world seen from a child's point of view. *Kewpie Doll* (1983) returns to similar material to that in *The Scent of Eucalyptus*, Adelaide in the years after the 1939–45 war. This time the emphasis on the uncomprehending innocence of the voyeuristic child, on physical ugliness and deformity and on sexual manipulation is greater. The sense of an artistic life being the ideal solution to and escape from the drabness of suburban life is also more emphasized. Barbara Hanrahan has reworked her realistic material to produce her characteristic air of a slightly sinister fairy tale, a story that leaps fantastically from the ordinary to the hallucinatory in a manner corresponding to her notion of the quality of artistic power.

A less gothic transmutation of outer reality occurs in *Tamarisk Row* (1974), the first novel of Gerald Murnane (1939–). The central figure, Clement Killeaton, is a boy who dreams about and creates for himself 'a country that is almost a perfect copy of Australia' as a refuge from the drabness of his own life. In a later novel, *The Plains* (1984), Murnane has the narrator, a film-maker, say that he looks 'for anything in the landscape that seemed to hint at some elaborate meaning behind appearances'. The plains of the title are a geographical feature of 'Inner Australia', which lies, as a country of the mind, beyond the populated coast of 'Outer Australia'. Murnane is, then, in the long tradition that uses literal inland Australia as a metaphor for a state of mind or of society. His distinction is that the 'literal' inland Australia is recognized from the start as unreal.

Writers of short fiction: Moorhouse and others

Towards the end of the 1960s many factors operated to effect a new approach to short fiction in Australia. Many of them were repressive or constraining factors that forced new initiatives to break out into new forms both of fiction and of publishing. The dissatisfaction of young people with Australia's involvement in the Vietnam War and the American alliance, the beginnings of a widespread use of prohibited hallucinogenic drugs, resentment at the prohibition of much literature and some political commentary published overseas, changing attitudes to sexual experimentation and to the publication of pornography, a sense of the disparity and inconsistency between what was available in film or television and what was available in print, and impatience with a Federal government that was tired and fumbling all produced an air of urgency about the need for change. The Vietnam War itself directed attention to the United States and to both political dissent and literary experimentation in that country and in other parts of the Americas. The fabulist work of Juan Luis Borges (1899–) and Donald Barthelme (1933–), the notion of literature as process, game or lie, and the possibilities for revelatory, confessional uses of literature all came to notice.

To find outlets for their new fiction, prose writers in the early 1970s often had to go beyond conventional and established institutions. Frank Moorhouse's first volume, *Futility and Other Animals* (1969), was published by a 'girlie' magazine in which some of the stories had appeared. Moorhouse, with Michael Wilding and Carmel Kelly, established a new fiction magazine, *Tabloid Story*, in 1972. It was a 'parasite' or 'piggyback' magazine, appearing, somewhat randomly, within the covers and among the regular content of various 'host' magazines. It served a valuable purpose in securing a large unaccustomed readership for many more-or-less experimental writers until 1984. Without the need for capital and with most of the costs of payment to contributors and typesetting paid by the Literature Board of the Australia Council, the editors – who varied over the years – could devote their attention to the primary business of selection. Small, short-lived, often duplicated magazines were also a feature of the early 1970s, and, although they mostly carried poetry, some did make space for stories.

Under the managership of Frank Thompson, the University of Queensland Press, already noted for the Paperback Poets series it began in 1970, branched into new prose fiction with the publication of Michael Wilding's *Aspects of the Dying Process* and Rodney Hall's *The Ship on the Coin* in 1972. Two new, small, 'alternative' presses, Wild and Woolley in Sydney and Outback in Melbourne, issued their first titles in 1974 and managed to attract even established writers. Some resentment was expressed by the Australian Book Publishers' Association at the grant of Literature Board subsidies to titles published by these presses, on the ground that the Board, by supporting work that had been rejected by the large established firms, was interfering in the literary market place. The largest firm, Angus and Robertson, was also suffering the loss of many of its best writers in the wake of a bitterly resented commercial takeover. But the effect of the new publishers was to goad the larger commercial presses into renewed activity, so that in the later 1970s there was substantial competition for fiction writers, both novelists and short-story writers. Above all, it was clear that a volume of short stories had once again become viable commercially, after nearly two decades of unsaleability.

Frank Moorhouse (1938–) had stories published in *Southerly, Westerly, Meanjin* and *Overland* from 1957 onwards, but found that 'As I developed away from the humanist tradition of the Australian story – sympathetic to the working class and kind to kangaroos – my stories were rejected from the literary magazines.' After a period of rejection between 1965 and 1970 he began to gain publication in the *Bulletin* and the politically liberal *Nation Review*. *Futility and Other Animals* (1969), though never banned, was often sold from under the counter because of its racy sexual scenes. It was also admired for its documentation of the inner-suburban alternative society. With *The Americans, Baby* (1972), the nature of what Moorhouse calls his 'discontinuous narrative' became clear. Some of the stories used characters with the same names as those in *Futility and Other Animals* in ways that suggested Moorhouse was simultaneously engaged on fragments of several novels each made up of discrete scenes or stories. But it was also obvious that the previously published stories had been selected and arranged to give coherence to this volume. Many of them dealt with people getting into social groupings or patterns that they were unable to cope with, or being dishonest even with themselves. The most frequently recurring character was Becker, the hypochondriac American Coca-Cola executive inevitably out of his depth in every Australian social gathering.

The Electrical Experience (1974) includes Becker, but only as a peripheral acquaintance of T. George McDowell, the proprietor of a country soft-drink factory. The stories combine in a richly detailed account of McDowell, the Australian equivalent of Babbitt or Becker, adherent of Progress, Rotary and civic spirit. But he too is out of his depth when he finds that neither he, his factory nor the town have any future. The format of this book, with its photographs, documents, and pages printed in white-on-black, extends Moorhouse's concept of pushing prose fiction to the borders of visual art and film.

Conference-ville (1976) narrows its focus to intellectuals attending a convention. It is an acerbic satire of the rituals, role-playing, gestures and power games of such settings. *Tales of Mystery and Romance* (1977), related in the first person by a narrator constantly aware of himself and constantly questioning the shape of his stories, covers a wider range, including relationships with ex-wives, family, women lovers, and Milton, a homosexual lover now seduced by spiritualism. Neither mystery nor romance proves to offer satisfaction to any of the characters.

The Everlasting Secret Family and Other Secrets (1980) provides a history of sexuality in four sections, covering the period from the 1930s to the 1970s. T. George McDowell and other characters from earlier volumes appear again, as do the now customary effect of disillusion and the sense of reaching an impasse. Moorhouse's belief that his work is a kind of endless dialogue 'with gender, with the notion of "commitment", with nationality, with self – and with form' is amply demonstrated. The documentary nature of his work, his fascination with tribal rituals and the possibilities they offer for revealing or obscuring human nature, becomes increasingly evident with each new volume.

Michael Wilding (1942–) is far less mimetic than Moorhouse. He is a fabulist, more concerned with the process of and the reasons for fictionalizing than with the object fictionalized. He writes more of sexual and other fantasies in surreal assemblages, though often with the same flat, dead-pan tone as Moorhouse. He is also committed to Marxism, and this causes him to be concerned with his characters' desire to gain control over their own lives and influence over the lives of others by the manipulation of language, in particular by the inventing of stories that embody and advocate their view of the world. He is also ideologically committed to a kind of cottage-industry view of literature, something that leads him into avoidance of smooth narrative surfaces; the deliberate retention of evidence of cuts, joins, and leaps; and preference for publication through individual or collective effort.

His short-story volumes, *Aspects of the Dying Process* (1972),

The West Midland Underground (1975), *Scenic Drive* (1976) and *The Phallic Forest* (1978), show a constant concern for experimentation. What remains through experiments that assimilate and discard the influence of Henry James, Jack Kerouac and Richard Brautigan is a slightly unreal, dreamy quality, a sense of being in a literary self-referential world that bears only faint resemblances to spontaneous life. His novels, *Living Together* (1974), *The Short Story Embassy* (1975) and *Pacific Highway* (1982), at first hint at and then embody dreams of a recovered Eden or earthly paradise, combining fantasy and ideological acceptability.

Murray Bail (1941–), author of a volume of short stories, *Contemporary Portraits, and Other Stories* (1975; republished as *The Drover's Wife, and Other Stories*, 1984), and a novel, *Homesickness* (1980), has a similar internationalist outlook to Wilding and a similar interest in the experimental and the surreal. He is wary of literature – and painting, for he is also an art critic – that 'is still primarily concerned with getting ourselves on our own two feet, of establishing our Australianness'. Influenced by Proust, Kafka, Hemingway, Patrick White and Michel Tournier, Bail's stories are reflexive, full of literary and artistic references and jokes, parodic and self-consciously modernist. They are spare in the presentation of their locales, but in any case locale is one of the aspects of story-telling that Bail calls in question. As he says in 'The Drover's Wife', an interrogation of Russell Drysdale's painting, 'It is the outback – but where exactly? South Australia? It could easily be Queensland, Western Australia, the Northern Territory. We don't know. You could never find that spot.'

Morris Lurie (1938–), the prolific author of short stories, novels, children's books, television scripts and international journalism, had a notable success with his first book, the novel *Rappaport* (1966). It is the breathlessly busy account, largely in dialogue, of a day in the life of Joe Rappaport, a Melbourne antique-dealer with a Walter-Mittyish tendency to fabulous daydreams. Lurie later came to regard it as 'all surfaces'. A later novel, *Flying Home* (1978), has the same comic and bizarre hyperbole and the same furious pace of narration, but a much deeper exploration of the spiritual hollowness of the homeless Jewish migrant who feels excluded from all family warmth. In several volumes of stories, notably *Happy Times* (1969) and *Dirty*

Friends (1981), he uses a similar international rootlessness as the setting-off point for fabulist ambition, consolation, and pathos. His children's stories, such as *The 27th Annual African Hippopotamus* (1968) and *Arlo the Dandy Lion* (1971), offer a more whimsical version of his fabulism.

Peter Carey (1943–) has a similar combination of realism crossing into fantasy and absurdism, but the pace of his narration is slower. After discarding some closely textured hieratic novel manuscripts, he began to specialize in short stories, managing to combine in one style the ritualistic and the spontaneous, the mandarin and the demotic, the poetic and the prosaic. In his first volume, *The Fat Man in History* (1974), which included the stories 'Crabs' and 'American Dreams', most of the characters are defeated or exploited by the demands and dreams of others. *War Crimes* (1979) has more surrealism and science fiction in stories such as 'Do You Love Me?', 'The Chance' and 'Exotic Pleasures', concerning, respectively, worlds in which people dematerialize, transform themselves genetically and come in contact with extra-terrestrial mystery.

Carey's novel *Bliss* (1981) veers again towards the realistic side of his balancing-act. Harry Joy, a man in advertising, dies briefly during a heart attack. On his return to life his perceptions retain something of an eternal quality. He is now dissatisfied with what he sees as a life of hell, advertising carcinogenic products, hypocritically accepting a stale marriage, pandering to the selfish dreams of his children. He finds a Virgilian guide through hell in the person of Honey Barbara, a drop-out and part-time prostitute who is full of dreams and ideals. Escaping with her help from the lowest level of hell, the asylum where he has been committed, he retreats to an idyllic rain forest where natural regeneration produces happiness. Like Wilding, Carey is fascinated by the power of stories to control and shape lives. *Bliss* is a novel conducted by stories, a novel in which events and situations such as marriage and the advertising-business are constituted by the assembly of legends and mythologies. The final state of bliss is constituted in part by stories told in the forest and by the forest, though in this section of the novel there is not the tart satire of the earlier depictions of capitalism and family politics.

Gerard Lee (1951–) was clearly influenced in his early stories by Moorhouse, Bail and Carey, as well as directly by their American counterparts. As in Moorhouse, the detached cool *faux-naïf* narrator is as often the object of irony as the denizens he describes – including Zen Buddhists and bellicose feminists. Lee's *Pieces for Glass Piano* (1978) has an abrasive and aggressive use of language, which is modified in his first novel, *True Love and How to Get It* (1982). It is an exercise in the sexual picaresque, with much benevolent social satire at the expense of several sub-cultures in Brisbane, such as hippies, punks and butch feminists.

A less experimental writer, but one who has absorbed many characteristics of the Australian short story from Lawson to White and beyond is James McQueen (1934–). He handles exact descriptions of environments well and has a melodramatic sense of atmosphere and emotion. The masculine voice of his stories in *The Escape Machine* (1981) and *Uphill Runner* (1984) and of his novel *Hook's Mountain* (1982) seems ill at ease with female characters but thoroughly at home with male vulnerability and sensitivity. His male characters tend to be trying to escape from family commitments, the aging process and the boredom of suburbia.

Novelists of the later 1970s

Elizabeth Jolley (1923–), a diarist and writer all her life, achieved her first book publication only in 1976. It was *Five Acre Virgin, and Other Stories*, later followed by two other collections, *The Travelling Entertainer, and Other Stories* (1979) and *Woman in a Lampshade* (1983). Jolley, brought up in the English Midlands in a family she describes as 'half English and three-quarters Viennese', migrated to Australia in 1959. Her stories and her novels, *Palomino* (1980), *The Newspaper of Claremont Street* (1981), *Mr Scobie's Riddle* (1983), *Miss Peabody's Inheritance* (1983) and *Milk and Honey* (1984), deal with displacement, transplantation, obsessive attachment to plots of land, homosexual attraction, death and decay, the sense of entrapment, and the struggle to survive. Some of the novels are closely related to particular stories, *Palomino* to 'The Libation', about a disappointing lesbian relationship, *The Newspaper of Claremont Street* to 'Pear Tree Dance', about a gossipy cleaning lady who dreams of a plot of land of her own, and *Mr Scobie's*

Riddle to 'Hilda's Wedding', about the night life in a bizarre hospital.

Milk and Honey seems to return for some of its details to a period of Elizabeth Jolley's life not previously much used for fictional purposes, her own childhood. It is set in a family, located outside Perth, that is European in custom and manners. The sweetness of the madeira and biscuits passed round during the musical evenings is chillingly at odds with the air of physical and mental sourness and decay that pervades the household, an air reminiscent of that surrounding the venal Matron Price and her old people's home in *Mr Scobie's Riddle*.

Elizabeth Jolley's fiction, with its precise narrative voice, almost dead-pan, but just slightly surprised at the horror, peculiarity and farce of what it describes, is full of eccentric characters, many speaking in strange ethnic, regional or class accents. In an interview in 1980 she said that her view of life was made up largely of 'ordinary men and women, some kinds of criminals, the sexually unconventional and those for whom there seems to be no place in the world'. Her wide-eyed prose is an admirable medium for snaring exotic characters and moments of high poignancy and farce. If she sometimes breaks the nervous tone of her narrative, it is because she is prepared to take large emotional risks.

Elizabeth Jolley is an admirer of Helen Garner (1942–), a younger writer also prepared to tackle the painful material of everyday life. *Monkey Grip* (1977) is a novel, set in Carlton, an inner suburb of Melbourne, about the sub-culture of subsistence, communal living and drug-taking. Its strength lies in its presentation of human relations interacting with the squalor that many characters accept as an index of righteousness or self-righteousness. Her two novellas, *Honour and Other People's Children* (1980), concern the difficulties of adjusting to divorce and remarriage when a child binds three adults together, and the attempts of two women to form a communal household based on honour.

Another novella, *The Children's Bach* (1984), is more closely and finely textured than her earlier works. Music is used as an index of sexuality in a work covering Garner's familiar territory of urban adults and children observing each other's shifts in emotional and social attachment. Characters counterpoint and separate, new subjects are introduced, some turn upside down, and old subjects return transformed in this study of modern love and sexuality. One of the finest character depictions, as so often in Garner's work, is that of an adolescent girl, Poppy, the cello-playing daughter of Elizabeth and her long-term but faithless lover Philip, a rock musician. Poppy observes and judges the adults with an innocent common sense far superior to most of their own judgements and self-assessments.

Robert Drewe (1943–) is a realist writer who manages to combine good journalistic description with more subtle and reticent observation, and black comedy with suspense and thriller elements. His first novel, *The Savage Crows* (1976), within an unsuccessful self-consciously literary framework, offers a commentary on the near-extermination of the Tasmanian Aborigines, and on the gruesome mutilation, supposedly for scientific purposes, of the body of the last full-blooded male Tasmanian in 1869. The material, including the studies of Wooraddy, Truganini and George Augustus Robinson, was later treated more passionately, lyrically and philosophically by Colin Johnson in *Doctor Wooreddy's Prescription for Enduring the Ending of the World*.

Drewe's *A Cry in the Jungle Bar* (1979) is set in Manila, with excursions to India, Sri Lanka and Bangladesh. Cullen is an Australian expert on water buffalo who works for a United Nations agency. He is a lumbering, apprehensive, puzzled man, still proud of his strength and fitness, but aware of his incapacity to control political or domestic events. The novel is a study of two sensitive people – Cullen and his wife, Margaret, who returns to Australia – living in a state of continuous tension in a country described by one character as having been 'three hundred years in a convent and forty in Hollywood'.

The Bodysurfers (1983) consists of twelve stories, many including the character David Lang, all set on the coast – in New South Wales, Western Australia and California. The concerns are marriage break-up, affairs ending in disappointment, expectations punctured, and desperation and crisis in the lives of middle-class professionals.

Another former journalist, Blanche d'Alpuget (1944–), set her first two novels, *Monkeys in the Dark* (1980) and *Turtle Beach* (1981), in South-east Asia, the first in Indonesia (in 1966, immediately after the period covered by Koch's *The Year of Living Dangerously*), the second in Malaysia. Her work is less

symbolic than Koch's, less male-oriented than Koch's or
Drewe's. It reveals a wider appreciation of recent military,
diplomatic, economic and political history in South-east Asia
than either of the other writers' works and it is also more
concerned with intellectual questions about religion, human
motivation and responsibility. Unlike Drewe and Koch, who
emphasize the alienness of the Australian journalist or official
when transported to Asia, Blanche d'Alpuget creates central
characters who penetrate energetically into the milieu. While
they are people of determination and prejudice, their ideas are
not blinkered by Australianness; they are, indeed, turned as
critically on Australian mores as on those of South-east Asia.
Blanche d'Alpuget's central characters, though having homes
and families in Australia, are unusually free of the chauvinism,
overt and covert, possessed by Drewe's and Koch's Australian
characters.

In *Turtle Beach*, the relations between sex and power are
inescapable. Many of the characters, including the Australian
journalist Judith Wilkes, seek power and fame, using sex more
as a product or symbol of power than as a means towards it.
Judith's animal-inhabited dreams are useful indicators of her
inner confusion and lack of self-possession, though their
over-use betrays a mannerism popular in Australian fiction as
a means of combating the criticism of externality or
superficiality. Koch's symbolism is another mannerism used
for a similar purpose.

11
The uniqueness of recent writing

Aboriginal writers

THE last twenty-five years have seen the development of two groups of writers not much represented before: Aboriginal writers in English and migrant writers in English or in European (and, more recently still, Asian) languages. Ironically, both oldest and newest Australians share the themes of displacement, alienation, loneliness and withdrawal already familiar from nineteenth-century writing about convicts and reluctant settlers.

The first major Aboriginal writer was Kath Walker (1920–), whose first volume of poetry, *We are Going* (1964), sold out within three days of publication. Subsequent volumes, *The Dawn is at Hand* (1966) and *My People: A Kath Walker Collection* (1970, revised 1981), also went into reprints. Her volume of legends from her own tribal area, *Stradbroke Dreamtime* (1972), and her illustrated children's book, *Father Sky and Mother Earth* (1981), represent further efforts to promote wider knowledge of Aboriginal culture.

The preservation and dissemination of Aboriginal culture, exposure of the injustices suffered by Aborigines at the hands of white settlers, and adjurations to right the wrongs and produce interracial harmony are the themes of most of her poems. Other poems tell of love, often thwarted by custom or misunderstanding. Walker's voice is more declamatory than musical, suited for oral recitation of the short, self-contained lines. Her work has touches of humour that leaven the horror, outrage and piteousness of her subjects, but her best poems are those, such as 'We are Going', that ironically contrast a sense of the epic Dreaming with the pathos of contemporary disenchantment and misery.

The poetry of Jack Davis (1917–), published in *The First-born, and Other Poems* (1970) and *Jagardoo: Poems from Aboriginal Australia* (1978), is full of poignant regret for the past and, in the second volume particularly, vehement protest about contemporary injustice. It is, however, in his two plays, *Kullark* (1979) and *The Dreamers* (1973, expanded 1982), that he has found his *métier*. In *Kullark* (published with *The Dreamers* in 1983), Davis covers 150 years of Aboriginal–European contact in Western Australia, with glimpses of an idyllic time before white settlement. It is folk drama in pageant form, with poetry, song, music, dance and pantomime.

The Dreamers, in Davis's words, 'deals with the life of an urban Aboriginal family from sun-rise in the morning until sun-down at night'. The focus of the play is Uncle Worru (played by Davis himself), the oldest member of the family and the only one who remembers what life was like in the bush. His poetic transpositions to this idyllic time provide a structure to the play and an ironic counterpoint to the compromise and unsatisfactory nature of modern urban Aboriginal life. It is a play of merciless exposure and criticism of blacks and whites, but above all a play of courage and hope.

Both plays are partly expressed in an Aboriginal *patois* that is a modified English incorporating many words of the Aboriginal language Nyoongah (or Bibbulmun). In *Kullark* some speeches are entirely in Nyoongah. The usual effect, however, is represented by this exchange between the two cousins Roy and Eli:

> ELI. How about a bottle of *gnoop* [the word for blood, now transferred to wine]?
> ROY. Bloody good idea. Take this cough off me chest.
> ELI. (*looking at the money* [put on the table by Dolly, Roy's wife, with instructions to buy food for lunch]). If we 'ad some *boondah* [stone, transferred to mean money]?
> ROY. No *choo* [shame]. Can't use this, gotta git tucker.

Kevin Gilbert (1933–) is the most vehement and the most self-critical of the Aboriginal poets. His *People ARE Legends* (1978) deals with the demand for land rights, the oppression of his people, the loss of Aboriginal spiritual life, the rape of black women by whites, and the problems of drunkenness. His poems evince a wide variety of mood and style, from the battle call of 'Look, Koori' to the pathos of 'The Contemporary Aboriginal' and the dialectical couplets of 'True' addressed to those, black and white, who differ from him, and to whom he says,

> Still, you *believe* and I know, I know
> That we all must tend the land we hoe
> And live to the dreams we dream . . . .

Gilbert is also noteworthy because his play *The Cherry Pickers* (written 1970, performed 1971), was the first play in English by an Aboriginal, and because of his vigorous polemical prose in *'Because a White Man'll Never Do It'* (1973).

The major Aboriginal novelist so far is Colin Johnson (1938–). *Wild Cat Falling* (1965) deals with the experiences and reminiscences of a nineteen-year-old Aboriginal, the child of a half-Aboriginal mother and a white father. Violence, including sexual violence, is part of the fabric of this novel (as of later Aboriginal novels). The narrator is involved in robbery and shooting and ends up on the run from the police.

It is the (unnamed) narrator's chameleon-like quality that makes him intensely vulnerable. He is able to assume the manners and outlook of almost any group he is with before beginning to satirize and then reject them. What he keeps reverting to is his sense of self-sufficiency and inviolability, which makes him detach himself from all groups in the end. He explores existentialism and nihilism as possibilities, frequently contemplates suicide as the only sensible choice, but seems ultimately to accept life.

Long Live Sandawara (1979) runs two narratives in parallel, one set in the contemporary Perth slums, the other in the Kimberley district of north-west Australia in the 1890s. The historical-novel strand concerns Sandawara, the leader of Aboriginal resistance to white settlement; in the contemporary strand (where armed opposition to white oppression proves equally futile) Sandawara is a model for Alan, the sixteen-year-old street fighter.

Doctor Wooreddy's Prescription for Enduring the Ending of the World (1983) is another historical novel, this time concerned with an Aboriginal man's experience of white invaders in Tasmania and Victoria. Wooreddy decides that these 'nums' (ghosts) must be manifestations of *Ria Warrawah*, the great spirit of evil and destruction. Their coming he interprets as an omen signalling the end of the world. None of his sufferings at the hands of the whites cause him to discard this notion; it is, indeed, true that all the Tasmanian Aborigines were dispossessed and alienated from both their land and their culture. In the end Wooreddy, now an old man who is certain of the impending destruction of the world, goes into a trance-like state as one of his companions is judicially murdered by jeering whites. Yet, for all the horrors and violence, this book, like Johnson's earlier novels, is neither uncritical of blacks nor entirely critical of whites. Robinson, the Chief Protector of Aborigines, is represented as a misguided but not unsympathetic man.

Archie Weller (1958–) is a younger novelist with better-developed qualities in narrative and dialogue than Johnson, but less interest in metaphysical problems. Encouraged by Jack Davis to pursue seriously the writing that he had intermittently tried from the age of twelve, he entered a novel manuscript, *The Day of the Dog*, for the 1980 *Australian*/Vogel Literary Award and had it highly commended. It was published in 1981.

The Day of the Dog concerns urban Aborigines in Perth, and their difficulties of unemployment, police persecution, imprisonment, heavy drinking, apathy and hopelessness. The novel begins with a celebration for Doug Dooligan's release from an eighteen-month stay in Fremantle gaol. His attempts to gain control of his life are thwarted by his petty criminal mates and the antipathy of whites. The young Nyoongah urbanites are

a new generation now of loud brash children. . . . No-one owns them. They are their own bosses. They have cobwebs in their hair and minds and, spiderlike, they dream up new dastardly deeds for their initiation. They paint on lies and blood from fights, to make themselves look elegant with patterns from their new Dreaming. They dance to their gods of flashing lights and hopes.

Doug's girl-friend Polly, on the run from the Community Welfare Department, is eventually caught. Doug, entrapped in theft and violence that eventually results in a murder, kills himself and his companions in a high-speed attempt to escape from the police.

The Day of the Dog, like Johnson's *Wild Cat Falling*, has some elements of autobiography in it. The novel of growing-up and the search for understanding of oneself and one's surroundings is a commonplace in white Australian literature. In black Australian literature it takes the distinctive quality of dealing in sex and violence, and the intrusion of the law into both.

Autobiographies also form a substantial part of black writing. In addition, there is a small number of works on the boundary of autobiography and fiction, notably *Wacvie* (1977) and *Welou, my Brother* (1984) by Faith Bandler, who is descended from Pacific islanders brought as labourers to Australia, and *Karobran: The Story of an Aboriginal Girl* (1978) by Monica Clare (1924–73).

Writers of non-English-speaking background

While all white Australian writers are migrants or the descendants of migrants, those who come from non-English-speaking countries commonly express feelings of alienation, loss and rejection akin to those of Aboriginal writers and the more disaffected of early British and Irish immigrants. Some, such as Judah Waten and David Martin, have been absorbed into the mainstream of publishers and readers in Australia. Some, notably Dimitris Tsaloumas, have chosen to write in their first language and to seek publication in their country of origin. With the large numbers of migrants coming to Australia since the late 1940s from countries such as Greece and Italy, substantial communities of bilingual writers and readers from specific countries have emerged, sometimes with their own publishing outlets. Short stories and poetry have been the preferred literary modes.

In the poems of Dimitris Tsaloumas (1921–) the landscape is mostly Mediterranean. Terraces with flagged courtyards containing pots of mint, basil and rosemary are surrounded by vineyards and olive groves. In the sea, men fish for octopus and dive for sponge. Ants, lizards and crickets catch the poet's eye as he alternately retreats into himself or seeks some wider, but still contained and disciplined, world outside himself to delight in. In this world the poet is often wryly crotchety at the unreasonable demands or thoughtlessness of family and friends, but always with a sense that his mockingly splenetic outbursts are directed partly at himself. In some poems there is also a sense of individual relationships being used as a metaphor for a muted form of comment against political repression and self-seeking.

In the much smaller number of poems with an Australian setting, Tsaloumas tends to find an insensitive and venal community. 'The Green Ants', for instance, is a satiric juxtaposition of the profound sanctity of the land to the Australian Aborigines and the arguments of 'enlightened' companies, economists and governments to mine it. 'Message', on the other hand, rejoices in the immortal, freedom-giving beauty of nature on land and sea in Australia, a land in which there is a path lacking 'a past in the hallucinations of captivity'.

Tsaloumas is disillusioned by such notions as progress, development, economic growth, media communication and modernity. He prophesies, like an Old Testament prophet during the Babylonian captivity, in favour of a return from barbarism to traditional standards of beauty, of respect for the environment and of conduct. He laments 'the illusions of newspapers' and, more generally, 'the meanness of these times'.

Tsaloumas gave up the writing of poetry when he came to Australia in 1953. Resuming ten years later, he subsequently had six volumes, written in Greek, published either in Melbourne (for political prudence) or in Greece. His first volume with an English text, *The Observatory: Selected Poems* (1983), a bilingual edition, won for him the National Book Council Award. A corrected edition was issued in 1984.

Born on the island of Leros in what were then the Italian-held Dodecanese, Tsaloumas is at home in Italian, Greek and English literature, both classical and modern. Kazantzakis, Seferis, Elytis, Empeirokos – and T. S. Eliot, whose work he encountered when he was in his early twenties – were his early models. When he resumed writing, his work had more solemnity, more substance and less self-indulgence. He has, in fact, become a highly intellectual poet, socially concerned, prophetic, without illusions, but not without hope or joy.

Pino Bosi (1933–) is known for his broadcasts in Italian and English, and for his short stories and poems. *The Checkmate, and Other Stories* (1973, 1983), covering a wide variety of circumstances and characters of many ethnic origins, has most of its narratives dependent on the clearing-away of some misconception or incomprehension.

Angelo Loukakis (1951–), who was born and educated in Australia, is a story-writer with settings mostly in Greece or in the Greek communities of Australia. His volume *For the Patriarch* (1981) concentrates its settings in the inner-suburban migrant communities of Sydney. Another writer of Greek ethnic origin, Spiro Zavos (1937–), sets some of his stories in *Faith of our Fathers* (1982) in Greek communities in New Zealand. Greek settings are not, of course, confined to writers of Greek origin. Most of the stories of Beverley Farmer (1941–) in *Milk* (1983) are about Greeks in Australia or Greeks and Australians in Greece.

The stories of Serge Liberman (1942–), a writer of Russian Jewish origin, have won many short-story awards. They are mostly about Jewish migrants, the narrator often being a doctor, scientist or writer whose educated, rational views of the world are shown to be inadequate to the human problems faced. His two collections are *On Firmer Shores* (1981) and *A Universe of Clowns* (1983).

The most prolific and widely published migrant writer is 'Banumbir Wongar' (Sreten Bozic). Much of his writing is on Aboriginal themes and there was, in fact, a misconception for some time that he was an Aboriginal. His best-known work is the stories of *The Track to Bralgu* (1978).

The most horrendous account of migrant experience in Australia is that of Rosa R. Cappiello. Her *Paese Fortunato* (1981) tells of a vile migrant hostel, a modern place of punishment or transportation. Inhabited by 'lesbians, pregnant women, old women ravers, loafers, junkies, slatterns, female vagabonds, misfits, widows', it is a staging-house on the way to a barely less depressing existence in run-down rooms and flats. In both its Italian original and its English translation, as *Oh Lucky Country* (1984), it has excited much literary attention (mostly favourable) and political attention (largely hostile). It injects a new element of disconcerting bitterness into the comfortable nostalgia that had prevailed in migrant writing. One of the difficulties of provocative rather than bland writing is that it may alienate part of the potential readership, which is likely to be uncommercially small anyway. One possibility for overcoming this difficulty is to seek support from a public sponsor, such as the Literature Board of the Australia Council. The new multicultural literary journal *Outrider* (1984–), edited by Manfred Jurgensen, has such support and may prove to be adventurous as well as eclectic.

Newly emerging writers

Sponsorship of literary awards expanded greatly in Australia during the 1970s. In 1974 both the *Age* newspaper and the National Book Council announced awards unlimited in genre. The New South Wales Premier's Awards for fiction, non-fiction and poetry offered even more substantial prize money from their institution in 1979. But the most imaginative award was the *Australian*/Vogel Literary Award, initiated in 1979 by Niels Stevns, founder of the Vogels bread company. Unlike almost all other major awards it encourages young writers by being awarded for a novel, historical work or biography in manuscript by a writer between the ages of eighteen and thirty (later raised to thirty-five). Its winners – all novelists – have included Paul Radley, Tim Winton, Nigel Krauth and Kate Grenville; its other discoveries have included Archie Weller. All have had their work published by George Allen and Unwin as part of the competition rules.

Paul Radley (1962–) jointly won the first *Australian*/Vogel Literary Award with *Jack Rivers and Me* (1980) and went on to write a kind of sequel, *My Blue Checker Corker and Me* (1982). Both are set in a small country town, based on his own home town of Boolaroo in New South Wales. The style is based on that of yarn-spinning in a country pub, with much delight in word games. *Jack Rivers and Me* is about a five-year-old boy, Peanut, his sister and his friend, Jack Rivers. Set in 1950, it begins with Peanut's first day at school, his observations of the world around him, and his experience of the intrusiveness of adults. *My Blue Checker Corker and Me*, with the same setting and some of the same characters, is centred on a ten-year-old boy who races pigeons, especially blue checkers. A third novel, about an adolescent, will follow.

Tim Winton (1960–) set *An Open Swimmer* (1982) in the south-east of Western Australia. Its action revolves around the sea, depicted as a transforming world of individual relationship with nature, and around spear fishing and the bush. The central character, Jerra Nilsam, approaches manhood tentatively and experimentally, learning to discard unusable parts of past relationships and be receptive to new and disturbing ones. The deft movement from outer to inner reality, the sense of the evanescence of experience and of sensation, and the brilliant images of decay, sudden change and beauty give this novel a distinctive quality.

Winton's second novel, *Shallows* (1984), is a fictional account of the last days of the whaling-industry in Western Australia. Its cast of characters is more numerous and varied than in *An Open Swimmer*, but it has the same swirl of half-understood emotions, the same carefully patterned construction, and the same opalescent description.

Nigel Krauth (1949–) jointly won the 1982 award with *Matilda, my Darling* (1983), a fictional account of Andrew Barton Paterson in 1895 at the time of the writing of 'Waltzing Matilda'. The life of the poet is set in a milieu of drought, bad feeling between squatters and itinerant pastoral workers, and a murder mystery. Krauth is adept at truth games, false trails, and dramatic irony between past and present. He is perhaps the most self-aware writer of all the Vogel winners.

Kate Grenville (1951–) was on the point of having her first collection of stories, *Bearded Ladies* (1984), published when she won the 1984 Vogel Award with the novel manuscript *Bea's Story*, in which a woman rejects convention in order to lead a life following her instincts. Both it and another work, *Dreamhouse*, are comedies in a largely realistic mode, though not without some self-awareness of the play between the fictionalized and the objective life of her characters. Kate Grenville's stories are of women pushed into careers, incidents or relationships, and too timid to protest much about it. In 'Meeting the Folks', for instance, the narrator, an Australian girl taken home by her insensitive French lover to meet his mother, encounters a loud, vulgar harridan who constantly belittles her and her far-off obscure country. Faced with yet another adverse comparison, the narrator reflects that 'I've never felt so affectionate towards that country with its diffidently graceful gumtrees . . . .'

The current fecundity of Australian fiction-writing is attested by another prize-winning book, *The Home Girls* (1982) by Olga Masters (1919–). These short stories, often set in small country towns during the period of the 1930s Depression, mostly concern women and the family. Masters's first novel, *Loving Daughters* (1984), is also set in a small country town, but its mood is less dark. It is a study of the possibilities of love, affection, and choice, involving two sisters, their father and brothers, and an unmarried English clergyman who believes himself in love with both sisters. He has, in fact, amalgamated their qualities in his mind into one perfect whole. Like many of the newly emerging writers of the 1980s (including Elizabeth Jolley and Tim Winton), Olga Masters writes a very economical, dramatically paced prose, with no trace of the over-indulgent verbosity of many of the social realists and some of the fabulists.

Publishing outlets

Poetry competitions have been less successful than novel competitions in drawing attention to promising new writers. They mostly offer only small prizes, generally awarded for a single poem. Even the Mattara Spring Festival Poetry Award (sponsored from Newcastle, NSW, since 1981), which offers a large prize and the likelihood of publication, has an air of predictability rather than discovery about its prize-winners.

Play-writing has been the most generously sponsored literary form in Australia for some years. Substantial sums are invested by the Theatre and Literature Boards of the Australia Council, the annual Australian National Playwrights Conference, and state- and local-government bodies in the form of commissions, readings, workshops and residencies, but, though the result is many hundreds of practitioners and would-be practitioners, the plays produced have been patchy, generally lacking the conciseness and concentration of much contemporary prose fiction. Play scripts also now have specialized presses such as Currency, Playlab, and Yackandandah, providing rapid and fairly cheap transition from performance script to print.

Despite the small circulation (averaging around 1000), the literary magazines provide the most stable and reliable means by which new authors are recognized. *Southerly* (1939–) and *Meanjin* (1940–), which, with the *Bulletin*, carried the main burden for many years, now have many more journals competing for the same finite list of writers and readers. *Quadrant* (1956–), which appears monthly, provides generous space for poetry and some space for fiction amid its right-wing political journalism. *Overland* (1954–), with the opposite political bias, is a more thoroughly literary journal, appearing quarterly. *Westerly* (1956–) is in many ways the most adventurous of the literary quarterlies, the one most likely to seek out and incorporate new ideas. *Scripsi* (1981–) is also an imaginative journal, sometimes with an odd assortment of the international and the Melburnian. *Inprint* (1977–), despite a circulation of only a few hundred, has attracted a great deal of experimental short-fiction writing. But the most sought-after place for publication is now probably the quarterly literary supplements edited with self-effacing eclecticism by Geoffrey Dutton (1922–), himself a prolific poet and prose-writer. From 1980 to 1984 they appeared in the *Bulletin*. From 1985 they will appear in the *Australian* newspaper. The other major metropolitan newspapers also find space for a poem in their Saturday editions and the *Age Monthly Review* began a literary supplement in 1984.

The literary magazines receive subsidies from the Literature Board of the Australia Council, a statutory body established in 1973 as a continuation of the Commonwealth Literary Fund (CLF). Whereas from 1908 to 1939 the CLF spent most of its limited funds in supporting writers too old to continue working and the distressed families of deceased writers, the direction both of the CLF and the Literature Board since 1939 has been to concentrate on nurturing literary creativity through fellowships, assistance to publishers and literary magazines, and the promotion of writing and reading through organizations, festivals and workshops. More recently, state-government arts bodies and some local-government authorities have also provided financial support for these purposes.

Further reading

History and social background

BOYD, ROBIN: *The Australian Ugliness* (Melbourne: Cheshire, 1960; Ringwood: Penguin, 1968, 1980).

CARROLL, JOHN (ed.): *Intruders in the Bush: The Australian Quest for Identity* (Melbourne: Oxford University Press, 1982).

CLARK, C. M. H.: *A History of Australia*, 5 vols so far published (Melbourne: Melbourne University Press, 1962–).

COVELL, ROGER: *Australia's Music: Themes of a New Society* (Melbourne: Sun Books, 1967).

DOCKER, JOHN: *Australian Cultural Elites: The Intellectual Traditions of Sydney and Melbourne* (Sydney: Angus & Robertson, 1974).

HORNE, DONALD: *The Lucky Country: Australia in the Sixties* (Ringwood: Penguin, 1964, 1968).

HANCOCK, W. K.: *Australia* (London: Benn, 1930; Brisbane: Jacaranda, 1961).

HUGHES, ROBERT: *The Art of Australia* (Ringwood: Penguin, 1966).

McCULLOCH, ALAN: *Encyclopaedia of Australian Art*, 2nd edn, 2 vols (Richmond: Hutchinson, 1984).

McQUEEN, HUMPHREY: *A New Britannia: An Argument concerning the Social Origins of Australian Radicalism and Nationalism* (Ringwood: Penguin, 1970).

——: *The Black Swan of Trespass: The Emergence of Modernist Painting in Australia to 1944* (Sydney: Alternative Publishing Cooperative, 1979).

PHILLIPS, A. A.: *The Australian Tradition: Studies in a Colonial Culture* (Melbourne: Cheshire, 1958, 1966).

SERLE, GEOFFREY: *From Deserts the Prophets Come: The Creative Spirit in Australia 1788–1972* (Melbourne: Heinemann, 1973).

SMITH, BERNARD: *Australian Painting 1788–1960/1970* (Melbourne: Oxford University Press, 1962, 1971).

——: *European Vision and the South Pacific 1768–1850* (Oxford: Clarendon Press, 1960, 1969).

STEPHENSEN, P. R.: *The Foundations of Culture in Australia: An Essay Towards National Self Respect* (Gordon: W. J. Miles, 1936).

TURNER, IAN (ed.): *The Australian Dream: A Collection of Anticipations about Australia from Captain Cook to the Present Day* (Melbourne: Sun Books, 1968).

WALKER, DAVID: *Dream and Disillusion: A Search for Cultural Identity* (Canberra: Australian National University Press, 1976).

WARD, RUSSEL: *The Australian Legend* (Melbourne: Oxford University Press, 1958, 1965).

Reference books

AUSTRALIAN LANGUAGE

BAKER, SIDNEY J.: *The Australian Language*, rev. edn (Sydney: Currawong, 1966; Melbourne: Sun Books, 1970).
Collins Dictionary of the English Language (special Australian consultant: G. A. Wilkes) (Sydney: Collins, 1979).
The Macquarie Dictionary (Sydney: Macquarie Library, 1981).
WILKES, G. A.: *A Dictionary of Australian Colloquialisms* (Sydney: Sydney University Press, 1978).

LITERARY BIBLIOGRAPHY

ANDREWS, BARRY G., and WILDE, WILLIAM H. (compilers): *Australian Literature to 1900: A Guide to Information Sources* (Detroit: Gale, 1980).
Australian Literary Studies (St Lucia): 'Annual Bibliography of Studies in Australian Literature' (May issue since 1964).
Bookmark: An Annual Diary and Directory (Melbourne: Australian Library Promotion Councl, 1974–).
BORCHARDT, D. H.: *Australian Bibliography: A Guide to Printed Sources of Information* (Sydney: Pergamon, 1976).
DAY, A. GROVE (compiler): *Modern Australian Prose, 1901–1975: A Guide to Information Sources* (Detroit: Gale, 1980).
HERGENHAN, LAURIE, *et al.*: *Selective Bibliography of Australian Books in Print* (Sydney: Literature Board of the Australia Council, [1984]).
JAFFA, HERBERT C. (compiler): *Modern Australian Poetry, 1920–1970: A Guide to Information Sources* (Detroit: Gale, 1979).
Journal of Commonwealth Literature (Oxford): 'Australia' in 'Annual Bibliography of Commonwealth Literature' (since 1965).
LOCK, FRED, and LAWSON, ALAN: *Australian Literature – A Reference Guide* (Melbourne: Oxford University Press, 1977, 1980).
MILLER, E. MORRIS, and MACARTNEY, FREDERICK T.: *Australian Literature: A Bibliography . . . to 1950* (Sydney: Angus & Robertson, 1956).
PRIESSNITZ, HORST: 'Australian Literature: A Preliminary Subject Checklist', *Australian Literary Studies*, 11 (1984) 513–40.

OTHER

The Australian Encyclopaedia, 2nd edn, 10 vols (Sydney: Angus & Robertson, 1958); 4th edn, 12 vols (Sydney: Grolier Society, 1983).
MURPHY, BRIAN: *A Dictionary of Australian History* (Sydney: McGraw-Hill, 1982; Fontana, 1983).
MURRAY-SMITH, STEPHEN (ed.): *The Dictionary of Australian Quotations* (Melbourne: Heinemann, 1984).

PIKE, DOUGLAS; NAIRN, BEDE; and SERLE, GEOFFREY (eds): *The Australian Dictionary of Biography*, 10 vols so far published (Melbourne: Melbourne University Press, 1966–).

WANNAN, BILL (compiler): *Australian Folklore: A Dictionary of Lore, Legends and Popular Allusions* (Sydney: Lansdowne, 1970).

Literary history and criticism

GENERAL

BARNES, JOHN (ed.): *The Writer in Australia: A Collection of Literary Documents, 1856 to 1964* (Melbourne: Oxford University Press, 1969).

BENNETT, BRUCE (ed.): *Cross Currents: Magazines and Newspapers in Australian Literature* (Melbourne: Longman Cheshire, 1981).

DOCKER, JOHN: *In a Critical Condition: Reading Australian Literature* (Ringwood: Penguin, 1984).

DUTTON, GEOFFREY (ed.): *The Literature of Australia* (Ringwood: Penguin, 1964, 1976).

——: *Snow on the Saltbush: The Australian Literary Experience* (Ringwood: Viking, 1984).

GIBSON, ROSS: *The Diminishing Paradise: Changing Literary Perceptions of Australia* (Sydney: Angus & Robertson, 1984).

GREEN, DOROTHY: *The Music of Love* (Ringwood: Penguin, 1984).

GREEN, H. M., *A History of Australian Literature*, 2 vols (Sydney: Angus & Robertson, 1961; rev. by Dorothy Green, 1984).

HADGRAFT, CECIL: *Australian Literature: A Critical Account to 1955* (London: Heinemann, 1960).

JOHNSTON, GRAHAME: *Annals of Australian Literature* (Melbourne: Oxford University Press, 1970).

—— (ed.): *Australian Literary Criticism* (Melbourne: Oxford University Press, 1962).

KIERNAN, BRIAN: *Criticism* (Melbourne: Oxford University Press, 1974).

KIRKBY, JOAN (ed.): *The American Model: Influence and Independence in Australian Poetry* (Sydney: Hale & Iremonger, 1982).

KRAMER, LEONIE (ed.): *The Oxford History of Australian Literature* (Melbourne: Oxford University Press, 1981).

MILLER, E. MORRIS: *Australian Literature from its Beginnings to 1935*, 2 vols (Melbourne: Oxford University Press, 1981).

Sydney: Sydney University Press, 1975).

PALMER, VANCE: *The Legend of the Nineties* (Melbourne: Melbourne University Press, 1954; illus. edn, Melbourne: Currey O'Neil, 1983).

SMITH, GRAEME KINROSS: *Australia's Writers* (Melbourne: Nelson, 1980).

SPECIAL SUBJECTS

HEALY, JOHN J.: *Literature and the Aborigine in Australia 1770–1975* (St Lucia: University of Queensland Press, 1978).

IKIN, VAN (ed.): *Australian Science Fiction* (St Lucia: University of Queensland Press, 1982).

JURGENSEN, MANFRED (ed.): *Ethnic Australia* (Brisbane: Phoenix Publications, 1981).

McFARLANE, BRIAN: *Words and Images: Australian Novels into Film* (Melbourne: Heinemann, 1983).

McVITTY, WALTER: *Innocence and Experience: Essays on Contemporary Australian Children's Writers* (Melbourne: Nelson, 1981).

MODJESKA, DRUSILLA: *Exiles at Home: Australian Women Writers 1925–1945* (Sydney: Angus & Robertson, 1981).

PIKE, ANDREW, and COOPER, ROSS: *Australian Film 1900–1977: A Guide to Feature Film Production* (Melbourne: Oxford University Press, 1980).

READE, ERIC: *The Australian Screen: A Pictorial History of Australian Film Making* (Melbourne: Lansdowne, 1975).

ROLFE, PATRICIA: *The Journalistic Javelin: An Illustrated History of the Bulletin* (Sydney: Wildcat Press, 1979 [1980]).

SAXBY, H. M.: *A History of Australian Children's Literature 1841–1941; 1941–1970*, 2 vols (Sydney: Wentworth Books, 1969, 1971).

STRATTON, DAVID: *The Last New Wave: The Australian Film Revival* (Sydney: Angus & Robertson, 1980).

SUMMERS, ANNE: *Damned Whores and God's Police: The Colonization of Women in Australia* (Ringwood: Penguin, 1975).

WALKER, SHIRLEY (ed.): *Who is She?: Images of Women in Australian Fiction* (St Lucia: University of Queensland Press, 1983).

WANNAN, BILL (ed.): *The Wearing of the Green: The Lore, Literature, Legend and Balladry of the Irish in Australia* (Melbourne: Lansdowne, 1965).

POETRY

GRAY, ROBERT, and LEHMANN, GEOFFREY (eds): *The Younger Australian Poets* (Sydney: Hale & Iremonger, 1983).

HALL, RODNEY (ed.): *The Collins Book of Australian Poetry* (Sydney: Collins, 1981).

HESELTINE, HARRY (ed.): *The Penguin Book of Australian Verse* (Ringwood: Penguin, 1972).

—— (ed.): *The Penguin Book of Modern Australian Verse* (Ringwood: Penguin, 1981).

JENNINGS, KATE (ed.): *Mother I'm Rooted: An Anthology of Australian Women Poets* (Melbourne: Outback Press, 1975).

McAULEY, JAMES: *A Map of Australian Verse* (Melbourne: Oxford University Press, 1975).

STEWART, DOUGLAS, and KEESING, NANCY (eds): *Australian Bush Ballads* (Sydney: Angus & Robertson, 1955).

——: *Old Bush Songs and Rhymes of Colonial Times*, enlarged and rev. from the collection of A. B. Paterson (Sydney: Angus & Robertson, 1957).

TRANTER, JOHN (ed.): *The New Australian Poetry* (St Lucia: Makar Press, 1979).

WRIGHT, JUDITH: *Preoccupations in Australian Poetry* (Melbourne: Oxford University Press, 1965).

FICTION

BURNS, D. R.: *The Directions of Australian Fiction: 1920–1974* (Sydney: Cassell, 1975).
GOLDSWORTHY, KERRYN (ed.): *Australian Short Stories* (Melbourne: J. M. Dent, 1983).
HAMILTON, K. G. (ed.): *Studies in the Recent Australian Novel* (St Lucia: University of Queensland Press, 1978).
HESELTINE, HARRY P. (ed.): *The Penguin Book of Australian Short Stories* (Ringwood: Penguin, 1976).
KIERNAN, BRIAN: *Images of Society and Nature: Seven Essays on Australian Novels* (Melbourne: Oxford University Press, 1971).
MOORHOUSE, FRANK (ed.): *The State of the Art: The Mood of Contemporary Australia in Short Stories* (Ringwood: Penguin, 1983).
RAMSON, W. S. (ed.): *The Australian Experience: Critical Essays on Australian Novels* (Canberra: Australian National University Press, 1974).

DRAMA

FITZPATRICK, PETER: *After 'The Doll': Australian Drama Since 1955* (Melbourne: Edward Arnold, 1979).
HOLLOWAY, PETER (ed.): *Contemporary Australian Drama: Perspectives since 1955* (Sydney: Currency Press, 1981).
LOVE, HAROLD (ed.): *The Australian Stage: A Documentary History* (Sydney: New South Wales University Press, 1984).
REES, LESLIE: *A History of Australian Drama*, 2 vols (Sydney: Angus & Robertson, 1973–8).
WILLIAMS, MARGARET: *Australia on the Popular Stage: 1829–1929* (Melbourne: Oxford University Press, 1983).

Chronological table

Abbreviations: *b.* = born; *d.* = dies; D = drama; P = prose; V = verse

DATE	AUTHOR AND TITLE	EVENT
1770		Captain Cook 'discovers' Australia and takes possession of the eastern coast (named New South Wales) for King George III
1774		Matthew Flinders *b.*
1776		J. H. Tuckey *b.*
1778		Gregory Blaxland *b.*
1782		Thomas Wells *b.*
1786		Barron Field *b.*
1788		First Fleet arrives in Australia and includes convicts Captain Arthur Phillip formally proclaims the colony of New South Wales at Sydney Cove First conflict between Aborigines and settlers at Rushcutter's Bay
1789	Anon. (ed.): *The Voyage of Governor Phillip to Botany Bay* [also contains Erasmus Darwin's 'A Visit of Hope to Sydney Cove near Botany Bay'] (P) Tench, Watkin (1758?): *A Narrative of the Expedition to Botany Bay* (P)	*The Voyage of Governor Phillip* is the first book about Australia to be published in London First dramatic production in Australia (George Farquhar's *The Recruiting Officer*) performed by convicts in Sydney
1790	White, John (1756?): *Journal of a Voyage to New South Wales* (P)	W. C. Wentworth *b.*
1791		Henry Savery *b.*
1792		William Howitt *b.*

DATE	AUTHOR AND TITLE	EVENT
1793	Hunter, John (1737): *An Historical Journal of the Transactions at Port Jackson and Norfolk Island* (P) Tench, Watkin (1758?): *A Complete Account of the Settlement at Port Jackson and Norfolk Island* (P)	The first book to deal only with the natural history of Australia (*Zoology and Botany of New Holland and the Isles Adjacent*, by George Shaw and James Edward Smith) published in London 1793–5
1794	Johnson, Richard (1753): *An Address to the Inhabitants of the Colonies, established in New South Wales and Norfolk Island* (P)	
1796		First theatre opened in Sydney by Robert Sidaway
1798	Collins, David (1756): *An Account of the English Colony in New South Wales*, vol. I (vol. II, 1802) (P)	Charles Rowcroft *b.*
1799		John Dunmore Lang *b.* 'Henry Melville' *b.*
1802		R. H. Horne *b.* The first book published in Australia, the *New South Wales General Standing Orders*, issued in Sydney by George Howe, the 'father' of printing in Australia
1803		W. Smith O'Brien *b.* Australia's first newspaper, the *Sydney Gazette* (1803–42), begins publication
1804	'C. S.' (?): 'The Vision of Melancholy, A Fragment' (V)	'The Vision of Melancholy' is first poem published locally (*Sydney Gazette*, 4 Mar)
1805	Tuckey (1776): *An Account of a Voyage to Establish a Colony at Port Phillip in Bass's Strait* (P)	Alexander Harris *b.*
1807		Charles Tompson *b.*
1808		Anna Maria Bunn *b.* W. H. Christie *b.*
1810	Robinson, Michael Massey (1744): *Odes* (V), in *Sydney Gazette*	C. T. Knowles *b.* David Collins *d.* Lachlan Macquarie begins term of office as Governor (1810–21)

DATE	AUTHOR AND TITLE	EVENT
1811	Mann, David Dickinson (1775?): *The Present Picture of New South Wales* (P)	
1813		Charles Harpur *b.*
1814	Flinders (1774): *A Voyage to Terra Australis* (P)	William Woolls *b.* Matthew Flinders *d.*
1815		Henry Parkes *b.* Mary T. Vidal *b.*
1816		John George Lang *b.* J. H. Tuckey *d.*
1818	Thomas Wells (1782): *Michael Howe, the Last and Worst of the Bushrangers of Van Diemen's Land* (P)	William Forster *b.*
1819	Field (1786): *First Fruits of Australian Poetry* (V) Wentworth (1790): *A Statistical, Historical and Political Description of the Colony of New South Wales and its Dependent Settlements in Van Diemen's Land* (P)	First book of verse locally published by George Howe
1820	Oxley, John (1785?): *Journals of Two Expeditions into the Interior of New South Wales* (P)	Raffaello Carboni *b.*
1821		S. P. Hill *b.* John Hunter *d.* The first locally produced magazine *Australian Magazine* 1821–2 published in Sydney by George Howe
1822		J. R. Houlding *b.* George French Angas *b.*
1823	Blaxland (1778): *A Journal of a Tour of Discovery across the Blue Mountains* (P) Wentworth (1790): *Australasia* (V)	Wentworth's *Australasia* was the first book of verse by an Australia-born author to be published in Britain
1824		J. L. Michael *b.* *Australian* (Sydney, 1824–48) founded, the first privately owned newspaper in the colony

DATE	AUTHOR AND TITLE	EVENT
1825		Catherine Spence *b*.
1826	Tompson (1807): *Wild Notes, from the Lyre of a Native Minstrel* (V)	T. A. Browne ('Rolf Boldrewood') *b*. Rachel Henning *b*. Michael Massey Robinson *d*. Tompson's *Wild Notes* (published in Sydney) was first book of verse by a native-born poet. First library in Australia established in Sydney
1827	'Pindar Juvenal': *The Van Diemen's Land Warriors* (V)	Caroline Leakey *b*. Richard Johnson *d*.
1828		D. H. Deniehy *b*. Richard Rowe *b*. John Oxley *d*. David Burn, *The Bushrangers* (D), produced in Edinburgh
1829	Savery (1791): *The Hermit in Van Diemen's Land* (P)	
1830	Savery (1791): *Quintus Servinton* (P)	Henry Kingsley *b*. Frederick Sinnett *b*. *Quintus Servinton* was the first novel written in Australia to be published in book form (in Hobart)
1831		Robert Sealy *b*. Charles Thatcher *b*. *Sydney Herald* begins (since 1842 titled *Sydney Morning Herald*)
1832	Woolls (1814): *The Voyage* (V)	John White *d*.
1833	Sturt (1795): *Two Expeditions into the Interior of South Australia* (P) Woolls (1814): *Australia* (V)	Adam Lindsay Gordon *b*. G. G. McCrae *b*. Watkin Tench *d*. Thomas Wells *d*. Theatre Royal (Sydney) founded (1833–8)
1834	'Melville' (1799): *The Bushrangers* (D)	Caroline Atkinson *b*.
1835	Thomas, E. H. (1801?): *The Bandit of the Rhine* (D)	James Brunton Stephens *b*. N. W. Swan *b*. *The Bandit of the Rhine* (now lost) was the first Australian play published in book form
1836		G. B. Barton *b*. Charles Darwin in Australia

DATE	AUTHOR AND TITLE	EVENT
1837		E. H. Thomas *d*.
1838	Bunn (1808): *The Guardian* (P) Woolls (1814): *Miscellanies in Prose and Verse* (P, V)	*The Guardian* was the first novel printed and published in New South Wales
1839		Henry Kendall *b*.
1840	Hill, Fidelia (1790?): *Poems and Recollections of the Past* (V)	First book of verse written by a woman published in Australia
1841	Christie (1808): *A Love Story* (P)	*A Mother's Offering to her Children* 'by a Lady Long Resident in NSW', first children's book
1842	Burn, David (1799?): *Plays and Fugitive Pieces* (D) Knowles (1810): *Salathiel* (D) Parkes (1815): *Stolen Moments* (V)	Henry Savery *d*. *Plays and Fugitive Pieces* was the first collection of plays to be published in Australia
1843	Hill, S. P. (1821): *Tarquin the Proud* (D) Rowcroft (1798): *Tales of the Colonies* (P)	Joseph Furphy *b*.
1844		Ada Cambridge *b*. J. B. O'Reilly *b*. C. T. Knowles *d*. Edward Geoghegan's *The Currency Lass* produced in Sydney
1845	Harpur (1813): *Thoughts: a Series of Sonnets* (V) McCombie, Thomas (1813?): *Arabin, or the Adventures of a Colonist in New South Wales* (P) Tucker (1808): *The Adventures of Ralph Rashleigh* (P) Vidal (1815): *Tales for the Bush* (P)	Ernest Favenc *b*.
1846	Rowcroft (1798): *The Bushranger of Van Diemen's Land* (P)	Marcus Clarke *b*. Mary Hannay Foott *b*. G. H. Gibson ('Ironbark') *b*. Barron Field *d*. *Argus* (Melbourne, 1846–1957) founded
1847	Harris (1805): *Settlers and Convicts* (P)	Catherine Martin *b*. T. H. Huxley in Australia 1847–9
1848		Jessie Catherine Couvreur ('Tasma') *b*.

DATE	AUTHOR AND TITLE	EVENT
1849	Harris (1805): *The Emigrant Family* (P)	
1850	Vidal (1815): *Cabramatta, and Woodleigh Farm* (P)	Thomas Arnold (brother of Matthew) in Australia 1950–6
1851		John Farrell *b.* Mrs Campbell Praed *b.* First of the goldrushes begins with the discovery of gold at Bathurst in New South Wales and at Ballarat and Bendigo in Victoria Goldrushes result in waves of immigration during the 1850s
1852		University of Sydney library established
1853	Harpur (1813): *The Bushrangers, and Other Poems* (D, V)	Gregory Blaxland *d.* Melbourne's public library established
1854	Howitt (1792): *A Boy's Adventures in the Wilds of Australia* (P) Spence (1825): *Clara Morison* (P)	Fidelia Hill *d.* *Age* (Melbourne) founded Uprising of miners at the Eureka Stockade (Ballarat)
1855	Carboni (1820): *The Eureka Stockade* (P) Lang, John George (1816): *The Forger's Wife* (P)	William Astley ('Price Warung') *b.* Louis Becke *b.* Catherine Stow (Mrs Langloh Parker) *b.* (?)
1856	Sinnett (1830): *The Fiction Fields of Australia* (P) Spence (1825): *Tender and True* (P)	J. F. Archibald *b.* Charles Rowcroft *d.* The first account of Australian literature, *The Fiction Fields of Australia*, published in *Journal of Australasia*, 1856–8
1857	Atkinson (1834): *Gertrude the Emigrant* (P) Howitt (1792): *Tallangetta, the Squatter's Home* (P) Michael (1824): *Songs Without Music* (V) Thatcher (1831): *Colonial Songster* (V)	Caroline Atkinson was the first Australia-born woman novelist Barbara Baynton *b.*
1858	Michael (1824): *Sir Archibald Yelverton* (V) Rowe (1828): *Peter Possum's Portfolio* (P, V)	Victor Daley *b.*

DATE	AUTHOR AND TITLE	EVENT
1859	Atkinson (1834): *Cowanda* (P) Kingsley (1830): *The Recollections of Geoffry Hamlyn* (P) Lang, John George (1816): *Botany Bay* (P) Leakey (1827): *The Broad Arrow* (P) Sealy (1831): *Scraps* (V)	Fergus Hume *b*.
1860	Deniehy (1828): *How I Became Attorney-General of New Barataria* (P) Michael (1824): *John Cumberland* (V) Vidal (1815): *Bengala* (P)	F. J. Broomfield *b*. A. A. G. Hales *b*.
1862	Harpur (1813): *A Poet's Home* (V) Kendall (1839): *Poems and Songs* (V)	Francis Adams *b*.
1863		George Essex Evans *b*.
1864	Gordon (1833): *The Feud* (V) Horne, R. H. (1802): *Prometheus the Firebringer* (V) Thatcher (1831): *Colonial Minstrel* (V)	A. B. ('Banjo') Paterson *b*. John George Lang *d*. *Australasian* (1864–1946) founded
1865	Harpur (1813): *The Tower of the Dream* (V) Kingsley (1830): *The Hillyars and the Burtons* (P) Spence (1825): *Mr Hogarth's Will* (P	E. G. Dyson *b*. Mary Gilmore *b*. A. G. Stephens *b*. D. H. Deniehy *d*. *Australian Journal* (1865–1958) founded
1866	Barton (1836): *The Poets and Prose Writers of New South Wales* and *Literature in New South Wales* (P) Horne, R. H. (1802): *The South Sea Sisters* (D)	Barcroft Boake *b*. Bernard O'Dowd *b*. Frederick Sinnett *d*. James Tucker *d*. Barton's books (published in Sydney) were the first book-length studies of Australian writing
1867	Gordon (1833): *Sea Spray and Smoke Drift* (V) Houlding (1822): *Australian Capers* (P) McCrae, G. G. (1833): *Mamba and The Story of Balladeadro* (V)	Henry Lawson *b*. Roderick Quinn *b*. Goldrushes in Queensland (1867–86) begin
1868	McCombie, Thomas (1813?): *Frank Henly, or Honest Industry Will Conquer* (P) Spence (1825): *The Author's Daughter* (P)	Randolph Bedford *b*. A. H. Davis ('Steele Rudd') *b*. Charles Harpur *d*. J. L. Michael *d*. Transportation of convicts ends
1869	Clarke (1846): *The Peripatetic Philosopher* and *Long Odds* (P) Kendall (1839): *Leaves From Australian Forests* (V)	E. J. Brady *b*. W. H. Ogilvie *b*. Thomas McCombie *d*. Charles Sturt *d*.

DATE	AUTHOR AND TITLE	EVENT
	Kingsley (1830): *Tales of Old Travel Renarrated* (P) Rowe (1828): *The Boy in the Bush* (P)	Mary T. Vidal *d*.
1870	Clarke (1846): *His Natural Life* (P), in the *Australian Journal* Gordon (1833): *Bush Ballads and Galloping Rhymes* (V) Houlding (1822): *Rural and City Life* (P)	C. J. Brennan *b*. Mrs Aeneas Gunn *b*. Ethel Robertson ('Henry Handel Richardson') *b*. Adam Lindsay Gordon *d*.
1871	Clarke (1846): *Old Tales of a Young Country* (P) Kingsley (1830): *Hetty, and Other Stories* (P) Stephens, James Brunton (1835): *Convict Once* (V)	J. Le Gay Brereton *b*. Louis Stone *b*. Anthony Trollope's first visit to Australia (1871–2)
1872	Kingsley (1830): *Hornby Mills and Other Stories* (P) Lang, John Dunmore (1799): *Poems Sacred and Secular* (V)	A. H. Adams *b*. John Shaw Neilson *b*. Ethel Turner *b*. Caroline Atkinson *d*. W. C. Wentworth *d*.
1873	Clarke (1846): *Holiday Peak* (P) McCrae, G. G. (1833): *The Man in the Iron Mask* (V) O'Reilly (1844): *Songs from the Southern Seas* (V) Stephens, James Brunton (1835): *The Godolphin Arabian* (V)	W. H. Christie *d*. 'Henry Melville' *d*. Anthony Trollope's *Australia and New Zealand* and *Harry Heathcote of Gangoil* published in London Edward William Cole opens first 'book arcade' in Melbourne
1874	Angas (1822): *The Wreck of the Admella* (V) Clarke (1846): *His Natural Life*, in book form (P) Kingsley (1830): *Reginald Hetherege* (P)	Alexander Harris *d*.
1875	Cambridge (1884): *The Manor House* (V) and *Up the Murray* (P) Clarke (1846): *'Twixt Shadow and Shine* (P) Swan (1835): *Tales of Australian Life* (P)	William Gosse Hay *b*. David Burn *d*. Raffaello Carboni *d*. Havelock Ellis in Australia (1875–79) Anthony Trollope's second visit
1876	Forster (1818): *The Weirwolf* (D) Stephens, James Brunton (1835): *A Hundred Pounds* (P)	C. J. Dennis *b*. Hugh McCrae *b*. Henry Kingsley *d*. Truganini, the last full-blood Tasmanian Aboriginal, dies in Hobart aged 73

DATE	AUTHOR AND TITLE	EVENT
1877	Clarke (1846): *Four Stories High* (P) Forster (1818): *The Brothers* (D)	
1878	'Boldrewood' (1826): *Ups and Downs* (P) Farrell (1851): *Ephemera: An Iliad of Albury* (V) Gibson (1846): *Southerly Busters* (V)	John Dunmore Lang *d.* Charles Thatcher *d.*
1879	O'Reilly (1844): *Moondyne* (P)	C. E. W. Bean *b.* Louis Esson *b.* Miles Franklin *b.* Norman Lindsay *b.* William Howitt *d.* Richard Rowe *d.* Anthony Trollope's *John Caldigate* published in London Joseph Conrad in Australia 1879, 1880, 1887, 1892, 1893
1880	Kendall (1839): *Songs from the Mountains* (V) Praed (1851): *An Australian Heroine* (P) Rowe (1828): *Roughing it in Van Diemen's Land* (P)	J. F. Archibald and John Haynes begin publishing the *Bulletin* Australia's most notorious bushranger, Ned Kelly, captured at Glenrowan and hanged Second wave of immigration during the 1880s
1881	Clarke (1846): *The Conscientious Stranger* and *The Mystery of Major Molineux and Human Repetends* (P) Kendall (1839): *Orara* (V) Praed (1851): *Policy and Passion* (P) Spence (1825): *Gathered In* (P)	E. F. O'Ferrall ('Kodak') *b.* Frank Wilmot ('Furnley Maurice') *b.* Marcus Clarke *d.* Caroline Leakey *d.*
1882	'Boldrewood' (1826): *Robbery under Arms* (P), in the *Sydney Mail* Farrell (1851): *Two Stories* (P) O'Reilly (1844): *Songs, Legends and Ballads* (V)	Frederic Manning *b.* William Forster *d.* Henry Kendall *d.*
1883	Harpur (1813): *Poems* (V) McCrae, G. G. (1833): *A Rosebud from the Garden of the Taj* (V)	Ethel Anderson *b.* William Blocksidge ('Baylebridge') *b.* Katharine Susannah Prichard *b.* Charles Tompson *d.*
1884	Clarke (*d.* 1881): *The Marcus Clarke Memorial Volume* (P) Forster (*d.* 1882): *Midas* (D)	R. H. Horne *d.* N. W. Swan *d.*

DATE	AUTHOR AND TITLE	EVENT
1885	Clarke (*d.* 1881): *For the Term of his Natural Life* (first edn to be so titled; P) Foott (1846): *Where the Pelican Builds* (V) Praed (1851): *The Head Station* (P)	Vance Palmer *b.*
1886	Adams, Francis (1862): *Australian Essays* (P) Clarke (*d.* 1881): *Sensational Tales* (P) Hume (1859): *The Mystery of a Hansom Cab* (P) Kendall (*d.* 1882): *Poems* (V) Praed (1851): *Miss Jacobsen's Chance* (P)	George French Angas *d.* J. F. Archibald editor of *Bulletin* 1886–1902
1887	Adams, Francis (1862): *Poetical Works* (V) Cambridge (1844): *Unspoken Thoughts* (V) Farrell (1851): *How he Died, and Other Poems* (V) O'Reilly (1844): *The Golden Secret* (P)	F. T. Macartney *b.* Jack McLaren *b.* *Boomerang* edited by William Lane 1887–92 Henry Lawson's first published poem, 'Song of the Republic', in the *Bulletin.*
1888	Adams, Francis (1862): *Songs of the Army of the Night* (V)	Arthur Upfield *b.* 'Rolf Boldrewood's' *Robbery under Arms* published as a book in London Henry Lawson's first story, 'His Father's Mate', published in the *Bulletin*
1889	Giles (1835): *Australia Twice Traversed* (P) Praed (1851): *The Romance of a Station* (P) 'Tasma' (1848): *Uncle Piper of Piper's Hill* (P)	Anna Maria Bunn *d.*
1890	Archibald (1856) and Broomfield (1860), eds: *A Golden Shanty: Prose and Verse by Bulletin Writers* (P, V) 'Boldrewood' (1826): *A Colonial Reformer, The Miner's Right* and *The Squatter's Dream* (P) Cambridge (1844): *A Marked Man* (P) Clarke (*d.* 1881): *The Austral Edition* (P) Hales (1860): *The Wanderings of a Simple Child* (P)	James Devaney *b.* Ion Idriess *b.* J. B. O'Reilly *d.* Robert Louis Stevenson in Australia 1890, 1891, 1893

DATE	AUTHOR AND TITLE	EVENT
	Martin, Catherine (1847): *An Australian Girl* (P) 'Tasma' (1848): *In her Earliest Youth; A Sydney Sovereign* (P)	
1891	'Boldrewood' (1826): *A Sydney-side Saxon* (P) Cambridge (1844): *The Three Miss Kings* (P) Evans (1863): *The Repentance of Magdalen Despar* (V) 'Tasma' (1848): *The Penance of Portia James* (P)	Rudyard Kipling in Australia The Queensland Shearers' Strike
1892	Adams, Francis (1862): *Australian Life* (P) 'Boldrewood' (1826): *Nevermore* (P) Cambridge (1844): *Not All in Vain* (P) Lane (1861): *The Working Man's Paradise* (P) 'Tasma' (1848): *A Knight of the White Feather* (P) 'Warung' (1855): *Tales of the Convict System* (P)	John Tierney ('Brian James') *b.* Barcroft Boake *d.* Lane's *The Working Man's Paradise* (published in Brisbane) written to raise funds for the families of unionists imprisoned during the Shearers' Strike
1893	Adams, Francis (1862): *The Australians* (P) Clarke (*d.* 1881): *Chidiock Tichbourne* (P) Favenc (1845): *The Last of Six* (P) Gibson (1846): *Ironbark Chips and Stockwhip Cracks* (V) Praed (1851): *Outlaw and Lawmaker* (P)	Martin Boyd *b.* Frank Dalby Davison *b.* Francis Adams *d.* William Woolls *d.*
1894	Becke (1855): *By Reef and Palm* (P) Lawson (1867): *Short Stories in Prose and Verse* (P) Neilson (1872): *The Tales we Never Hear* (V) Stephens, A. G. (1865): *A Queenslander's Travel-notes* (P) Turner, Ethel (1872): *Seven Little Australians* (P) 'Warung' (1855): *Tales of the Early Days* (P)	Jean Devanny *b.* H. V. Evatt *b.*
1895	'Boldrewood' (1826): *The Sphinx of Eaglehawk* (P) Cambridge (1844): *Fidelis* (P) Paterson (1864): *The Man from Snowy River* (V)	Leonard Mann *b.* Mark Twain in Australia Words and music of 'Waltzing Matilda' first sung in public; the words were written by 'Banjo' Paterson

DATE	AUTHOR AND TITLE	EVENT
	Praed (1851): *Mrs Tregaskiss* (P) 'Tasma' (1848): *Not Counting the Cost* (P)	Angus & Robertson begin regular publishing with *The Man from Snowy River*
1896	Brereton (1871): *The Song of Brotherhood* and *Perdita* (V) Dyson (1865): *Rhymes from the Mines* (V) Favenc (1845): *The Moccasins of Silence* (P) Lawson (1867): *While the Billy Boils* (P); *In the Days When the World was Wide* (V) Parker (1855?): *Australian Legendary Tales* (P)	Joan Lindsay *b.* Sir Henry Parkes *d.* A. G. Stephens editor of *Bulletin* 'Red Page' 1896–1906
1897	Boake (*d.* 1892): *Where the Dead Men Lie* (V) Brennan (1870): *XVIII Poems* and *XXI Poems (1893–1897): Towards the Source* (V) Brereton (1871): *Sweetheart Mine* (V) Cambridge (1844): *At Midnight* (P) Farrell (1851): *Australia to England* (V) Praed (1851): *Nulma* (P) Quinn (1867): *Mostyn Stayne* (P) 'Tasma' (1848): *A Fiery Ordeal* (P) 'Warung' (1855): *Tales of the Old Regime* (P)	Marjorie Barnard *b.* Flora Eldershaw *b.* Jessie Catherine Couvreur ('Tasma') *d.*
1898	'Boldrewood' (1826): *A Romance of Canvas Town* and *Plain Living* (P) Cambridge (1844): *Materfamilias* (P) Daley (1858): *At Dawn and Dusk* (V) Dyson (1865): *Below and On Top* (P) Evans (1863): *Loraine, and Other Verses* (V) Ogilvie (1869): *Fair Girls and Gray Horses* (V) 'Warung' (1855): *Tales of the Isle of Death* and *Half-Crown Bob, and Tales of the Riverine* (P)	Ethel Pedley *d.* The Australian Constitution approved by referendum
1899	Brady (1869): *The Ways of Many Waters* (V) Brereton (1871): *Landlopers* (P) Favenc (1845): *My Only Murder* (P) Pedley, Ethel (?1860): *Dot and the Kangaroo* (P) Quinn (1867): *The Hidden Tide* (V) 'Rudd' (1868): *On our Selection* (P)	*The Bookfellow* (1899–1925) founded by A. G. Stephens Formation of the Australian Literature Society

DATE	AUTHOR AND TITLE	EVENT
1900	'Boldrewood' (1826): *The Babes in the Bush* (P) Lawson (1867): *On the Track and Over the Sliprails* (P); *Verses, Popular and Humorous* (V)	Jack Lindsay *b*. British Parliament passes an act to constitute the Commonwealth of Australia; all states join the Federation Two Aboriginal brothers, Jimmie and Joe Governor, and Jackie Underwood kill seven whites in New South Wales (see Keneally's *The Chant of Jimmie Blacksmith*, 1972)
1901	'Boldrewood' (1826): *In Bad Company* (P) Dyson (1865): *The Gold Stealers* (P) Franklin (1879): *My Brilliant Career* (P) Hay (1875): *Stifled Laughter* (P) Lawson (1867): *Joe Wilson and His Mates* (P) Quinn (1867): *The Circling Hearths* (V) Stephens, A. G. (1865), ed.: *The Bulletin Story Book* (P); *The Bulletin Reciter* (V)	Eleanor Dark *b*. Henrietta Drake-Brockman *b*. Xavier Herbert *b*. Kenneth Slessor *b*. G. B. Barton *d*. Proclamation of the Federal Constitution First national election Legislation enacted to prohibit permanent settlement by non-Europeans ('White Australia' policy)
1902	Baynton (1862): *Bush Studies* (P) 'Boldrewood' (1826): *The Ghost Camp* (P) Brereton (1871): *Oithona* (V) Lawson (1867): *Children of the Bush* Paterson (1864): *Rio Grande's Last Race* (V) Praed (1851): *Dwellers by the River* (P) Stephens, A. G. (1865): *Oblation* (V) Stephens, James Brunton (1835): *Poetical Works* (V); *My Chinee Cook and Other Humorous Verses* (V)	Dymphna Cusack *b*. Robert D. FitzGerald *b*. Florence James *b*. Alan Marshall *b*. Christina Stead *b*. James Brunton Stephens *d*.
1903	Bedford (1868): *True Eyes and the Whirlwind* (P) Cambridge (1844): *Thirty Years in Australia* (P) Furphy (1843): *Such is Life: Being Certain Extracts from the Diary of Tom Collins* (P) O'Dowd (1866): *Dawnward?* (V) Praed (1851): *Fugitive Anne* (P) 'Rudd' (1868): *Our New Selection* (P)	*Steele Rudd's Magazine* (1903–27) founded
1904	Farrell (*d*. 1904): *My Sundowner, and Other Poems* (V) 'Rudd' (1868): *Sandy's Selection* (P)	John Morrison *b*. Brian Penton *b*. F. N. Ratcliffe *b*.

DATE	AUTHOR AND TITLE	EVENT
	Stephens, A. G. (1865): *The Red Pagan* (P)	John Farrell *d.*
1905	Bedford (1868): *The Snare of Strength* (P) 'Boldrewood' (1826): *The Last Chance* (P) Favenc (1845): *Voices of the Desert* (V) Furphy (1843): *Rigby's Romance* (P) Lawson (1867): *When I was King* (V) Paterson (1864), ed.: *Old Bush Songs* (V) Praed (1851): *The Maid of the River* (P)	Victor Daley *d.* Lothian Publishing Co. founded in Melbourne
1906	Dyson (1865): *Fact'ry 'Ands* and *In the Roaring Fifties* (P) Evans (1863): *The Secret Key, and Other Verses* (V) O'Dowd (1866): *The Silent Land* (V) Paterson (1864): *An Outback Marriage* (P) Praed (1851): *The Lost Earl of Ellan* (P) 'Rudd' (1868): *Back at our Selection* (P)	Cyril Pearl *b.* A. H. Adams editor of *Bulletin* 'Red Page' 1906–9
1907	Baynton (1862): *Human Toll* (P) Hay (1875): *Herridge of Reality Swamp* (P) O'Dowd (1866): *Dominions of the Boundary* (V) Praed (1851): *The Luck of the Leura* (P)	Ralph de Boissiere *b.* Gavin Casey *b.* A. D. Hope *b.* John O'Grady ('Nino Culotta') *b.* *Lone Hand* (1907–21) founded
1908	Banfield (1852): *The Confessions of a Beachcomber* (P) Brereton (1871): *Sea and Sky* (V) Daley (1858): *Poems* (V) Gunn (1870): *We of the Never Never* (P) 'Richardson' (1870): *Maurice Guest* (P) Sorenson (1869): *The Squatter's Ward* (P)	Eve Langley *b.* Colin Simpson *b.* Ernest Favenc *d.* Commonwealth Literary Fund founded
1909	Franklin (1879): *Some Everyday Folk and Dawn* (P) McCrae, Hugh (1876): *Satyrs and Sunlight: Silvarum Libri* (V)	Ronald McKie *b.* G. E. Evans *d.*

DATE	AUTHOR AND TITLE	EVENT
	O'Dowd (1866): *The Seven Deadly Sins* (V)	
	Praed (1851): *A Summer Wreath* (P)	
	'Rudd' (1868): *Stocking our Selection* (P)	
1910	Bean (1879): *On the Wool Track* (P)	Alan Moorehead *b*.
	Blocksidge (1883): *Moreton Miles*; *Southern Songs*; *A Northern Trail* and *The New Life* (V)	Catherine Spence *d*. Mitchell Library (Sydney) opens
	Brereton (1871): *To-morrow* (D)	
	Bruce (1878): *A Little Bush Maid* (P)	
	Esson (1879): *Bells and Bees* (V)	
	Gilmore (1865): *Marri'd* (V)	
	Lawson (1867): *The Rising of the Court* (P)	
	Praed (1851): *Opal Fire* (P)	
	'Richardson' (1870): *The Getting of Wisdom* (P)	
	Spence (*d*. 1910): *An Autobiography* (P)	
1911	Bean (1879): *The Dreadnought of the Darling* (P)	William Hart-Smith *b*.
	Bedford (1868): *Billy Pagan, Mining Engineer* (P)	Hal Porter *b*. Olaf Ruhen *b*.
	Daley (*d*. 1905): *Wine and Roses* (V)	Dal Stivens *b*.
	Dyson (1865): *Benno and Some of the Push* (P)	Judah Waten *b*. William Astley ('Price Warung') *d*.
	Lawson (1867): *Mateship* (P)	Up to 300,000 migrants (mostly British) arrive 1911–14
	Stone (1871): *Jonah* (P)	
1912	Cambridge (1844): *The Retrospect* (P)	George Johnston *b*.
	Esson (1879): *Red Gums* (V); *The Time is not yet Ripe* and *Three Short Plays – The Woman Tamer, Dead Timber, The Sacred Place* (D)	Roland Robinson *b*. Kylie Tennant *b*. Patrick White *b*. Joseph Furphy *d*.
	Gibson (1846): *Ironbark Splinters from the Australian Bush* (V)	
	Gordon (*d*. 1870): *Poems* (V)	
	Hay (1875): *Captain Quadring* (P)	
	O'Dowd (1866): *The Bush* (V)	
1913	Brennan (1870): *Poems 1913* (V)	John Blight *b*.
	Brennan (1870): and Brereton (1871): *A Mask* (D)	Mary Durack *b*. Rex Ingamells *b*.
	Cambridge (1844): *The Hand in the Dark* (V)	Kenneth Mackenzie *b*. Barbara McNamara ('Elizabeth
	Dennis (1876): *Backblock Ballads* (V)	O'Conner') *b*.
	Lawson (1867): *Triangles of Life* (P)	Douglas Stewart *b*.
	Lindsay, Norman (1879): *A Curate in Bohemia* (P)	Donald Stuart *b*. Louis Becke *d*.

DATE	AUTHOR AND TITLE	EVENT
	Prichard (1883): *Clovelly Verses* (V) Stephens, A. G. (1865): *Bill's Idees* (P)	
1914	Adams, A. H. (1872): *Three Plays for the Australian Stage – The Wasters, Galahad Jones, Mrs Pretty and the Premier* (D) Blocksidge (1883): *Life's Testament* (V) Dyson (1865): *Spat's Fact'ry* (P)	Peter Cowan *b*. Russel Ward *b*. Rachel Henning *d*. Australia joins Britain in World War I (1914–18)
1915	Dennis (1876): *The Songs of a Sentimental Bloke* (V) McCrae, G. G. (1833): *The Fleet and Convoy* (V) Mawson (1882): *The Home of the Blizzard* (P) Palmer, Vance (1885): *The Forerunners* (V); *The World of Men* (P) Praed (1851): *Lady Bridget in the Never Never Land* (P) Prichard (1883): *The Pioneers* (P) Stone, Louis (1871): *Betty Wayside* (P)	David Campbell *b*. C. M. H. Clark *b*. T. A. G. Hungerford *b*. John Manifold *b*. David Martin *b*. Judith Wright *b*. T. A. Browne ('Rolf Boldrewood') *d*. Australian and New Zealand Army Corps (ANZACs) at Gallipoli
1916	Blocksidge (1883): *A Wreath* (V) Dennis (1876): *The Moods of Ginger Mick* (V) Furphy (*d*. 1912): *Poems* (V) Neilson (1872): *Old Granny Sullivan* (V) Praed (1851): *Sister Sorrow* (P) Prichard (1883): *Windlestraws* (P)	George R. Turner *b*. Morris West *b*. *Birth* (ed. Bernard O'Dowd, Vance Palmer and others, 1916–22) founded
1917	Baynton (1862): *Cobbers* (P) Bedford (1868): *The Silver Star* (P) Dennis (1876): *Doreen* and *The Glugs of Gosh* (V) 'Maurice' (1881): *To God: From the Weary Nations* (V) Paterson (1864): *Saltbush Bill, J.P.* (V); *Three Elephant Power* (P) 'Richardson' (1870): *Australia Felix* (P)	Nancy Cato *b*. Jon Cleary *b*. Frank Hardy *b*. Sumner Locke-Elliott *b*. James McAuley *b*; William Lane *d*.
1918	Brennan (1870): *A Chant of Doom* (V) Dennis (1876): *Digger Smith* (V) Gibbs (1877): *Snugglepot and Cuddlepie* (P) Gilmore (1865): *The Passionate Heart* (V)	Mary Hannay Foott *d*. J. R. Houlding *d*.

DATE	AUTHOR AND TITLE	EVENT
	Hay (1875): *The Escape of the Notorious Sir William Heans* (P) Lindsay, Norman (1879): *The Magic Pudding* (P) McCrae, G. G. (1833): *John Rous* (P)	
1919	Bedford (1868): *Aladdin and the Boss Cockie* (P) Brereton (1871): *The Burning Marl* (V) Dennis (1876): *Jim of the Hills* (V) Neilson (1872): *Heart of Spring* (V)	Nene Gare *b.* Olga Masters *b.* J. F. Archibald *d.* *Smith's Weekly* (1919–50) founded
1920	Boyd, Martin (1893): *Retrospect* (V) Esson (1879): *Dead Timber – The Drovers* and three earlier plays (D) Kendall (*d.* 1882): *Poems* (V) McCrae, Hugh (1876): *Colombine* (V) 'Maurice' (1881): *Eyes of Vigilance* and *Ways and Means* (V) Palmer, Vance (1885): *The Camp* (V); *The Shantykeeper's Daughter* (P) Quinn (1867): *Poems* (V)	Donald Horne *b.* Rosemary Dobson *b.* Gwen Harwood *b.* Colin Thiele *b.* Kath Walker *b.* Louisa Lawson *d.*
1921	Bean (1879): *The Story of Anzac, The Official History of Australia in the War of 1914–18*, vol. i (P) Dennis (1876): *A Book for Kids* (V) 'Maurice' (1881): *Arrows of Longing* (V) O'Dowd (1866): *Alma Venus!* (V) O'Ferrall (1881): *Bodger and the Boarders* (P) Paterson (1864): *Collected Verse* (V) Prichard (1883): *Black Opal* (P)	Eric Lambert *b.* Ray Lawler *b.* Ivan Southall *b.* Dimitris Tsaloumas *b.* Patricia Wrightson *b.* G. H. Gibson ('Ironbark') *d.*
1922	Gilmore (1865): *Hound of the Road* (P) Macartney (1887): *Something for Tokens* (V) McCrae, Hugh (1876): *Idyllia* (V) Palmer, Vance (1885): *The Boss of Killara* (P)	Geoffrey Dutton *b.* Henry Lawson *d.* Legislation for assisted passage leads to a further 300,000 migrants during the 1920s Melbourne University Press established
1923	Martin, Catherine (1847): *The Incredible Journey* (P) Neilson (1872): *Ballad and Lyrical Poems* (V) Palmer, Vance (1885): *The Enchanted Island* (P)	Dorothy Hewett *b.* Eric Rolls *b.* D. H. Lawrence's *Kangaroo* published in London *Vision* (ed. Jack Lindsay, Kenneth Slessor and others, 1923–4) founded Opening of first public radio station (2 SB Sydney)

DATE	AUTHOR AND TITLE	EVENT
1924	Brereton (1871): *The Carillon Poems* (V) Dennis (1876): *Rose of Spadgers* (V) Palmer, Vance (1885): *Cronulla* and *The Outpost* (P); *The Black Horse* (D) Slessor (1901): *Thief of the Moon* (V)	David Rowbotham *b*. D. H. Lawrence and M. L. Skinner, *The Boy in the Bush* (published in London)
1925	Boyd, Martin (1893): *Love Gods* (P) Gilmore (1865): *The Tilted Cart* (V) Lawson (*d*. 1922): *Poetical Works* (V) 'Richardson' (1870): *The Way Home* (P)	Thea Astley *b*. Vincent Buckley *b*. Francis Webb *b*. E. F. O'Ferrall ('Kodak') *d*. *The Australian Encyclopaedia*, ed. Arthur Jose, 2 vols (Angus & Robertson, 1925–6)
1926	Boyd, Martin (1893): *Brangane* (P) McLaren (1887): *My Crowded Solitude* (P) Prichard (1883): *Working Bullocks* (P) Slessor (1901): *Earth-visitors* (V)	Ada Cambridge *d*.
1927	Devaney (1890): *The Currency Lass* (P) FitzGerald (1902): *The Greater Apollo* (V) Neilson (1872): *New Poems* (V)	David Ireland *b*. Alan Seymour *b*. G. G. McCrae *d*.
1928	Boyd, Martin (1893): *The Montforts* (P) Brereton (1871): *Swags Up!* (V); *The Temple on the Hill* (D) Evans (*d*. 1909): *Collected Verse* (V) Franklin (1879): *Up the Country* (P) McCrae, Hugh (1876): *Satyrs and Sunlight* (V) Palmer, Vance (1885): *The Man Hamilton* (P) Prichard (1883): *The Wild Oats of Han* (P)	Bruce Beaver *b*. Richard Beynon *b*. Elizabeth Harrower *b*. *London Aphrodite* (ed. Jack Lindsay and P. R. Stephensen 1928–9) founded in London Charles Kingsford Smith makes first trans-Pacific flight in the 'Southern Cross' Formation of the Fellowship of Australian Writers
1929	Devaney (1890): *The Vanished Tribes* (P) Dyson (1865): *The Golden Shanty* (P) 'Eldershaw, M. Barnard': *A House is Built* (P) FitzGerald (1902): *To Meet the Sun* (V) Hay (1875): *Strabane of the Mulberry Hills* (P) Manning (1882): *The Middle Parts of Fortune: Somme and Ancre* [abridged edn 1930 titled *Her Privates We*] (P)	Ray Mathew *b*. Peter Porter *b*. Barbara Baynton *d*. The Great Depression (1929–34) begins

DATE	AUTHOR AND TITLE	EVENT
	Prichard (1883): *Coonardoo* (P) 'Richardson' (1870): *Ultima Thule* (P)	
1930	Franklin (1879): *Ten Creeks Run* (P) Gilmore (1865): *The Wild Swan* (V) Lindsay, Norman (1879): *Redheap* (P) Lower (1903): *Here's Luck* (P) Palmer, Vance (1885): *Men are Human* and *The Passage* (P) Prichard (1883): *Haxby's Circus* (P) 'Richardson' (1870): *The Fortunes of Richard Mahony* – the three novels published in 1917, 1925, 1929 (P)	Geoffrey Blainey *b.* Bruce Dawe *b.* Peter Kenna *b.*
1931	Brereton (1871): *So Long, Mick* (D) Davison (1893): *Forever Morning* and *Man-shy* (P) 'Eldershaw, M. Barnard': *Green Memory* (P) Franklin (1883): *Old Blastus of Bandicoot* and *Back to Bool Bool* (P) Gilmore (1865): *The Rue Tree* (V) Idriess (1890): *Lasseter's Last Ride* (P) Palmer, Vance (1885): *Separate Lives* (P) Upfield (1888): *The Sands of Windee* (P)	Shirley Hazzard *b.* Peter Mathers *b.* Barry Oakley *b.* E. G. Dyson *d.* *Manuscript: A Miscellany of Art and Letters* (Geelong, 1931–5) founded
1932	Dark (1901): *Slow Dawning* (P) Gilmore (1865): *Under the Wilgas* (V) Idriess (1890): *Flynn of the Inland* (P) Lindsay, Norman (1879): *Miracles by Arrangement* and *The Cautious Amorist* (P) Mann, Leonard (1895): *Flesh in Armour* (P) Palmer, Vance (1885): *Daybreak* (P) Prichard (1883): *Kiss on the Lips* (P); *The Earth Lover* (V) Slessor (1901): *Cuckooz Contrey* (V)	Christopher Koch *b.* C. J. Brennan *d.* Fergus Hume *d.* Australia's national broadcasting network (the ABC) begins
1933	Davison (1893): *The Wells of Beersheba* (P) Franklin (1879): *Bring the Monkey* (P) Lindsay, Norman (1879): *Saturdee* (P) O'Ferrall (*d.* 1925): *Stories* (P) Slessor (1901): *Darlinghurst Nights* (V)	Kevin Gilbert *b.* John Le Gay Brereton *d.* A. G. Stephens *d.*

DATE	AUTHOR AND TITLE	EVENT
1934	'Baylebridge' (1883): *Love Redeemed* (V) Boyd, Martin (1893): *Scandal of Spring* (P) Dark (1901): *Prelude to Christopher* (P) Lindsay, Norman (1879): *Pan in the Parlour* (P) 'Maurice' (1881): *Melbourne Odes* (V) Neilson (1872): *Collected Poems* (V) Palmer, Vance (1885): *The Swayne Family; Sea and Spinifex* (P) Penton (1904): *Landtakers* (P) 'Richardson' (1870): *The End of a Childhood* (P) 'Rudd' (1868): *Green Grey Homestead* (P) Stead (1902): *The Salzburg Tales* and *Seven Poor Men of Sydney* (P)	Barry Humphries *b.* James McQueen *b.* David Malouf *b.* Chris Wallace-Crabbe *b.*
1935	Boyd, Martin (1893): *The Lemon Farm* (P) Dennis (1876): *The Singing Garden* (P, V) Mann, Leonard (1895): *Human Drift* (P) Palmer, Vance (1885): *Hurricane* (P) Tennant (1912): *Tiburon* (P) White, Patrick (1912): *The Ploughman, and Other Poems* (V)	Rodney Hall *b.* Thomas Keneally *b.* Thomas Shapcott *b.* Randolph Stow *b.* A. H. Davis ('Steele Rudd') *d.* Frederick Manning *d.* Mrs Campbell Praed *d.* Louis Stone *d.*
1936	Boyd, Martin (1893): *The Painted Princess* (P) Dark (1901): *Return to Coolami* (P) Davison (1893): *Children of the Dark People* (P) Devanny (1894): *Sugar Heaven* (P) 'Eldershaw, M. Barnard': *The Glasshouse* (P) Franklin (1879): *All That Swagger* (P) Ingamells (1913): *Forgotten People* (V) Paterson (1864): *The Shearer's Colt* (P) Stead (1902): *The Beauties and Furies* (P) Stivens (1911): *The Tramp* (P)	A. H. Adams *d.* C. J. Dennis *d.* A. A. G. Hales *d.* National Library begins issuing *Annual Catalogue of Australian Publications* (1936–60)
1937	Boyd, Martin (1893): *The Picnic* (P) Dark (1901): *Sun across the Sky* (P)	Catherine Martin *d.* *Venture* (ed. Rex Ingamells, Adelaide, 1937–40) founded

DATE	AUTHOR AND TITLE	EVENT
	'Eldershaw, M. Barnard': *Plaque with Laurel* (P)	
	Hay (1875): *The Mystery of Alfred Doubt* (P)	
	Mackenzie (1913): *Our Earth* (V); *The Young Desire It* (P)	
	Mann, Leonard (1895): *A Murder in Sydney* (P)	
	Palmer, Vance (1885): *Legend for Sanderson* (P)	
	Prichard (1883): *Intimate Strangers* (P)	
1938	Boyd, Martin (1893): *Night of the Party* (P)	Colin Johnson *b*.
	Brennan (*d*. 1932): *Twenty-three Poems* (V)	Morris Lurie *b*.
	Dark (1901): *Waterway* (P)	Frank Moorhouse *b*.
	Evatt (1894): *Rum Rebellion* (P)	Les A. Murray *b*.
	FitzGerald (1902): *Moonlight Acre* (V)	C. J. Dennis *d*.
	Herbert (1901): *Capricornia* (P)	*Jindyworobak Anthology* (1938–53) begins
	Ingamells (1913): *Sun-Freedom* (V)	
	Lindsay, Norman (1879): *Age of Consent* (P)	
	Mackenzie (1913): *Chosen People* (P)	
	Mann, Leonard (1895): *The Plumed Voice* (V)	
	Neilson (1872): *Beauty Imposes* (V)	
	Ratcliffe (1904): *Flying Fox and Drifting Sand* (P)	
	Stead (1902): *House of All Nations*	
1939	'Baylebridge' (1883): *Sextains* and *This Vital Flesh* (V)	*Southerly* (Sydney) begins.
	Boyd, Martin (1893): *A Single Flame* (P)	Douglas Stewart literary editor of the *Bulletin* 1939–61
	Franklin, Miles (1879) and Cusack (1902): *Pioneers on Parade* (P)	Australia at war 1939–45
	Gilmore (1865): *Battlefields* (V)	
	McCrae, Hugh (1876): *Poems* (V)	
	Mann, Leonard (1895): *Mountain Flat* (P)	
	'Richardson' (1870): *The Young Cosima* (P)	
	Slessor (1901): *Five Bells* (V)	
	Tennant (1912): *Foveaux* (P)	
	White, Patrick (1912): *Happy Valley* (P)	
1940	Boyd, Martin (1893): *Nuns in Jeopardy* (P)	Jack Hibberd *b*. Geoffrey Lehmann *b*.

DATE	AUTHOR AND TITLE	EVENT
	Davison (1893): *The Woman at the Mill* (P)	Langloh Parker d.
	Ingamells (1913): *Memory of Hills* (V)	*Angry Penguins* (ed. Max Harris and others, 1940–6) founded
	Neilson (1872): *To the Men of the Roads* (V)	*Meanjin* (Brisbane, then Melbourne) begins with C. B. Christesen as first editor
	Palmer, Vance (1885): *National Portraits* (P)	
	Prichard (1883): *Brumby Innes* (D)	
	Stead (1902): *The Man who Loved Children* (P)	
	Stewart (1913): *Elegy for an Airman* (V)	
1941	Dark (1901): *The Timeless Land* (P)	Murray Bail b.
	Gilmore (1865): *The Disinherited* (V)	Roger McDonald b.
	Macartney (1887): *Preferences* (V)	Randolph Bedford d.
	Manifold (1915): *The Death of Ned Kelly* (V)	F. J. Broomfield d.
	Mann, Leonard (1895): *Poems from the Mask* (V)	A. B. ('Banjo') Paterson d.
	O'Dowd (1866): *Poems* (V)	Douglas Stewart editor of *Bulletin* 'Red Page' 1941–61
	Prichard (1883): *Moon of Desire* (P)	*Coast to Coast* (1941–73) founded
	Stewart (1913): *Sonnets to the Unknown Soldier* (V)	*Poetry: A Quarterly of Australian and New Zealand Verse* (ed. Flexmore Hudson, 1941–7) founded
	Tennant (1912): *The Battlers* (P)	
	White, Patrick (1912): *The Living and the Dead* (P)	
1942	Casey (1907): *It's Harder for Girls* (P)	Ron Blair b.
	Ingamells (1913): *News of the Sun* (V)	Helen Garner b.
	Langley (1908): *The Pea Pickers* (P)	Humphrey McQueen b.
	Mann, Leonard (1885): *The Go-Getter* (P)	Michael Wilding b.
	Porter, Hal (1911): *Short Stories* (P)	David Williamson b.
	Stewart (1913): *Ned Kelly* (D)	William Blocksidge ('Baylebridge') d.
		John Shaw Neilson d.
		Frank Wilmot ('Furnley Maurice') d.
1943	Barnard, Marjorie (1897): *The Persimmon Tree* (P)	Peter Carey b.
	Casey (1907): *Birds of a Feather* (P)	Robert Drewe b.
	Hart-Smith (1911): *Columbus Goes West* (V)	John Tranter b.
	Ingamells (1913): *Content are the Quiet Ranges* and *Unknown Land* (V)	Louis Esson d.
	Neilson (1872): *Lines Written in Memory of Adam Lindsay Gordon* (V)	*Australian New Writing* (1943–6) founded
	Stewart (1913): *Ned Kelly* (D)	*Barjai* (1943–7) founded
	Tennant (1912): *Ride on Stranger* and *Time Enough Later* (P)	

DATE	AUTHOR AND TITLE	EVENT
1944	Cowan (1914): *Drift* (P) Dobson (1920): *In a Convex Mirror* (V) Dutton (1922): *Night Flight and Sunrise* (V) McCrae, Hugh (1876): *Forests of Pan* (V) Mackenzie, Kenneth (1913): *The Moonlit Doorway* (V) 'Ern Malley': *The Darkening Ecliptic* (V) Manifold (1915): *Trident* (V) Mann, Leonard (1895): *The Delectable Mountains* (V) Marshall (1902): *These are my People* (P) Prichard (1883): *Potch and Colour* (P) Slessor (1901): *One Hundred Poems* (V) Stewart 1913); *A Girl with Red Hair* (P); *The Fire on the Snow and The Golden Lover* (D)	Robert Adamson *b.* Alex Buzo *b.* Blanche D'Alpüget *b.* David Foster *b.* The 'Ern Malley hoax' against *Angry Penguins* (ed. Max Harris) occurs
1945	Blight (1913): *The Old Pianist* (V) Casey (1907): *Downhill is Easier* (P) Dark (1901): *The Little Company* (P) Gilmore (1865): *Pro Patria Australia* (V) Hart-Smith (1911): *Harvest* (V) Lindsay, Norman (1879): *The Cousin from Fiji* (P) McCrae, Hugh (1876): *Voice of the Forest* (V) West (1916): *Moon in my Pocket* (P)	John Docker *b.* John Romeril *b.* William Gosse Hay *d.* The Australian Book Council, later National Book Council, formed in Sydney
1946	Boyd, Martin (1893): *Lucinda Brayford* (P) Davison (1893): *Dusty* (P) Esson (*d.* 1943): *The Southern Cross* (D) Franklin (1879): *My Career Goes Bung* (P) McAuley (1917): *Under Aldebaran* (V) Manifold (1915): *Selected Verse* (V) Marshall (1902): *Tell us about the Turkey, Jo* (P) Prichard (1883): *The Roaring Nineties* (P) Stead (1902): *Letty Fox, her Luck* (P) Stewart (1913): *The Dosser in Springtime* (V) Stivens (1911): *The Courtship of Uncle Henry* (P)	Ethel Robertson ('Henry Handel Richardson') *d.* Children's Book of the Year Award begins

DATE	AUTHOR AND TITLE	EVENT
	Tennant (1912): *Lost Haven* (P)	
	Wright (1915): *The Moving Image* (V)	
1947	Casey (1907): *The Wits are Out* (P)	Peter Kocan *b.*
	'Eldershaw, M. Barnard': *Tomorrow and Tomorrow* (P)	Post-war European immigration programme begins
	Lindsay, Norman (1879): *Halfway to Anywhere* (P)	
	Morrison (1904): *Sailors Belong Ships* (P)	
	Neilson (*d.* 1942): *Unpublished Poems* (V)	
	Palmer, Vance (1885): *Hail Tomorrow* (D); *Cyclone* (P)	
	Stewart (1913): *Glencoe* (V); *Shipwreck* (D)	
1948	Dark (1901): *Storm of Time* (P)	Michael Dransfield *b.*
	Dobson (1920): *The Ship of Ice* (V)	
	Drake-Brockman (1901): *Sydney or the Bush* (P)	
	Furphy (*d.* 1912): *The Buln-Buln and the Brolga* (P)	
	Gilmore (1865): *Selected Verse* (V)	
	Harpur (*d.* 1868): *Rosa: Love Sonnets to Mary Doyle* (V)	
	McCrae, Hugh (1876): *Story Book Only* (P)	
	Marshall (1902): *Ourselves Writ Strange* (P)	
	Palmer, Vance (1885): *Golconda* (P)	
	Park (19??): *The Harp in the South* (P)	
	Prichard (1883): *Golden Miles* (P)	
	Stead (1902): *A Little Tea, a Little Chat* (P)	
	Webb (1925): *A Drum for Ben Boyd* (V)	
	White, Patrick (1912): *The Aunt's Story* (P)	
1949	Boyd, Martin (1893): *Such Pleasure* (P)	Roderick Quinn *d.*
	Campbell (1915): *Speak with the Sun* (V)	
	FitzGerald (1902): *Heemskerck Shoals* (V)	
	Marshall (1902): *How Beautiful are thy Feet; Pull down the Blind* (P)	
	Morrison (1904): *The Creeping City* (P)	
	Park (19): *Poor Man's Orange* (P)	
	Wright (1915): *Woman to Man* (V)	

DATE	AUTHOR AND TITLE	EVENT
1950	Casey (1907): *City of Men* (P) Franklin (1879): *Prelude to Waking* (P) Hardy (1917): *Power without Glory* (P) 'James, Brian' (1892): *The Advancement of Spencer Button* (P) Lindsay, Norman (1879): *Dust or Polish?* (P) Marshall (1902): *Bumping into Friends* (P) Morrison (1904): *Port of Call* (P) Prichard (1883): *Winged Seeds* (P)	Louis Nowra *b.*
1951	Cusack (1902) and Florence James (1902): *Come in Spinner* (P) Ingamells (1913): *The Great South Land* (V) McCrae, Hugh (1876): *The Ship of Heaven* (D) Mackenzie, Kenneth (1913): *Dead Men Rising* (P) Stivens (1911): *Jimmy Brockett* (P)	Kate Grenville *b.* Angelo Loukakis *b.* Brian Penton *d.* Defamation suit over Frank Hardy's *Power without Glory*
1952	Boyd, Martin (1893): *The Cardboard Crown* (P) Braddon (1921): *The Naked Island* (P) De Boissiere (1907): *Crown Jewel* (P) FitzGerald (1902): *Between Two Tides* (V) Henning (1826): *The Letters*, ed. David Adams (P) Hungerford (1915): *The Ridge and the River* (P) Marshall (1902): *People of the Dreamtime* (P) Stead (1902): *The People with the Dogs* (P) Stewart (1913): *Sun Orchids* (V) Tennant (1912): *Tether a Dragon* (D) Waten (1911): *Alien Son* (P) Webb (1925): *Leichhardt in Theatre* (V)	E. J. Brady *d.* *Ern Malley's Journal* (ed. Max Harris and others, 1952–5) founded *The Realist Writer* (ed. Bill Wannan, subsequently Stephen Murray-Smith, 1952–4) founded
1953	Brennan (*d.* 1932): *The Burden of Tyre* (V) 'Caddie': *Caddie, a Sydney Barmaid* (P) Dark (1901): *No Barrier* (P) FitzGerald (1902): *This Night's Orbit* (V) Martin, David (1915): *From Life* (V)	Steve Sewell *b.* Bernard O'Dowd *d.*

DATE	AUTHOR AND TITLE	EVENT
	Stivens (1911): *The Gambling Ghost* (P)	
	Tennant (1912): *The Joyful Condemned* (P)	
	Webb (1925): *Birthday* (V)	
	Wright (1915): *The Gateway* (V)	
1954	Blight (1913): *The Two Suns Met* (V)	Miles Franklin *d.*
	Buckley (1925): *The World's Flesh* (V)	Jack McLaren *d.*
	Franklin (1879): *Cockatoos* (P)	*Overland* (Melbourne, ed. Stephen Murray-Smith) founded
	Gilmore (1865): *Fourteen Men* (V)	*Poetry Magazine* (Sydney, 1954–71; later *New Poetry*) founded
	Lambert (1921): *The Veterans* (P)	
	Langley (1908): *White Topee* (P)	
	Mackenzie (1913): *The Refuge* (P)	
	Palmer, Vance (1885): *The Legend of the Nineties* (P)	
	Waten (1911): *The Unbending* (P)	
1955	Boyd, Martin (1893): *A Difficult Young Man* (P)	Rex Ingamells *d.*
	Hope (1907): *The Wandering Islands* (V)	Kenneth Mackenzie ('Seaforth Mackenzie') *d.*
	Marshall (1902): *I Can Jump Puddles* (P)	First performance of Ray Lawler *Summer of the Seventeenth Doll*
	Morrison (1904): *Black Cargo* (P)	
	Niland (1917): *The Shiralee* (P)	
	Palmer, Vance (1885): *Let the Birds Fly* (P)	
	Stewart (1913): *The Birdsville Track* (V)	
	Stivens (1911): *Ironbark Bill* (P)	
	White, Patrick (1912): *The Tree of Man* (P)	
	Wright (1915): *The Two Fires* (V)	
1956	Anderson, Ethel (1883): *At Parramatta* (P)	Flora Eldershaw *d.*
	Campbell (1915): *The Miracle of Mullion Hill* (V)	*Quadrant* (Sydney), ed. James McAuley, begins
	De Boissiere (1907): *Rum and Coca-Cola* (P)	*Westerly* (Perth) begins
	Franklin (*d.* 1954): *Gentlemen at Gyang Gyang* (P)	Television begins in Sydney with ABC and TCN-9
	McAuley (1917): *A Vision of Ceremony* (V)	
	Marshall (1902): *How's Andy Going?* (P)	
	Porter, Hal (1911): *The Hexagon* (V)	
	Stow (1935): *A Haunted Land* (P)	
	Tennant (1912): *The Honey Flow* (P)	
	Upfield (1888): *Man of Two Worlds* (P)	

DATE	AUTHOR AND TITLE	EVENT
1957	Boyd, Martin (1893): *Outbreak of Love* (P) Harrower (1928): *Down in the City* (P) Lawler (1921): *The Summer of the Seventeenth Doll* (D) Mann, Leonard (1895): *Elegiac, and Other Poems* (V) Palmer, Vance (1885): *Seedtime* and *The Rainbow Bird* (P) Slessor (1901): *Poems* (P) Stivens (1911): *The Scholarly Mouse* (P) Stow (1935): *Act One* (V); *The Bystander* (P) Waten (1911): *Shares in Murder* (P) White, Patrick (1912): *Voss* (P)	*Australian Letters* (ed. Max Harris, Geoffrey Dutton and others, 1957–68) founded Miles Franklin Award begins with *Voss*
1958	Astley (1925): *Girl with a Monkey* (P) Cato (1917): *All the Rivers Run* (P) Cowan (1914): *The Unploughed Land* (P) O'Grady, John ('Nino Culotta') (1907) Hardy (1917): *The Four-legged Lottery* (P) Harrower (1928): *The Long Prospect* (P) Koch (1932): *The Boys in the Island* (P) Martin, David (1915): *Poems 1938–1958* (V) Pearl (1906): *Wild Men of Sydney* (P) Porter, Hal (1911): *A Handful of Pennies* (P) Ruhen (1911): *Naked under Capricorn* (P) Stewart (1913): *Four Plays* (D) Stivens (1911): *The Wide Arch* (P) Stow (1935): *To the Islands* (P) Ward (1914): *The Australian Legend* (P)	Archie Weller *b.* Ethel Anderson *d.* Mary Grant Bruce *d.* Hugh McCrae *d.* Ethel Turner *d.* *Melbourne Critical Review* begins, since 1965 titled the *Critical Review* *Nation* (1958–72) begins National Institute of Dramatic Art (NIDA) established at University of New South Wales
1959	Campbell (1915): *Evening Under Lamplight* (P) Durack (1913): *Kings in Grass Castles* (P) FitzGerald (1902): *The Wind at your Door* (V) Hart-Smith (1911): *Poems of Discovery* (V) Herbert (1901): *Seven Emus* (P)	Vance Palmer *d.*

DATE	AUTHOR AND TITLE	EVENT
	Hewett (1923): *Bobbin Up* (P)	
	Mann, Leonard (1895): *Andrea Caslin* (P)	
	Palmer, Vance (1885): *The Big Fellow* (P)	
	Prichard (1883): *N'Goola* (P)	
	Stuart (1913): *Yandy* (P)	
	Wallace-Crabbe (1934): *The Music of Division* (V)	
	West (1916): *The Devil's Advocate* (P)	
	Wright (1915): *The Generations of Men* (P)	
1960	Astley (1925): *A Descant for Gossips* (P)	Tim Winton *b.*
	Beynon (1928): *The Shifting Heart* (D)	National Library of Australia becomes an autonomous body
	Boyd, Robin (1919): *The Australian Ugliness* (P)	Adelaide Festival of the Arts established
	Harrower (1928): *The Catherine Wheel* (P)	First performance of Alan Seymour's *The One Day of the Year*
	Hope (1907): *Poems* (V)	
	'O'Conner' (1913): *The Irishman* (P)	
	Stewart (1913): *Fisher's Ghost* (D); ed., *Voyager Poems* (V)	
1961	Beaver (1928): *Under the Bridge* (V)	Mrs Aeneas Gunn *d.*
	Buckley (1925): *Masters in Israel* (V)	*Australian Book Review*, 1st ser. (1961–74) founded
	Clark, C. M. H. (1915): *A History of Australia*, vol. i (P)	*Australian National Bibliography* begins
	Cook (1929): *Wake in Fright* (P)	
	Gare (1919): *The Fringe Dwellers* (P)	
	Hall (1935): *Penniless Till Doomsday* (V)	
	Herbert (1901): *Soldiers' Women* (P)	
	Manifold (1915): *Nightmares and Sunhorses* (V)	
	Mathew (1929): *A Bohemian Affair* (P)	
	Porter, Hal (1911): *The Tilted Cross* (P)	
	Porter, Peter (1929): *Once Bitten, Twice Bitten* (V)	
	Shapcott (1935): *Time on Fire* (V)	
	Stuart (1913): *The Driven* (P)	
	Waten (1911): *Time of Conflict* (P)	
	Webb (1925): *Socrates, and Other Poems* (V)	
	White, Patrick (1912): *Riders in the Chariot* (P)	

DATE	AUTHOR AND TITLE	EVENT
1962	Astley (1925): *The Well Dressed Explorer* (P) Boyd, Martin (1893): *When Blackbirds Sing* (V) Campbell (1915): *Poems* (V) Casey (1907): *Amid the Plenty* (P) Dawe (1930): *No Fixed Address* (V) Dutton (1922): *Flowers and Fury* (V) FitzGerald (1902): *Southmost Twelve* (V) Martin, David (1915): *The Young Wife* (P) Morrison (1904): *Twenty-three* (P) Porter, Hal (1911): *A Bachelor's Children* (P) Seymour (1927): *The One Day of the Year* (D) Stewart (1913): *Rutherford; The Garden of Ships* (V) Stow (1935): *Outrider* (V) Turner, George (1916): *The Cupboard under the Stairs* (P) Wright (1915): *Birds* (V)	Paul Radley *b.* Jean Devanny *d.* Dame Mary Gilmore *d.* *Makar* (St Lucia, 1962–79) founded First chair of Australian literature established at Sydney University, held by G. A. Wilkes and, from 1968, by Leonie Kramer Australia joins USA in Vietnam War 1962–72
1963	Blight (1913): *A Beachcomber's Diary* (V) Hall (1935): *Forty Beads on a Hangman's Rope* (V) Hardy (1917): *Legends from Benson's Valley* (P) Harwood (1920): *Poems* (V) Hazzard (1931): *Cliffs of Fall* (P) Herbert (1901): *Larger than Life* and *Disturbing Element* (P) Locke-Elliott (1917): *Careful, He Might Hear You* (P) Moorehead (1910): *Cooper's Creek* (P) Porter, Hal (1911): *The Watcher on the Cast-iron Balcony* (P); *The Tower* (D) Prichard (1883): *Child of the Hurricane* (P) Stow (1935): *Tourmaline* (P) Thiele (1920): *Storm Boy* (P) West (1916): *The Shoes of the Fisherman* (P) Wright (1915): *Five Senses* (V)	W. H. Ogilvie *d.* *Australian Literary Studies* (ed. L. T. Hergenhan) founded *Southern Review* (Adelaide) founded *Oz* (ed. Richard Walsh and Richard Neville, 1963–5) founded Australian Society of Authors formed with Dal Stivens as President *Art and Australia* founded Penguin Australia begins
1964	Beaver (1928): *Seawall and Shoreline* (V) Cato (1917): *The Sea Ants* (P) Cowan (1914): *Summer* (P)	Gavin Casey *d.* Nettie Palmer *d.* *Australian* founded *Poetry Australia* (Sydney) founded

DATE	AUTHOR AND TITLE	EVENT
	Davison (1893): *The Road to Yesterday* (P)	
	Horne, Donald (1921): *The Lucky Country: Australia in the Sixties* (P)	
	Johnston (1912): *My Brother Jack* (P)	
	Keneally (1935): *The Place at Whitton* (P)	
	McAuley (1917): *Captain Quiros* (V)	
	Shapcott (1935): *The Mankind Thing and Sonnets 1960–63* (V)	
	Walker (1920): *We are Going* (V)	
	Waten (1911): *Distant Land* (P)	
	Webb (1925): *The Ghost of the Cock* (V)	
	White, Patrick (1912): *The Burnt Ones* (P)	
	Wright (1915): *City Sunrise* (V)	
1965	Astley (1925): *The Slow Natives* (P)	P. R. ('Inky') Stephensen *d.*
	Boyd, Martin (1893): *Day of my Delight* (P)	Sun Books begins
	Cowan (1914): *The Empty Street* (P)	
	Dawe (1930): *A Need of Similar Name* (V)	
	FitzGerald (1902): *Forty Years' Poems* (V)	
	Johnson (1938): *Wild Cat Falling* (P)	
	Keneally (1923): *The Fear* (P)	
	Koch (1923): *Across the Sea Wall* (P)	
	Martin, David (1915): *The Hero of Too* (P)	
	Murray (1938) & Lehmann (1940): *The Ilex Tree* (V)	
	Porter, Hal (1911): *The Cats of Venice* (P)	
	Porter, Peter (1929): *Poems Ancient and Modern* (V)	
	Southall (1921): *Ash Road* (P)	
	Stow (1935): *The Merry-go-round in the Sea* (P)	
	White, Patrick (1912): *Four Plays* (D)	
1966	Beaver (1928): *You Can't Come Back* (V)	Eric Lambert *d.*
	Blainey (1930): *The Tyranny of Distance* (P)	*Australian Dictionary of Biography* begins
	Buckley (1925): *Arcady and Other Places* (V)	
	Cowan (1914): *Seed* (P)	
	Harrower (1928): *The Watch Tower* (P)	

DATE	AUTHOR AND TITLE	EVENT
	Hazzard (1931): *The Evening of the Holiday* (P) Hope (1907): *Collected Poems 1930–65* (V) Lurie (1938): *Rappaport* (P) Mathers (1931): *Trap* (P) Porter, Hal (1911): *The Paper Chase* (P); *The Professor* (D) Stead (1902): *Dark Places of the Heart* (P) Walker (1920): *The Dawn is at Hand* (V) White, Patrick (1912): *The Solid Mandala* (P) Wright (1915): *The Other Half* (V); *The Nature of Love* (P)	
1967	Beaver (1928): *Open at Random* (V) Dutton (1922): *Poems Soft and Loud* (V) Hall (1935): *Eyewitness* (V) Hazzard (1931): *People in Glass Houses* (P) Keneally (1935): *Bring Larks and Heroes* (P) Lindsay, Joan (1896): *Picnic at Hanging Rock* (P) Prichard (1883): *Happiness* and *Subtle Flame* (P) Shapcott (1935): *A Taste of Salt Water* (V) Stead (1902): *The Puzzleheaded Girl* (P) Stewart (1913): *Collected Poems* (V) Tennant (1912): *Tell Morning This* (P) Wallace-Crabbe (1934): *The Rebel General* (V)	Referendum ends constitutional discrimination against Aborigines by record 90% vote Cecil Mann *d.* D'Arcy Niland *d.*
1968	Astley (1925): *A Boat Load of Home Folk* (P) Blight (1913): *My Beachcombing Days* (V) Davison (1893): *The White Thorntree* (P) Dawe (1930): *An Eye for a Tooth* (V) Hall (1935): *The Autobiography of a Gorgon* and *The Law of Karma* (V) Ireland (1927): *The Chantic Bird* (P) Keneally (1935): *Three Cheers for the Paraclete* (P) Lehmann (1940): *A Voyage of Lions* (V)	C. E. W. Bean *d.* Henrietta Drake-Brockmann *d.* Dorothea Mackellar *d.*

DATE	AUTHOR AND TITLE	EVENT
	Lindsay, Norman (1879): *Rooms and Houses* (P)	
	Martin, David (1915): *The Idealist* (V)	
	Porter, Hal (1911): *Elijah's Ravens* (V)	
	Stivens (1911): *Three Persons Make a Tiger* (P)	
	West (1916): *The Tower of Babel* (P)	
1969	Beaver (1928): *Letters to Live Poets* (V)	Norman Lindsay *d.*
	Boyd, Martin (1893): *The Tea Time of Love* (P)	Katharine Susannah Prichard *d.*
	Dawe (1930): *Beyond the Subdivisions* (V)	*Australian Author* (Sydney) founded
	Hope (1907): *New Poems: 1965–1969* (V)	
	Keneally (1935): *The Survivor* (P)	
	Johnston (1912): *Clean Straw for Nothing* (P)	
	Lurie (1938): *Happy Times* (P)	
	McAuley (1917): *Surprises of the Sun* (V)	
	Moorhouse (1939): *Futility and Other Animals* (P)	
	Murray (1938): *The Weatherboard Cathedral* (V)	
	Rolls (1925): *They All Ran Wild* (P)	
	Shapcott (1935): *Inwards to the Sun* (V)	
	Webb (1925): *Collected Poems* (V)	
	West (1916): *The Heretic* (P)	
1970	Adamson (1944): *Canticles on the Skin* (V)	Frank Dalby Davison *d.*
	Campbell (1915): *The Branch of Dodona* (V)	James Devaney *d.*
	Hall (1935): *Heaven, in a Way* (V)	George Johnston *d.*
	Hazzard (1931): *The Bay of Noon* (P)	Norman Lindsay *d.*
	Hope (1907): *Dunciad Minor* (V)	Nimrod Theatre founded by John Bell and Ken Horler
	Oakley (1931): *A Salute to the Great McCarthy; Let's Hear it for Prendergast* (P)	University of Queensland Press begins extensive publishing of Australian literature
	McQueen, Humphrey (1942): *A New Britannia* (P)	
	Porter, Hal (1911): *Mr Butterfry and Other Tales of New Japan* (P)	
	Serventy (19??): *Dryandra* (P)	
	Stivens (1911): *A Horse of Air* (P)	
	Walker (1920): *My People* (V, P)	
	White, Patrick (1912): *The Vivisector* (P)	

DATE	AUTHOR AND TITLE	EVENT
1971	Adamson (1944): *The Rumour* (V) Buzo (1944): *Macquarie* (D) Dawe (1930): *Condolences of the Season* (V) Hardy (1917): *The Outcasts of Foolgarah* (P) Ireland (1927): *The Unknown Industrial Prisoner* (P) Johnston (d. 1970): *A Cartload of Clay* (P) Keneally (1935): *A Dutiful Daughter* (P) McAuley (1917): *Collected Poems 1936–1970* (V) Porter, Hal (1911): *The Right Thing* (P) Wright (1915): *Collected Poems 1942–1970* (V)	Frank Clune *d.* Kenneth Slessor *d.* John Tierney ('Brian James') *d.* *LiNQ* (Townsville) founded Currency Press, the first company to publish only Australian plays, founded in Sydney by Katharine Brisbane and Philip Parsons
1972	Astley (1925): *The Acolyte* (P) Dransfield (1949): *Drug Poems* and *The Inspector of Tides* (V) Hewett (1923): *The Chapel Perilous* (D) Hope (1907): *Collected Poems 1930–1970* (V) Ireland (1927): *The Flesheaters* (P) Keneally (1930): *The Chant of Jimmie Blacksmith* (P) Kenna (1930): *The Slaughter of St Teresa's Day* (D) Mathers (1931): *The Wort Papers* (P) Moorhouse (1939): *The Americans, Baby* (P) Murray (1938): *Poems against Economics* (V) Porter, Peter (1929): *After Martial* and *Preaching to the Converted* (V) Tranter (1943): *Red Movie* (V) Wilding (1942): *Aspects of the Dying Process* (P) Williamson (1942): *The Removalists* (D)	Martin Boyd *d.* *Tabloid Story* founded First Labor Party government for 23 years formed by E. G. Whitlam
1973	Buzo (1944): *Norm and the Ahmed, Rooted, The Roy Murphy Show: Three Plays* (D) Cowan (1914): *The Tins* (P) Hibberd (1940): *A Stretch of the Imagination* (D) Kenna (1930): *A Hard God* (D) Romeril (1945): *I Don't Know Who to Feel Sorry For* (D)	Michael Dransfield *d.* Francis Webb *d.* Patrick White awarded Nobel Prize for literature Literature Board (subsequently within Australia Council) replaces the Commonwealth Literary Fund Opening of Sydney Opera House

DATE	AUTHOR AND TITLE	EVENT
	Stead (1902): *The Little Hotel* (P)	
	West (1916): *The Salamander* (P)	
	White, Patrick (1912): *The Eye of the Storm* (P)	
	Williamson (1942): *Don's Party* (D)	
	Wright (1915): *Alive: Poems 1971–72* (V)	
	Wrightson (1921): *The Nargun and the Stars* (P)	
1974	Astley (1925): *A Kindness Cup* (P)	*SPAN* founded
	Beaver (1928): *Lauds and Plaints* (V)	Wild and Woolley (Sydney) begin
	Carey (1943): *The Fat Man in History* (P)	publishing new Australian writing
	Docker (1945): *Australian Cultural Elites* (P)	New Labor government introduces immigration policy which effectively ends 'White Australia'
	Foster (1944): *The Pure Land* (P)	policy
	Hibberd (1940): *Dimboola* (D)	The *Age* Book of the Year Award
	Ireland (1927): *Burn* (P)	begins
	Keneally (1935): *Blood Red, Sister Rose* (P)	National Book Council Awards begin
	McKie (1909): *The Mango Tree* (P)	Patrick White Award begins
	Malouf (1934): *Neighbours in a Thicket* (V)	
	Moorhouse (1939): *The Electrical Experience* (P)	
	Murray (1938) *Lunch and Counter Lunch* (V)	
	Porter, Hal (1911): *Fredo Fuss Love Life* (P)	
	Stuart (1913): *Prince of my Country* (P)	
	West (1916): *Harlequin* (P)	
	White, Patrick (1912): *The Cockatoos* (P)	
	Wilding (1942): *Living Together* (P)	
1975	Bail (1941): *Contemporary Portraits* (P)	Dymphna Cusack d.
	Beaver (1928): *Odes and Days* (V)	*Hecate: A Women's Interdisciplinary Journal* (St Lucia) founded
	Blight (1913): *Hart* (V)	Whitlam Government dismissed by
	Campbell, David (1915): *Deaths and Pretty Cousins* (V)	Governor-General
	Dawe (1930): *Just a Dugong at Twilight* (V)	
	Dransfield (d. 1973): *Memoirs of a Velvet Urinal* (V)	
	Hall (1935): *A Place among People* (V)	
	Hardy (1917): *But the Dead are Many* (P)	
	Herbert (1901): *Poor Fellow my Country* (P)	
	Hope (1907): *A Late Picking* (V)	

DATE	AUTHOR AND TITLE	EVENT
	Keneally (1935): *Gossip from the Forest* (P)	
	Malouf (1934): *Johnno* (P)	
	Oakley (1931): *Bedfellows* and *The Feet of Daniel Mannix* (D)	
	Romeril (1945): *The Floating World* (D)	
	Tranter (1943): *The Alphabet Murders* (V)	
	Wilding (1942): *The Short Story Embassy* and *The West Midland Underground* (P)	
1976	Blair (1942): *The Christian Brothers* (D)	James McAuley d.
	Buzo (1944): *Martello Towers* (D)	
	Buckley (1925): *Golden Builders* (V)	
	Drewe (1943): *The Savage Crows* (P)	
	Ireland (1927): *The Glass Canoe* (P)	
	Keneally (1935): *Season in Purgatory* (P)	
	Oakley (1931): *A Lesson in English* (D)	
	Shapcott (1935): *Seventh Avenue Poems* (V)	
	Stead (1902): *Miss Herbert (The Suburban Wife)* (P)	
	Stivens (1911): *The Unicorn* (P)	
	West (1916): *The Navigator* (P)	
	White, Patrick (1912): *A Fringe of Leaves* (P)	
	Williamson (1942): *A Handful of Friends* (D)	
	Wright (1915): *Fourth Quarter* (V)	
1977	Adamson (1944): *Cross the Border* (V)	*Journal of Australian Studies* (ed. Bob Bessant) founded
	Dutton (1922): *A Body of Words* (V)	Hale and Iremonger begin publishing Australian literature
	Elliott (1917): *Water under the Bridge* (P)	Formation of the Association for the Study of Australian Literature (ASAL)
	FitzGerald (1902): *Product: Later Verses* (V)	
	Hanrahan (1939): *The Albatross Muff* (P)	
	Keneally (1935): *A Victim of the Aurora* (P)	
	Marshall (1902): *The Complete Stories of Alan Marshall* (P)	
	McCullough (1937): *The Thorn Birds* (P)	
	Moorhouse (1939): *Tales of Mystery and Romance* (P)	
	Oakley (1931): *Walking through Tigerland* (P)	

DATE	AUTHOR AND TITLE	EVENT
	Park (19): *Swords and Crowns and Rings* (P)	
1978	Jessica Anderson (19): *Tirra Lirra by the River* (P)	*Australian Book Review*, 2nd ser.
	Beaver (1928): *Death's Directives* (V)	
	Dawe (1930): *Sometimes Gladness* (V)	
	Dransfield (d. 1973): *Voyage into Solitude* (V)	
	Garner (1942): *Monkey Grip* (P)	
	Gilbert (1933): *People ARE Legends* (V)	
	Hanrahan (1939): *Where All the Queens Strayed* (P)	
	Koch (1932): *The Year of Living Dangerously* (P)	
	Lehmann (1940): *Ross' Poems* (V)	
	Malouf (1934): *An Imaginary Life* (P)	
	Murray (1938): *Ethnic Radio* (V)	
	Nowra (1950): *Inner Voices* (D)	
	Porter, Peter (1929): *The Cost of Seriousness* (V)	
	Stead (1902): *Letty Fox: Her Luck* (P)	
	Tranter (1943): *Crying in Early Infancy: One Hundred Sonnets* (V)	
	White, Patrick (1912): *Big Toys* (D)	
1979	Astley (1925): *Hunting the Wild Pineapple* (P)	David Campbell *d.*
	Beaver (1928): *As it was . . .* (P); *Selected Poems* (V)	Ion Idriess *d.* New South Wales Premier's Literary Awards begin
	Buckley (1925): *The Pattern* and *Late Winter Child* (V)	
	Buzo (1944): *Makassar Reef* (D)	
	Carey (1943): *War Crimes* (P)	
	Cowan (1914): *Mobiles* (P)	
	Drewe (1943): *A Cry in the Jungle Bar* (P)	
	Hanrahan (1939): *The Peach Groves* (P)	
	Ireland (1927): *A Woman of the Future* (P)	
	Johnson (1938): *Long Live Sandawara* (P)	
	Keneally (1935): *Confederates; Passenger* (P)	
	McDonald (1941): *1915* (P)	
	Nowra (1950): *Visions* (D)	
	Stow (1935): *Visitants* (P)	
	Tranter (1943): *Dazed in the Ladies Lounge* (V)	
	White, Patrick (1912): *The Twyborn Affair* (P)	

DATE	AUTHOR AND TITLE	EVENT
1980	Anderson (19): *the Impersonators* (P) Bail (1941): *Homesickness* (P) Blight (1913): *The New City Poems* (V) Dransfield (*d.* 1973): *The Second Month of Spring* (V) Garner (1942): *Honour and Other People's Children* (P) Hanrahan (1939): *The Frangipani Gardens* (P) Hazzard (1931): *The Transit of Venus* (P) Keneally (1935): *The Cut-rate Kingdom* (P) Kocan (1947): *The Treatment* (P) Malouf (1934): *First Things Last* (V) Moorhouse (1939): *The Everlasting Secret Family and Other Secrets* (P) Murray (1938): *The Boys who Stole the Funeral: A Novel Sequence* (V) Oakley (1931): *The Great God Mogadon and Other Plays* (D) Radley (1962): *Jack Rivers and Me* (P) Stow (1935): *The Girl Green as Elderflower* (P)	*The Australian*/Vogel National Literary Award begins
1981	Carey (1943): *Bliss* (P) D'Alpuget (1944): *Turtle Beach* (P) Facey (1894): *A Fortunate Life* (P) Foster (1944): *Moonlite* (P) Hall (1935): *The Most Beautiful World: Fictions and Sermons* (V) Harwood (1920): *The Lion's Bride* (V) Hope (1907): *Antechinus: Poems 1975–1980* (V) Ireland (1927): *City of Women* (P) Kenna (1930): *Furtive Love* (D) Lehmann (1940): *Nero's Poems* (V) Loukakis (1951): *For the Patriarch* (P) Lurie (1938): *Dirty Friends* (P) Martin, David (1915): *Foreigners* (P) Nowra (1950): *Inside the Island* and *The Precious Woman* (D) Oakley (1931): *Marsupials and Politics: Two Comedies* (D) Porter, Hal (1911): *The Clairvoyant Goat* (P) Porter, Peter (1929): *English Subtitles* (V)	Leonard Mann *d.* John O'Grady ('Nino Culotta') *d.* *The Macquarie Dictionary*, the first general dictionary compiled in Australia, published

DATE	AUTHOR AND TITLE	EVENT
	Rolls (1923): *A Million Wild Acres* (P)	
	Weller (1958): *The Day of the Dog* (P)	
	White, Patrick (1912): *Flaws in the Glass: A Self-portrait* (P)	
1982	Adamson (1944): *The Law at Heart's Desire* (V)	Jim McNeil *d.*
	Astley (1925): *An Item from the Late News* (P)	Albert Facey *d.*
		Thomas Keneally awarded the Booker Prize
	Hall (1935): *Just Relations* (P)	*Australian Short Stories* ed. Bruce Pascoe begins
	Hanrahan (1939): *Dove* (P)	
	Keneally (1935): *Schindler's Ark* (P)	
	Lee (1951): *True Love and How to Get It* (P)	
	McDonald (1941): *Slipstream* (P)	
	Malouf (1934): *Child's Play with Eustace and the Prowler* and *Fly Away Peter* (P)	
	Masters (1919): *The Home Girls* (P)	
	Morrison (1904): *North Wind* (P)	
	Radley (1962): *My Blue Checker Corker and Me* (P)	
	Robinson (1912): *Selected Poems* (V)	
	Romeril (1945): *Bastardy* (D)	
	Shapcott (1935): *The Birthday Gift* (P)	
	Waten (1911): *Scenes of Revolutionary Life* (P)	
	Wilding (1942): *Pacific Highway* (P)	
	Winton (1960): *An Open Swimmer* (P)	
1983	Blair (1942): *Marx* and *Last Day in Woolloomooloo* (D)	Colin Simpson *d.*
	Buckley (1925): *Cutting Green Hay* (P)	Christina Stead *d.*
	Cato (1917): *Forefathers* (P)	Alan Moorehead *d.*
	Davis (1917): *Kullark* and *The Dreamers* (D)	
	Dawe (1930): *Sometimes Gladness*, 2nd edn (V); *Over Here, Harv!* (P)	
	Drewe (1943): *The Bodysurfers* (P)	
	Foster (1944): *Plumbum* (P)	
	Hanrahan (1939): *Kewpie Doll* (P)	
	Johnson, Colin (1938): *Doctor Wooreddy's Prescription for Enduring the Ending of the World* (P)	
	Jolley (1923): *Woman in a Lampshade*, *Mr Scobie's Riddle* and *Miss Peabody's Inheritance* (P)	
	Kocan (1947): *The Cure* (P)	
	Murray (1938): *The People's Otherworld* (V)	

DATE	AUTHOR AND TITLE	EVENT
	Nowra (1950): *Sunrise* (D)	
	Porter, Peter (1929): *Collected Poems* (V)	
	Sewell (1953): *Traitors* (D)	
	Shapcott (1935): *Welcome!* (V)	
	Tennant (1912): *Tantavallon* (P)	
	Tsaloumas (1921): *The Observatory* (V)	
	White, Patrick (1912): *Signal Driver* (D)	
	Williamson (1942): *The Perfectionist* (D)	
1984	Cappiello (19??): *Oh Lucky Country* (P)	A. Bertram Chandler *d.*
	Docker (1945): *In a Critical Condition* (P)	Alan Marshall *d.*
	Garner (1942): *The Children's Bach* (P)	Hal Porter *d.*
		Xavier Herbert *d.*
	Grenville (1951): *Bearded Ladies* (P)	*Outrider* (ed. Manfred Jurgensen) founded
	Ireland (1927): *Archimedes and the Seagle* (P)	Australian-owned publisher Rigby ceases operations and is subsequently sold to Kevin Weldon
	Jolley (1923): *Milk and Honey* (P)	
	McQueen, James (1934): *Uphill Runner* (P)	
	Malouf (1934): *Harland's Half Acre* (P)	
	Masters (1919): *Loving Daughters* (P)	
	Mathers (1931): *A Change for the Better* (P)	
	Shapcott (1935): *White Stag of Exile* (P)	
	Stow (1935): *The Suburbs of Hell* (P)	
	Winton (1960): *Shallows* (P)	

Index